CW01021257

JONATHAN HICKMAN
WRITER

NICK PITARRA
ARTIST

JORDIE BELLAIRE
COLORS

RUS WOOTON
LETTERS

WITH

RYAN BROWNE
ARTIST (CHAPTER 10)

IMAGE COMICS, INC.
Robert Kirkman – Chief Operating Officer
Erik Larsen – Chief Financial Officer
Todd McFarlane – President
Marc Silvestri – Chief Executive Officer
Jim Valentino – Vice-President

Eric Stephenson – Publisher
Ron Richards – Director of Business Development
Jennifer de Guzman – Director of Trade Book Sales
Kat Salazar – Director of PR & Marketing
Corey Murphy – Director of Retail Sales
Jeremy Sullivan – Director of Digital Sales
Emilio Bautista – Sales Assistant
Branwyn Bigglestone – Senior Accounts Manager
Emily Miller – Accounts Manager
Jessica Ambriz – Administrative Assistant
Tyler Shainline – Events Coordinator
David Brothers – Content Manager
Jonathan Chan – Production Manager
Drew Gill – Art Director
Meredith Wallace – Print Manager
Monica Garcia – Senior Production Artist
Jenna Savage – Production Artist
Addison Duke – Production Artist
Tricia Ramos – Production Assistant
IMAGECOMICS.COM

SCIENCE.
BAD.

MP

THE MANHATTAN PROJECTS

I AM NOT MY
BROTHER

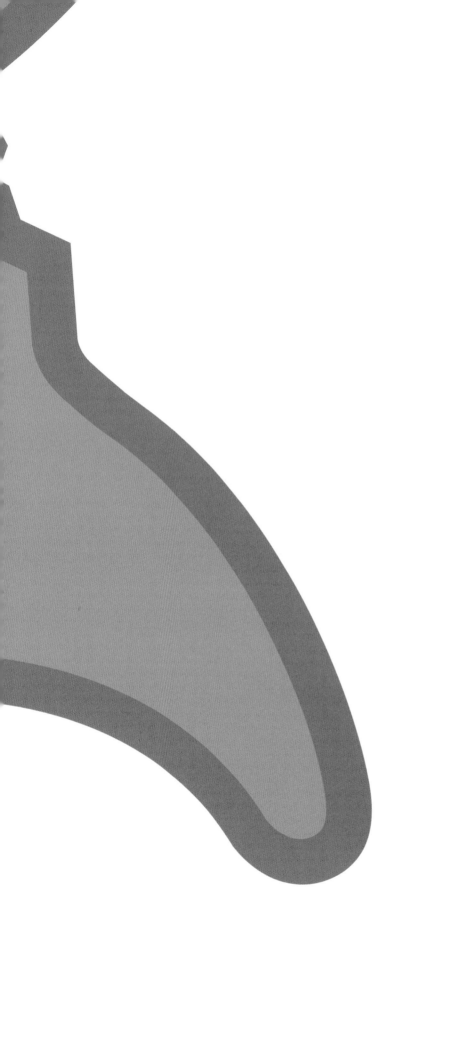

"I WAS SURROUNDED BY THOSE WILLING TO SACRIFICE ALL OF MANKIND IF DOING SO ACHIEVED THEIR GOALS. EVIL DEEDS BY EVIL MEN THAT ONLY I COULD PREVENT.

MOURN THEN THE PASSING OF THE WORLD. FOR WHEN THE TIME CAME, I COULD FIND NO GOOD IN MYSELF, ONLY MISCHIEF."

CLAVIS AUREA
THE RECORDED FEYNMAN | **VOL. 4**

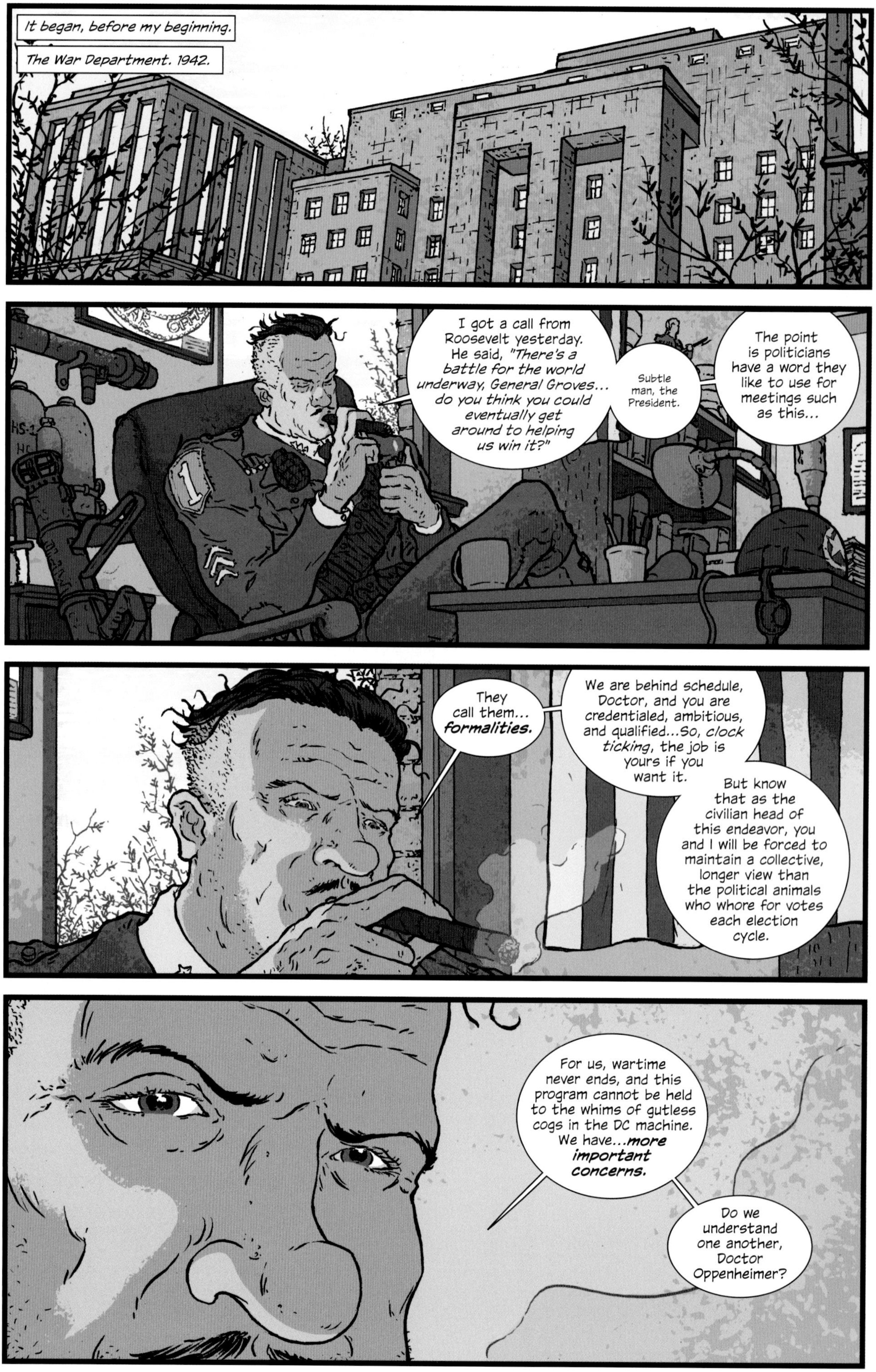
It began, before my beginning.
The War Department. 1942.
I got a call from Roosevelt yesterday. He said, "There's a battle for the world underway, General Groves... do you think you could eventually get around to helping us win it?"
Subtle man, the President.
The point is politicians have a word they like to use for meetings such as this...
They call them... formalities.
We are behind schedule, Doctor, and you are credentialed, ambitious, and qualified...So, clock ticking, the job is yours if you want it.
But know that as the civilian head of this endeavor, you and I will be forced to maintain a collective, longer view than the political animals who whore for votes each election cycle.
For us, wartime never ends, and this program cannot be held to the whims of gutless cogs in the DC machine. We have...more important concerns.
Do we understand one another, Doctor Oppenheimer?

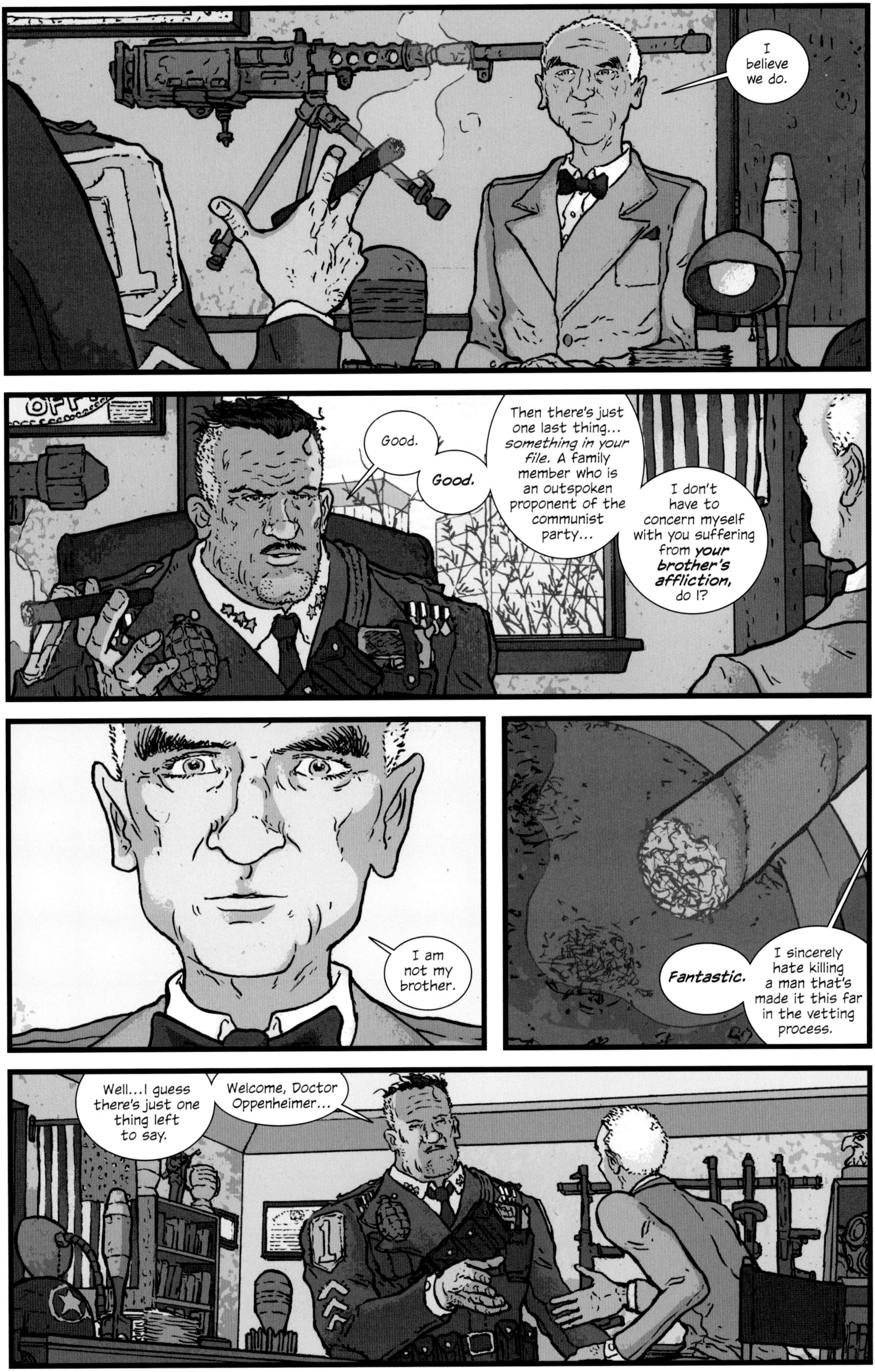
I believe we do.
Good.
Good.
Then there's just one last thing... *something in your file.* A family member who is an outspoken proponent of the communist party...
I don't have to concern myself with you suffering from ***your brother's affliction,*** do I?
I am not my brother.
Fantastic.
I sincerely hate killing a man that's made it this far in the vetting process.
Well...I guess there's just one thing left to say.
Welcome, Doctor Oppenheimer...

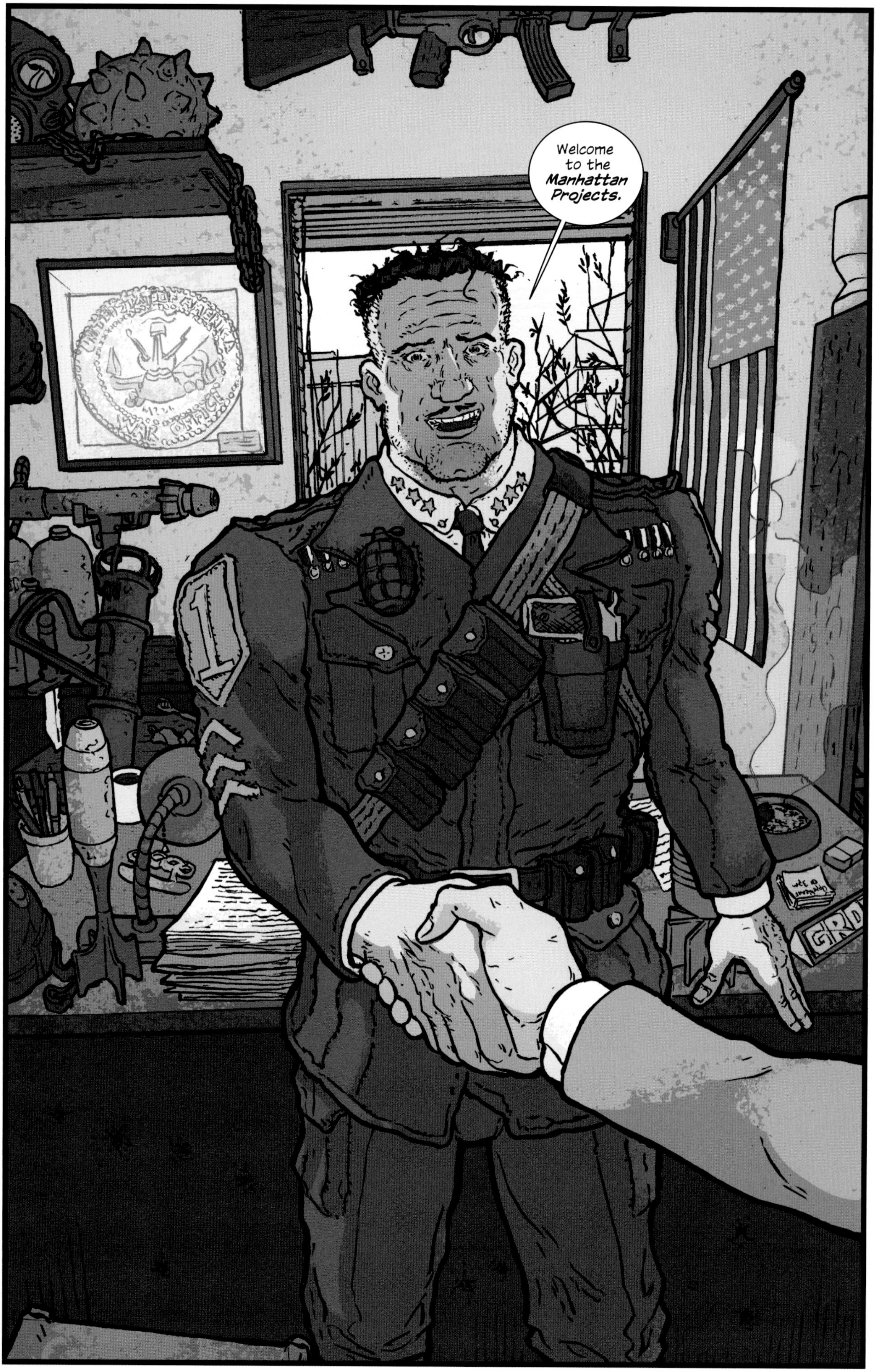
Welcome to the *Manhattan Projects.*

"ON MY FIRST DAY, I WAS GIVEN A GOVERNMENT-ISSUED DISASTER PACKET.

IT INCLUDED: A SOLAR-POWERED RADIO BEACON, ANTIBIOTICS, A CYANIDE CAPSULE, AN ETERNAL FLAME, A COLLAPSABLE KNIFE, AN INFINITY PEN, AND A JOURNAL."

CLAVIS AUREA
THE RECORDED FEYNMAN | **VOL. 1**

01

INFINITE OPPENHEIMERS

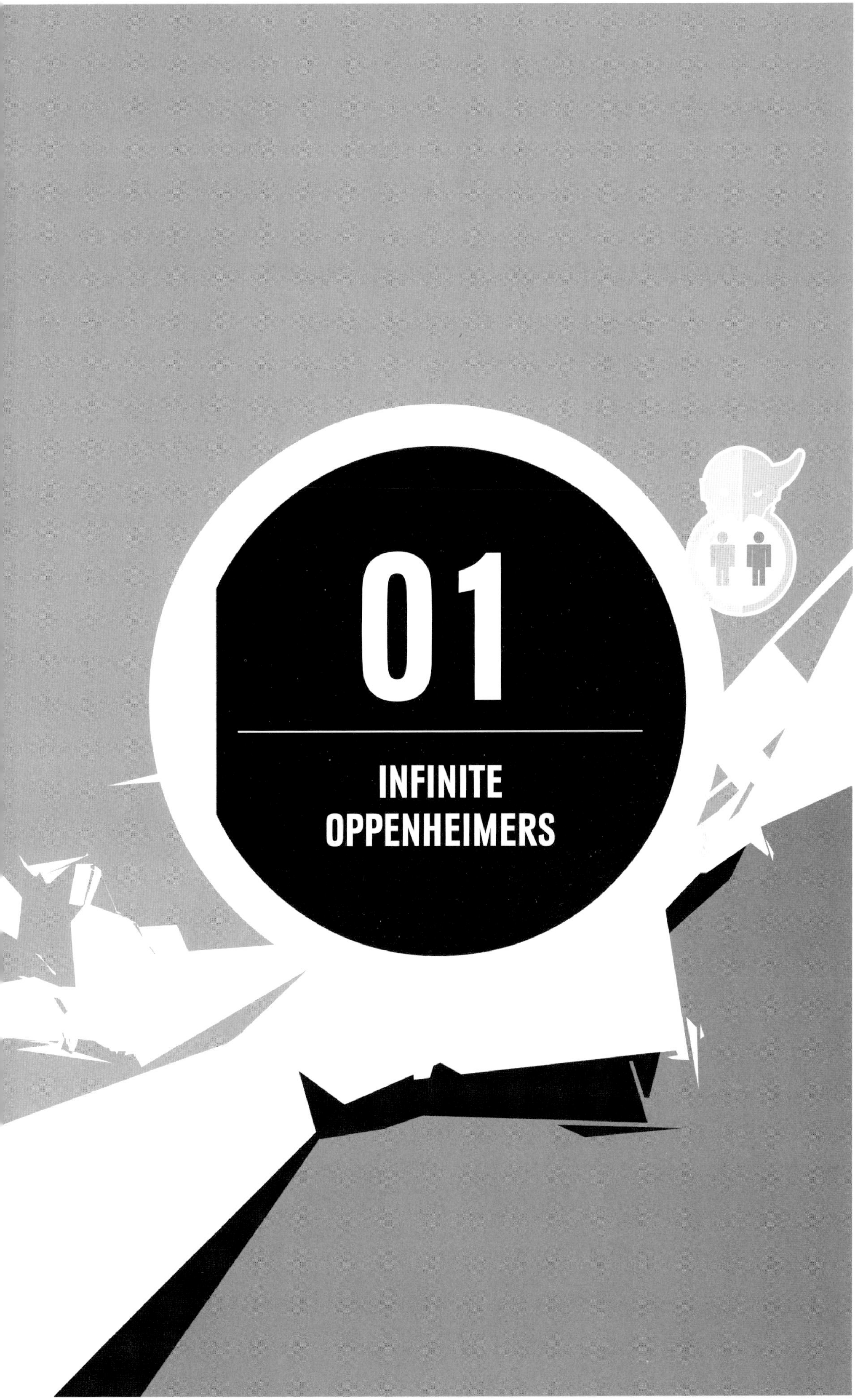

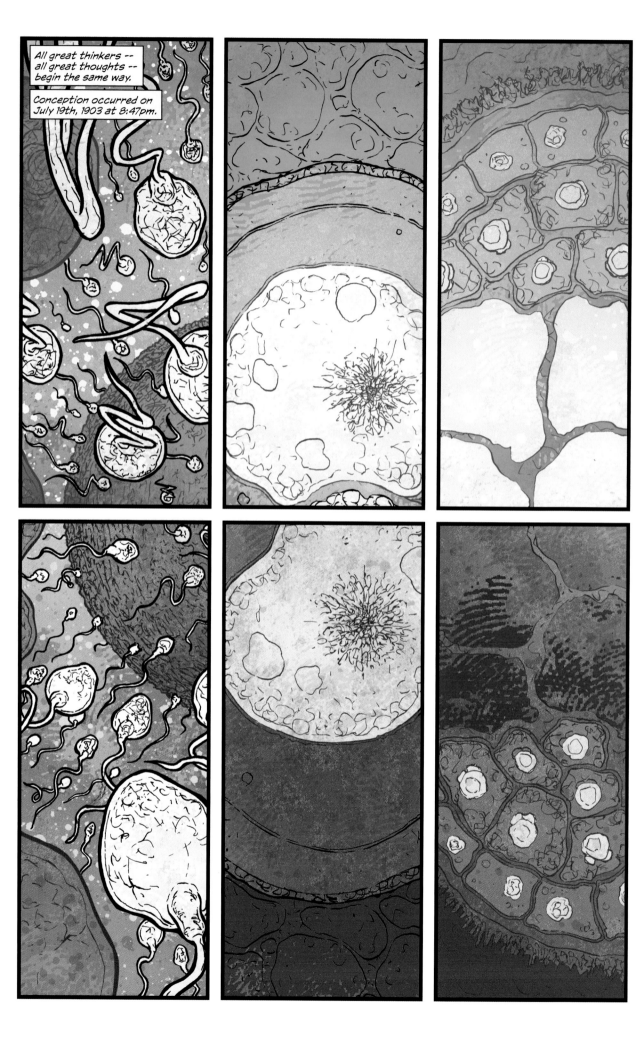

All great thinkers --
all great thoughts --
begin the same way.

Conception occurred on
July 19th, 1903 at 8:47pm.

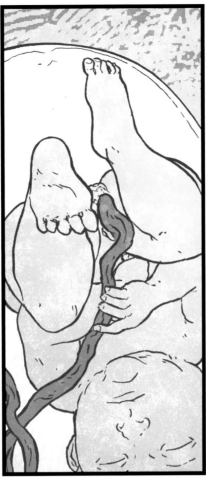

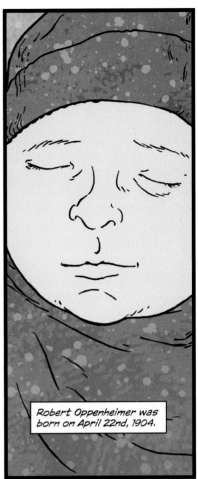

Robert Oppenheimer was born on April 22nd, 1904.

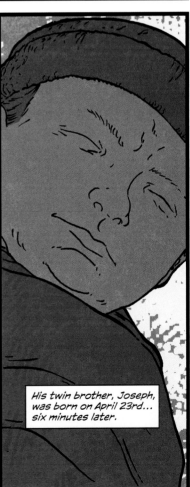

His twin brother, Joseph, was born on April 23rd... six minutes later.

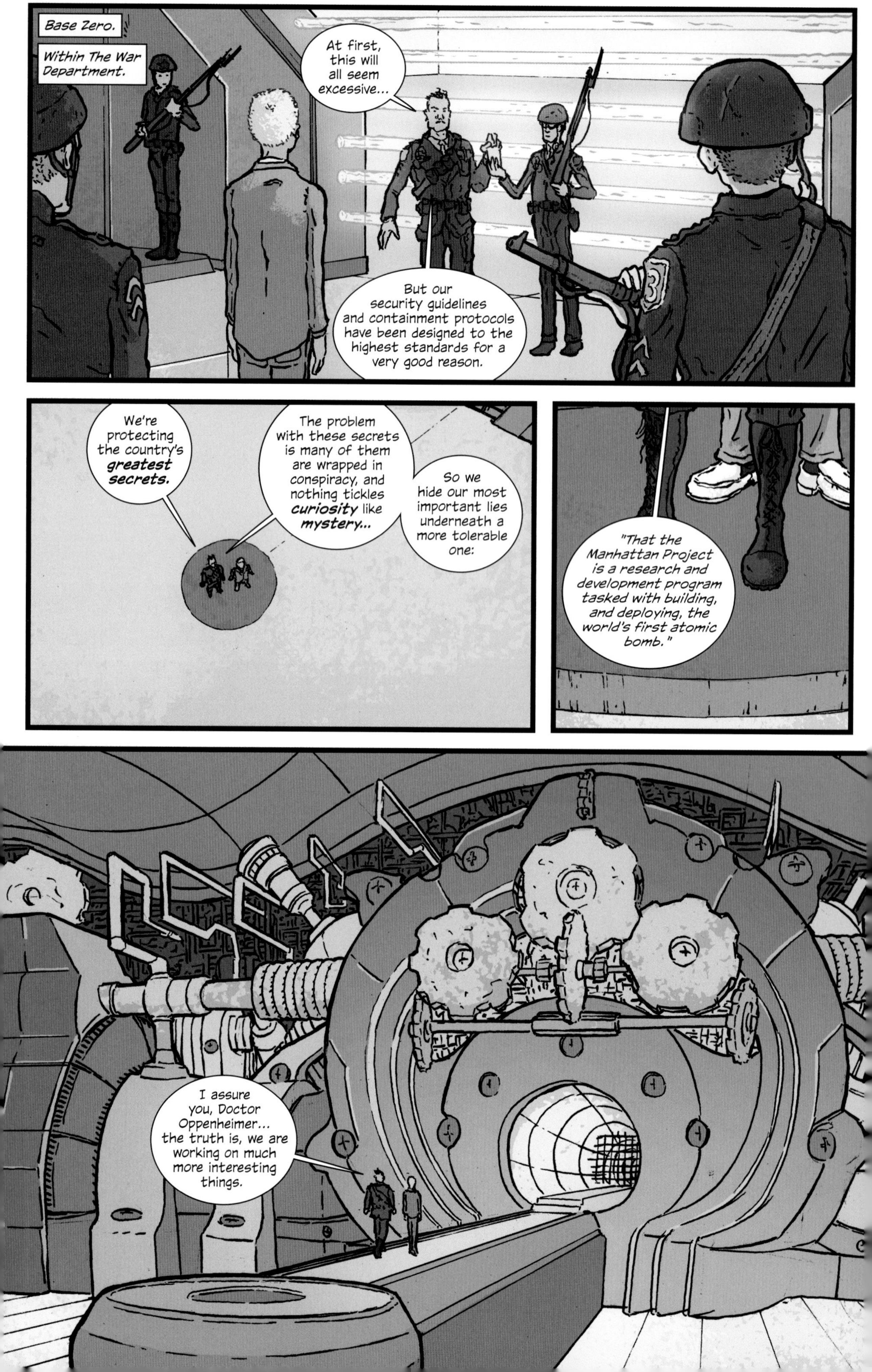
Base Zero.
Within The War Department.
At first, this will all seem excessive...
But our security guidelines and containment protocols have been designed to the highest standards for a very good reason.
We're protecting the country's **greatest secrets.**
The problem with these secrets is many of them are wrapped in conspiracy, and nothing tickles **curiosity** like **mystery...**
So we hide our most important lies underneath a more tolerable one:
"That the Manhattan Project is a research and development program tasked with building, and deploying, the world's first atomic bomb."
I assure you, Doctor Oppenheimer... the truth is, we are working on much more interesting things.

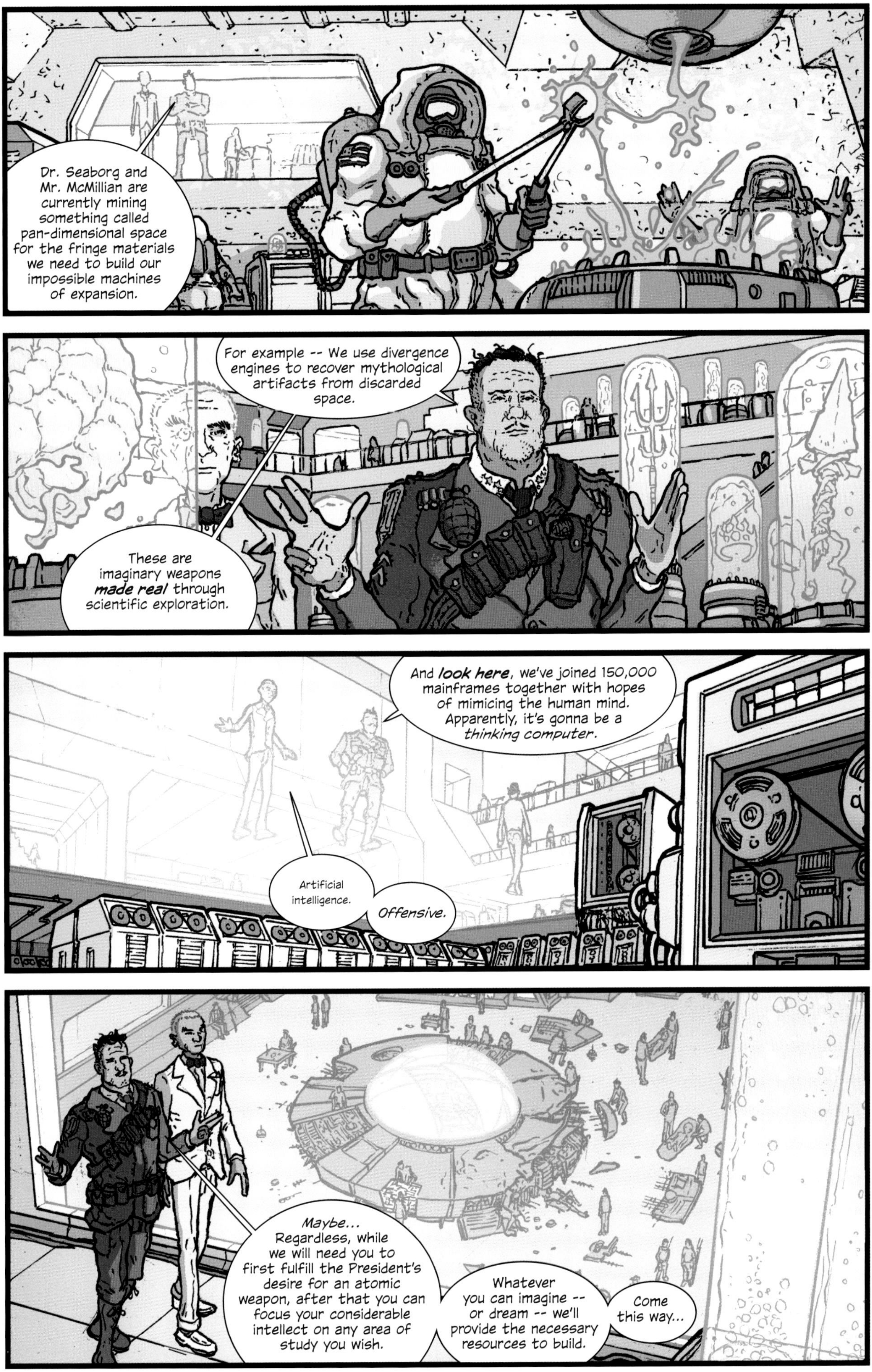
Dr. Seaborg and Mr. McMillian are currently mining something called pan-dimensional space for the fringe materials we need to build our impossible machines of expansion.
For example -- We use divergence engines to recover mythological artifacts from discarded space.
These are imaginary weapons *made real* through scientific exploration.
And *look here*, we've joined 150,000 mainframes together with hopes of mimicing the human mind. Apparently, it's gonna be a *thinking computer*.
Artificial intelligence.
Offensive.
Maybe... Regardless, while we will need you to first fulfill the President's desire for an atomic weapon, after that you can focus your considerable intellect on any area of study you wish.
Whatever you can imagine -- or dream -- we'll provide the necessary resources to build.
Come this way...

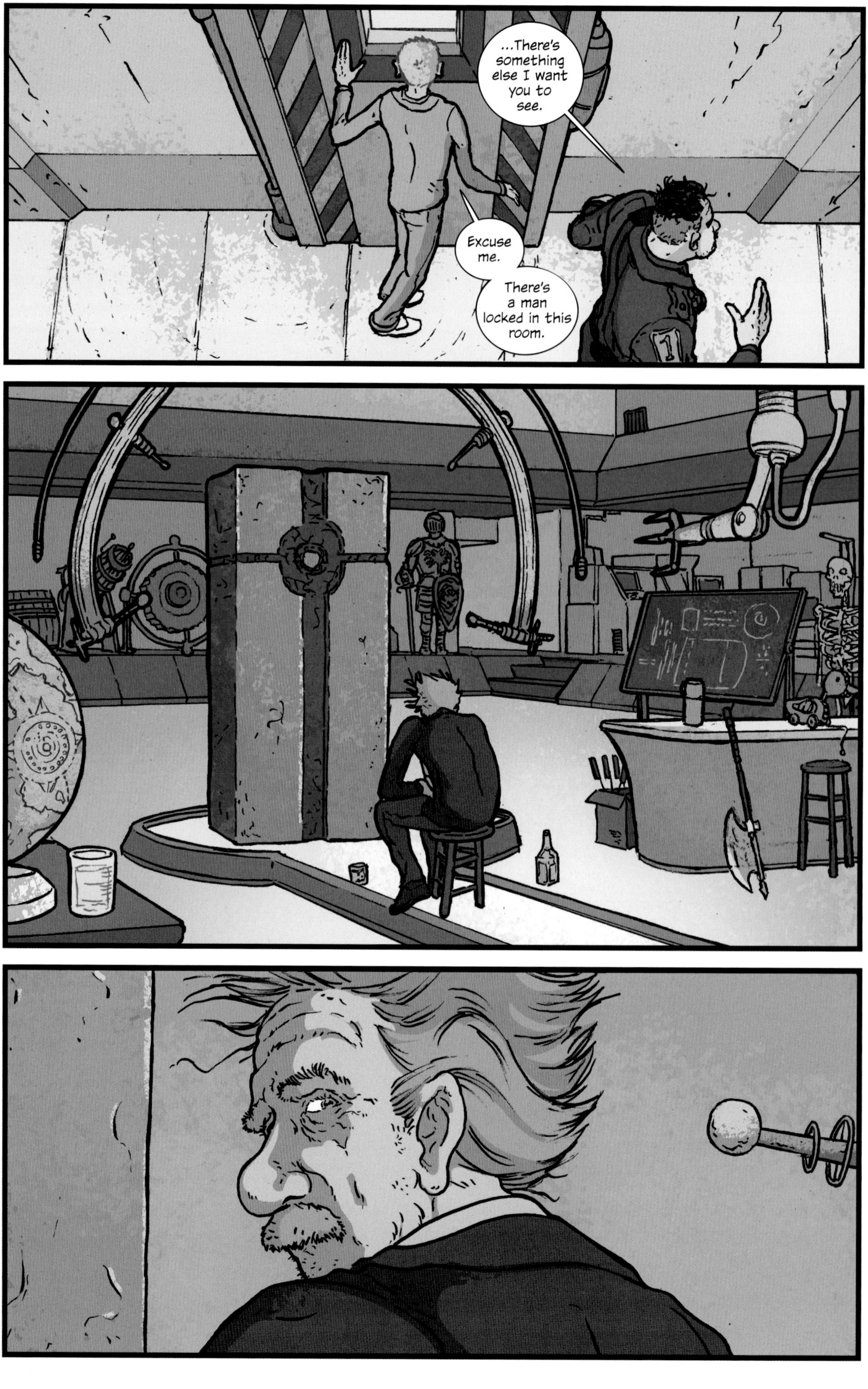
...There's something else I want you to see.
Excuse me.
There's a man locked in this room.
1

Yes, there most certainly is -- and for very good reason.
But don't you worry about him...
He only gets out when I'm good and damned ready.
Now... what you're going to-- *FEH!*
Hmm. 112 decibels.
We can listen to this for six more minutes before experiencing irreversible hearing loss.
It's not your ears you should be worried about, Doctor...
The proximity alarm means something has entered our airspace.
Early warning detected a single object on a collision course, sir.
Who would dare attack us here?
On a ***collision course***? Who do you think, soldier...?
It's the goddamn Japanese.

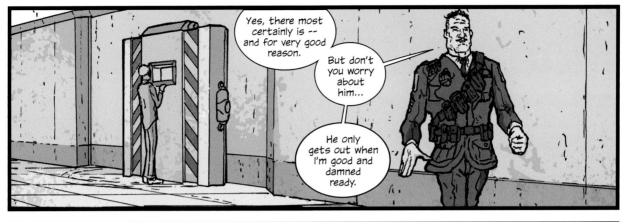

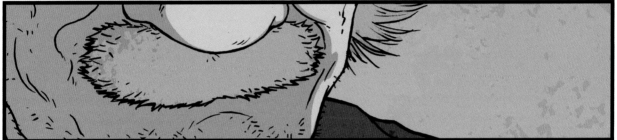

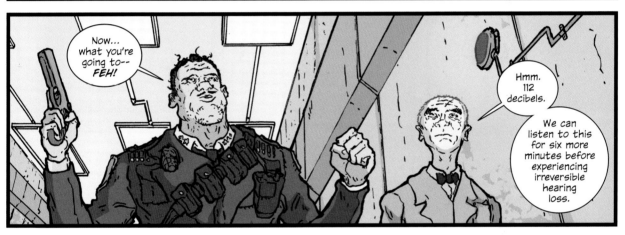

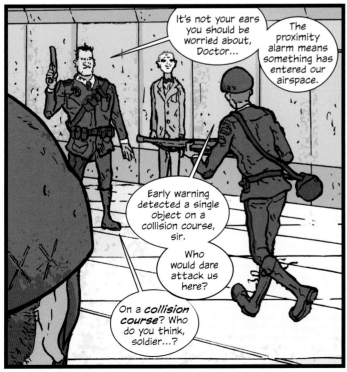

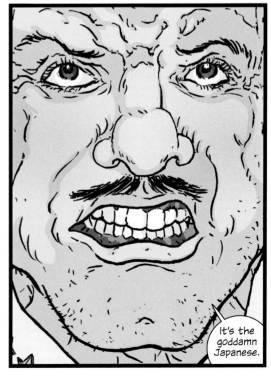

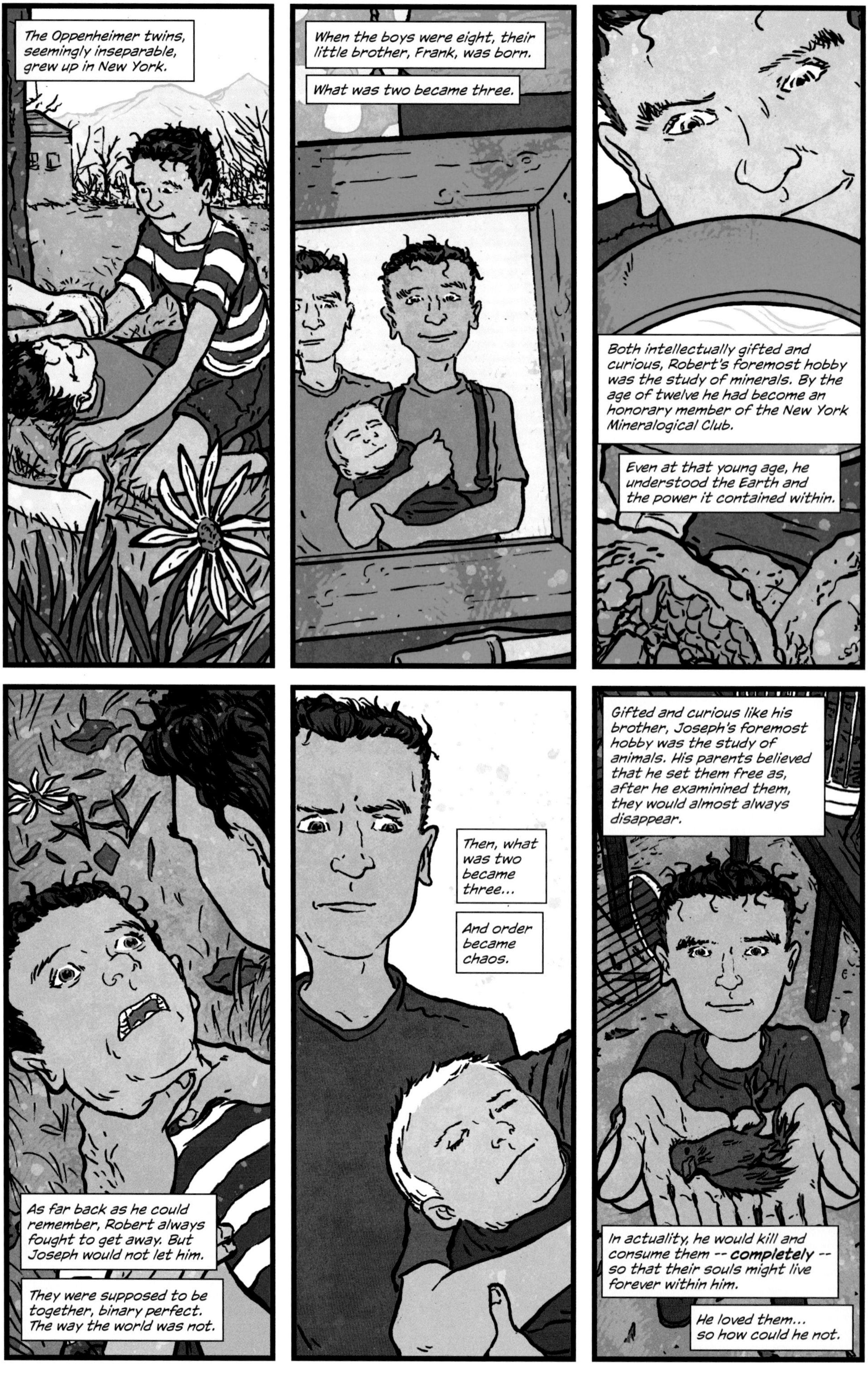
The Oppenheimer twins, seemingly inseparable, grew up in New York.
When the boys were eight, their little brother, Frank, was born.
What was two became three.
Both intellectually gifted and curious, Robert's foremost hobby was the study of minerals. By the age of twelve he had become an honorary member of the New York Mineralogical Club.
Even at that young age, he understood the Earth and the power it contained within.
As far back as he could remember, Robert always fought to get away. But Joseph would not let him.
They were supposed to be together, binary perfect. The way the world was not.
Then, what was two became three...
And order became chaos.
Gifted and curious like his brother, Joseph's foremost hobby was the study of animals. His parents believed that he set them free as, after he examined them, they would almost always disappear.
In actuality, he would kill and consume them -- **completely** -- so that their souls might live forever within him.
He loved them... so how could he not.

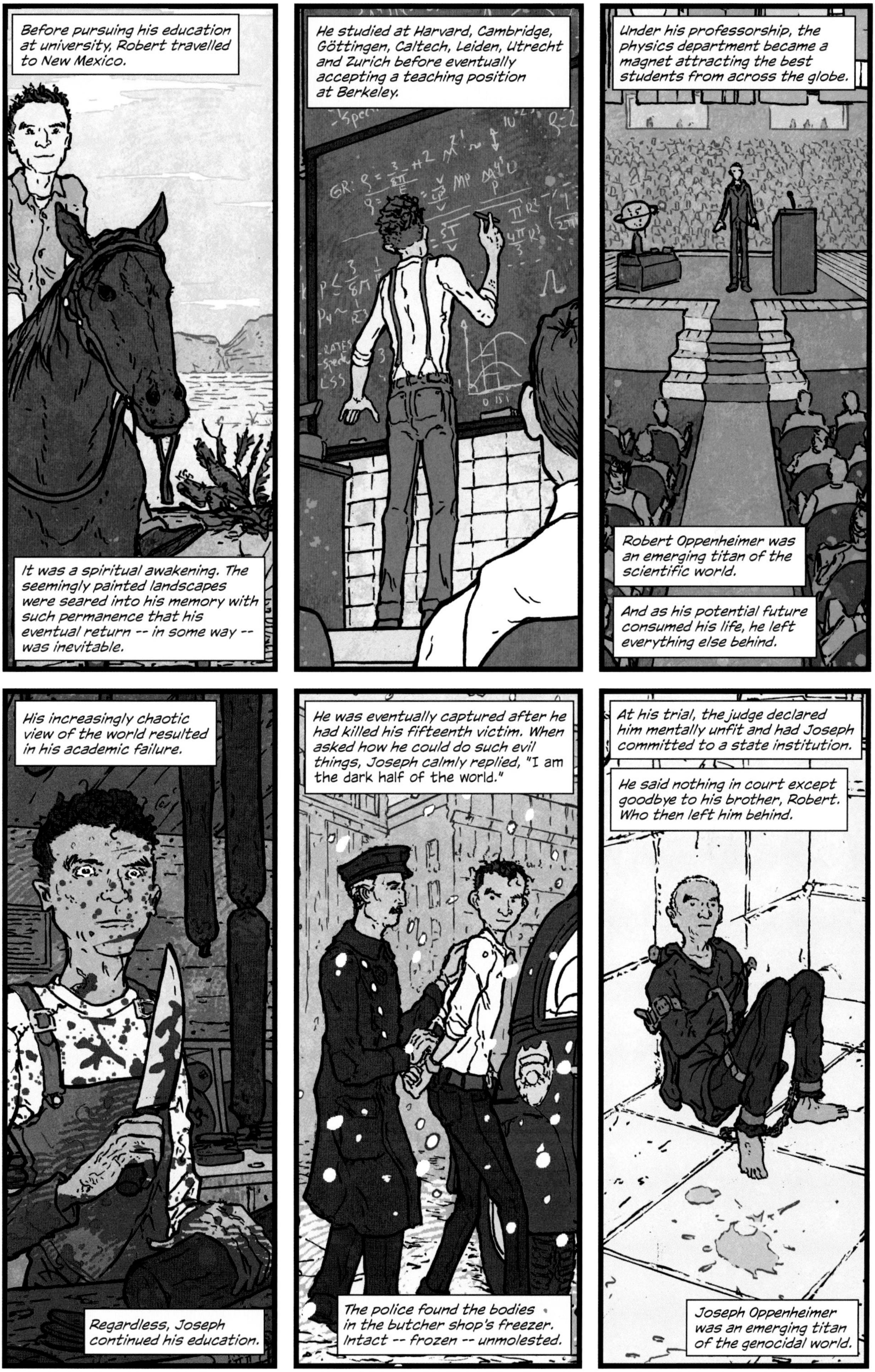
Before pursuing his education at university, Robert travelled to New Mexico.
It was a spiritual awakening. The seemingly painted landscapes were seared into his memory with such permanence that his eventual return -- in some way -- was inevitable.
He studied at Harvard, Cambridge, Göttingen, Caltech, Leiden, Utrecht and Zurich before eventually accepting a teaching position at Berkeley.
Under his professorship, the physics department became a magnet attracting the best students from across the globe.
Robert Oppenheimer was an emerging titan of the scientific world.
And as his potential future consumed his life, he left everything else behind.
His increasingly chaotic view of the world resulted in his academic failure.
Regardless, Joseph continued his education.
He was eventually captured after he had killed his fifteenth victim. When asked how he could do such evil things, Joseph calmly replied, "I am the dark half of the world."
The police found the bodies in the butcher shop's freezer. Intact -- frozen -- unmolested.
At his trial, the judge declared him mentally unfit and had Joseph committed to a state institution.
He said nothing in court except goodbye to his brother, Robert. Who then left him behind.
Joseph Oppenheimer was an emerging titan of the genocidal world.

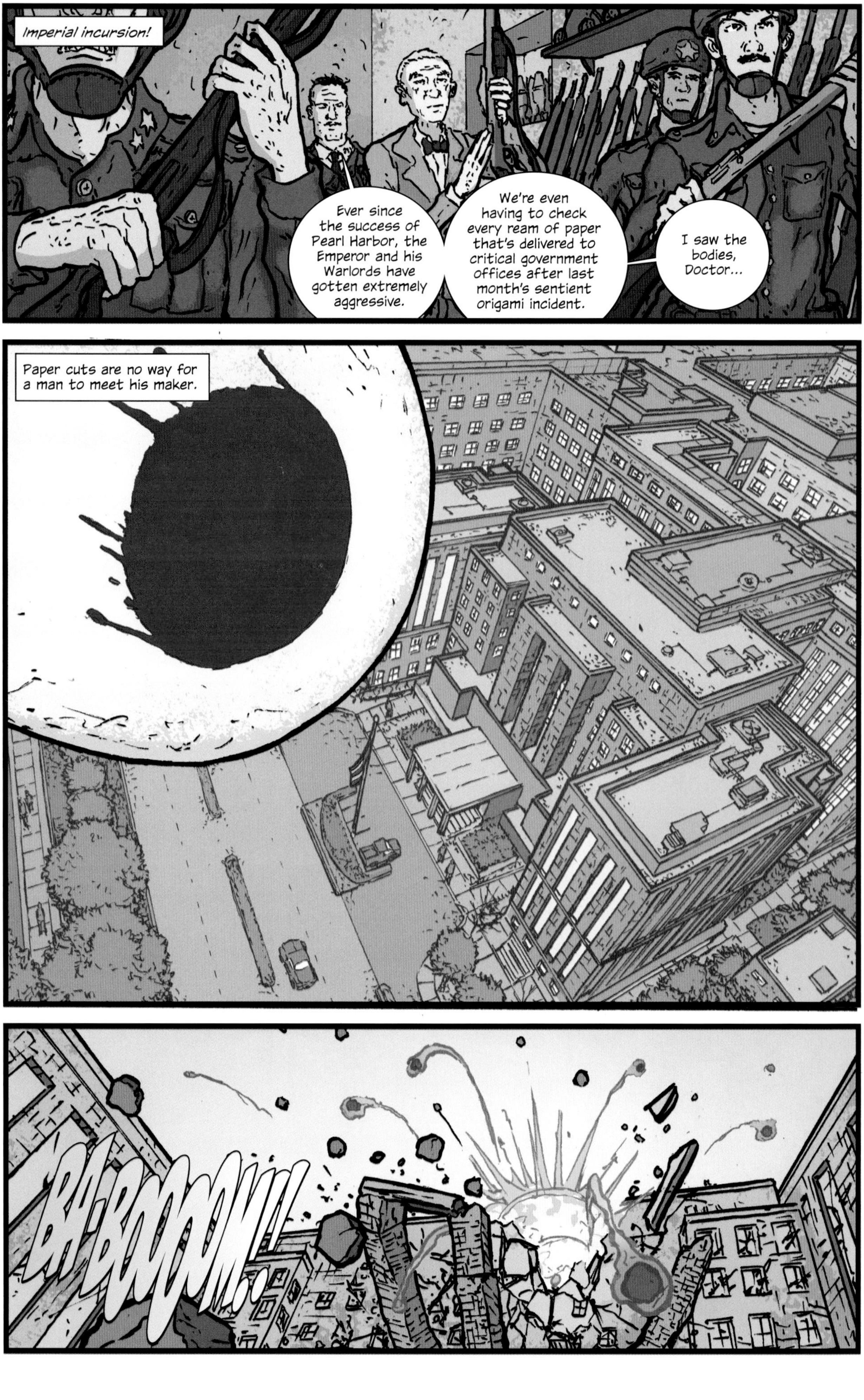
Imperial incursion!
Ever since the success of Pearl Harbor, the Emperor and his Warlords have gotten extremely aggressive.
We're even having to check every ream of paper that's delivered to critical government offices after last month's sentient origami incident.
I saw the bodies, Doctor...
Paper cuts are no way for a man to meet his maker.
BA-BOOOOOM!!!

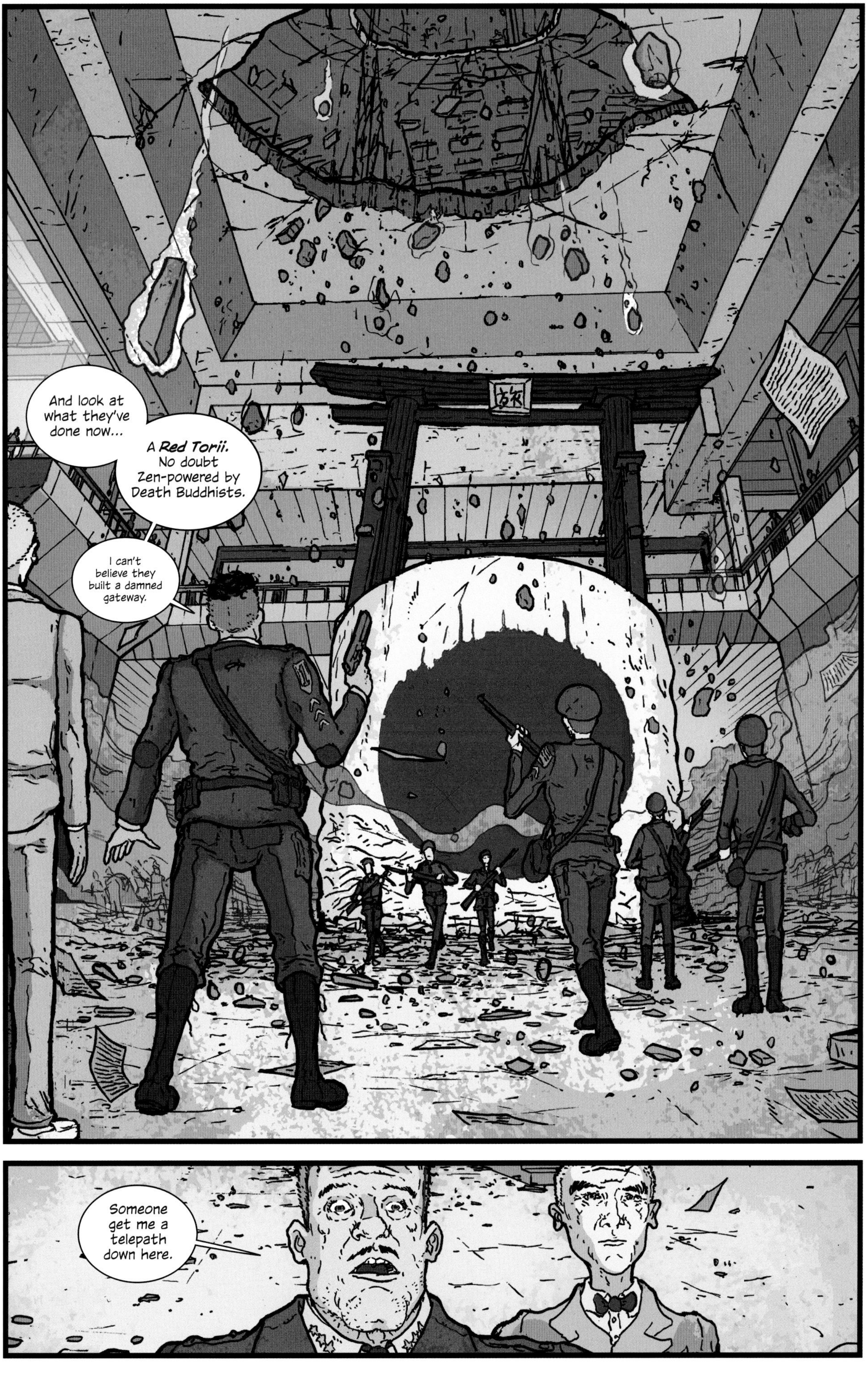
And look at what they've done now...
A *Red Torii.* No doubt Zen-powered by Death Buddhists.
I can't believe they built a damned gateway.
Someone get me a telepath down here.

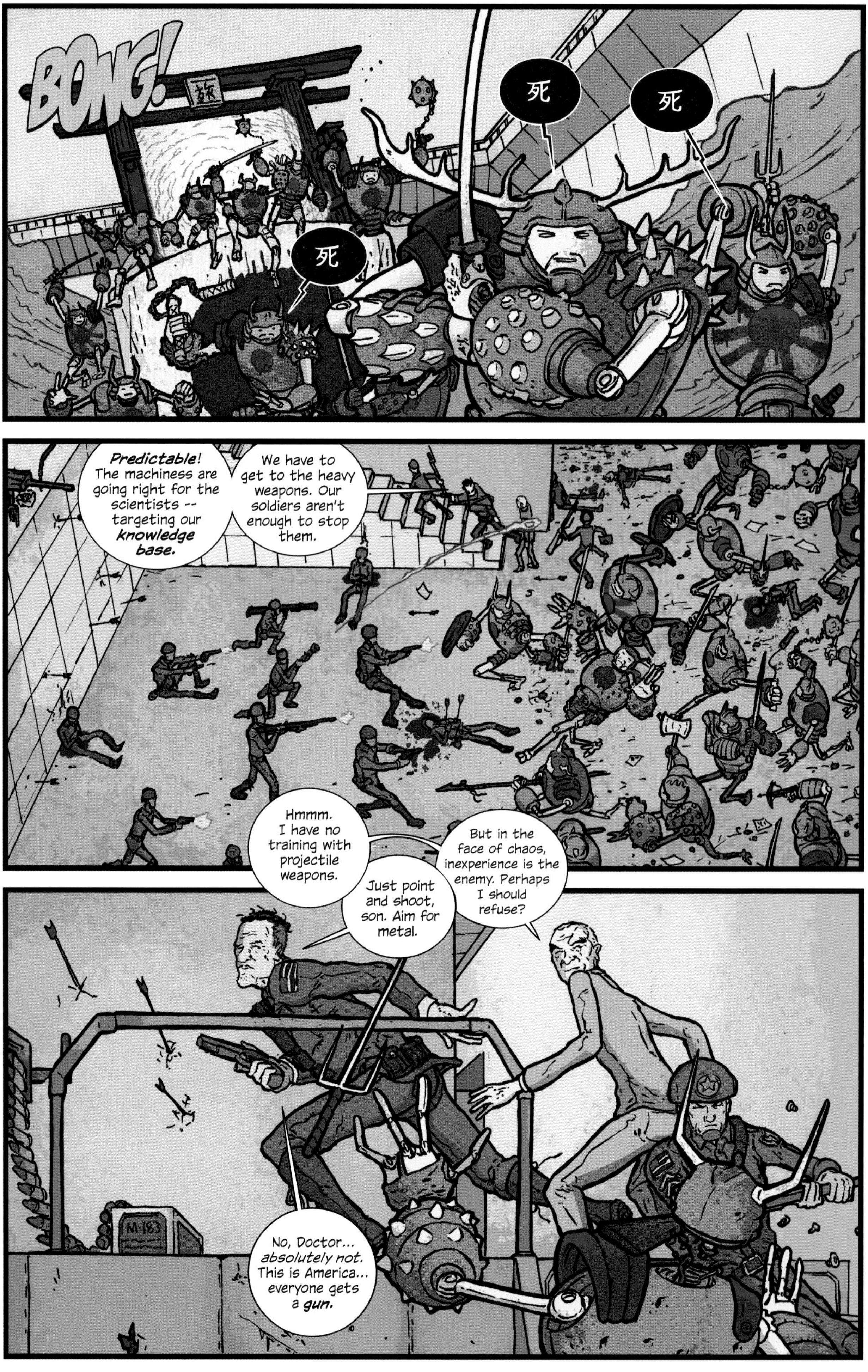
BONG!
死
死
死
Predictable! The machiness are going right for the scientists -- targeting our knowledge base.
We have to get to the heavy weapons. Our soldiers aren't enough to stop them.
Hmmm. I have no training with projectile weapons.
But in the face of chaos, inexperience is the enemy. Perhaps I should refuse?
Just point and shoot, son. Aim for metal.
No, Doctor... absolutely not. This is America... everyone gets a gun.
M-183

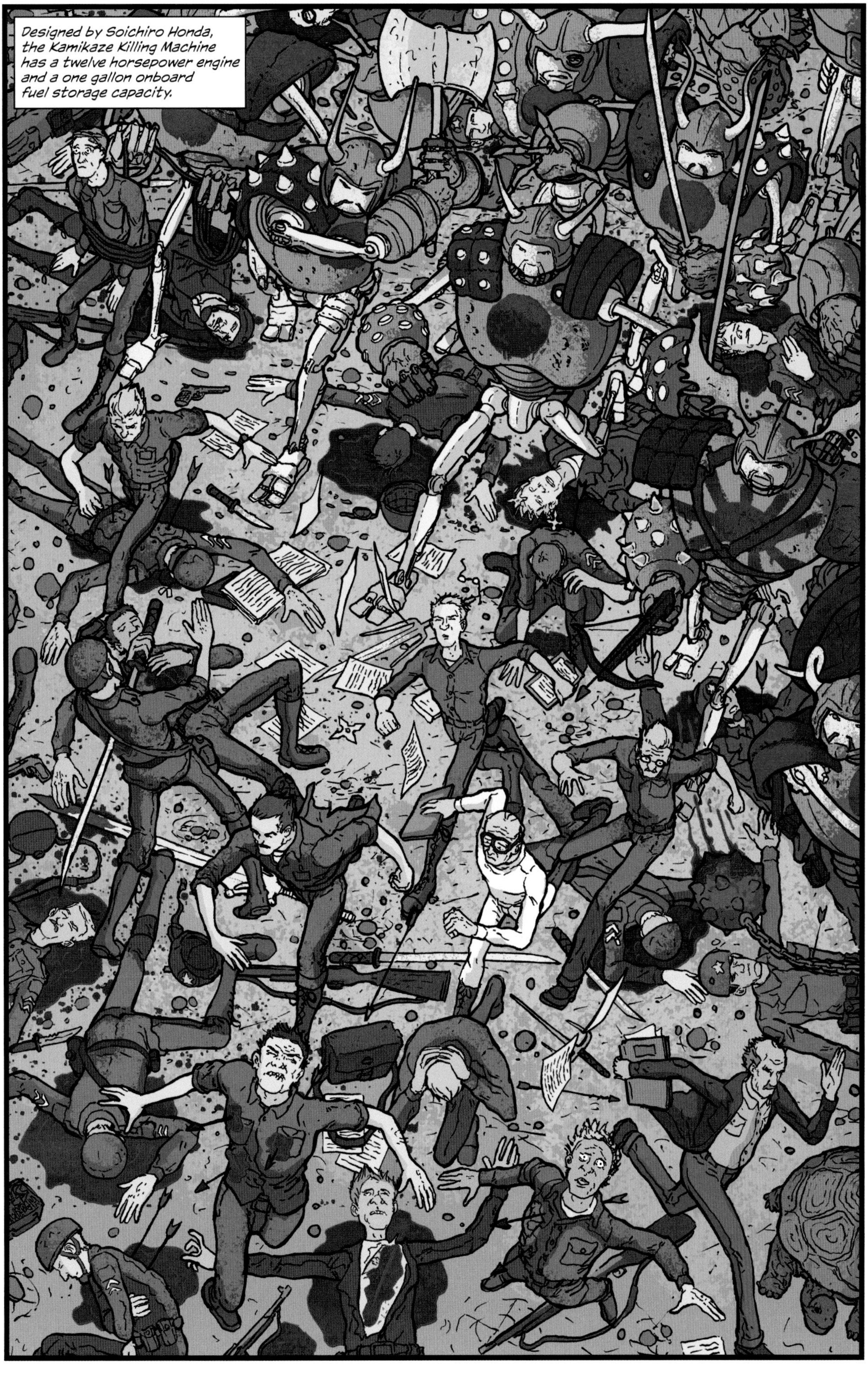
Designed by Soichiro Honda,
the Kamikaze Killing Machine
has a twelve horsepower engine
and a one gallon onboard
fuel storage capacity.

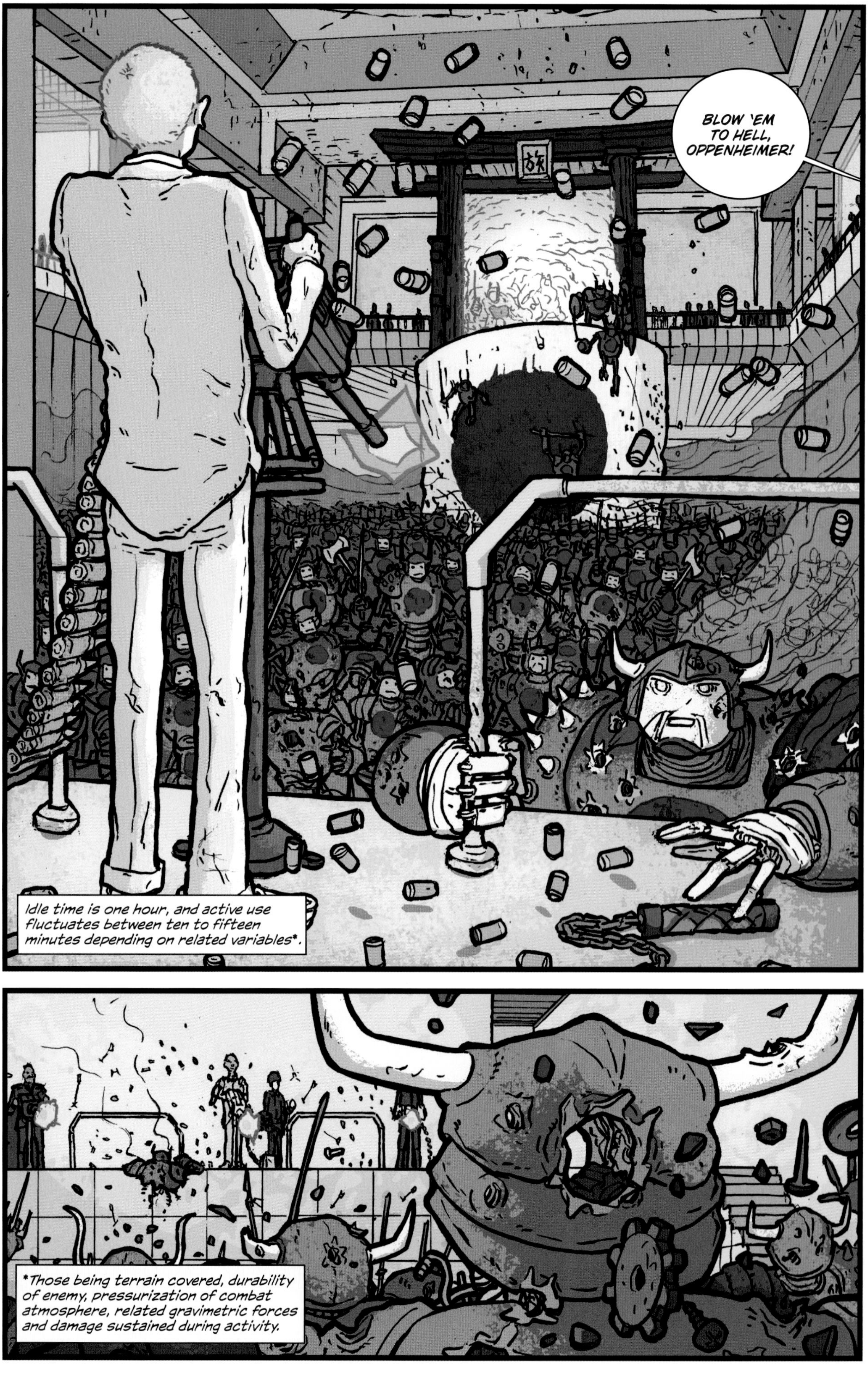
BLOW 'EM TO HELL, OPPENHEIMER!
Idle time is one hour, and active use fluctuates between ten to fifteen minutes depending on related variables*.
*Those being terrain covered, durability of enemy, pressurization of combat atmosphere, related gravimetric forces and damage sustained during activity.

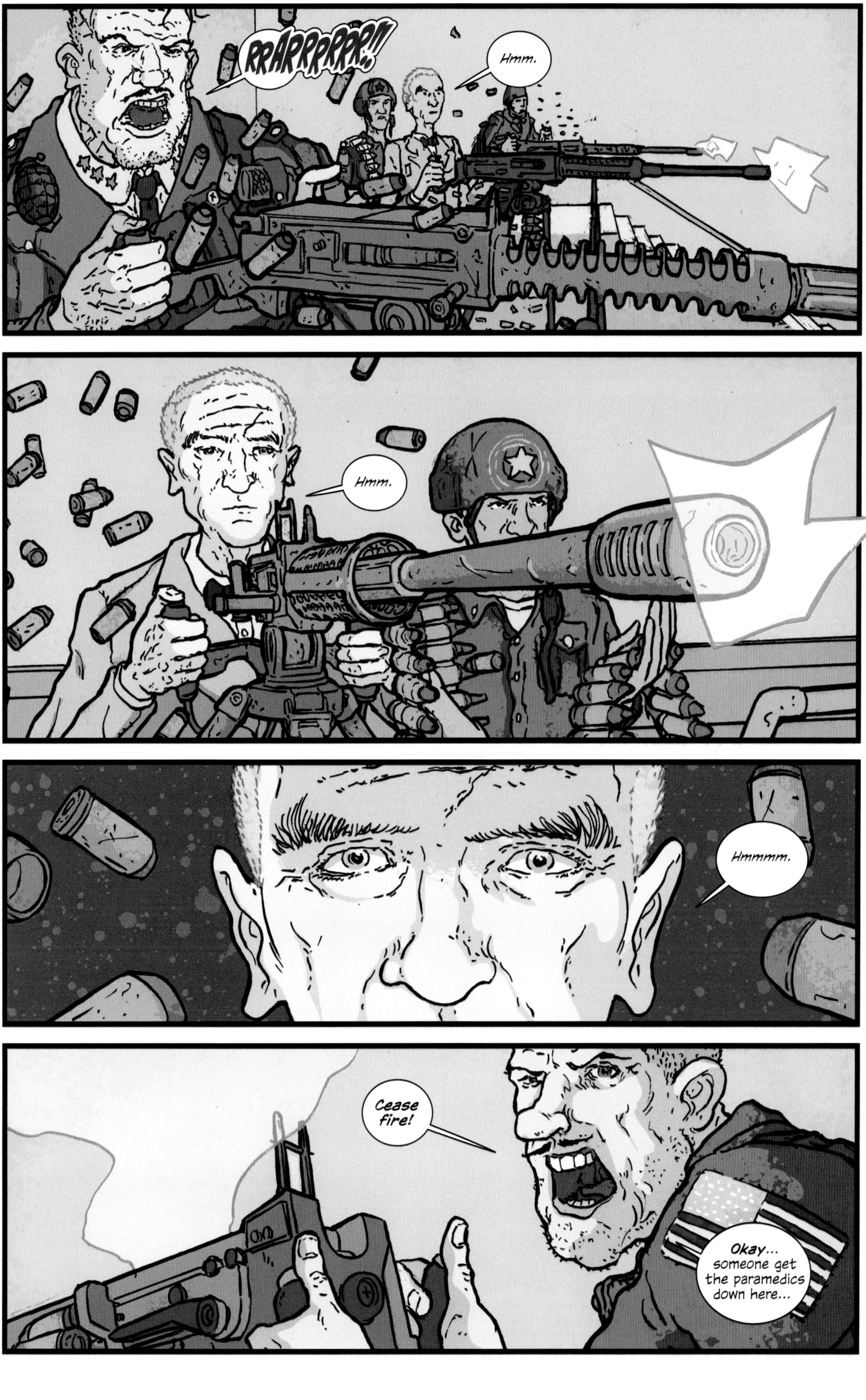
RRARRRRRR!!
Hmm.
Hmm.
Hmmmm.
Cease fire!
Okay... someone get the paramedics down here...

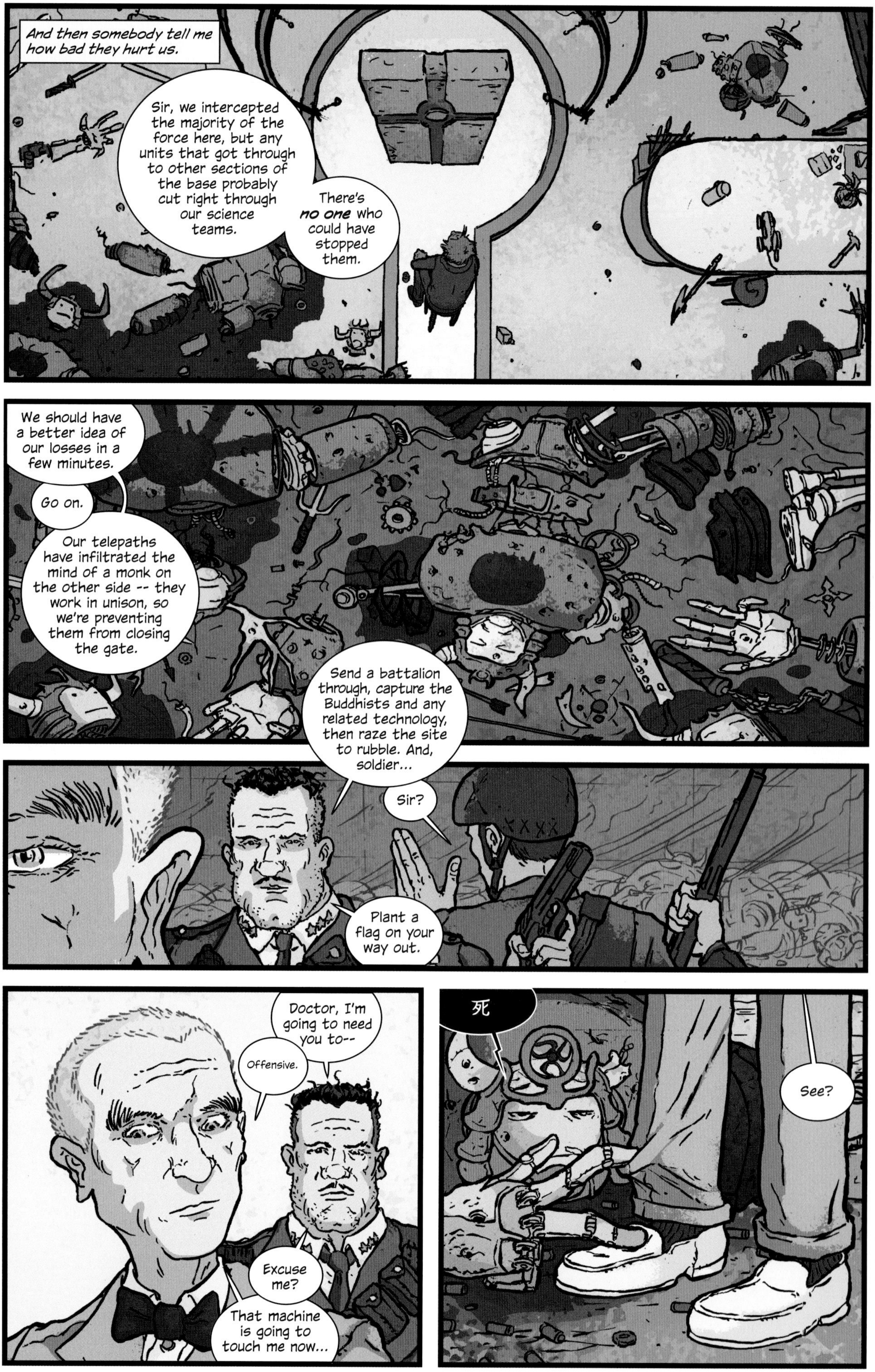
And then somebody tell me how bad they hurt us.
Sir, we intercepted the majority of the force here, but any units that got through to other sections of the base probably cut right through our science teams.
There's *no one* who could have stopped them.
We should have a better idea of our losses in a few minutes.
Go on.
Our telepaths have infiltrated the mind of a monk on the other side -- they work in unison, so we're preventing them from closing the gate.
Send a battalion through, capture the Buddhists and any related technology, then raze the site to rubble. And, soldier...
Sir?
Plant a flag on your way out.
Doctor, I'm going to need you to--
Offensive.
Excuse me?
That machine is going to touch me now...
死
See?

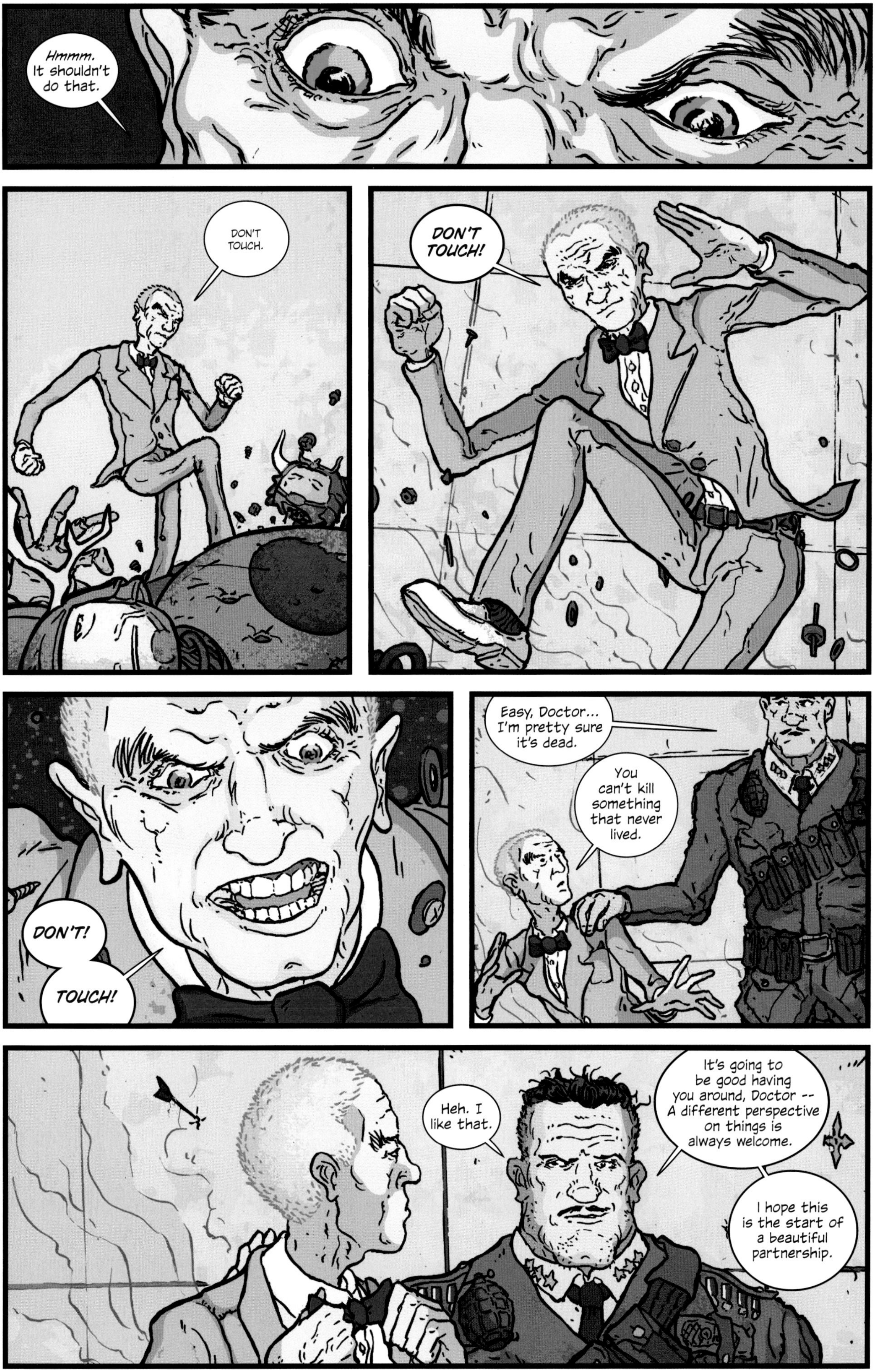
Hmmm.
It shouldn't
do that.
DON'T
TOUCH.
DON'T
TOUCH!
DON'T!
TOUCH!
Easy, Doctor...
I'm pretty sure
it's dead.
You
can't kill
something
that never
lived.
Heh. I
like that.
It's going to
be good having
you around, Doctor --
A different perspective
on things is
always welcome.
I hope this
is the start of
a beautiful
partnership.

In the years after the establishment of the Berkeley physics department, Robert continued to have success follow success.

He helped build great machines...

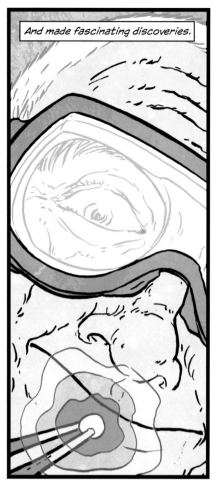

And made fascinating discoveries.

All of his accomplishments eventually culminating in his invitation to be the civilian head of the Manhattan Projects.

It was the best day of his life.

Joseph consumed Robert -- *completely* -- so that his soul might live forever within him.

He loved his brother... so how could he not.

There's just one last thing...

I don't have to concern myself with you suffering from your *brother's affliction*, do I?

The twins light and dark halves warred. And in that war, the Oppenheimer shattered.

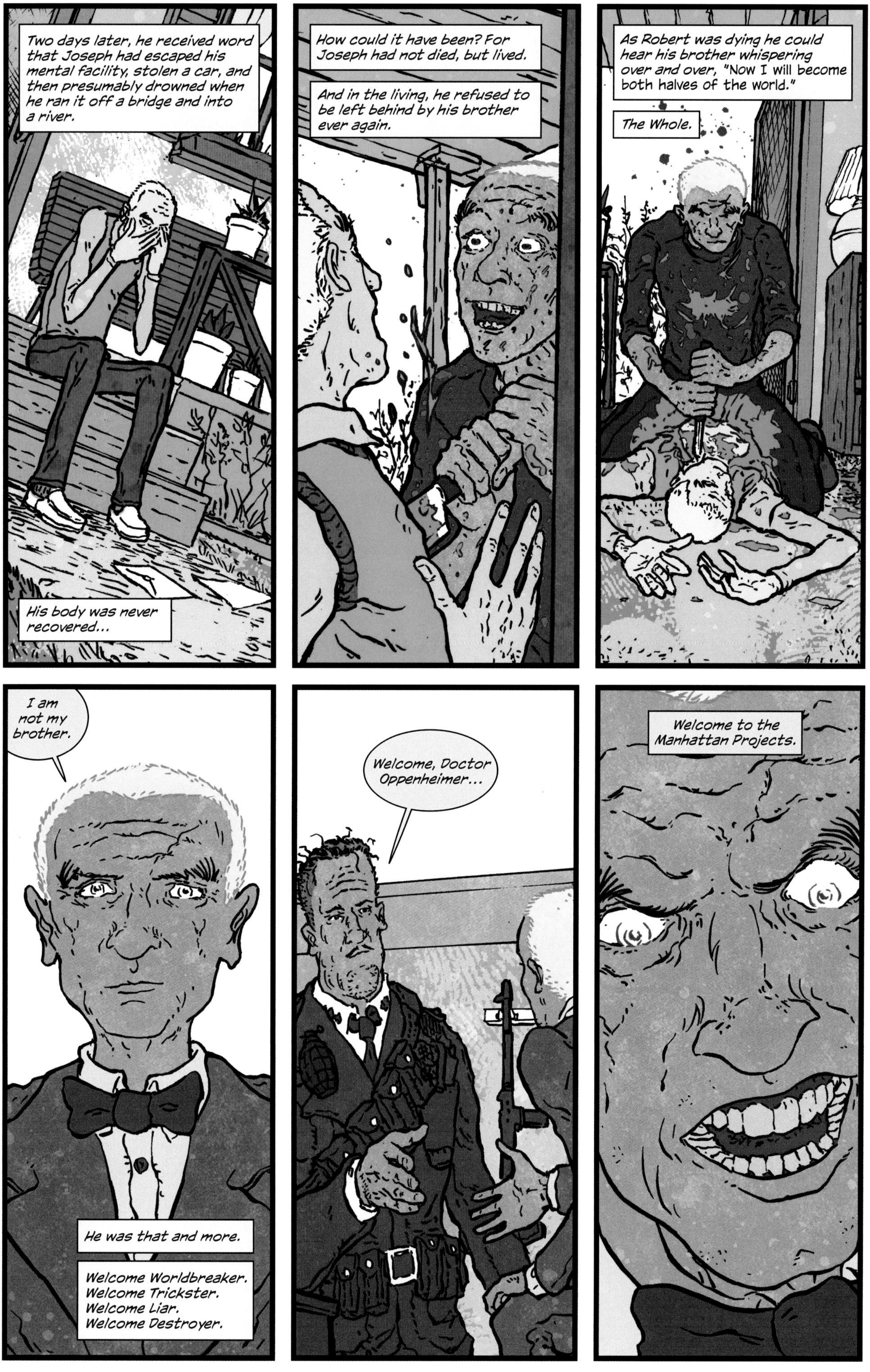
Two days later, he received word that Joseph had escaped his mental facility, stolen a car, and then presumably drowned when he ran it off a bridge and into a river.
His body was never recovered...
How could it have been? For Joseph had not died, but lived.
And in the living, he refused to be left behind by his brother ever again.
As Robert was dying he could hear his brother whispering over and over, "Now I will become both halves of the world."
The Whole.
I am not my brother.
He was that and more.
Welcome Worldbreaker.
Welcome Trickster.
Welcome Liar.
Welcome Destroyer.
Welcome, Doctor Oppenheimer...
Welcome to the Manhattan Projects.

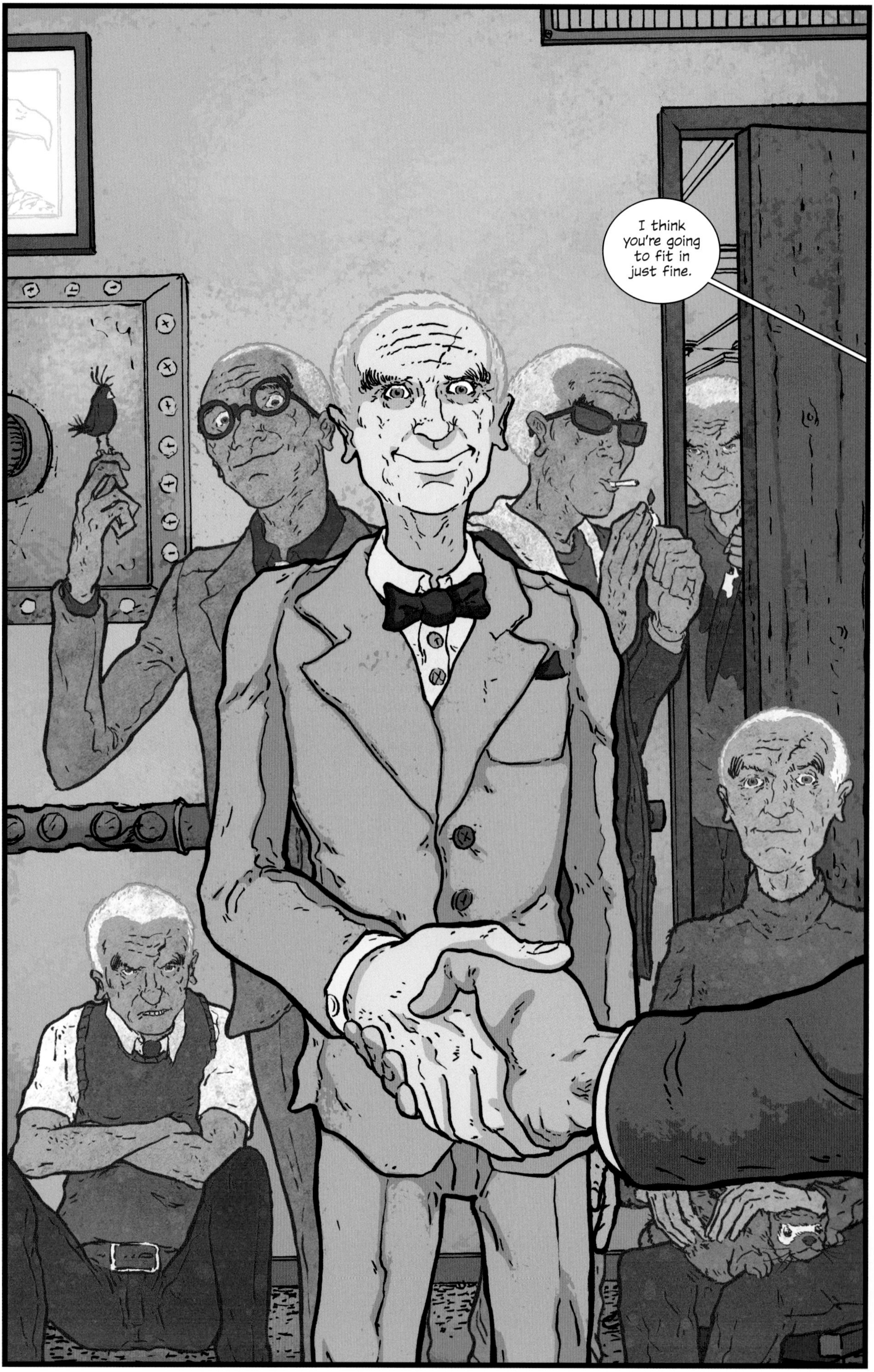
I think you're going to fit in just fine.

"IN THE BEGINNING, WHEN I FIRST
JOINED THE PROJECTS – BEFORE HIS
INTERNAL CIVIL WAR, BEFORE THE GREAT
CULLING, BEFORE THE AMALGAMATED
OPPENHEIMER COALESCED, THIRTY-TWO
DISTINCT VERSIONS OF THE DOCTOR
EXISTED.

FROM THERE, THE RATE OF FRACTURE
INCREASED EXPONENTIALLY, AND BY
1968 THAT NUMBER WAS VIRTUALLY
ENDLESS."

CLAVIS AUREA
THE RECORDED FEYNMAN | **VOL. 1**

I HOPE YOU LIKE NEW
EXPERIENCES

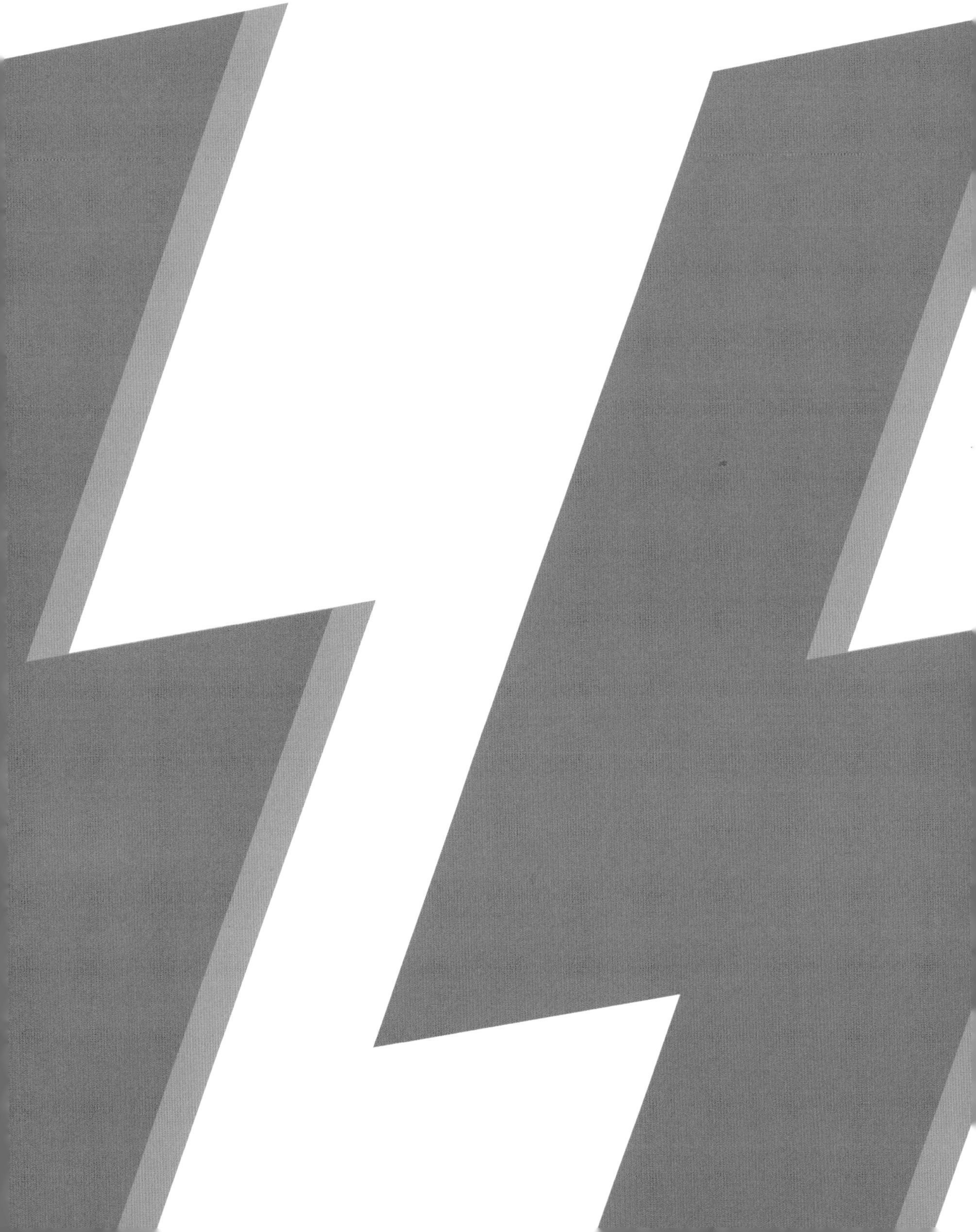

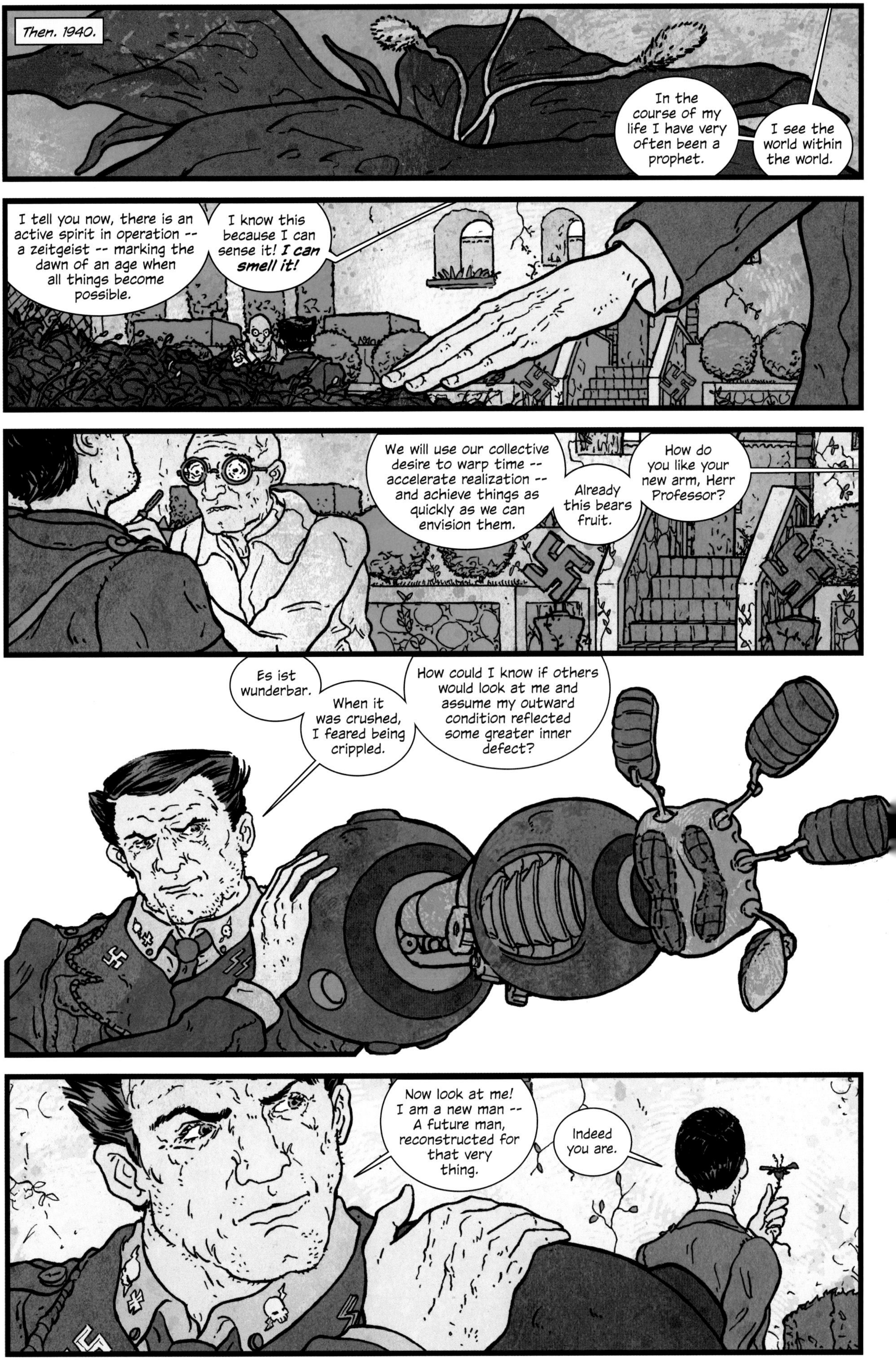
Then. 1940.
In the course of my life I have very often been a prophet.
I see the world within the world.
I tell you now, there is an active spirit in operation -- a zeitgeist -- marking the dawn of an age when all things become possible.
I know this because I can sense it! *I can smell it!*
We will use our collective desire to warp time -- accelerate realization -- and achieve things as quickly as we can envision them.
Already this bears fruit.
How do you like your new arm, Herr Professor?
Es ist wunderbar.
When it was crushed, I feared being crippled.
How could I know if others would look at me and assume my outward condition reflected some greater inner defect?
Now look at me! I am a new man -- A future man, reconstructed for that very thing.
Indeed you are.

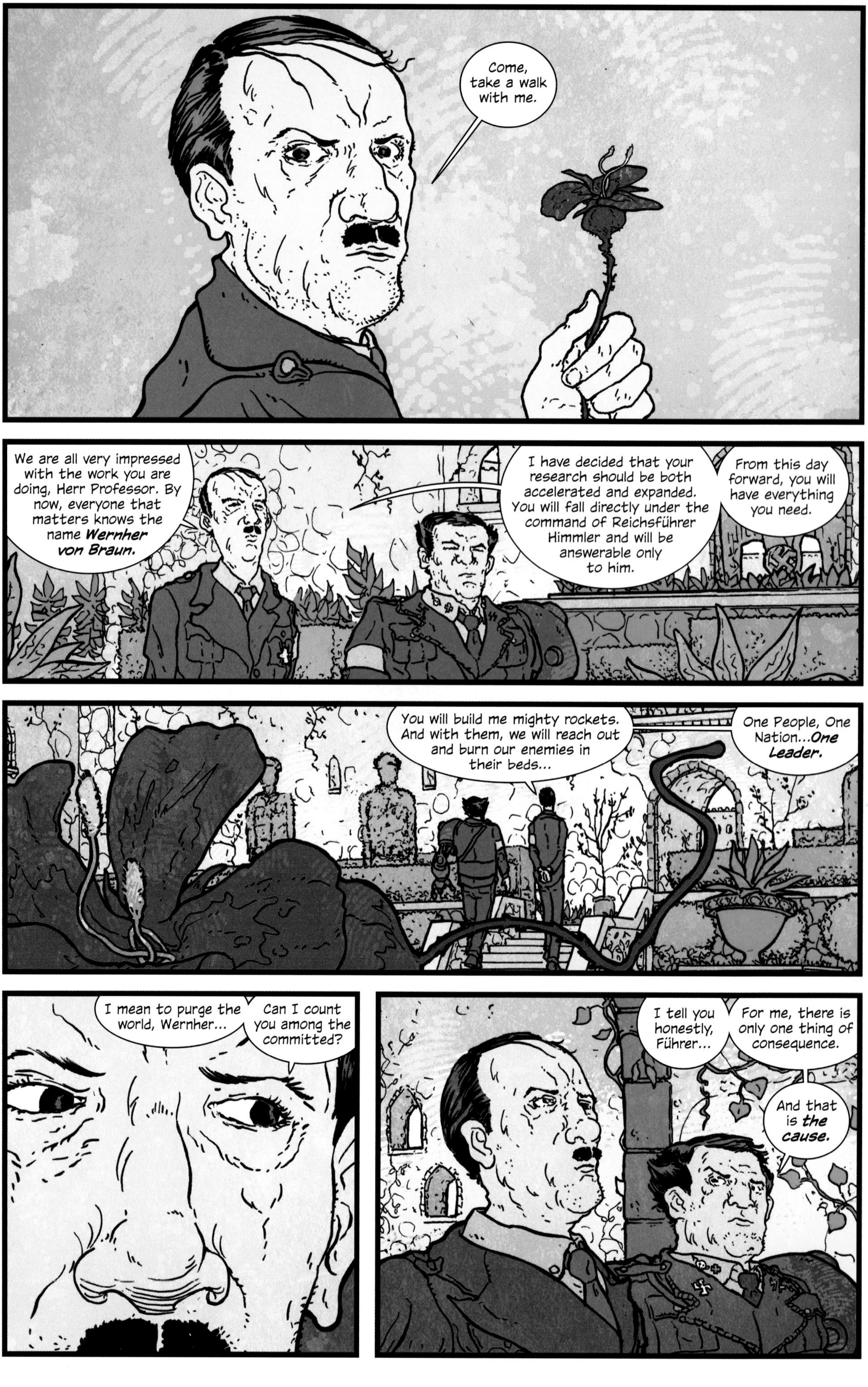
Come, take a walk with me.
We are all very impressed with the work you are doing, Herr Professor. By now, everyone that matters knows the name **Wernher von Braun.**
I have decided that your research should be both accelerated and expanded. You will fall directly under the command of Reichsführer Himmler and will be answerable only to him.
From this day forward, you will have everything you need.
You will build me mighty rockets. And with them, we will reach out and burn our enemies in their beds...
One People, One Nation...**One Leader.**
I mean to purge the world, Wernher...
Can I count you among the committed?
I tell you honestly, Führer...
For me, there is only one thing of consequence.
And that is **the cause.**

"NEVER FORGET, WE OWE THE FUTURE TO THE FASCISTS."

CLAVIS AUREA
THE RECORDED FEYNMAN | **VOL. 1**

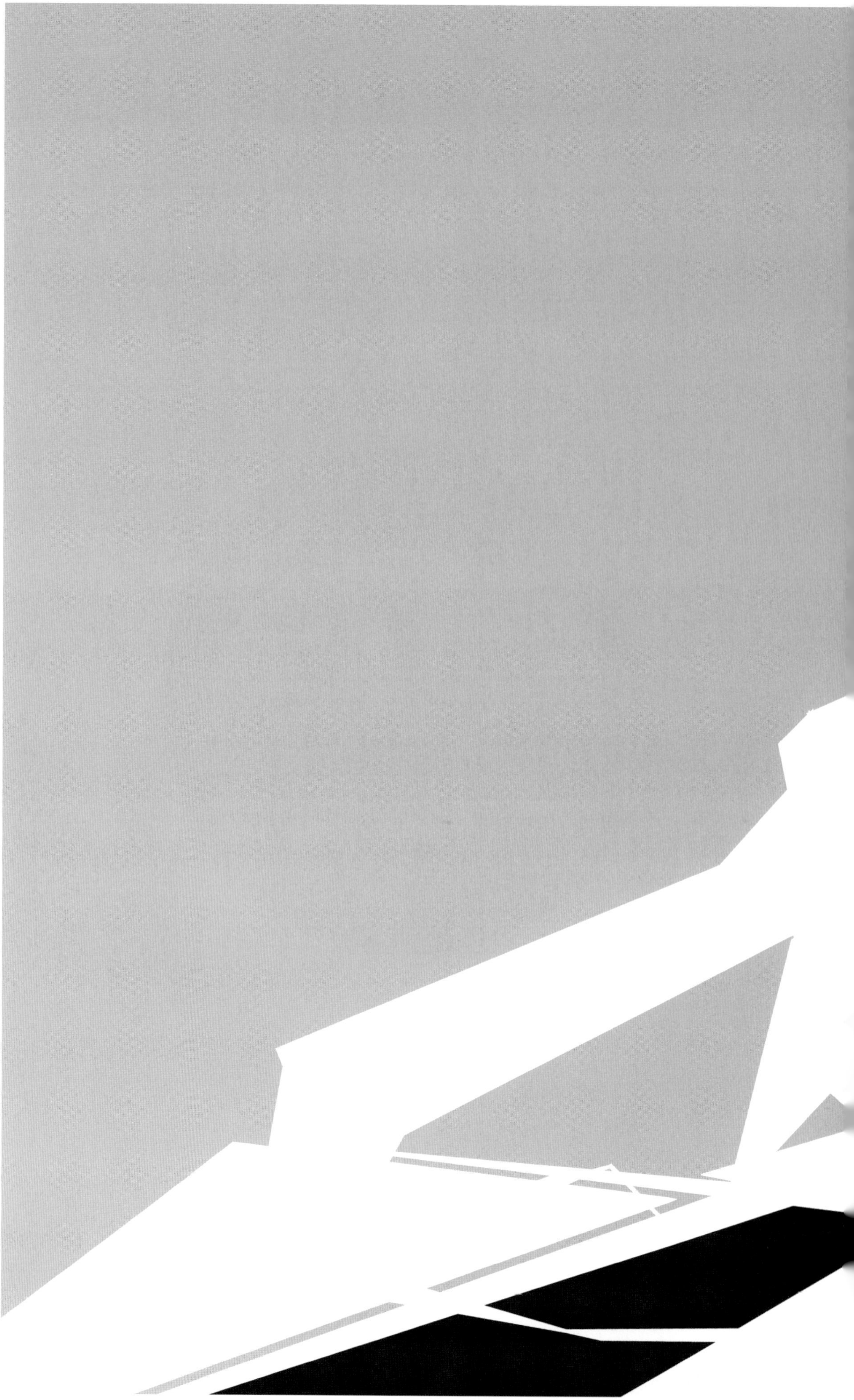

02

ROCKET MAN

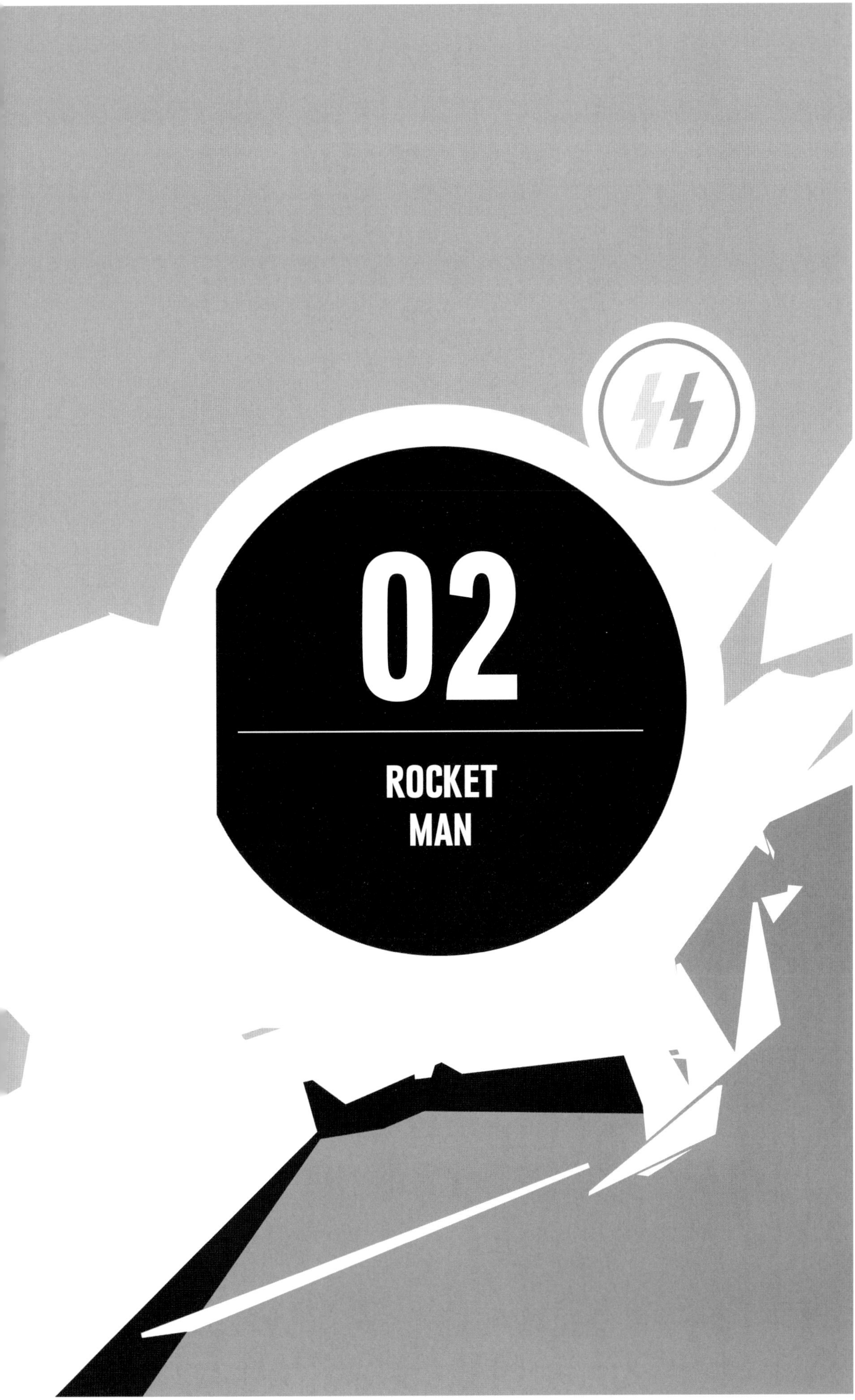

"I APOLOGIZE IF I'M EXCEEDINGLY FORMAL, BUT I FIND IT A NECESSARY COPING MECHANISM. YOU SEE, I SUFFER FROM AN EMBARRASSINGLY MUNDANE AFFLICTION THAT, WHEN UNADDRESSED, RESULTS IN A SHAMEFUL LACK OF MANNERS.

I AM CURSED WITH BURDEN OF ALWAYS BEING RIGHT."

CLAVIS AUREA
THE RECORDED FEYNMAN | **VOL. 1**

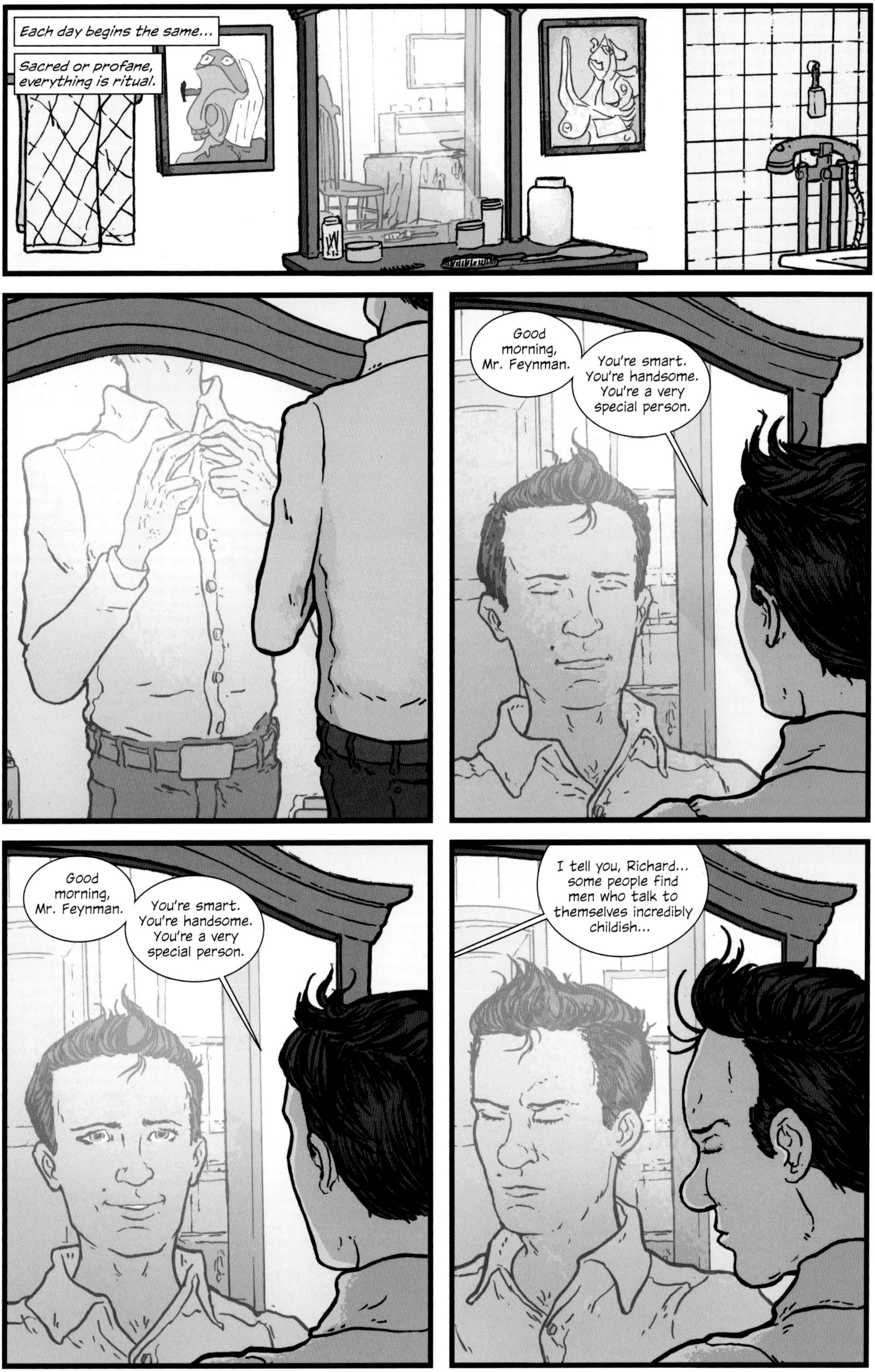
Each day begins the same...
Sacred or profane, everything is ritual.
Good morning, Mr. Feynman.
You're smart. You're handsome. You're a very special person.
Good morning, Mr. Feynman.
You're smart. You're handsome. You're a very special person.
I tell you, Richard... some people find men who talk to themselves incredibly childish...

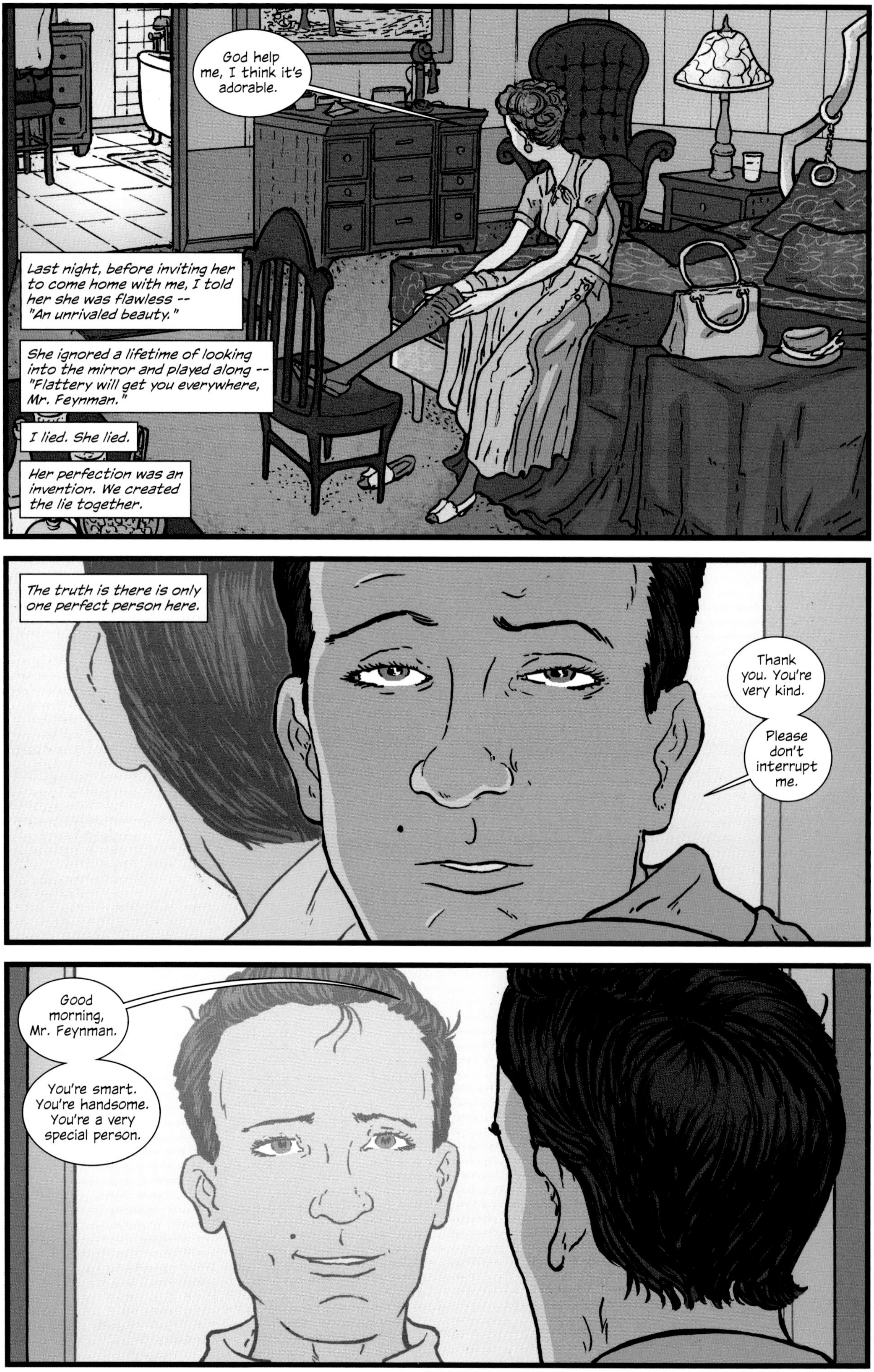
God help me, I think it's adorable.
Last night, before inviting her to come home with me, I told her she was flawless -- "An unrivaled beauty."
She ignored a lifetime of looking into the mirror and played along -- "Flattery will get you everywhere, Mr. Feynman."
I lied. She lied.
Her perfection was an invention. We created the lie together.
The truth is there is only one perfect person here.
Thank you. You're very kind.
Please don't interrupt me.
Good morning, Mr. Feynman.
You're smart. You're handsome. You're a very special person.

Now.

The War Department.

Welcome back, Doctor.

The transport chamber is ready...

Ah! Excellent. Molecular deconstruction and reassembly all before breakfast.

Did you know that we actually lose .005 percent of our body mass every time we use the gateway?..

Where do you think it goes, Captain?

Hrmp! I have no idea, sir...but this communication came through for you an hour ago.

I've been instructed to make sure you read it before you leave for Los Alamos.

Uh-huh...now you have to ask yourself, is the loss from water transitioning between states? Or is it something more exotic, like...

Wait...

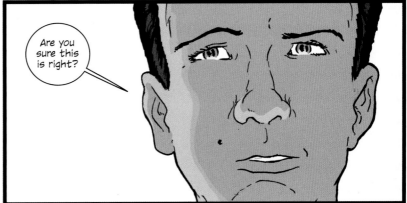

Are you sure this is right?

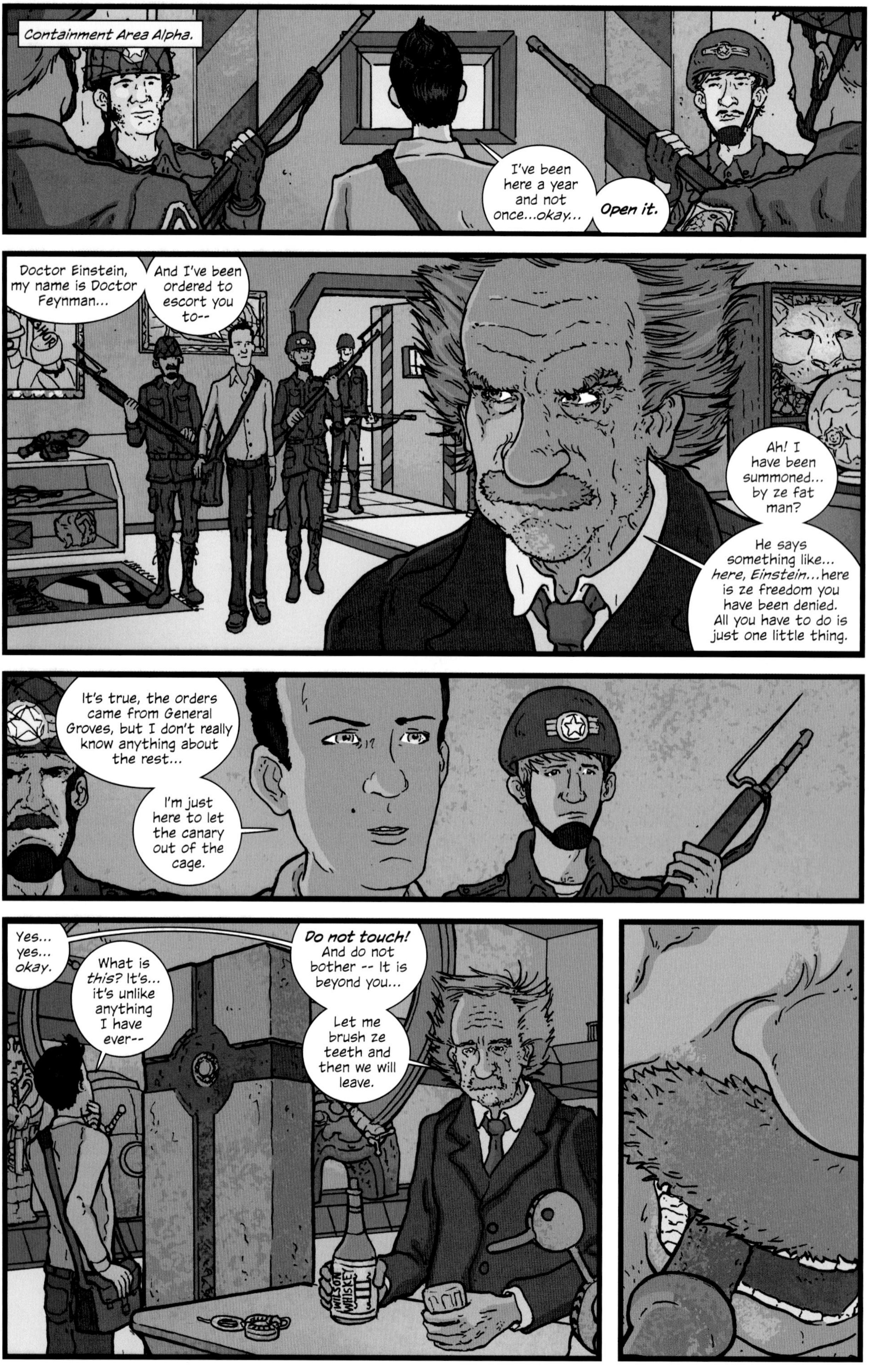
Containment Area Alpha.
I've been here a year and not once...okay...
Open it.
Doctor Einstein, my name is Doctor Feynman...
And I've been ordered to escort you to--
Ah! I have been summoned... by ze fat man?
He says something like... here, Einstein...here is ze freedom you have been denied. All you have to do is just one little thing.
It's true, the orders came from General Groves, but I don't really know anything about the rest...
I'm just here to let the canary out of the cage.
What is this? It's... it's unlike anything I have ever--
Do not touch! And do not bother -- It is beyond you...
Yes... yes... okay.
Let me brush ze teeth and then we will leave.
WILSON WHISKEY

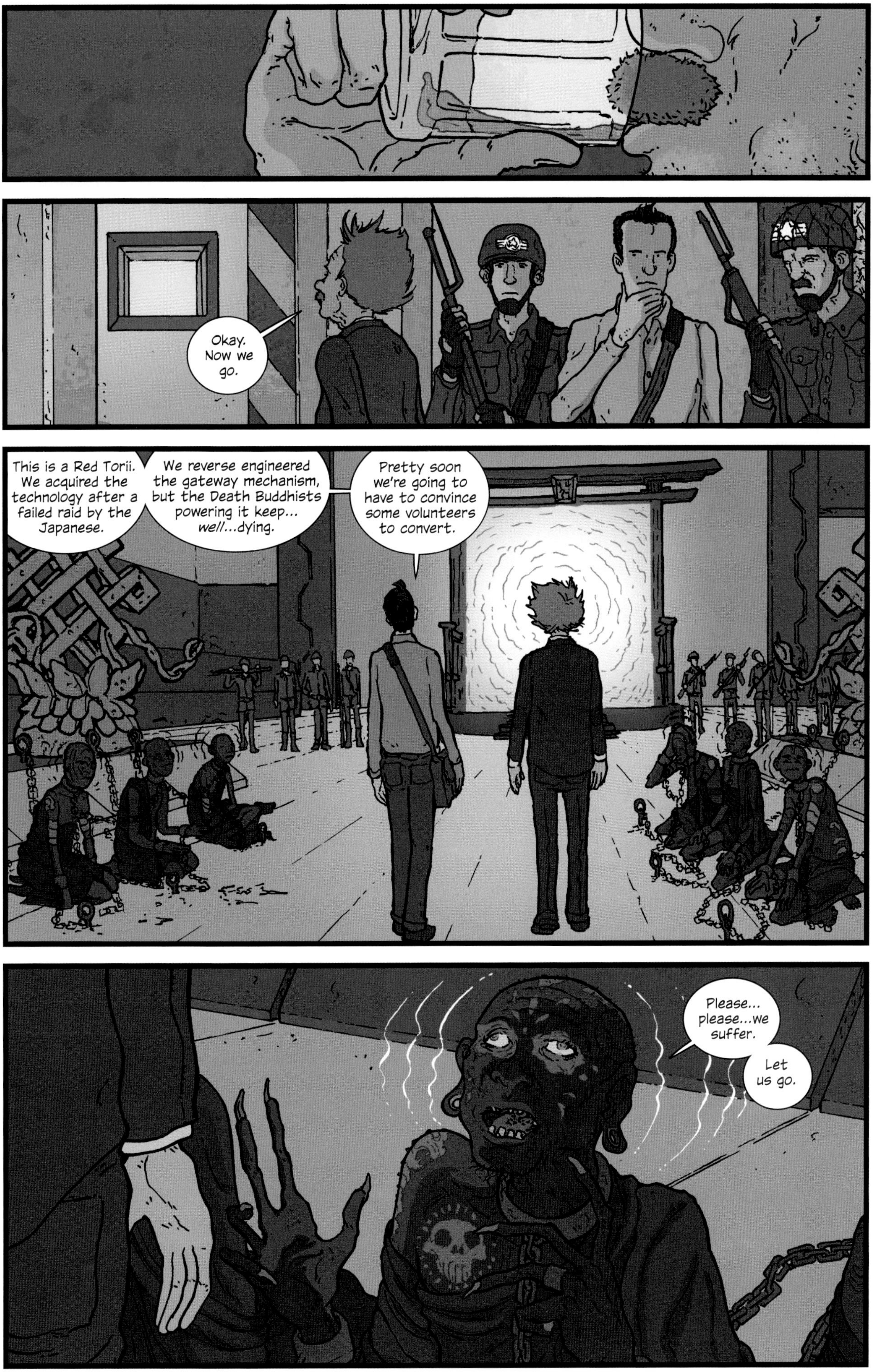
Okay. Now we go.
This is a Red Torii. We acquired the technology after a failed raid by the Japanese.
We reverse engineered the gateway mechanism, but the Death Buddhists powering it keep... *well*...dying.
Pretty soon we're going to have to convince some volunteers to convert.
Please... please...we suffer.
Let us go.

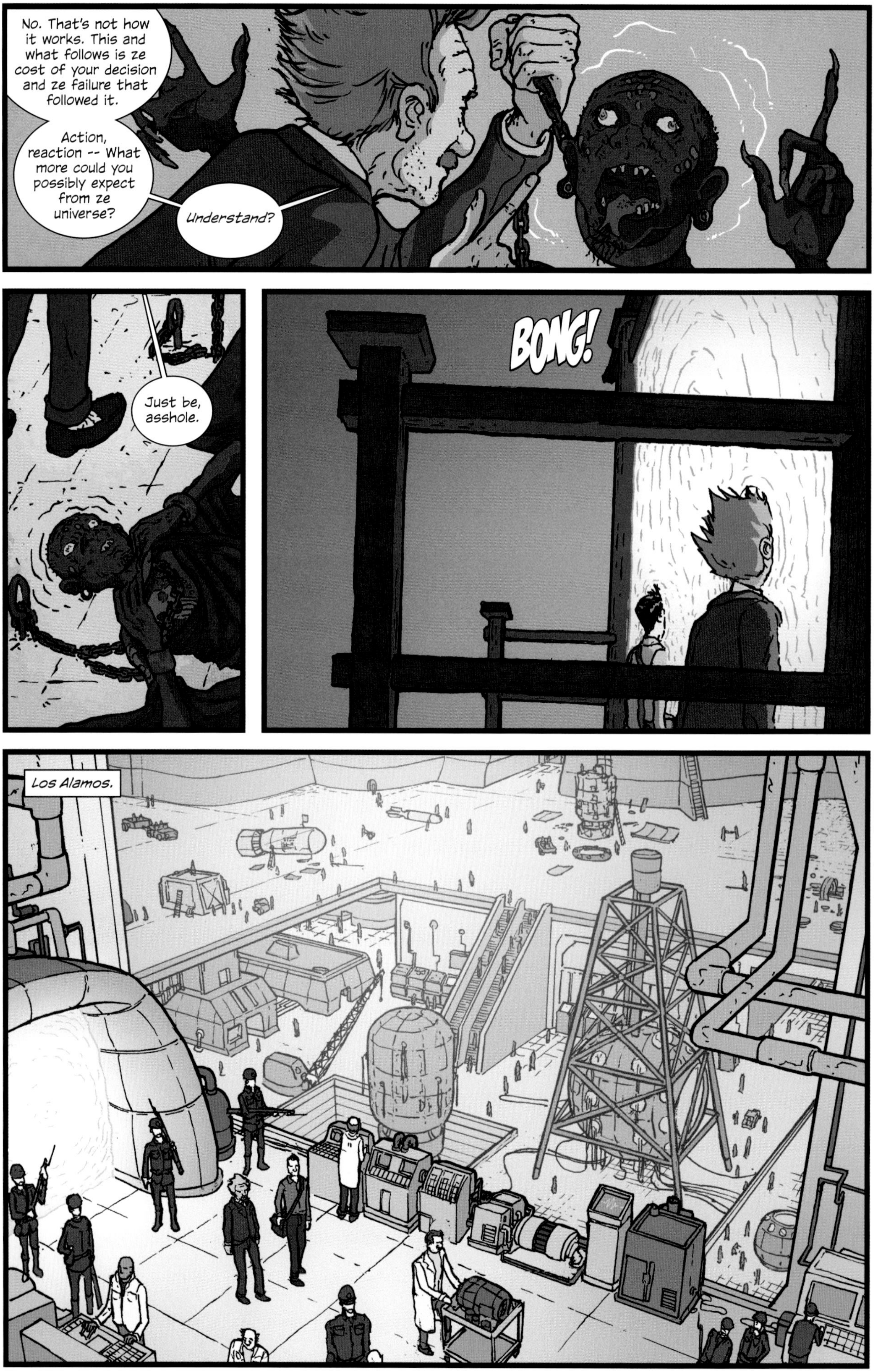
No. That's not how it works. This and what follows is ze cost of your decision and ze failure that followed it.
Action, reaction -- What more could you possibly expect from ze universe?
Understand?
Just be, asshole.
BONG!
Los Alamos.

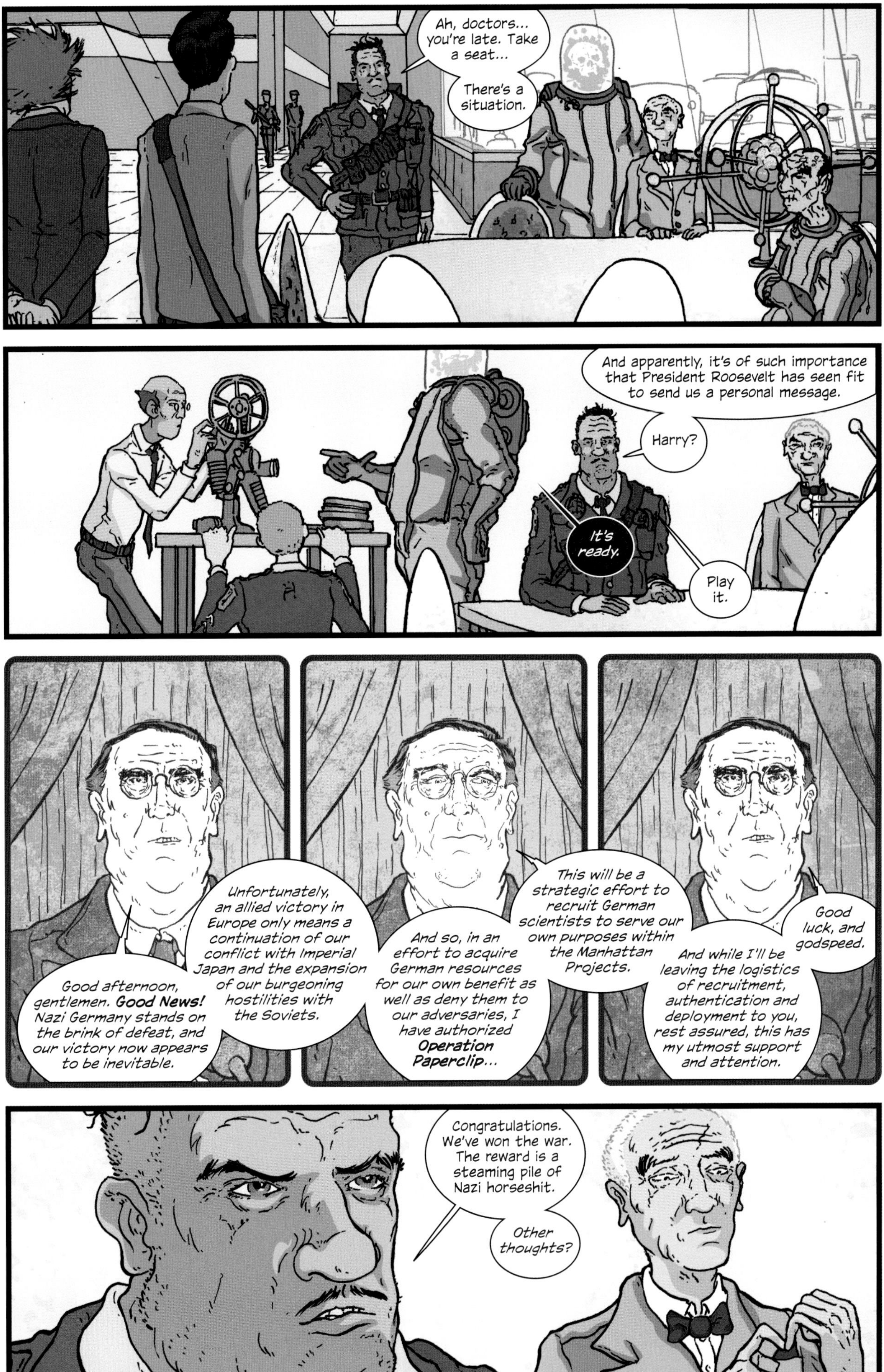
Ah, doctors... you're late. Take a seat...
There's a situation.
And apparently, it's of such importance that President Roosevelt has seen fit to send us a personal message.
Harry?
It's ready.
Play it.
Good afternoon, gentlemen. **Good News!** Nazi Germany stands on the brink of defeat, and our victory now appears to be inevitable.
Unfortunately, an allied victory in Europe only means a continuation of our conflict with Imperial Japan and the expansion of our burgeoning hostilities with the Soviets.
And so, in an effort to acquire German resources for our own benefit as well as deny them to our adversaries, I have authorized **Operation Paperclip**...
This will be a strategic effort to recruit German scientists to serve our own purposes within the Manhattan Projects.
And while I'll be leaving the logistics of recruitment, authentication and deployment to you, rest assured, this has my utmost support and attention.
Good luck, and godspeed.
Congratulations. We've won the war. The reward is a steaming pile of Nazi horseshit.
Other thoughts?

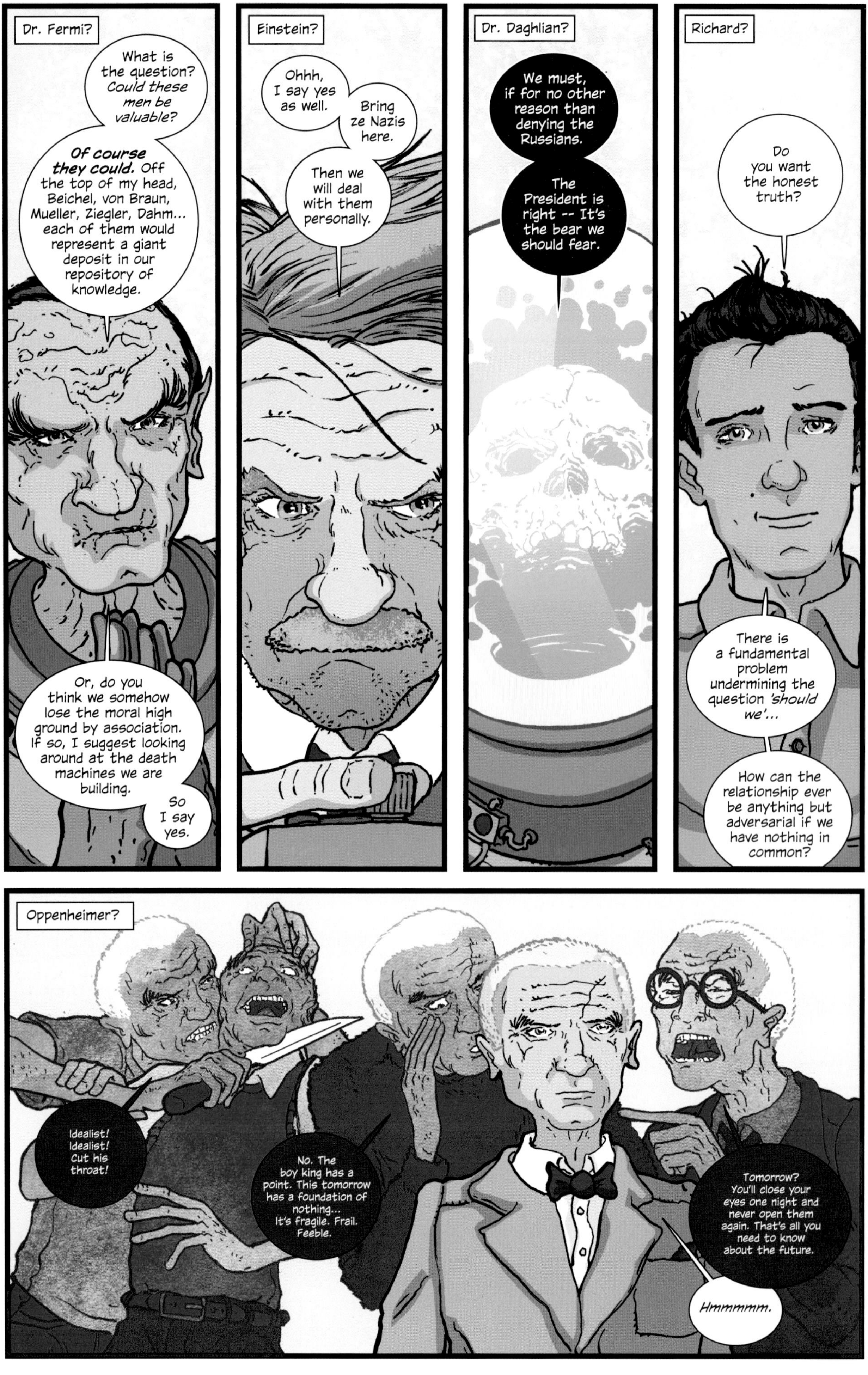

Dr. Fermi?
What is the question? *Could these men be valuable?*
Of course they could. Off the top of my head, Beichel, von Braun, Mueller, Ziegler, Dahm... each of them would represent a giant deposit in our repository of knowledge.
Or, do you think we somehow lose the moral high ground by association. If so, I suggest looking around at the death machines we are building.
So I say yes.
Einstein?
Ohhh, I say yes as well.
Bring ze Nazis here.
Then we will deal with them personally.
Dr. Daghlian?
We must, if for no other reason than denying the Russians.
The President is right -- It's the bear we should fear.
Richard?
Do you want the honest truth?
There is a fundamental problem undermining the question *'should we'*...
How can the relationship ever be anything but adversarial if we have nothing in common?
Oppenheimer?
Idealist! Idealist! Cut his throat!
No. The boy king has a point. This tomorrow has a foundation of nothing... It's fragile. Frail. Feeble.
Tomorrow? You'll close your eyes one night and never open them again. That's all you need to know about the future.
Hmmmmm.

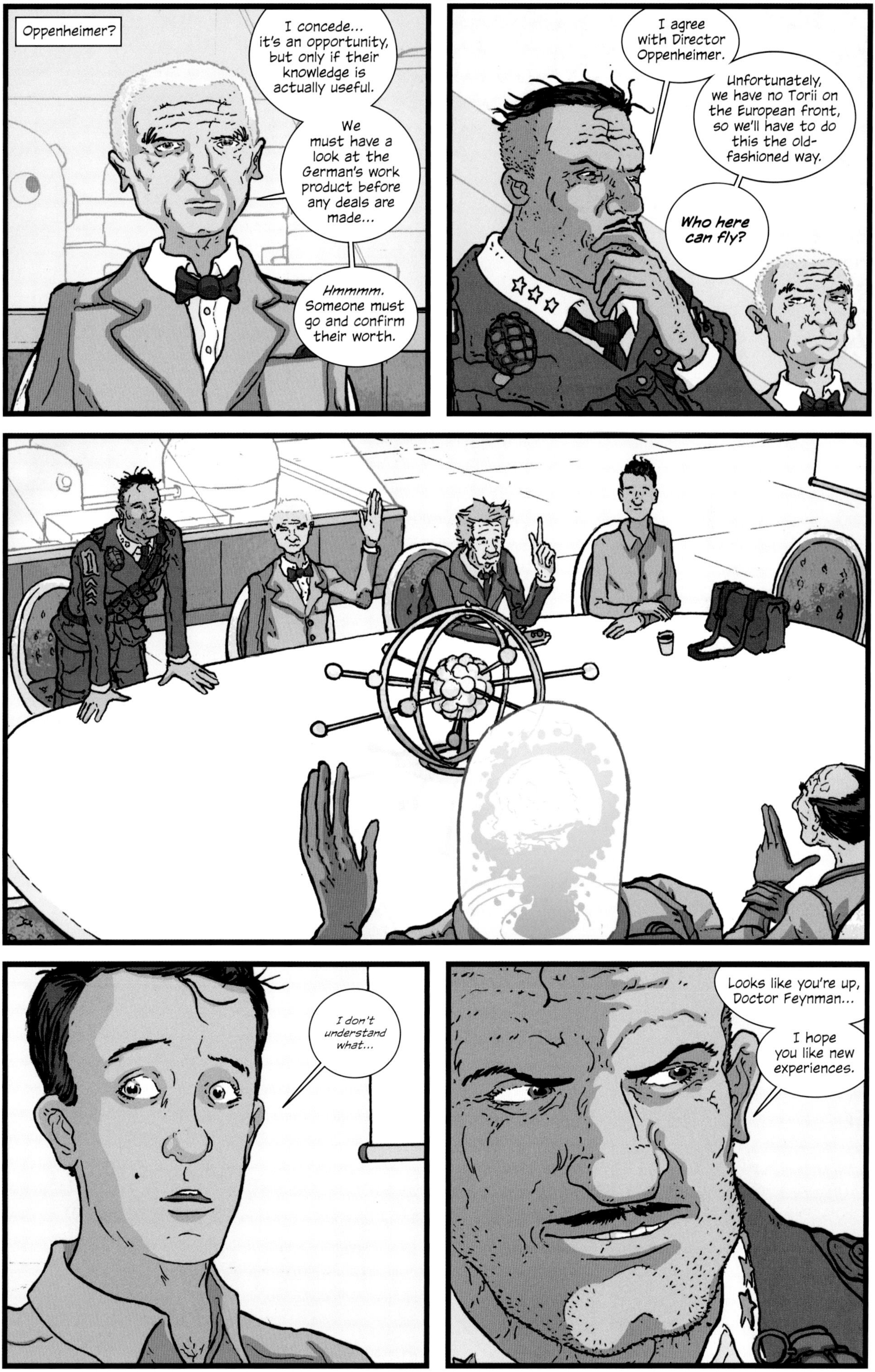
Oppenheimer?
I concede... it's an opportunity, but only if their knowledge is actually useful.
We must have a look at the German's work product before any deals are made...
Hmmmm. Someone must go and confirm their worth.
I agree with Director Oppenheimer.
Unfortunately, we have no Torii on the European front, so we'll have to do this the old-fashioned way.
Who here can fly?
I don't understand what...
Looks like you're up, Doctor Feynman...
I hope you like new experiences.

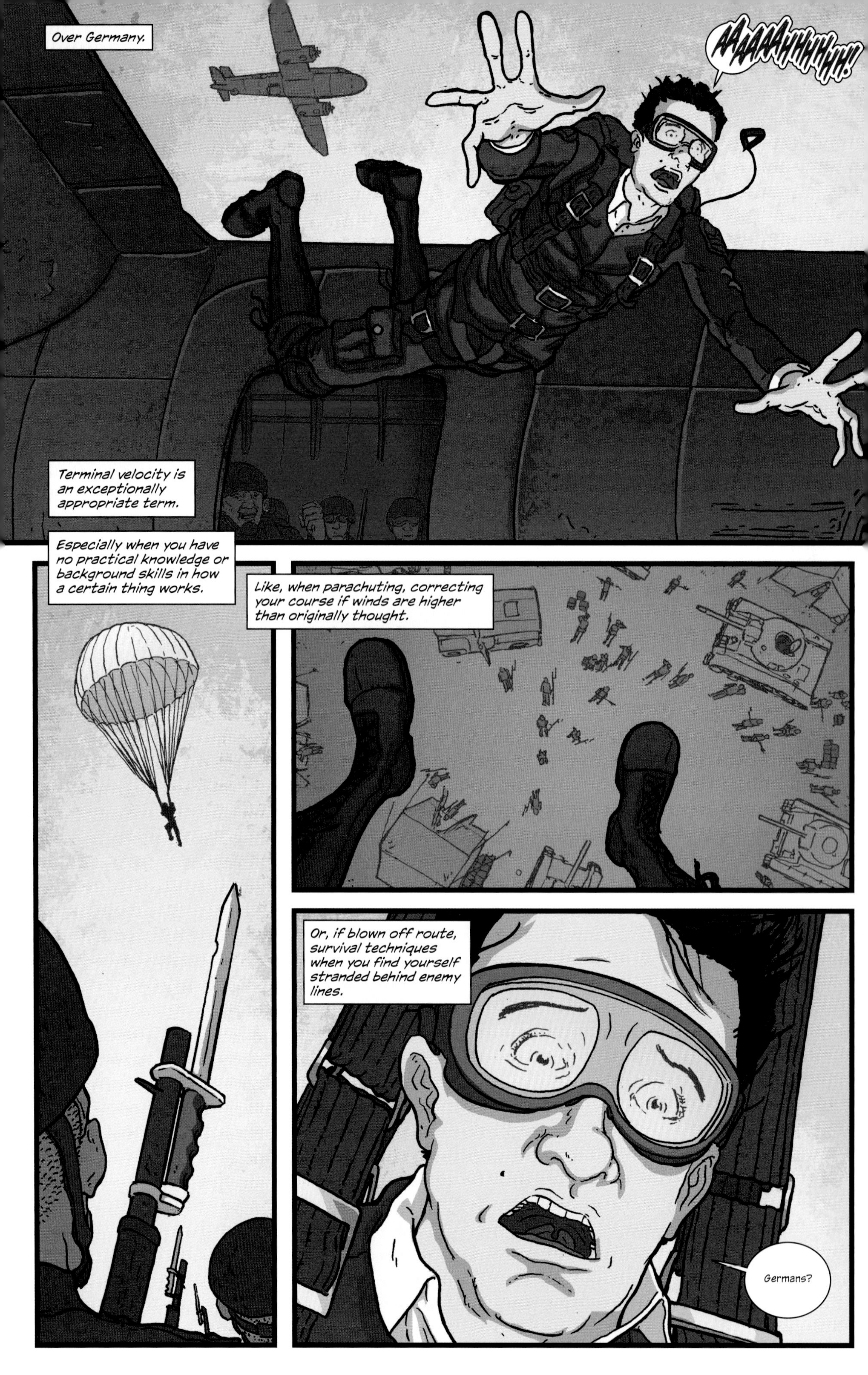
Over Germany.
AAAAAAHHHHHH!
Terminal velocity is an exceptionally appropriate term.
Especially when you have no practical knowledge or background skills in how a certain thing works.
Like, when parachuting, correcting your course if winds are higher than originally thought.
Or, if blown off route, survival techniques when you find yourself stranded behind enemy lines.
Germans?

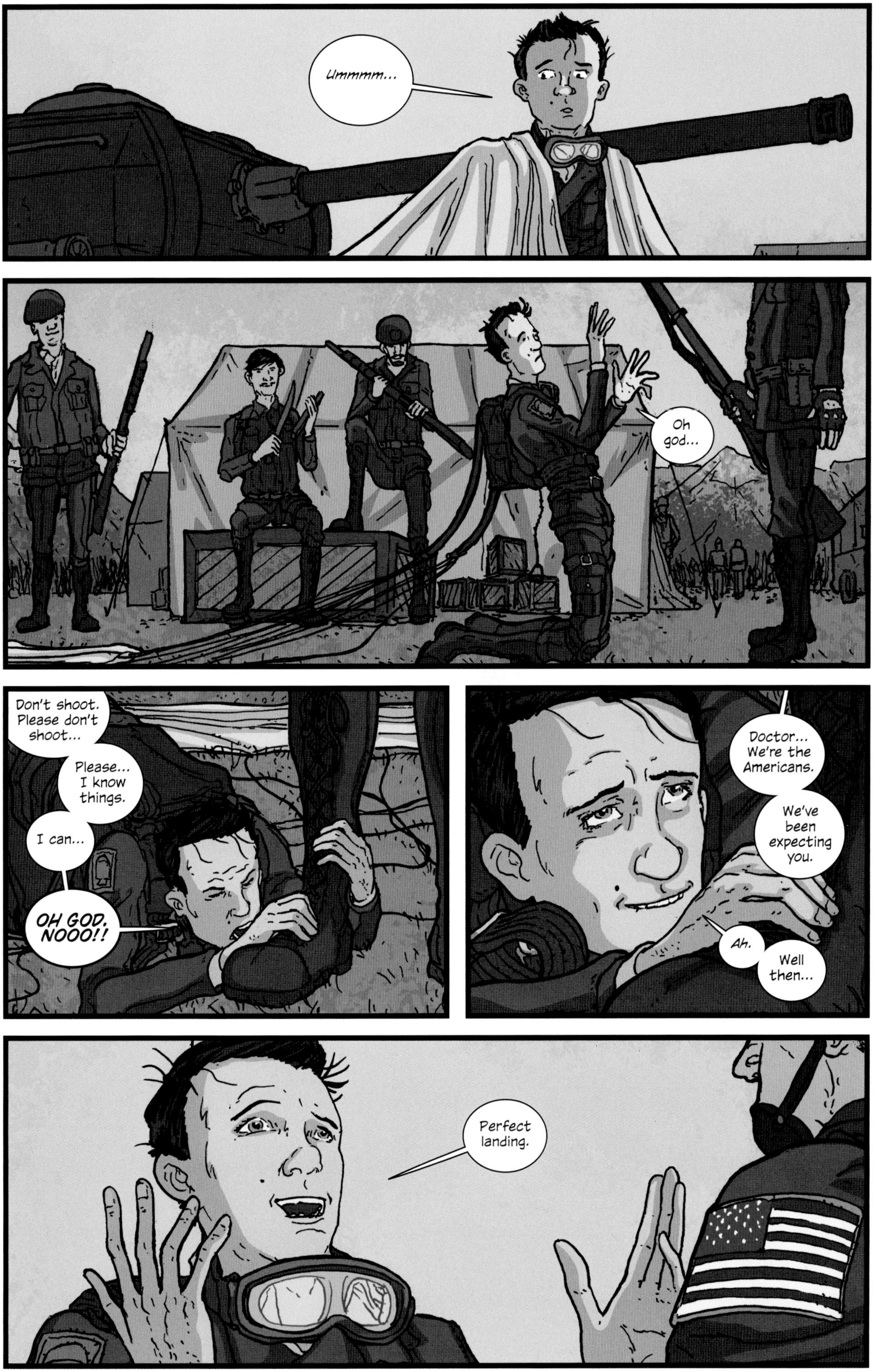
Ummmm...
Oh god...
Don't shoot. Please don't shoot...
Please... I know things.
I can...
OH GOD. NOOO!!
Doctor... We're the Americans.
We've been expecting you.
Ah.
Well then...
Perfect landing.

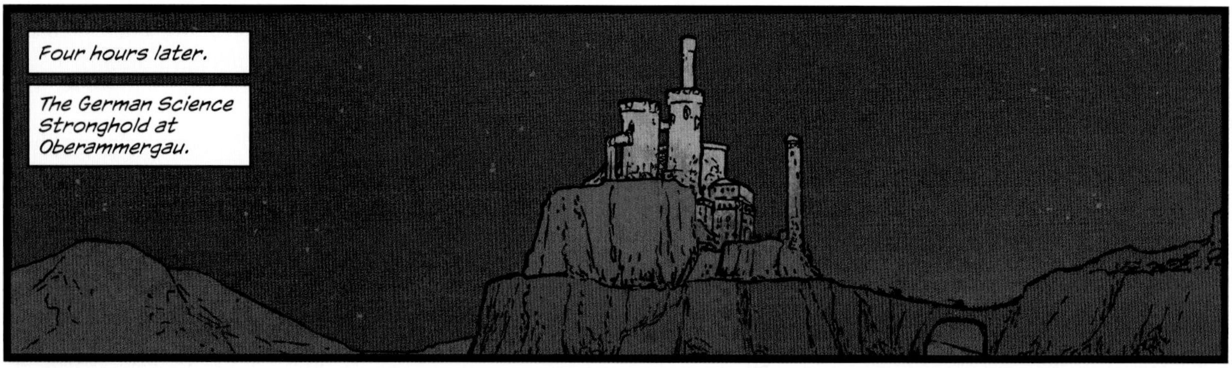
Four hours later.
The German Science Stronghold at Oberammergau.

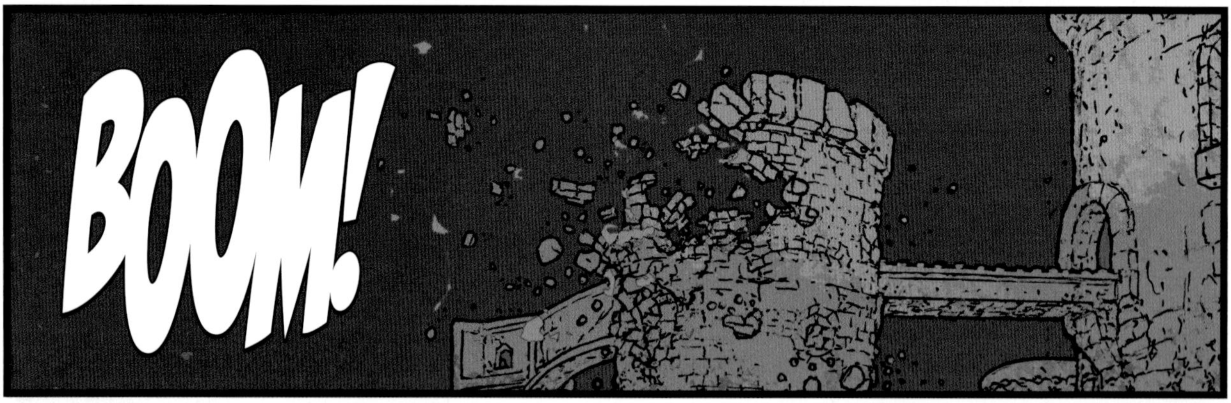
BOOM!

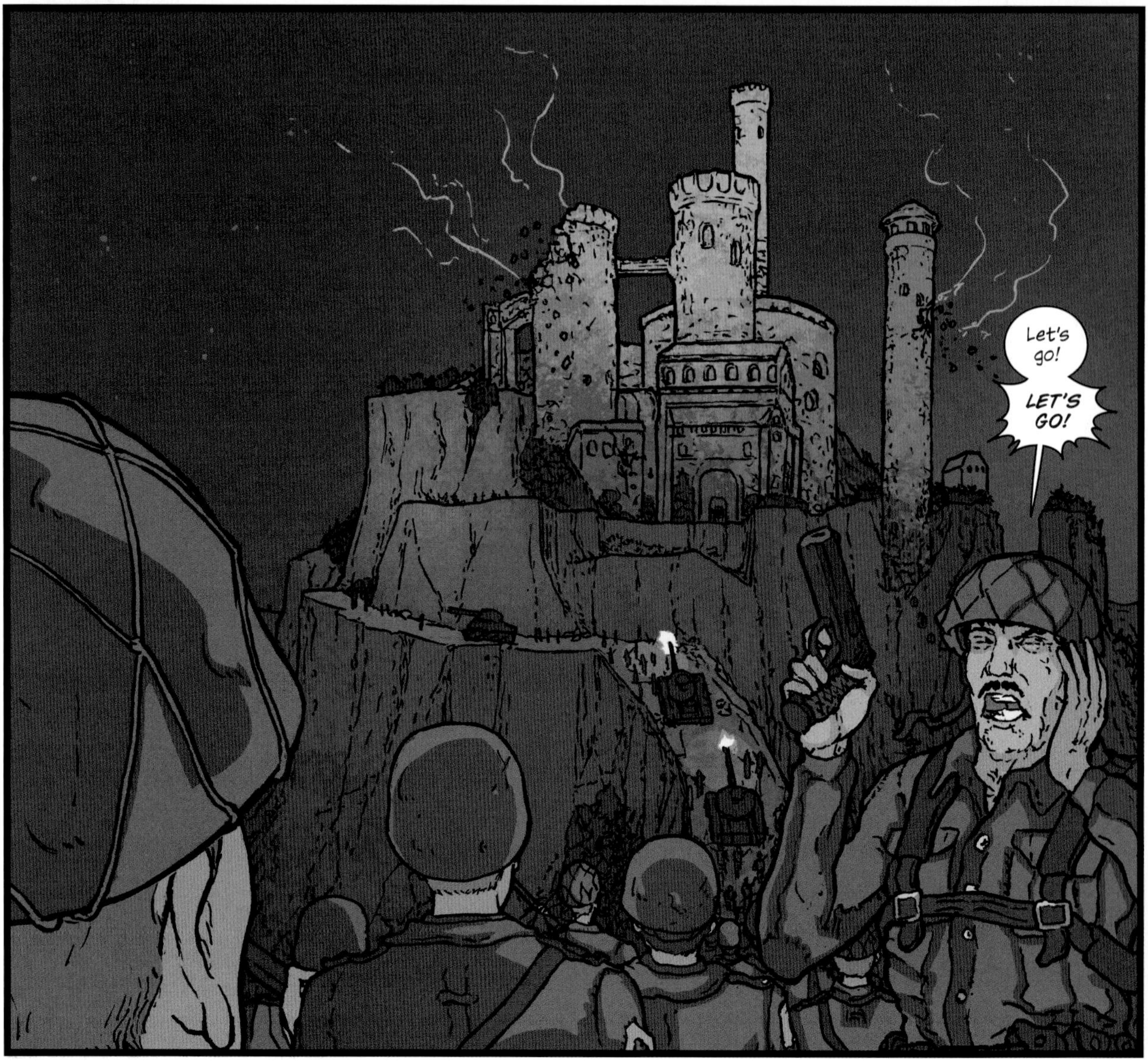
Let's go!
LET'S GO!

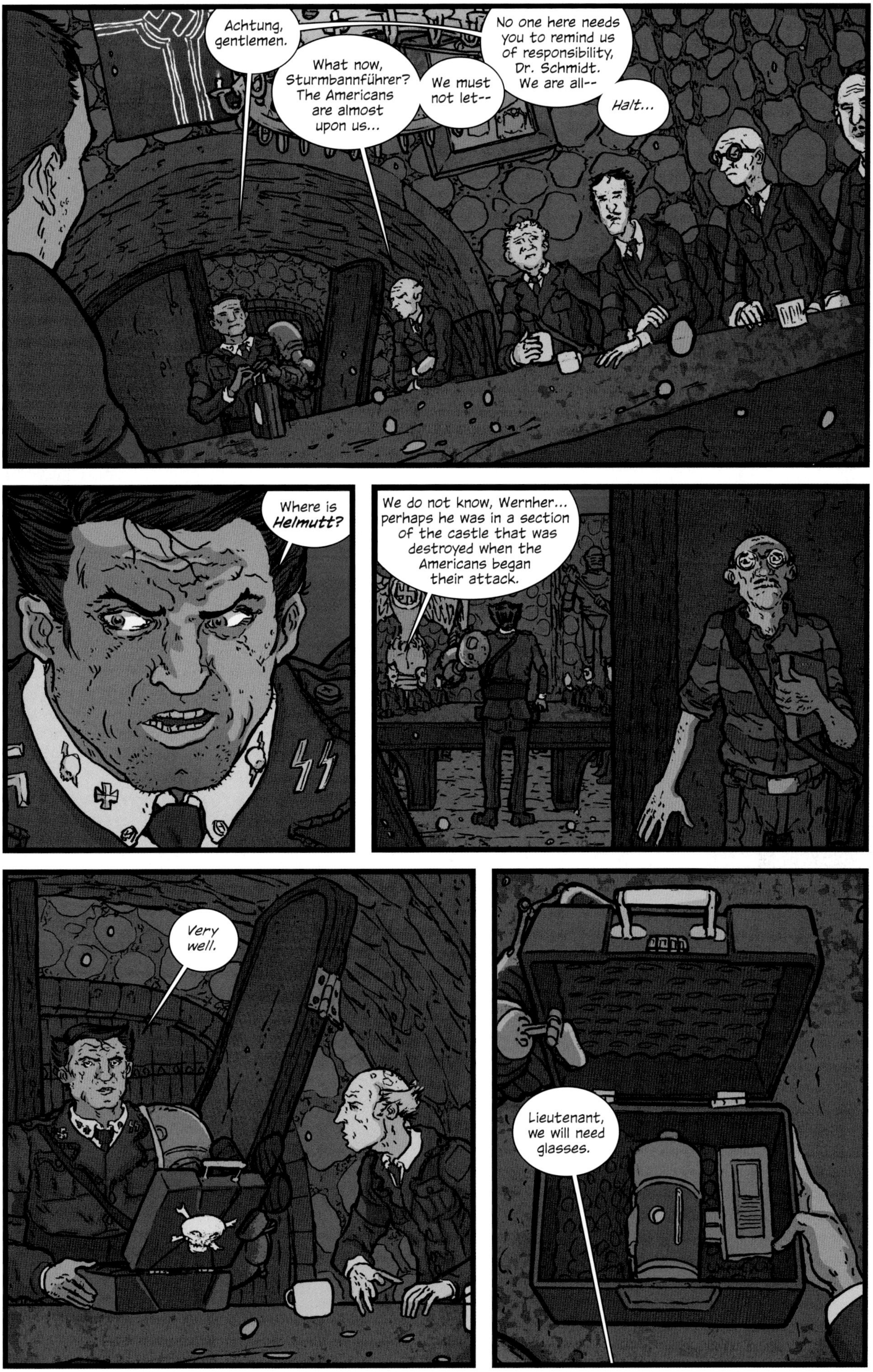
Achtung, gentlemen.
What now, Sturmbannführer? The Americans are almost upon us...
We must not let--
No one here needs you to remind us of responsibility, Dr. Schmidt. We are all--
Halt...
Where is Helmutt?
We do not know, Wernher... perhaps he was in a section of the castle that was destroyed when the Americans began their attack.
Very well.
Lieutenant, we will need glasses.

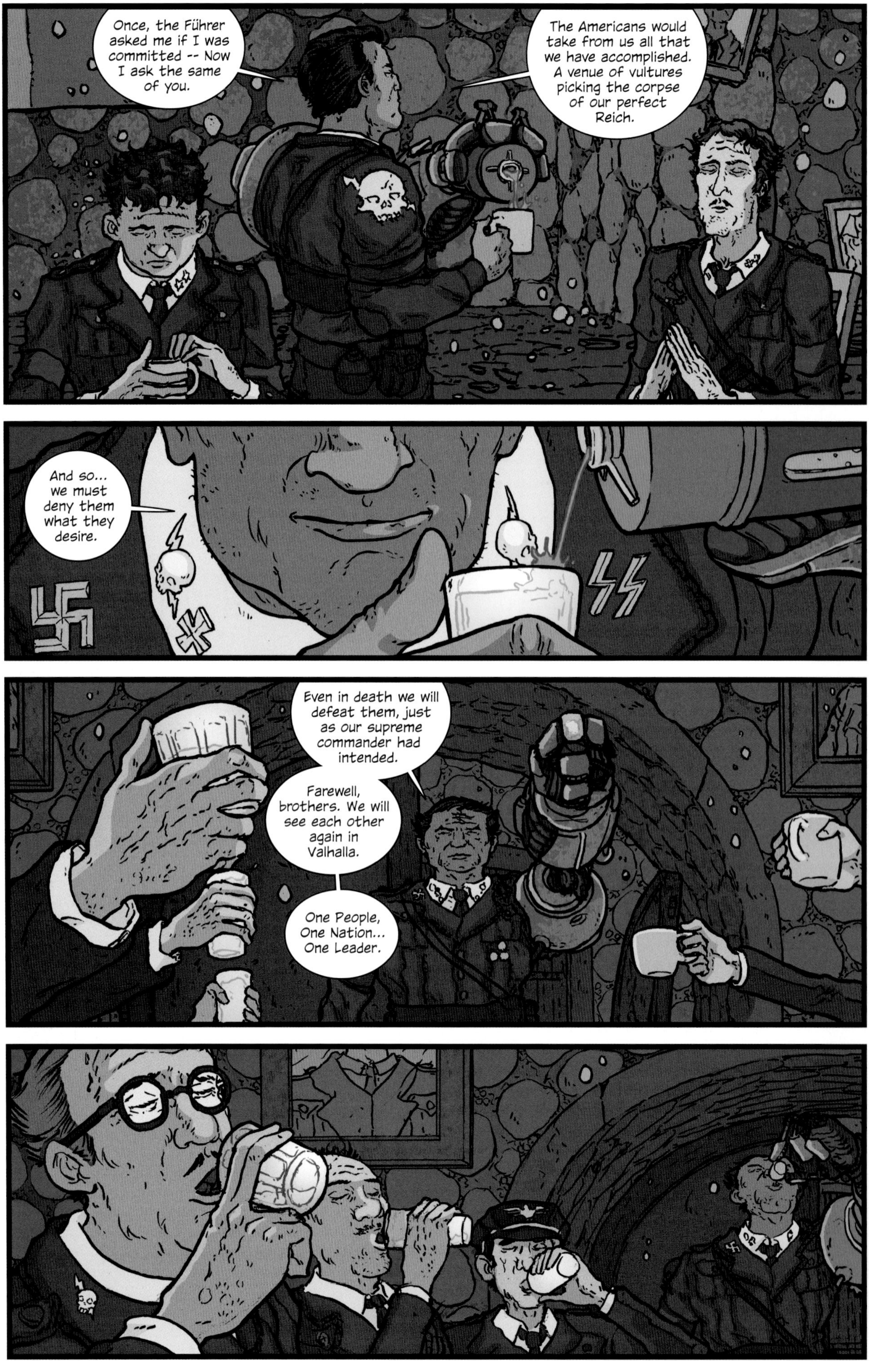

Once, the Führer asked me if I was committed -- Now I ask the same of you.
The Americans would take from us all that we have accomplished. A venue of vultures picking the corpse of our perfect Reich.
And so... we must deny them what they desire.
Even in death we will defeat them, just as our supreme commander had intended.
Farewell, brothers. We will see each other again in Valhalla.
One People, One Nation... One Leader.

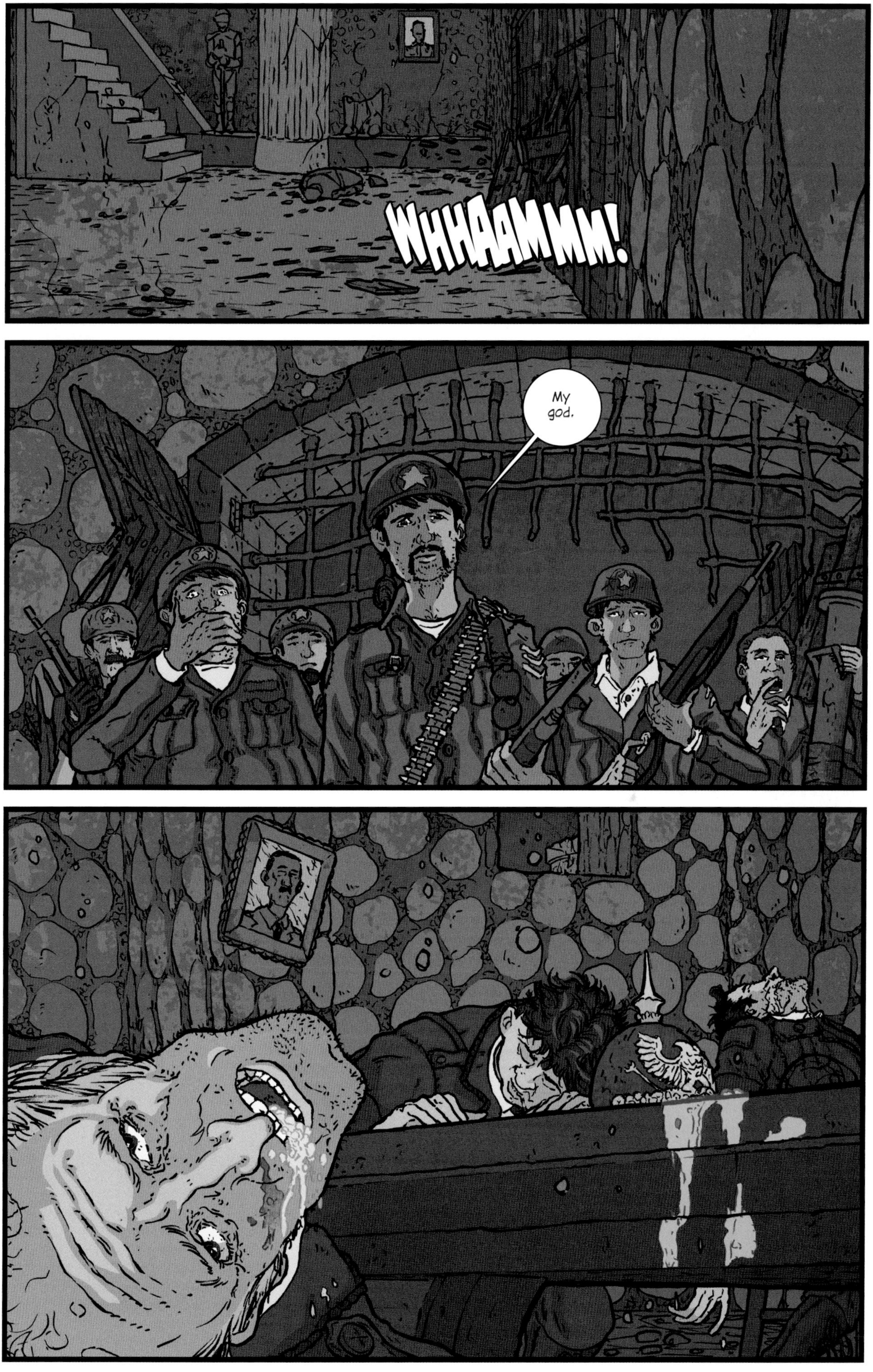
WHHAAMMM!
My god.

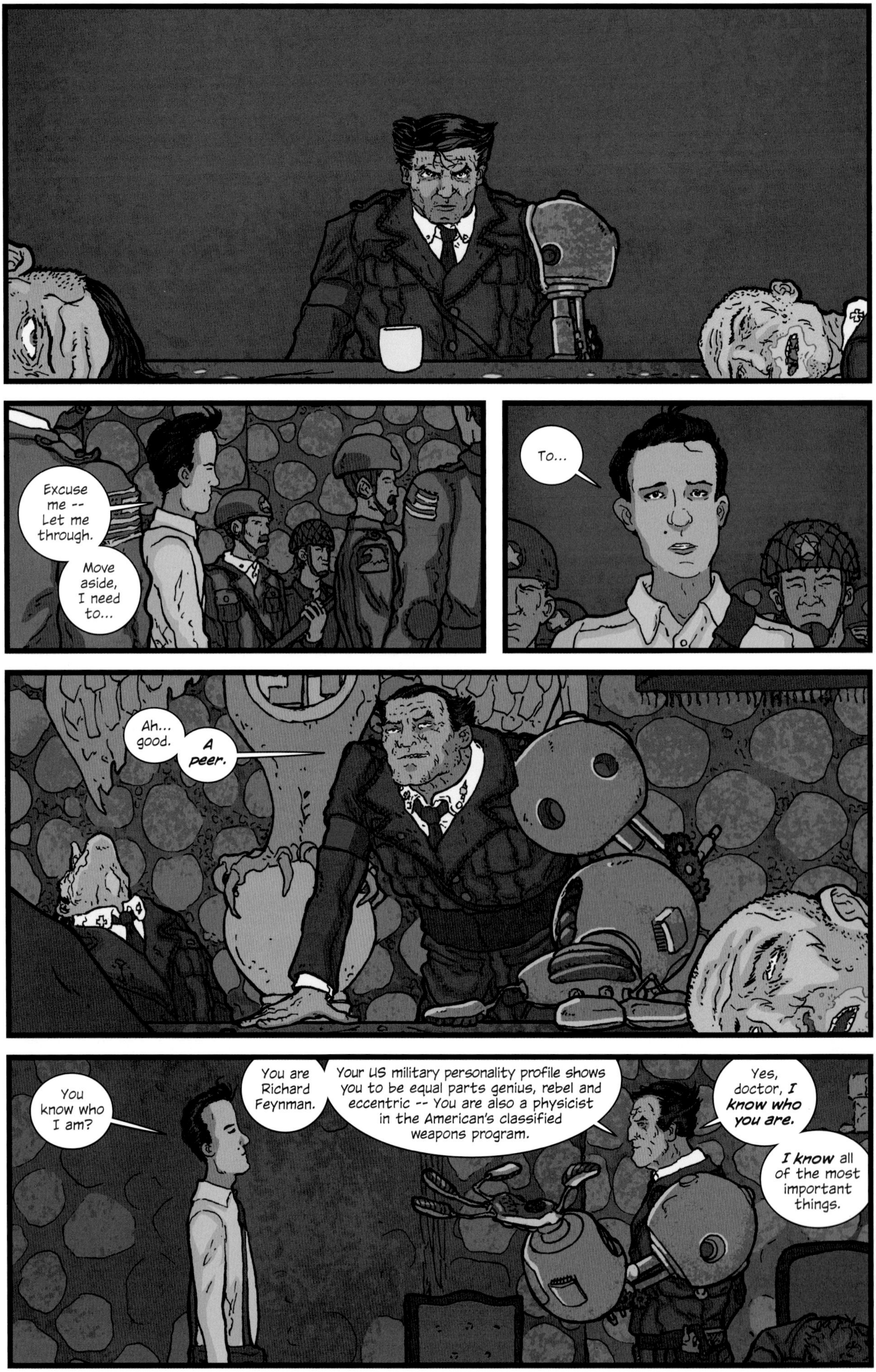
Excuse me -- Let me through.
Move aside, I need to...
To...
Ah... good.
A peer.
You know who I am?
You are Richard Feynman.
Your US military personality profile shows you to be equal parts genius, rebel and eccentric -- You are also a physicist in the American's classified weapons program.
Yes, doctor, I know who you are.
I know all of the most important things.

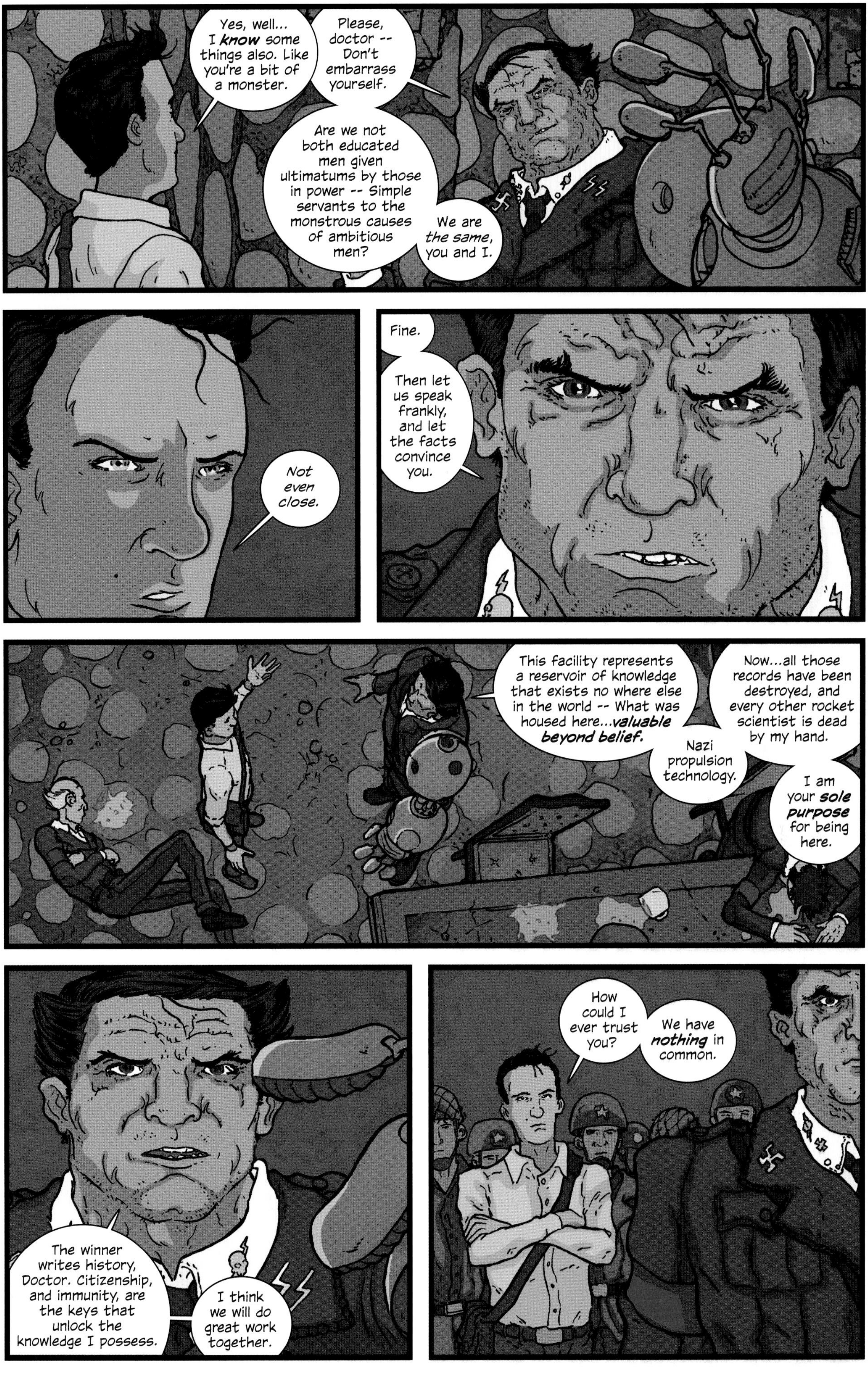
Yes, well... I *know* some things also. Like you're a bit of a monster.
Please, doctor -- Don't embarrass yourself.
Are we not both educated men given ultimatums by those in power -- Simple servants to the monstrous causes of ambitious men?
We are *the same*, you and I.
Not even close.
Fine.
Then let us speak frankly, and let the facts convince you.
This facility represents a reservoir of knowledge that exists no where else in the world -- What was housed here...*valuable beyond belief.*
Nazi propulsion technology.
Now...all those records have been destroyed, and every other rocket scientist is dead by my hand.
I am your *sole purpose* for being here.
The winner writes history, Doctor. Citizenship, and immunity, are the keys that unlock the knowledge I possess.
I think we will do great work together.
How could I ever trust you?
We have *nothing* in common.

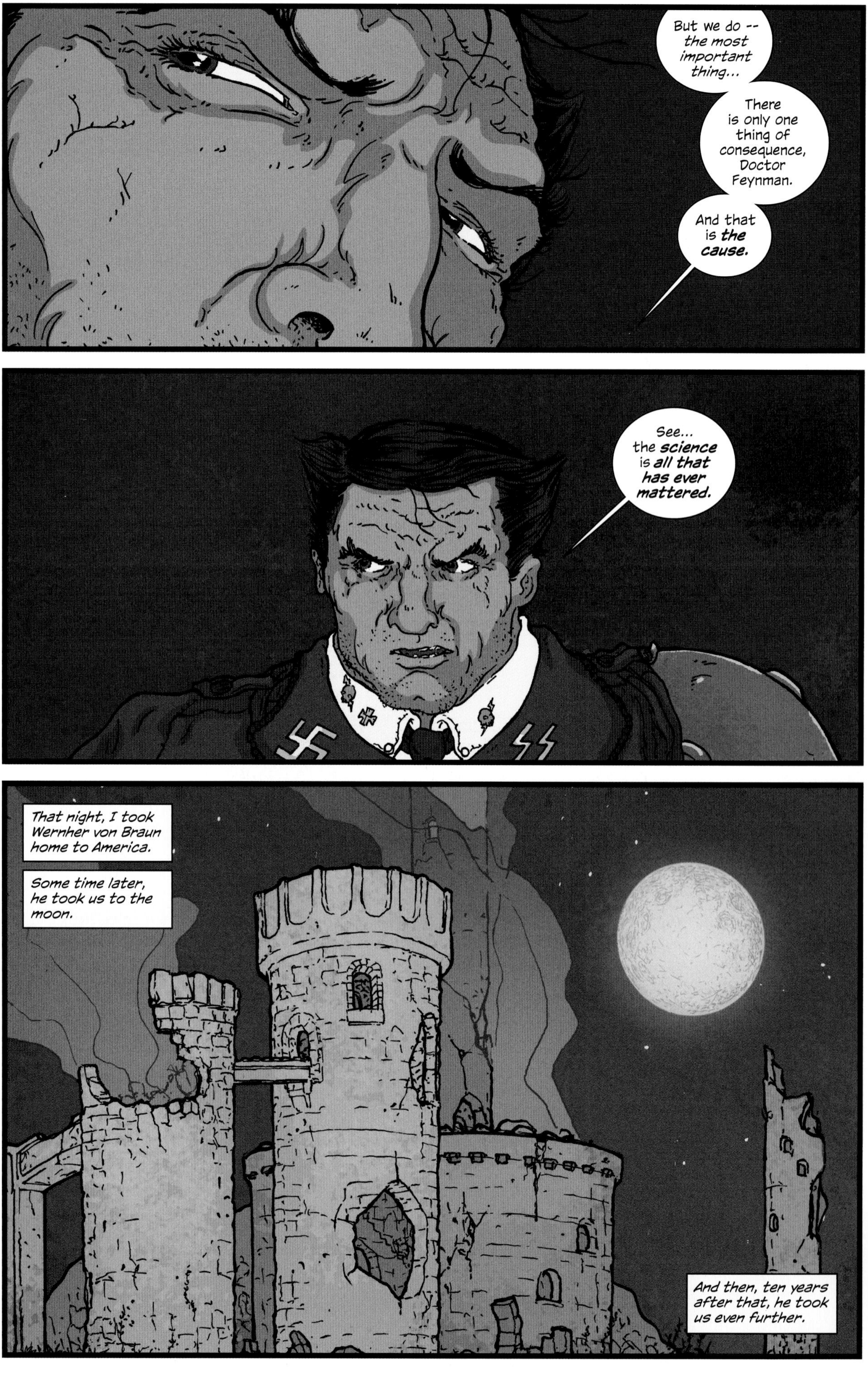
But we do -- the most important thing...
There is only one thing of consequence, Doctor Feynman.
And that is **the cause.**
See... the **science** is **all that has ever mattered.**
That night, I took Wernher von Braun home to America.
Some time later, he took us to the moon.
And then, ten years after that, he took us even further.

"THE EXPLORATORY, FOREVER-CLASS FRIGATE, UTDF VON BRAUN, LEFT THE SOLAR SYSTEM IN THE YEAR 1997.

IT NEVER RETURNED."

CLAVIS AUREA
THE RECORDED FEYNMAN | **VOL. 3**

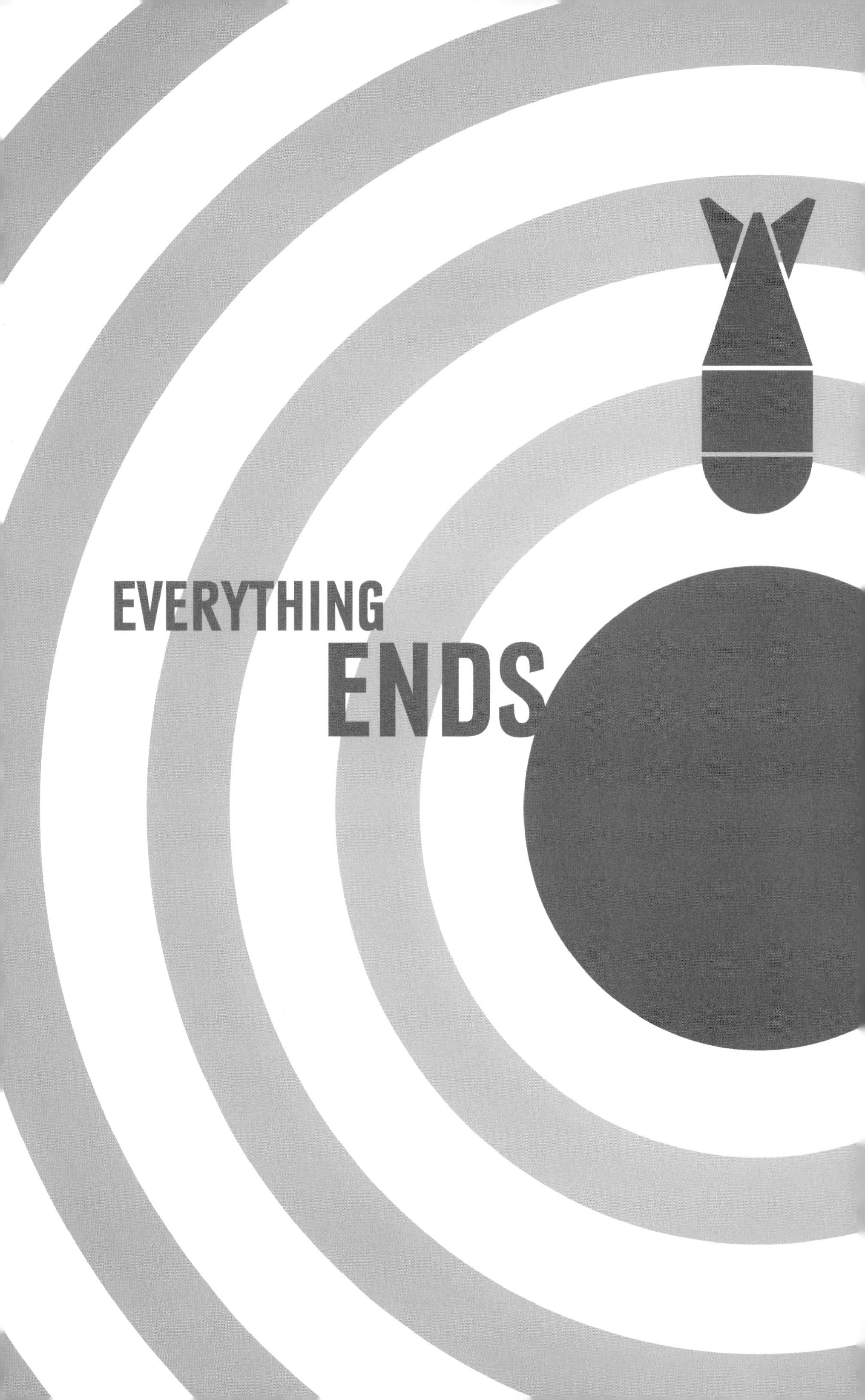
EVERYTHING
ENDS

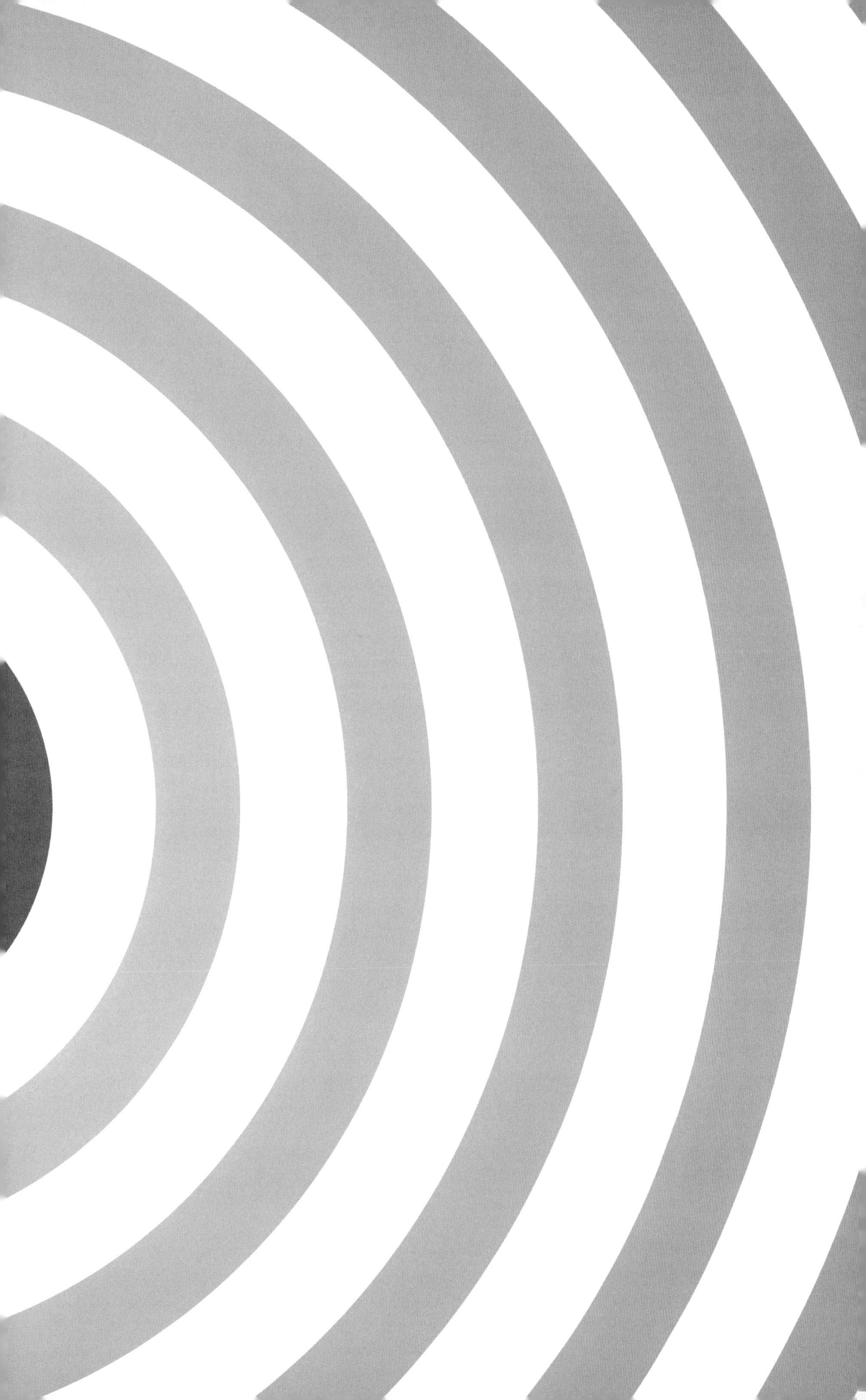

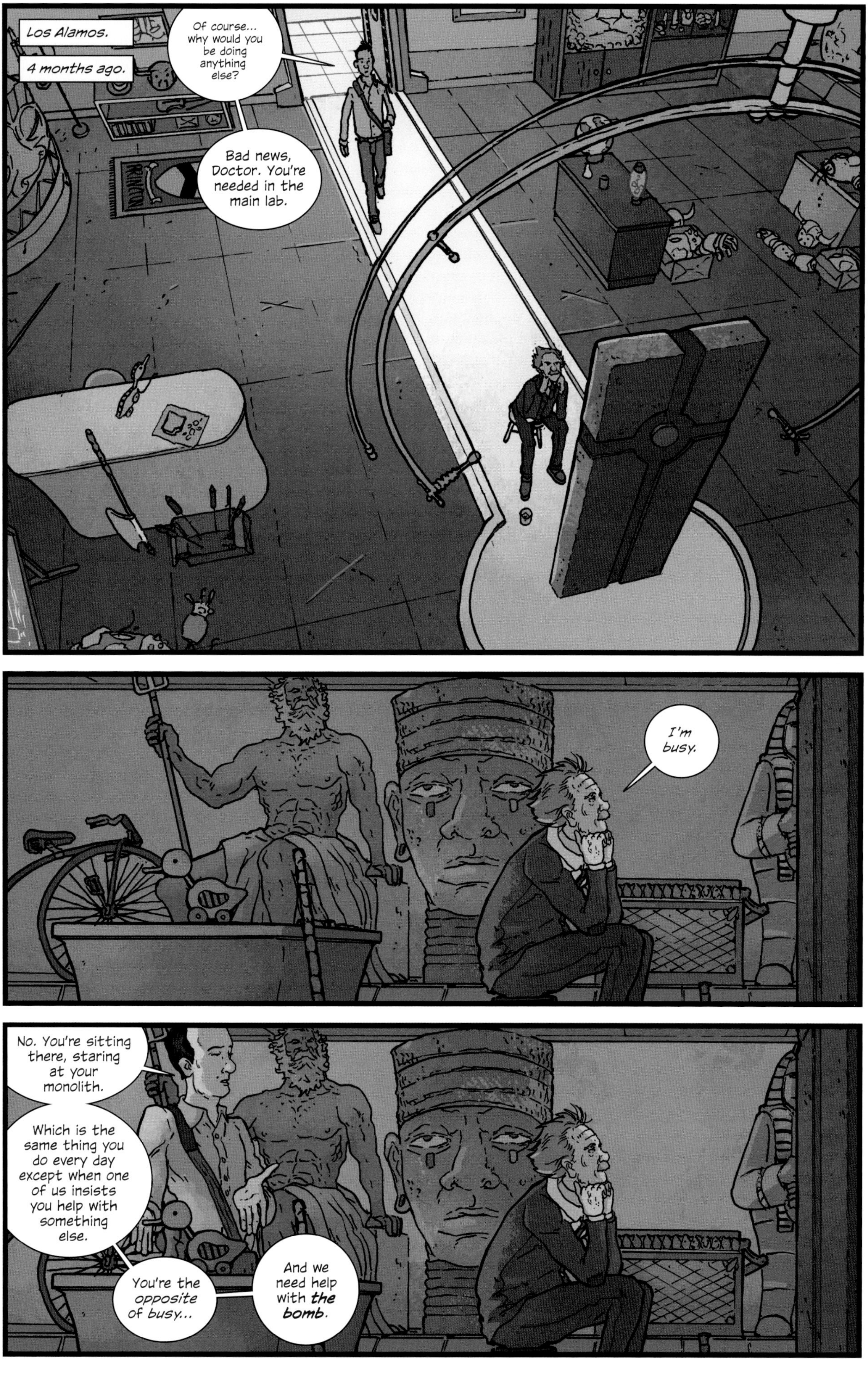
Los Alamos.
4 months ago.
Of course... why would you be doing anything else?
Bad news, Doctor. You're needed in the main lab.
I'm busy.
No. You're sitting there, staring at your monolith.
Which is the same thing you do every day except when one of us insists you help with something else.
You're the opposite of busy...
And we need help with the bomb.

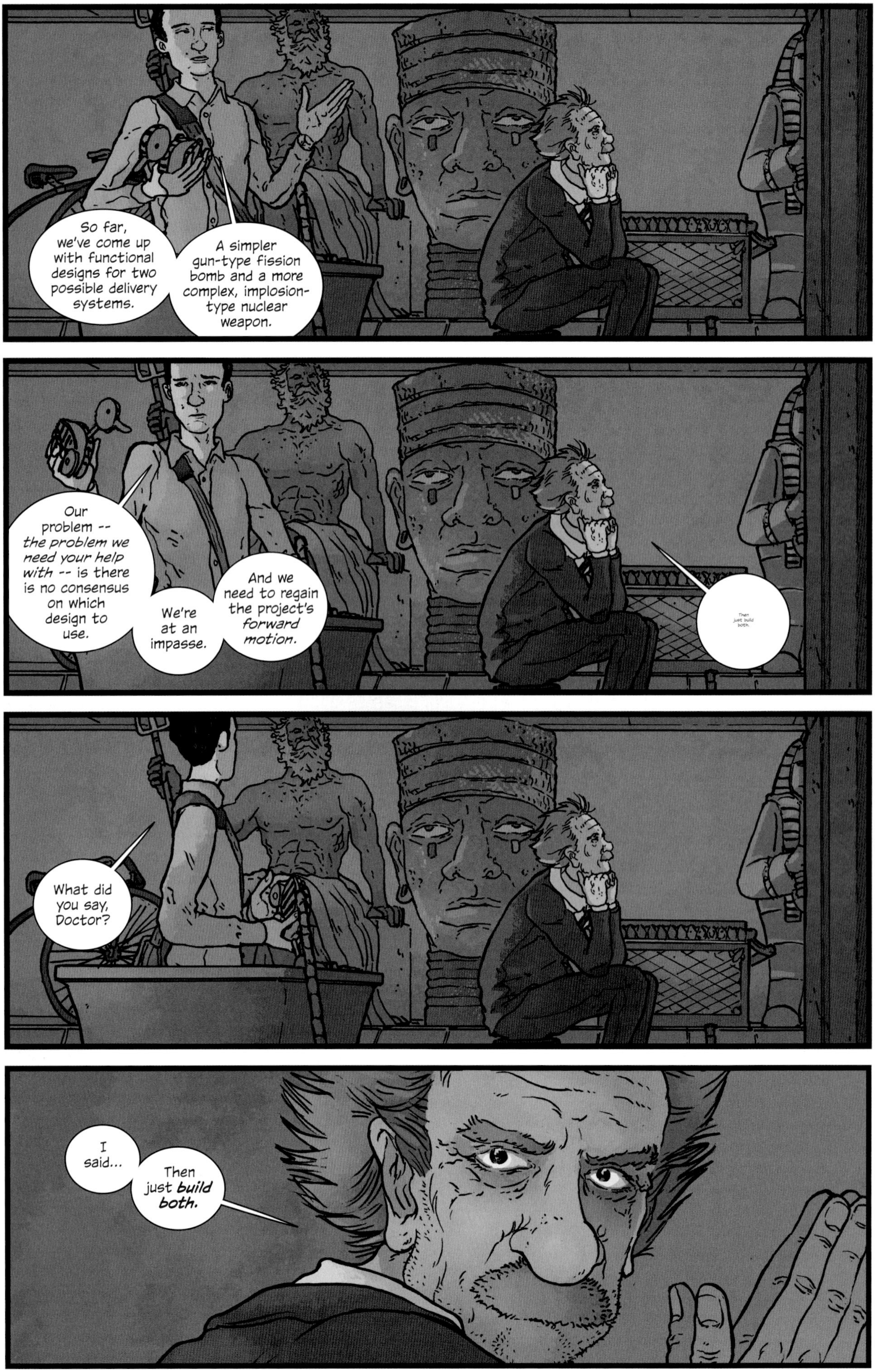
So far, we've come up with functional designs for two possible delivery systems.
A simpler gun-type fission bomb and a more complex, implosion-type nuclear weapon.
Our problem -- *the problem we need your help with* -- is there is no consensus on which design to use.
We're at an impasse.
And we need to regain the project's *forward motion*.
Then just build both.
What did you say, Doctor?
I said...
Then just ***build both.***

"THE BOMB MADE US RECKLESS. IT MADE US ARROGANT. IT MADE US STOP BELIEVING IN THE POSSIBILITY THAT ANYTHING COULD BE DONE.

INSTEAD, WE KNEW IT."

CLAVIS AUREA
THE RECORDED FEYNMAN

VOL. 1

03

THE
BOMB

"WHAT AM I GUILTY OF?

AN INTIMATE FAMILIARITY WITH THE NECESSITY OF FICTION. TRUTH IS MY WIFE, BUT LIES ARE MY MISTRESS. "

CLAVIS AUREA
THE RECORDED FEYNMAN | **VOL. 4**

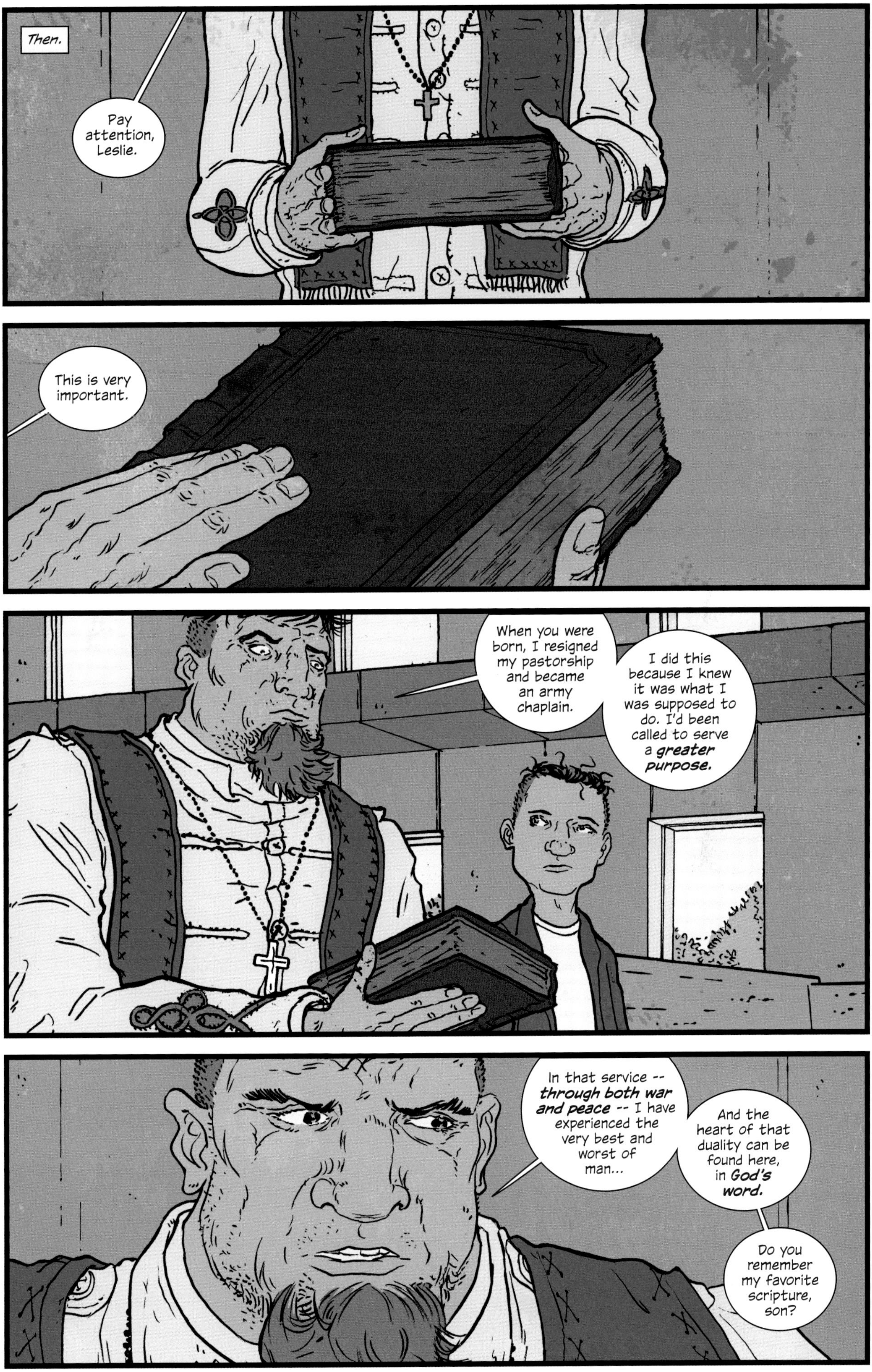
Then.
Pay attention, Leslie.
This is very important.
When you were born, I resigned my pastorship and became an army chaplain.
I did this because I knew it was what I was supposed to do. I'd been called to serve a *greater purpose.*
In that service -- *through both war and peace* -- I have experienced the very best and worst of man...
And the heart of that duality can be found here, in *God's word.*
Do you remember my favorite scripture, son?

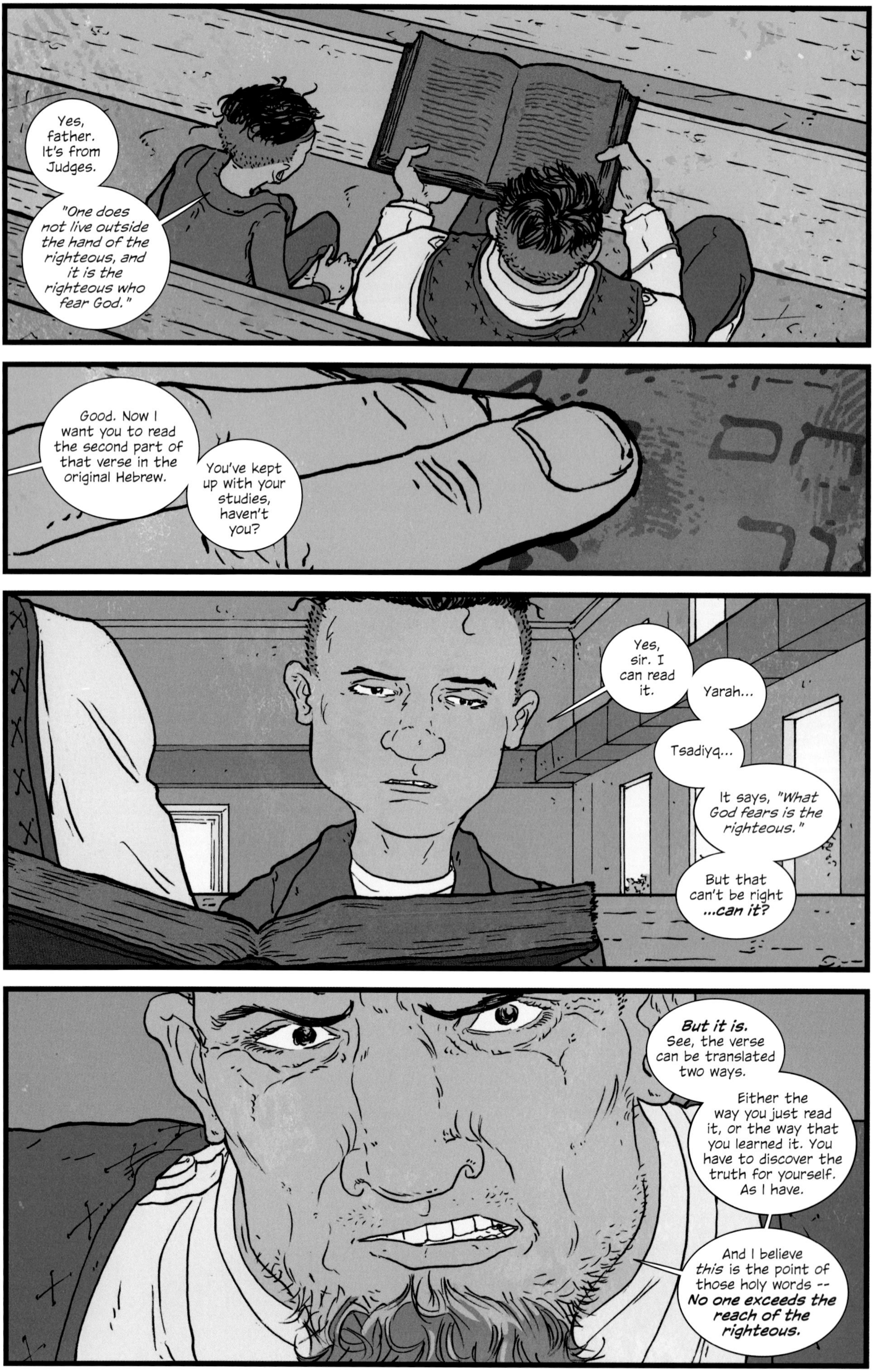
Yes, father. It's from Judges.
"One does not live outside the hand of the righteous, and it is the righteous who fear God."
Good. Now I want you to read the second part of that verse in the original Hebrew.
You've kept up with your studies, haven't you?
Yes, sir. I can read it.
Yarah...
Tsadiyq...
It says, "What God fears is the righteous."
But that can't be right ...can it?
But it is. See, the verse can be translated two ways.
Either the way you just read it, or the way that you learned it. You have to discover the truth for yourself. As I have.
And I believe this is the point of those holy words -- No one exceeds the reach of the righteous.

Los Alamos.

Now.

Uranium. Sweet, sweet plutonium.

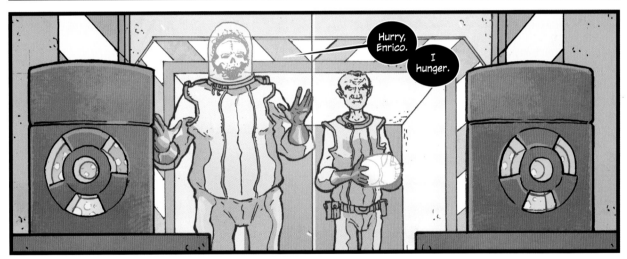

Hurry, Enrico. I hunger.

Yes, well... considering your current state, I think I'll take my time and get good and properly suited up.

Best to be prudent, don't you think.

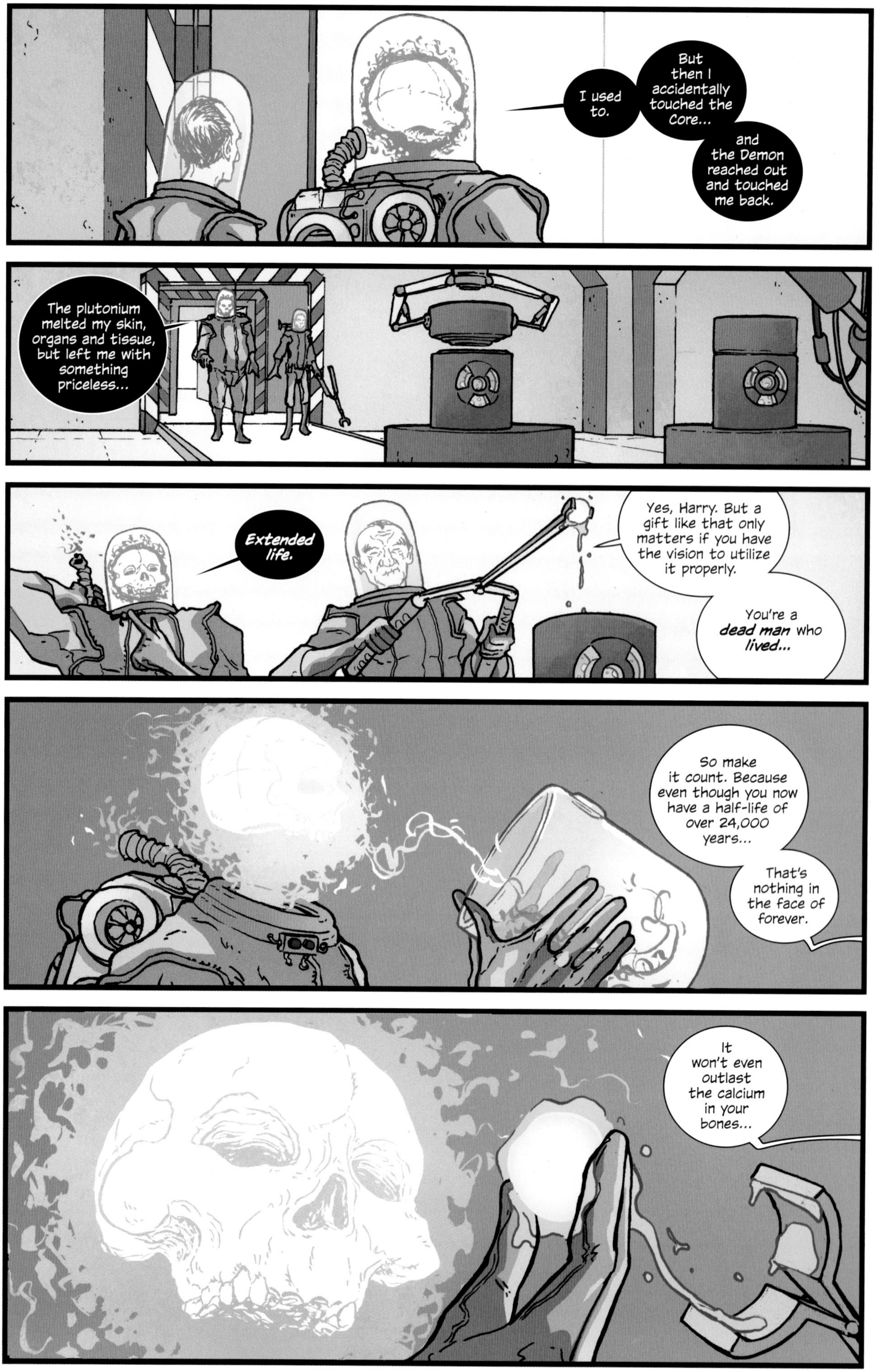
I used to.
But then I accidentally touched the Core...
and the Demon reached out and touched me back.
The plutonium melted my skin, organs and tissue, but left me with something priceless...
Extended life.
Yes, Harry. But a gift like that only matters if you have the vision to utilize it properly.
You're a dead man who lived...
So make it count. Because even though you now have a half-life of over 24,000 years...
That's nothing in the face of forever.
It won't even outlast the calcium in your bones...

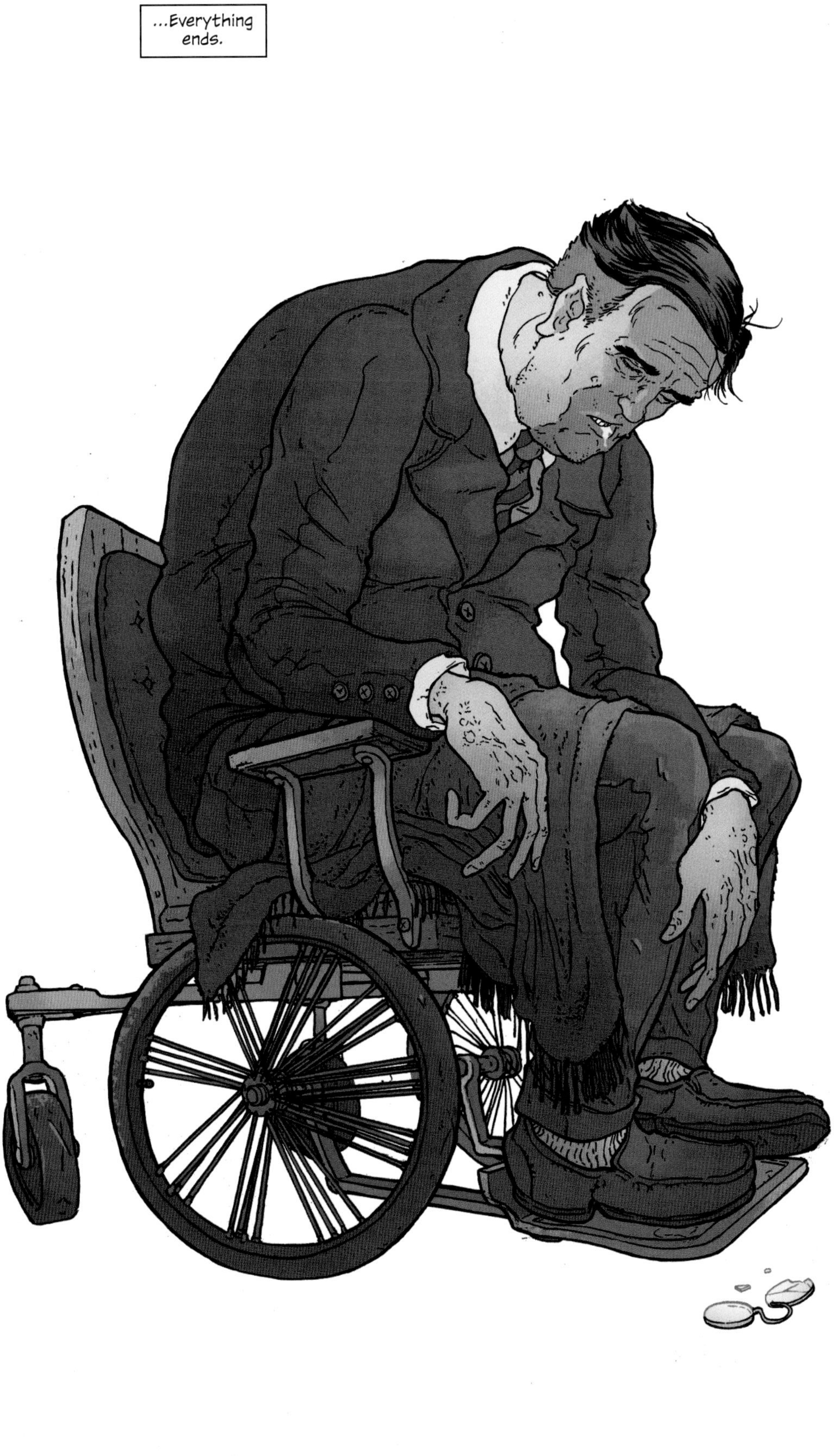
...Everything ends.

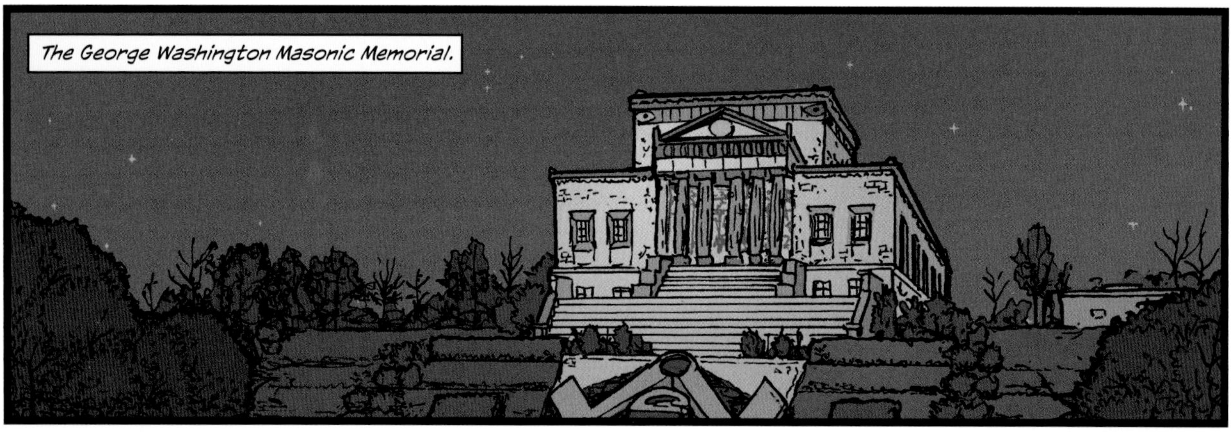
The George Washington Masonic Memorial.

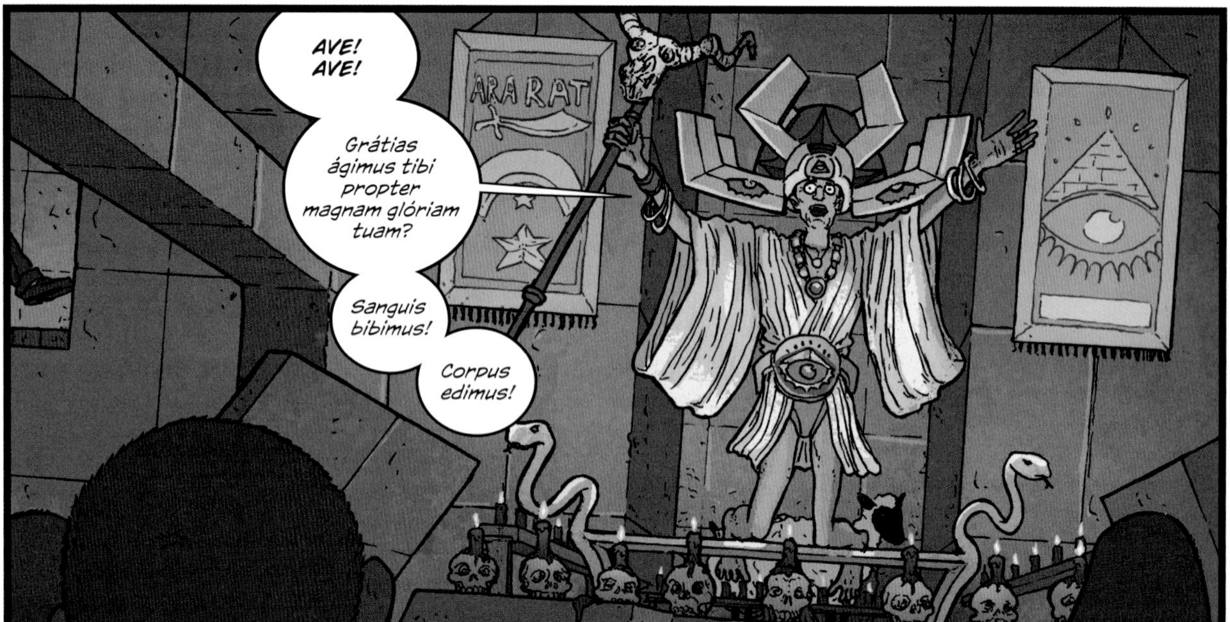
AVE! AVE!
Grátias ágimus tibi propter magnam glóriam tuam?
Sanguis bibimus!
Corpus edimus!
ARA RAT

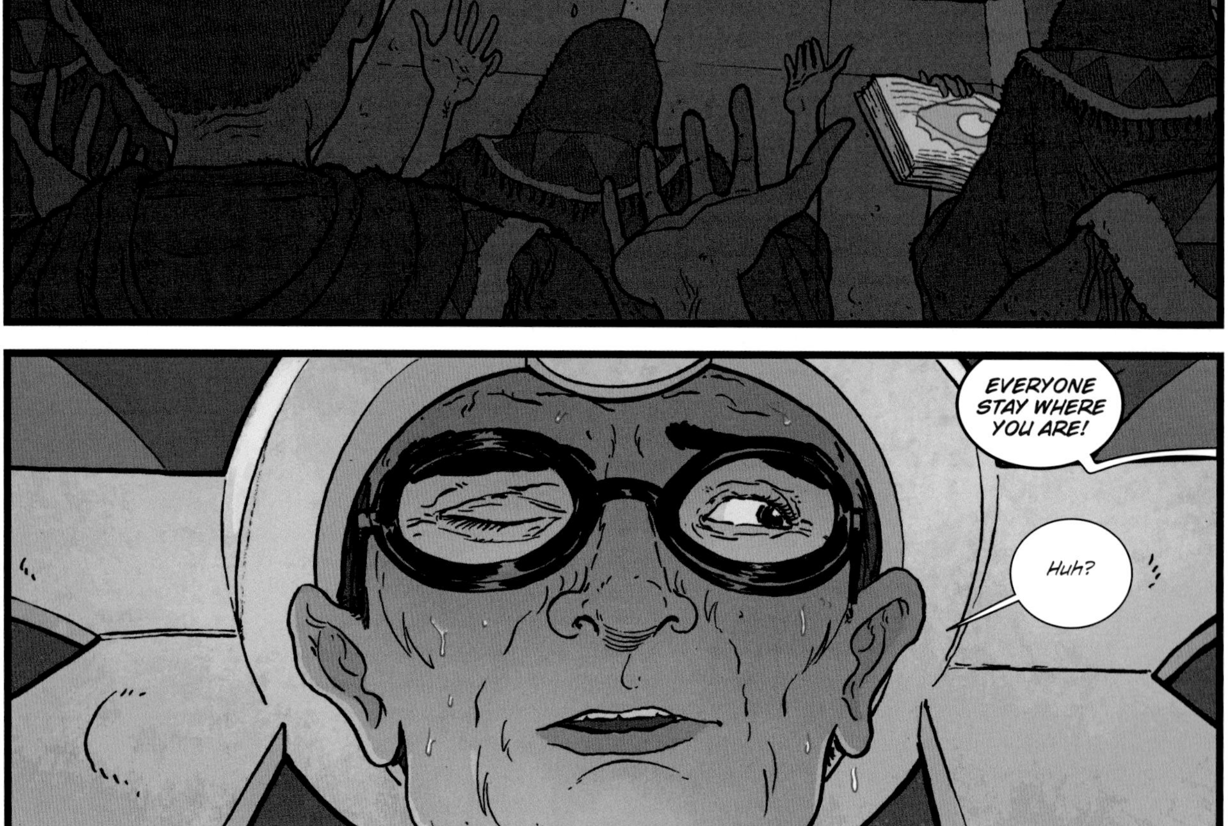
EVERYONE STAY WHERE YOU ARE!
Huh?

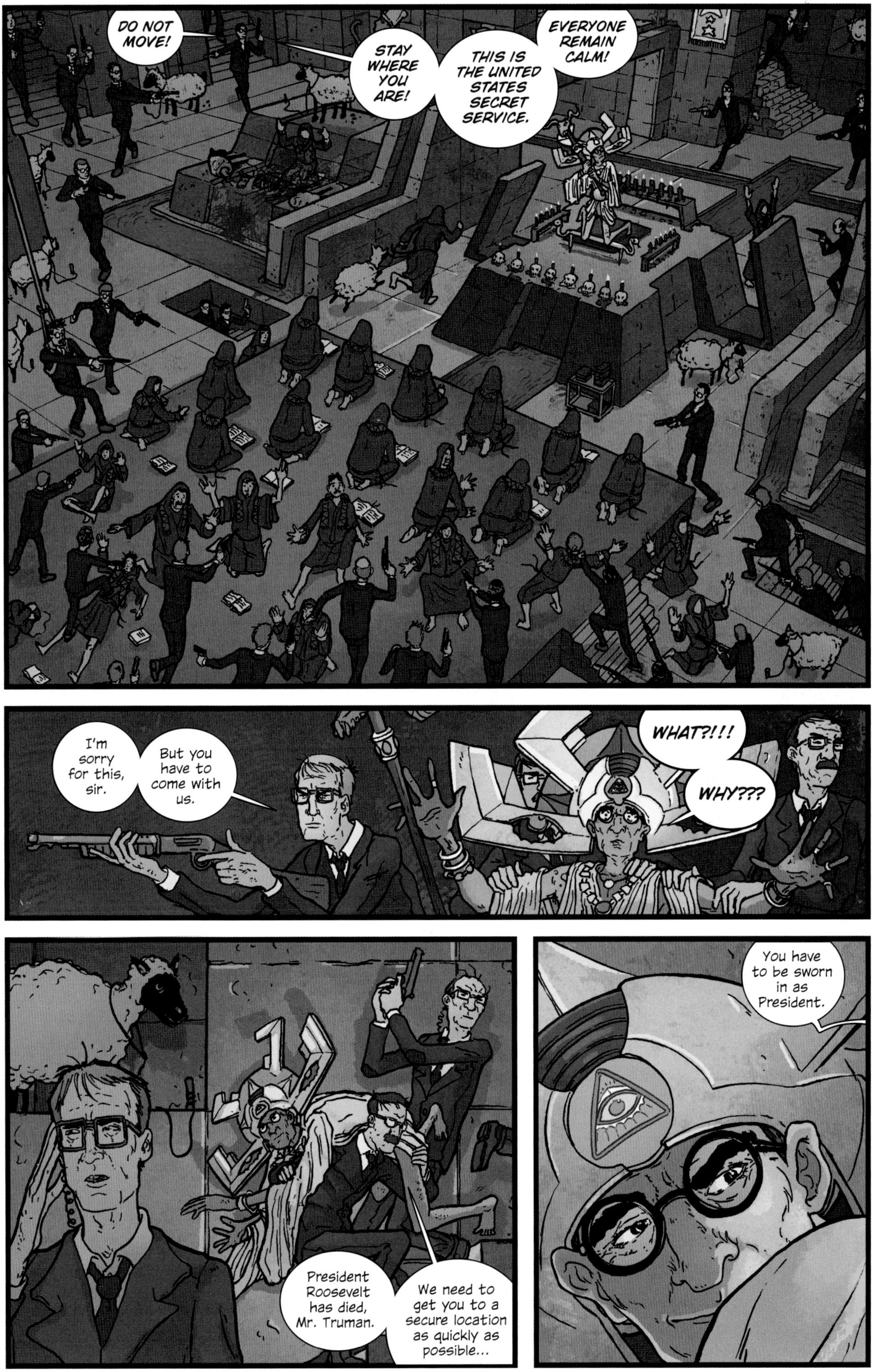
DO NOT MOVE!
STAY WHERE YOU ARE!
THIS IS THE UNITED STATES SECRET SERVICE.
EVERYONE REMAIN CALM!
I'm sorry for this, sir.
But you have to come with us.
WHAT?!!!
WHY???
President Roosevelt has died, Mr. Truman.
We need to get you to a secure location as quickly as possible...
You have to be sworn in as President.

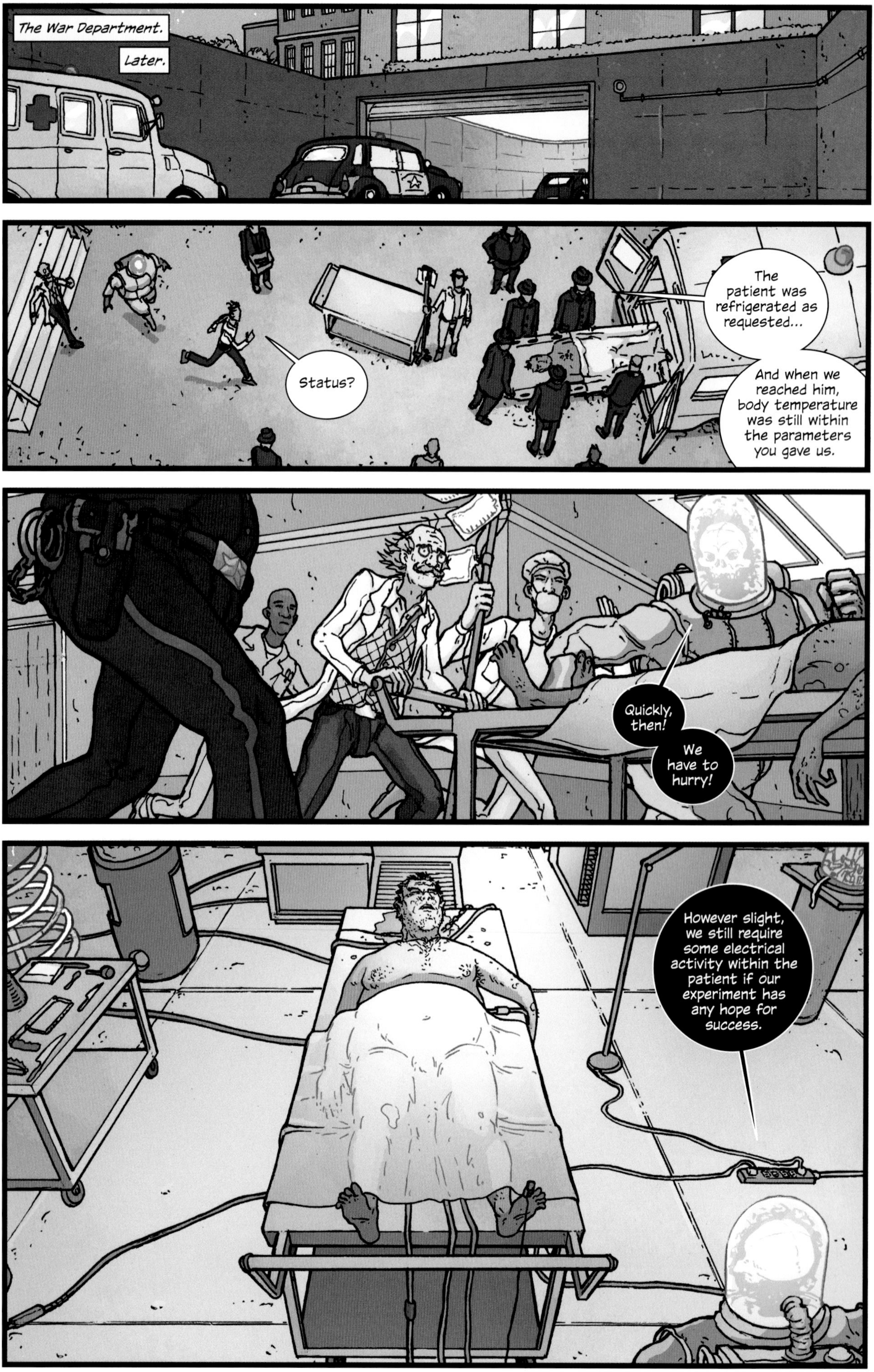

The War Department.
Later.
Status?
The patient was refrigerated as requested...
And when we reached him, body temperature was still within the parameters you gave us.
Quickly, then!
We have to hurry!
However slight, we still require some electrical activity within the patient if our experiment has any hope for success.

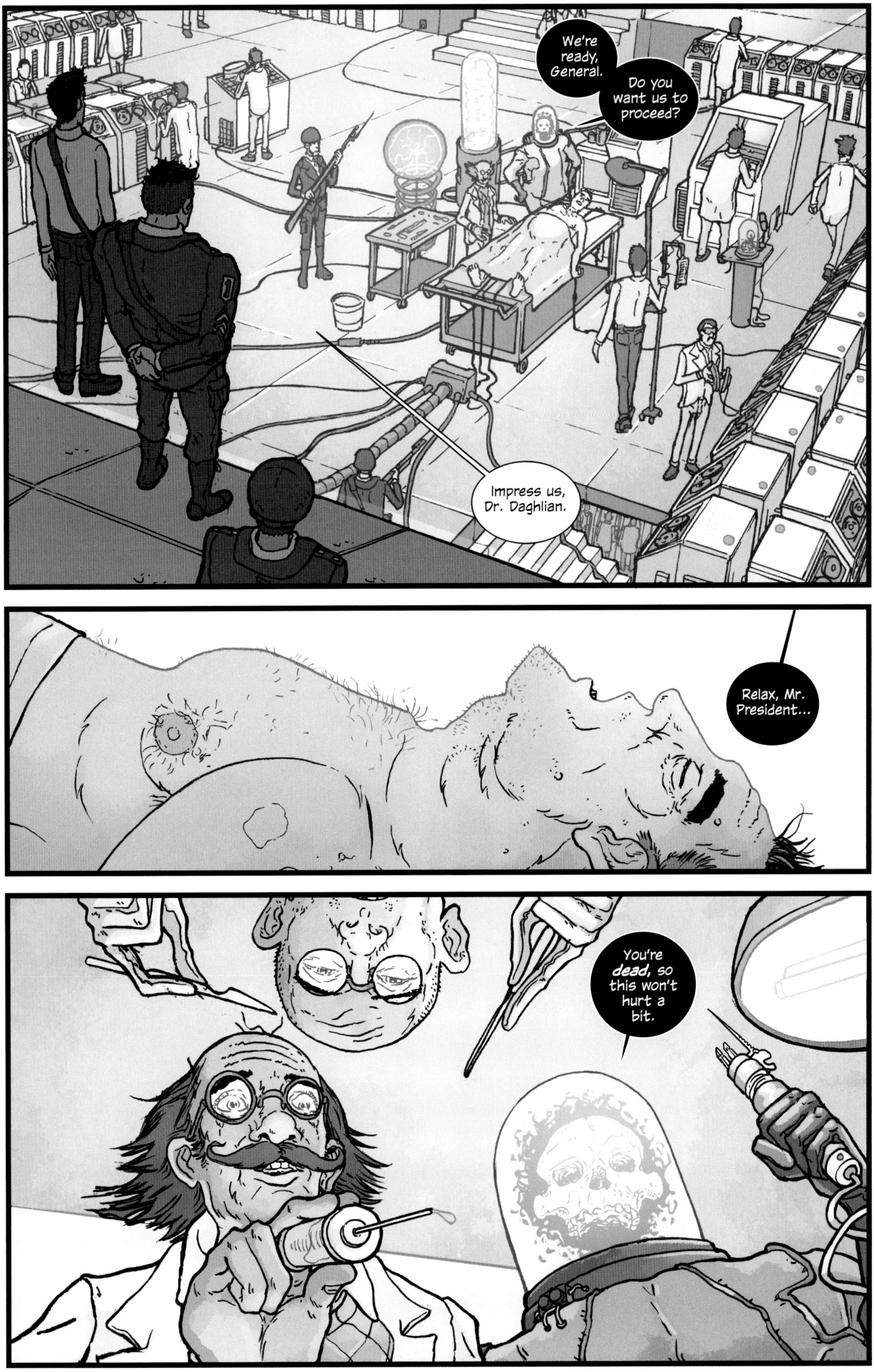
We're ready, General.
Do you want us to proceed?
Impress us, Dr. Daghlian.
Relax, Mr. President...
You're *dead*, so this won't hurt a bit.

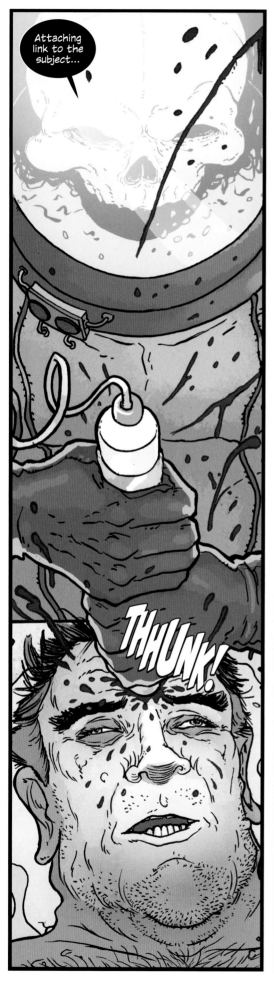

Attaching link to the subject...

THHUNK!

...attempting a connection.

I can't believe we're doing this...

Should we be doing this?

Are we even allowed to do this?

Doctor Feynman, do you see anyone stoppin' us?

Excuse me, General. You wanted me to--

Yeah. It's time?

Yes, sir.

All right. Lead the way, Captain.

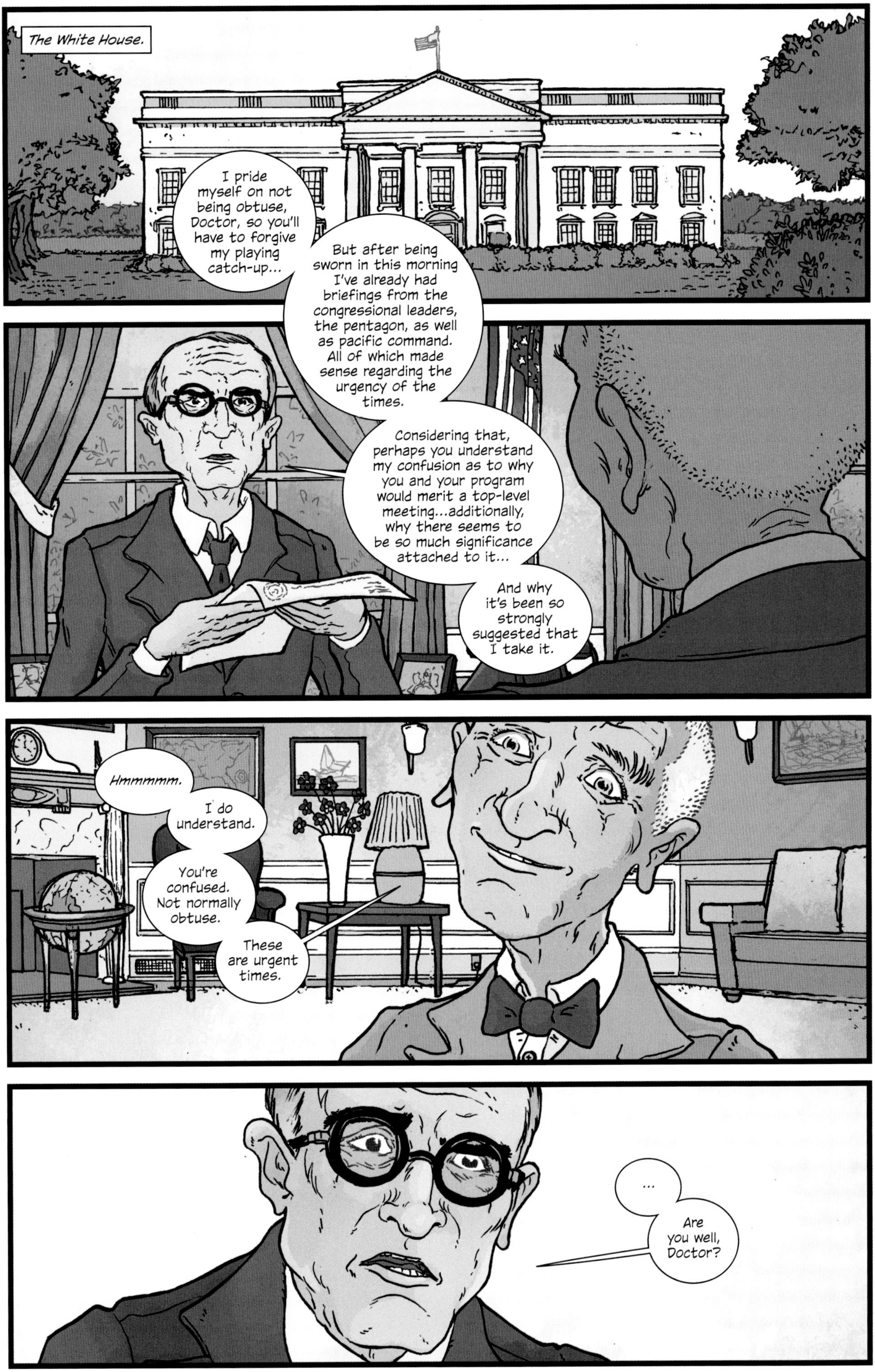
The White House.
I pride myself on not being obtuse, Doctor, so you'll have to forgive my playing catch-up...
But after being sworn in this morning I've already had briefings from the congressional leaders, the pentagon, as well as pacific command. All of which made sense regarding the urgency of the times.
Considering that, perhaps you understand my confusion as to why you and your program would merit a top-level meeting...additionally, why there seems to be so much significance attached to it...
And why it's been so strongly suggested that I take it.
Hmmmmm.
I do understand.
You're confused. Not normally obtuse.
These are urgent times.
...
Are you well, Doctor?

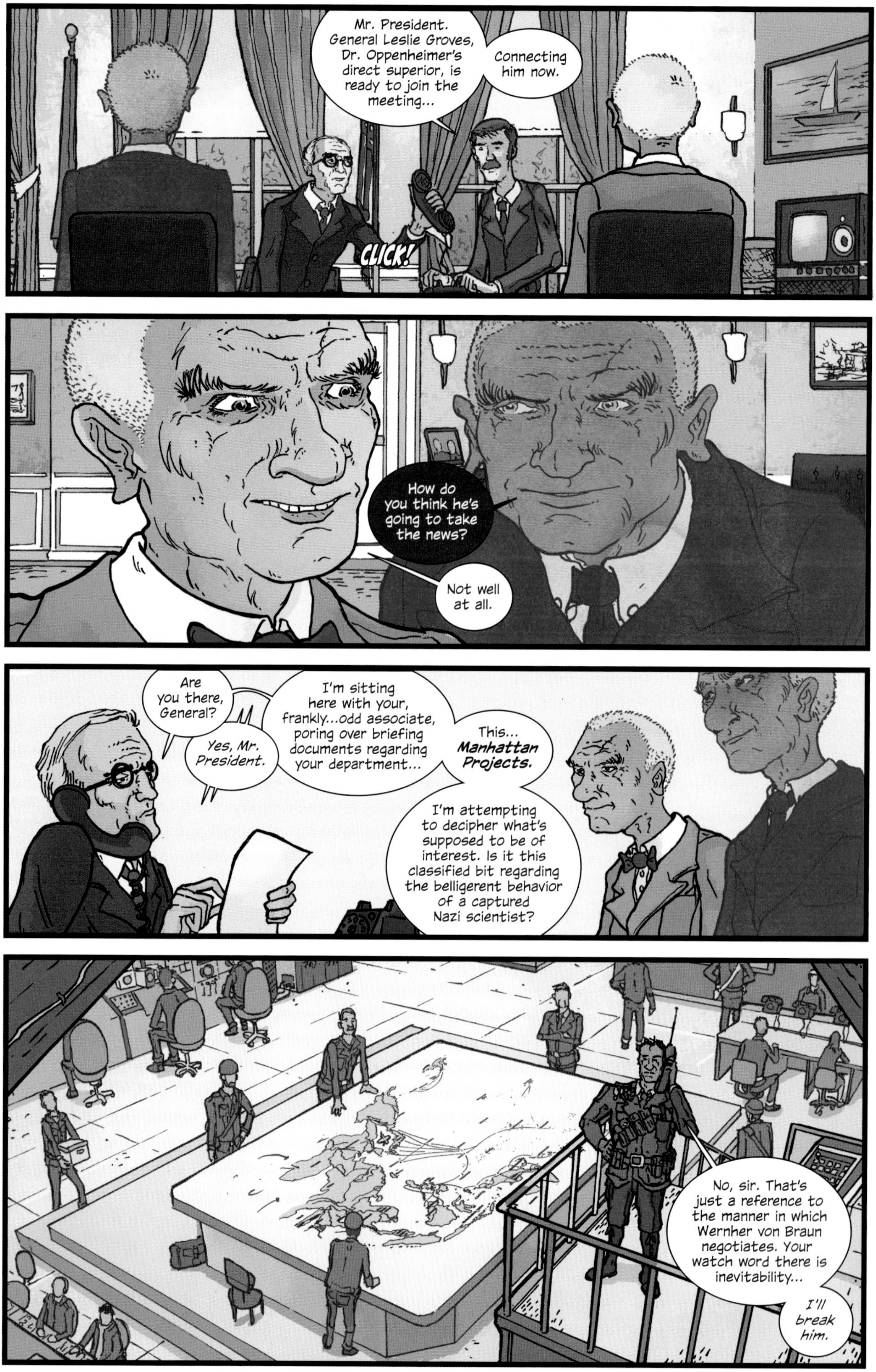
Mr. President. General Leslie Groves, Dr. Oppenheimer's direct superior, is ready to join the meeting...
Connecting him now.
CLICK!
How do you think he's going to take the news?
Not well at all.
Are you there, General?
Yes, Mr. President.
I'm sitting here with your, frankly...odd associate, poring over briefing documents regarding your department...
This... *Manhattan Projects.*
I'm attempting to decipher what's supposed to be of interest. Is it this classified bit regarding the belligerent behavior of a captured Nazi scientist?
No, sir. That's just a reference to the manner in which Wernher von Braun negotiates. Your watch word there is inevitability...
I'll break him.

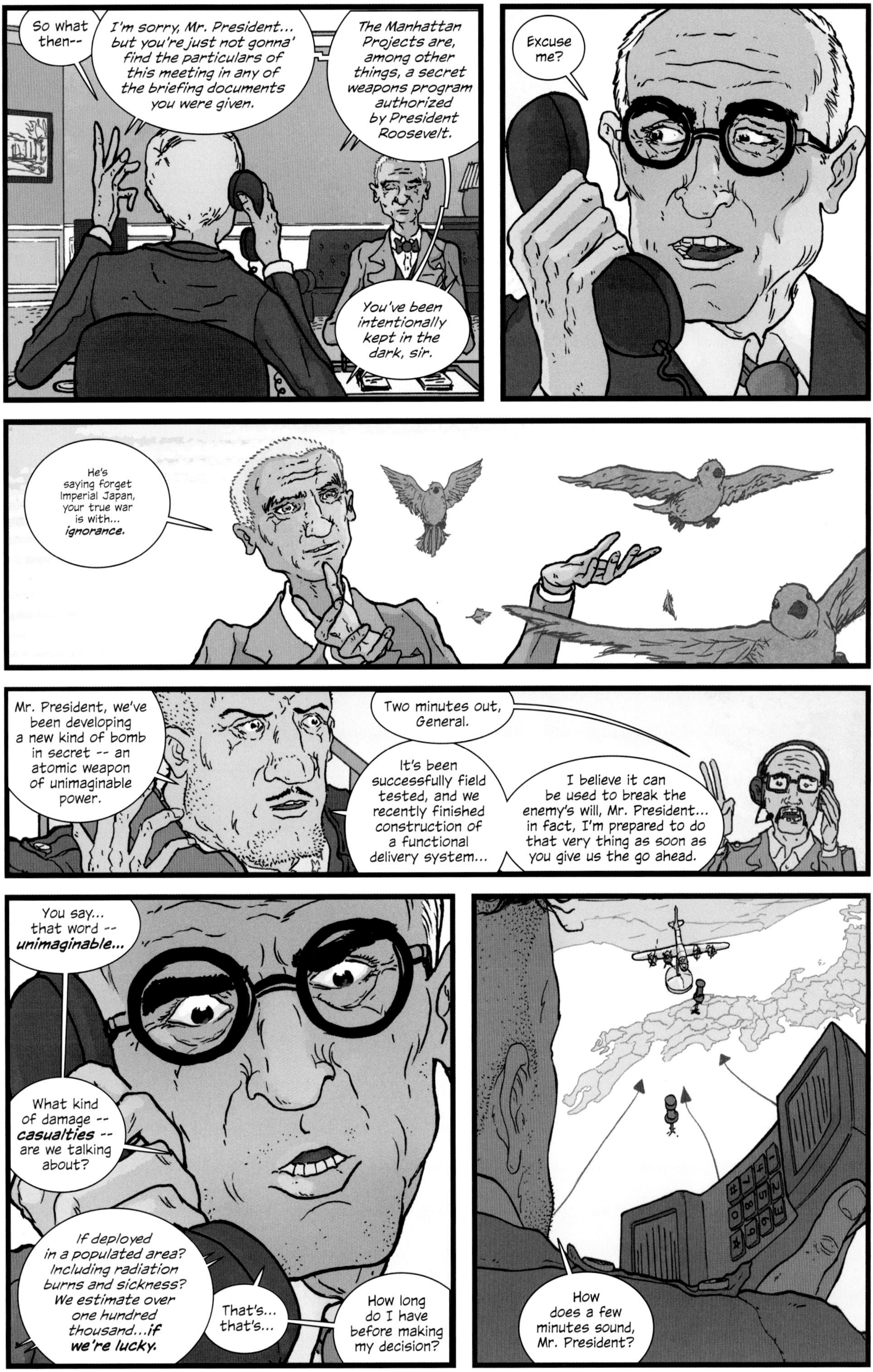

So what then--
I'm sorry, Mr. President... but you're just not gonna' find the particulars of this meeting in any of the briefing documents you were given.
The Manhattan Projects are, among other things, a secret weapons program authorized by President Roosevelt.
You've been intentionally kept in the dark, sir.
Excuse me?
He's saying forget Imperial Japan, your true war is with... ignorance.
Mr. President, we've been developing a new kind of bomb in secret -- an atomic weapon of unimaginable power.
Two minutes out, General.
It's been successfully field tested, and we recently finished construction of a functional delivery system...
I believe it can be used to break the enemy's will, Mr. President... in fact, I'm prepared to do that very thing as soon as you give us the go ahead.
You say... that word -- unimaginable...
What kind of damage -- casualties -- are we talking about?
If deployed in a populated area? Including radiation burns and sickness? We estimate over one hundred thousand... if we're lucky.
That's... that's...
How long do I have before making my decision?
How does a few minutes sound, Mr. President?

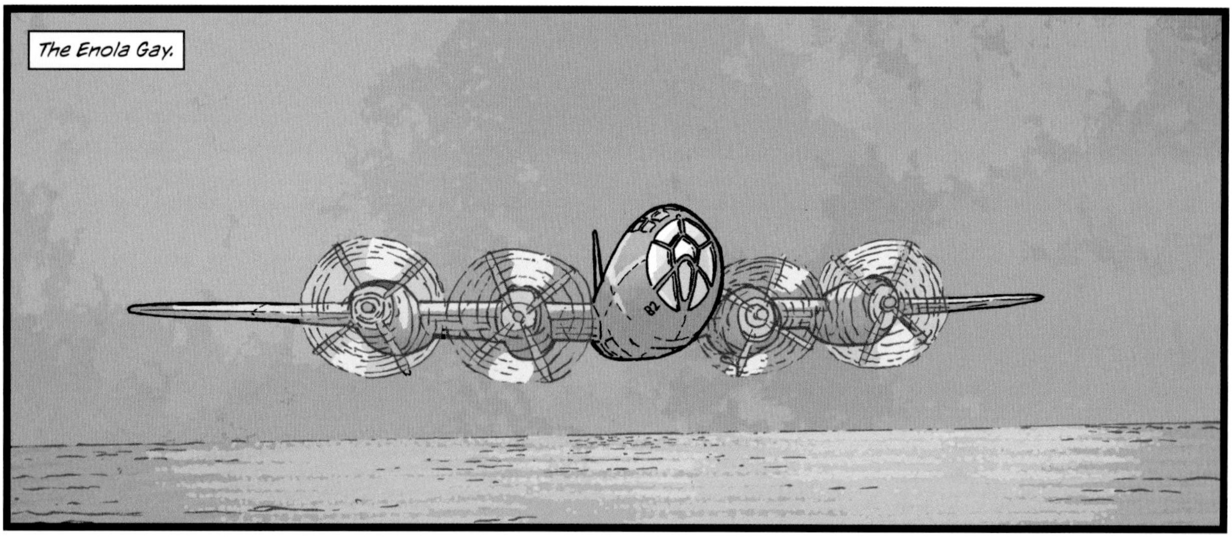
The Enola Gay.

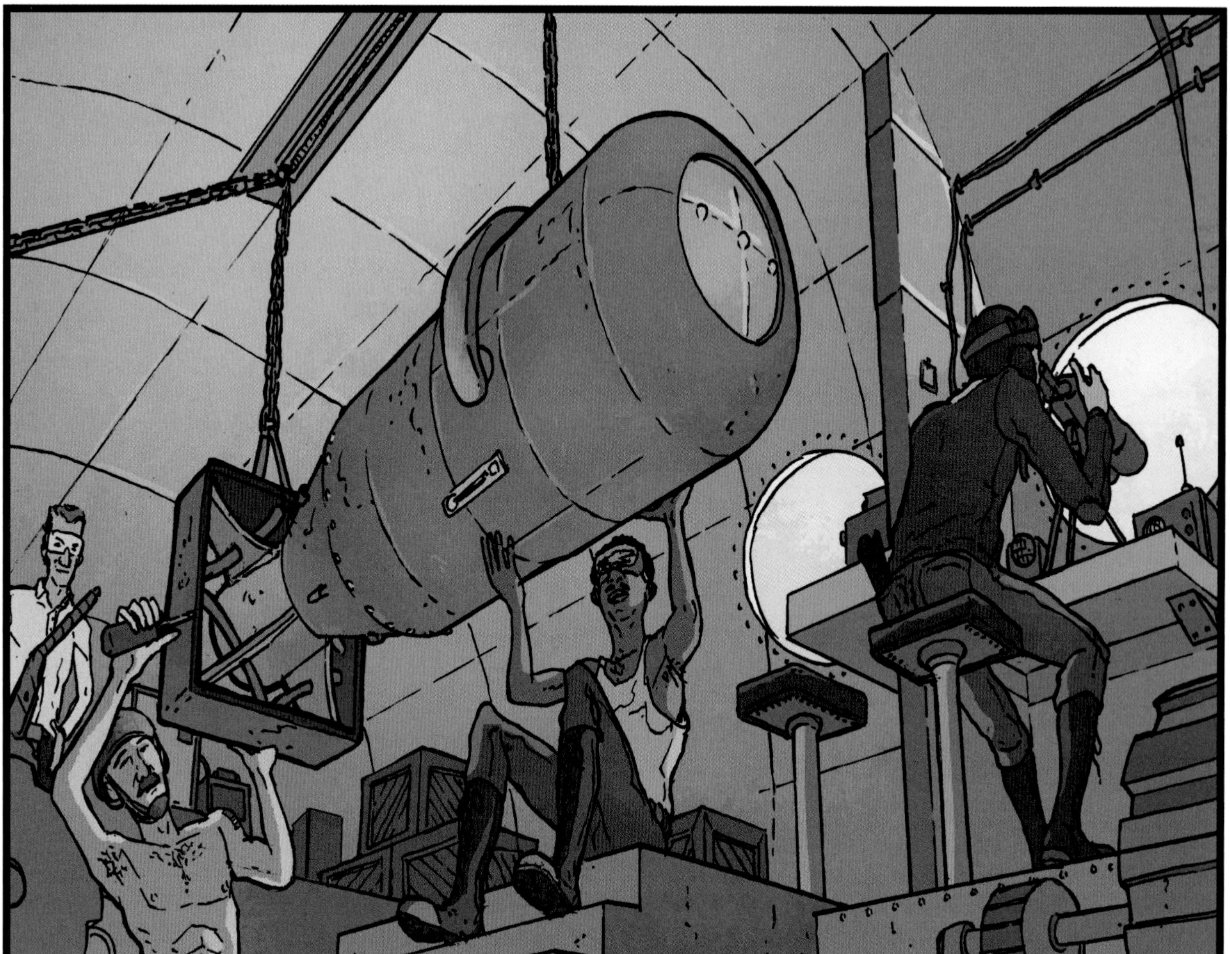

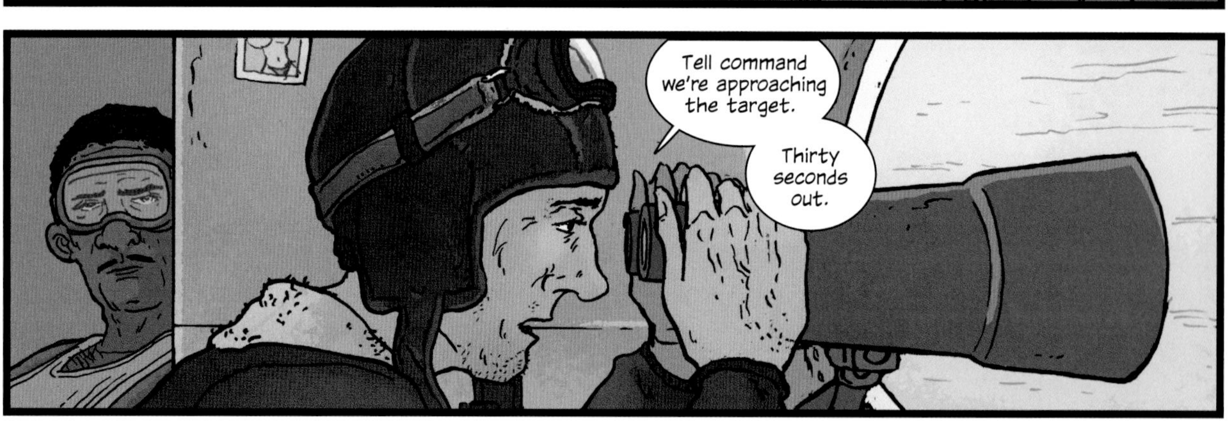
Tell command we're approaching the target.
Thirty seconds out.

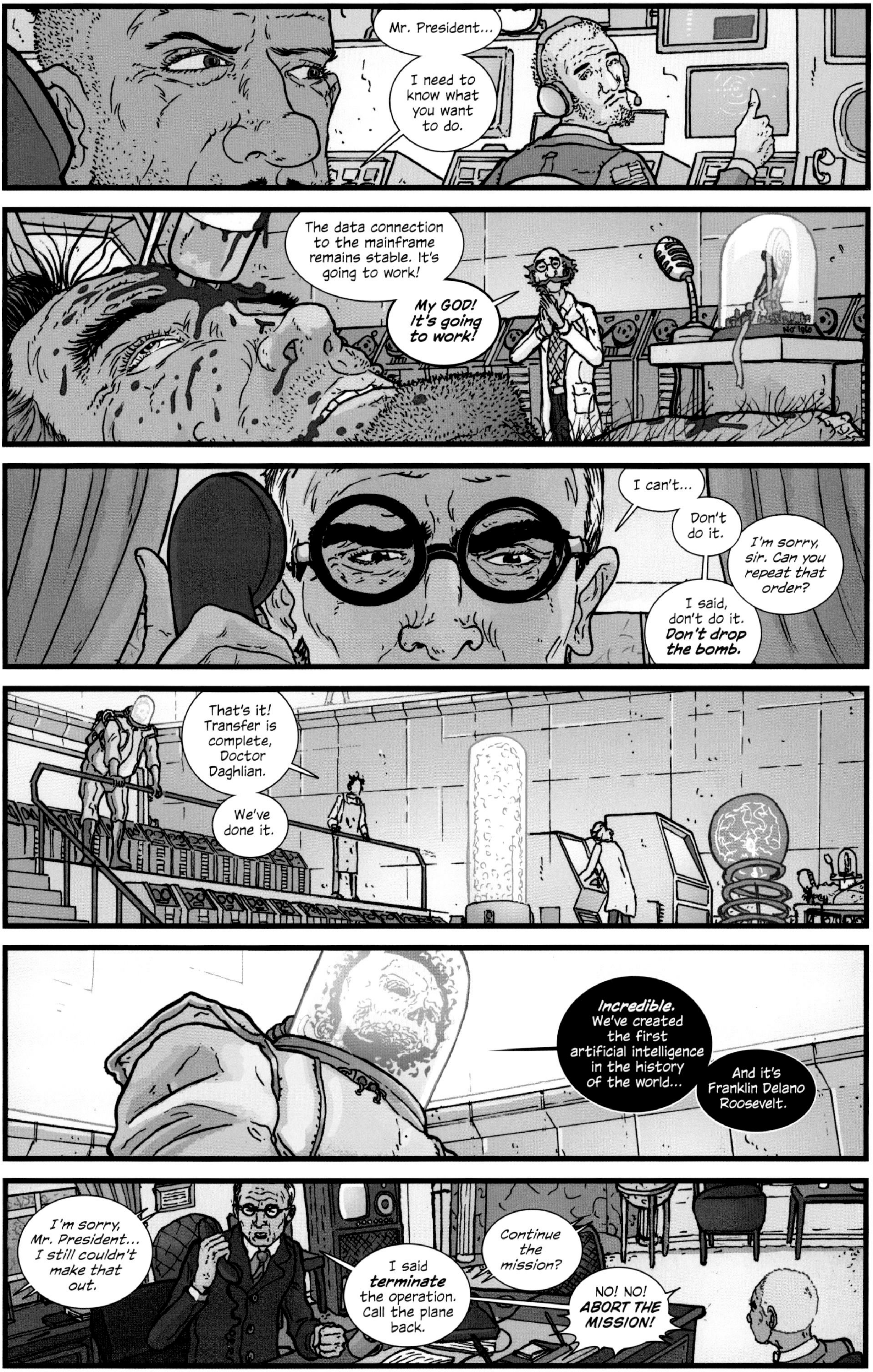

Mr. President...
I need to know what you want to do.
The data connection to the mainframe remains stable. It's going to work!
My GOD! It's going to work!
I can't...
Don't do it.
I'm sorry, sir. Can you repeat that order?
I said, don't do it. Don't drop the bomb.
That's it! Transfer is complete, Doctor Daghlian.
We've done it.
Incredible. We've created the first artificial intelligence in the history of the world...
And it's Franklin Delano Roosevelt.
I'm sorry, Mr. President... I still couldn't make that out.
I said terminate the operation. Call the plane back.
Continue the mission?
NO! NO! ABORT THE MISSION!

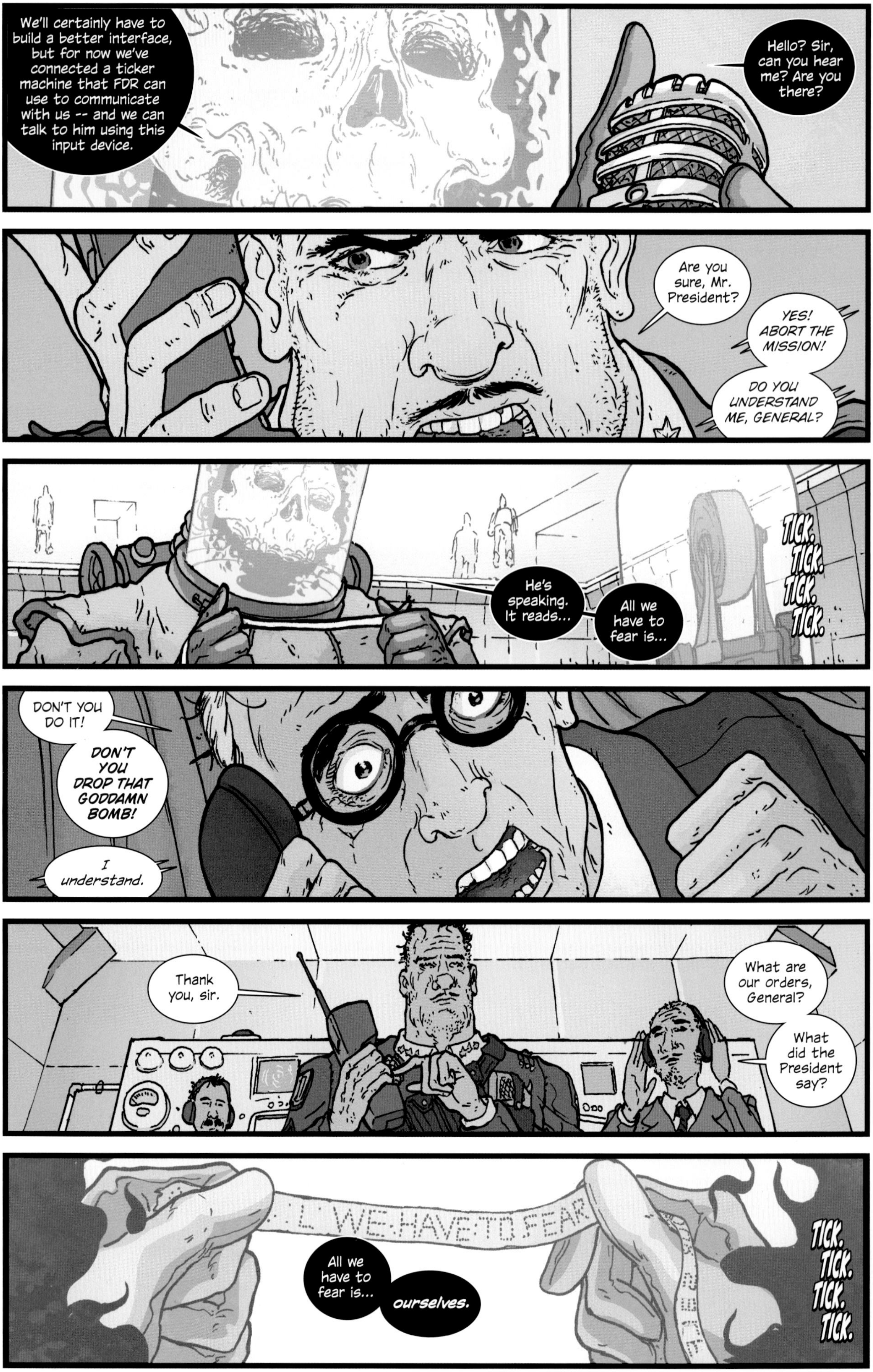
We'll certainly have to build a better interface, but for now we've connected a ticker machine that FDR can use to communicate with us -- and we can talk to him using this input device.
Hello? Sir, can you hear me? Are you there?
Are you sure, Mr. President?
YES! ABORT THE MISSION!
DO YOU UNDERSTAND ME, GENERAL?
He's speaking. It reads...
All we have to fear is...
TICK. TICK. TICK. TICK.
DON'T YOU DO IT!
DON'T YOU DROP THAT GODDAMN BOMB!
I understand.
Thank you, sir.
What are our orders, General?
What did the President say?
L WE HAVE TO FEAR
All we have to fear is...
ourselves.
TICK. TICK. TICK. TICK.

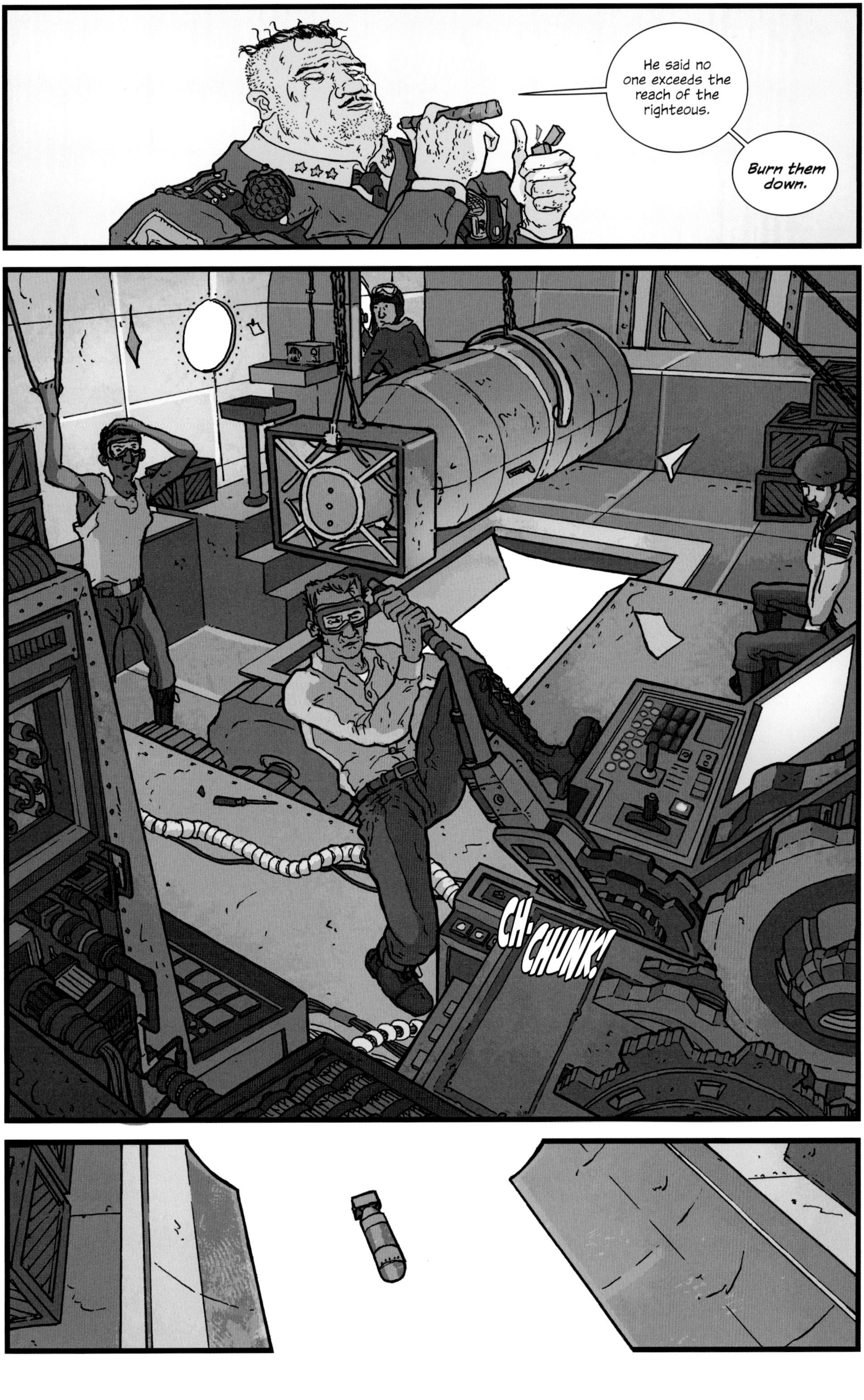
He said no one exceeds the reach of the righteous.
Burn them down.
CH-CHUNK!

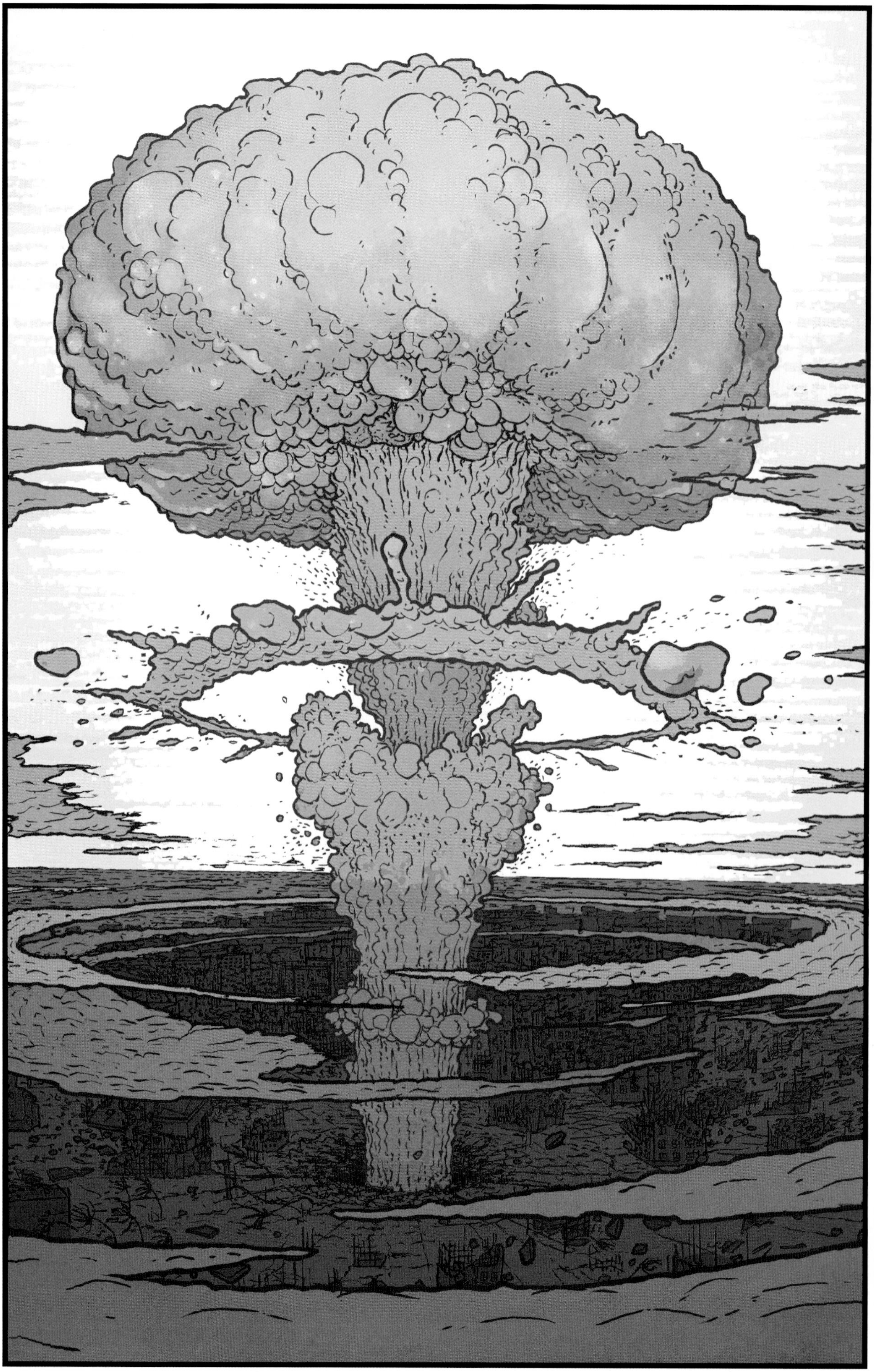

"AFTER HIROSHIMA, AT THE URGING OF GENERAL GROVES AND DIRECTOR OPPENHEIMER, THE FDR ARTIFICIAL INTELLIGENCE ESTABLISHED A SHADOW GOVERNMENT OF THE UNITED STATES."

CLAVIS AUREA
THE RECORDED FEYNMAN

VOL. 1

THE DOOR OPENED
WIDER

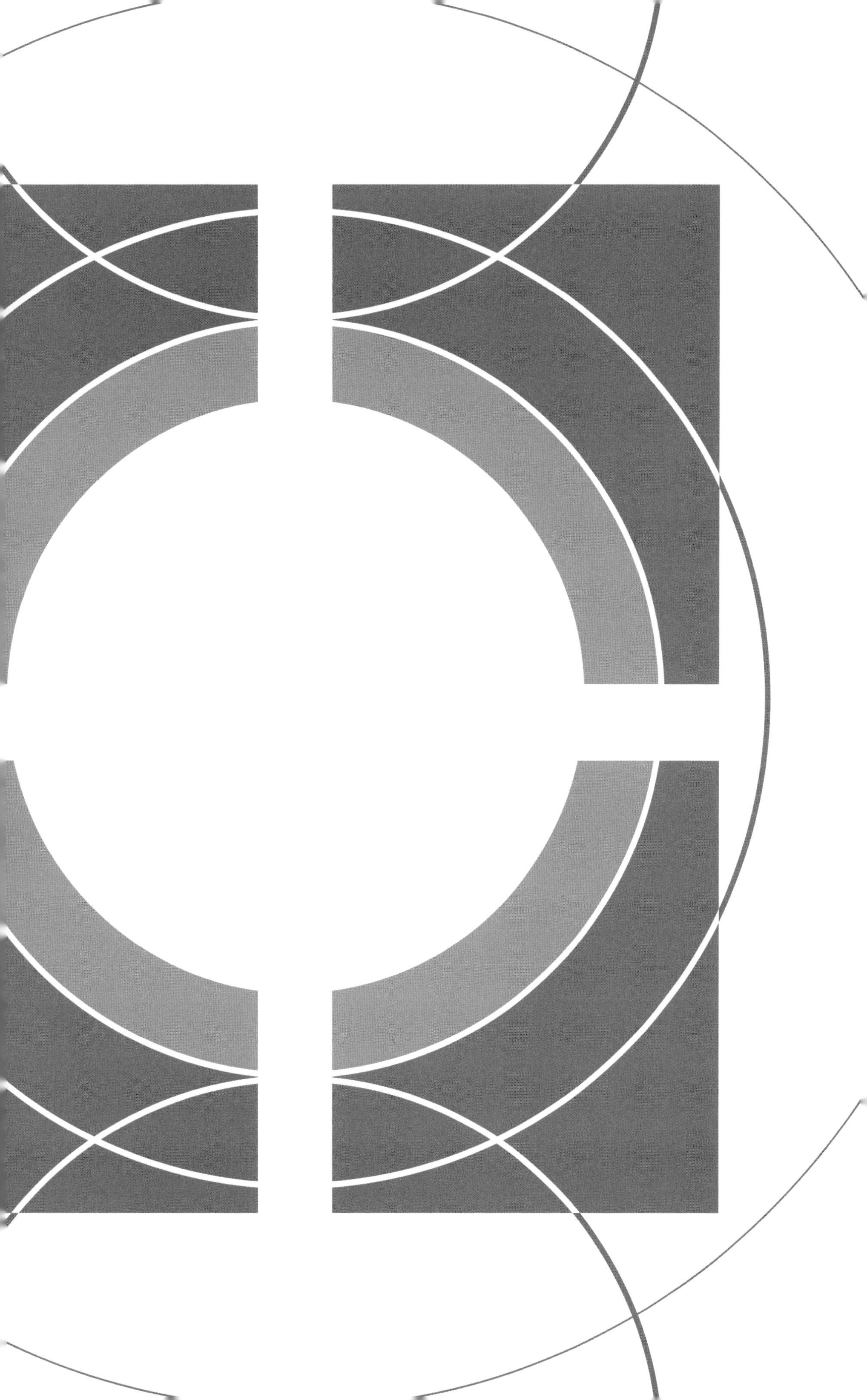

"A HUMAN BEING IS A PART OF THE WHOLE, CALLED BY US 'UNIVERSE', A PART LIMITED IN TIME AND SPACE. "

- ALBERT EINSTEIN

CLAVIS AUREA
THE RECORDED FEYNMAN | VOL. 1

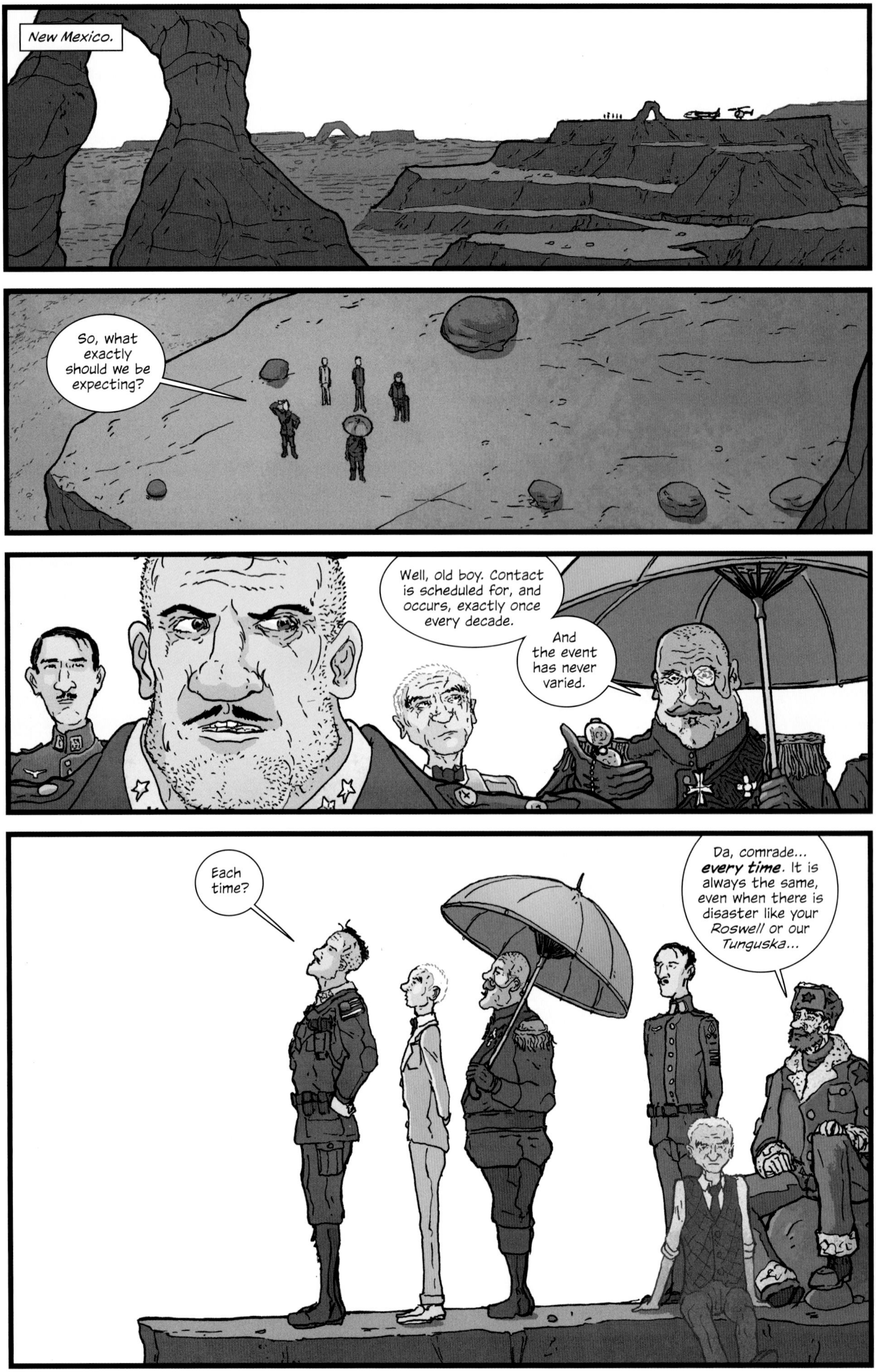
New Mexico.
So, what exactly should we be expecting?
Well, old boy. Contact is scheduled for, and occurs, exactly once every decade.
And the event has never varied.
Each time?
Da, comrade... ***every time***. It is always the same, even when there is disaster like your *Roswell* or our *Tunguska*...

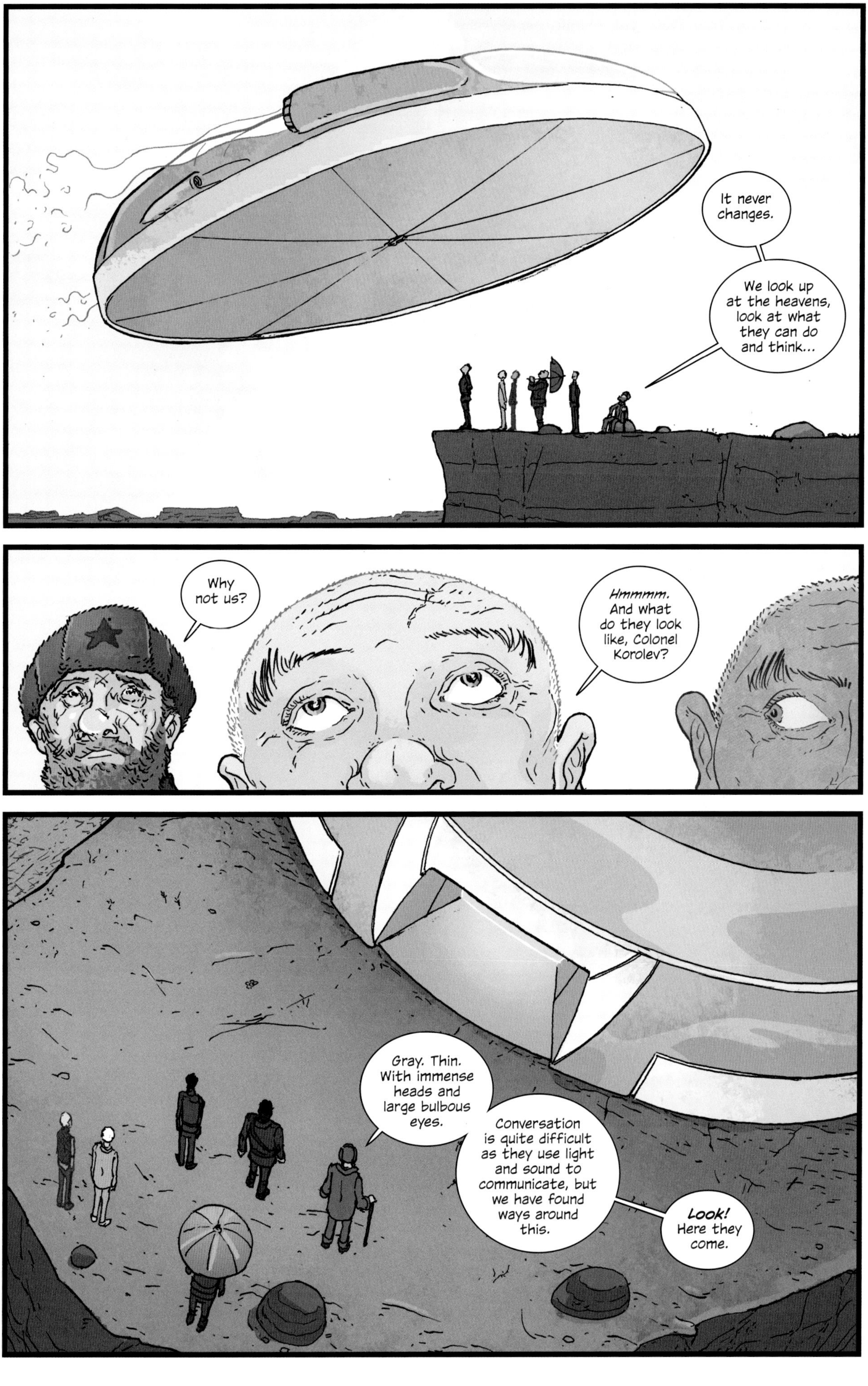
It never changes.
We look up at the heavens, look at what they can do and think...
Why not us?
Hmmmm. And what do they look like, Colonel Korolev?
Gray. Thin. With immense heads and large bulbous eyes.
Conversation is quite difficult as they use light and sound to communicate, but we have found ways around this.
Look! Here they come.

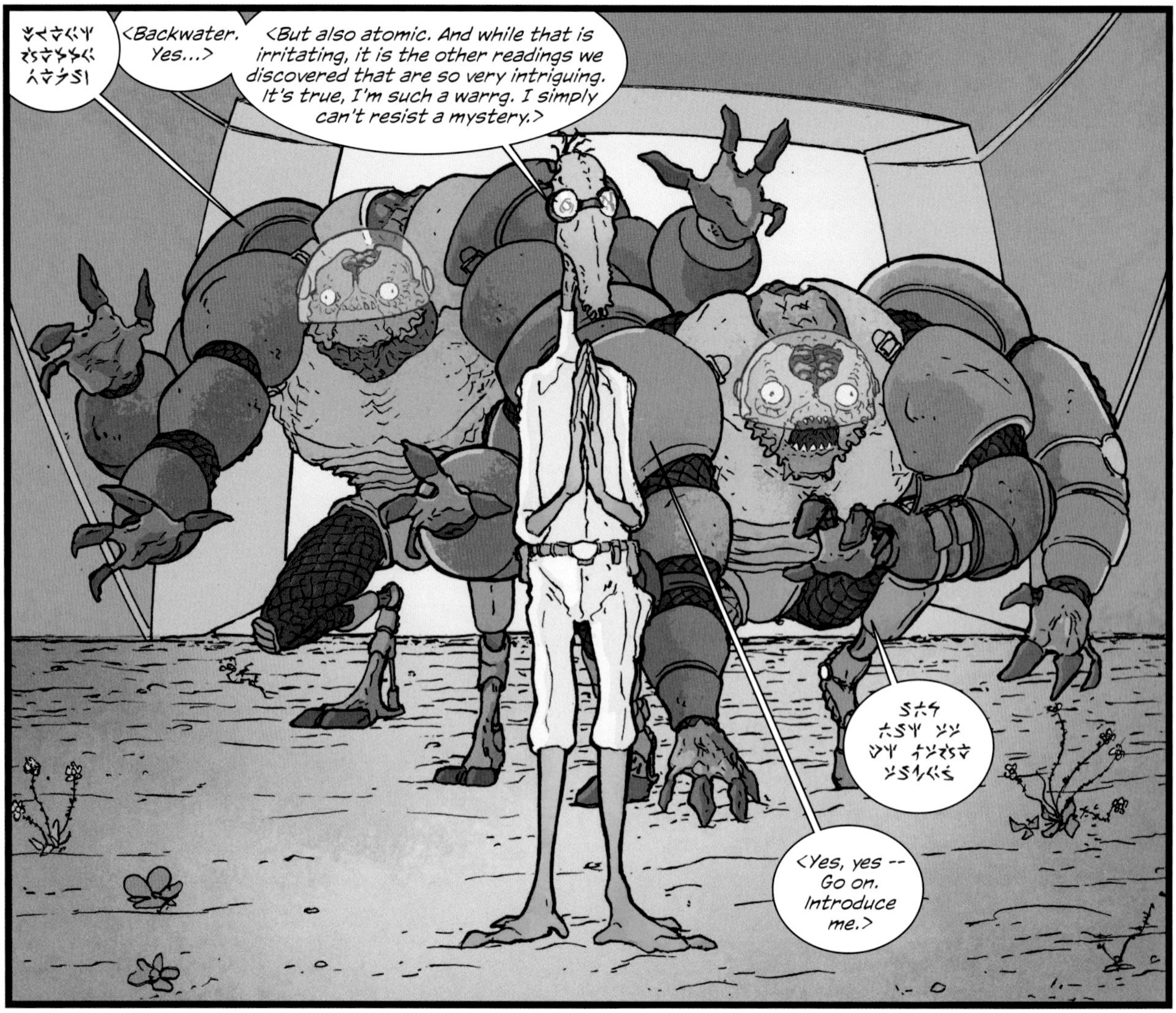
<Backwater. Yes...>
<But also atomic. And while that is irritating, it is the other readings we discovered that are so very intriguing. It's true, I'm such a warrg. I simply can't resist a mystery.>
<Yes, yes -- Go on. Introduce me.>

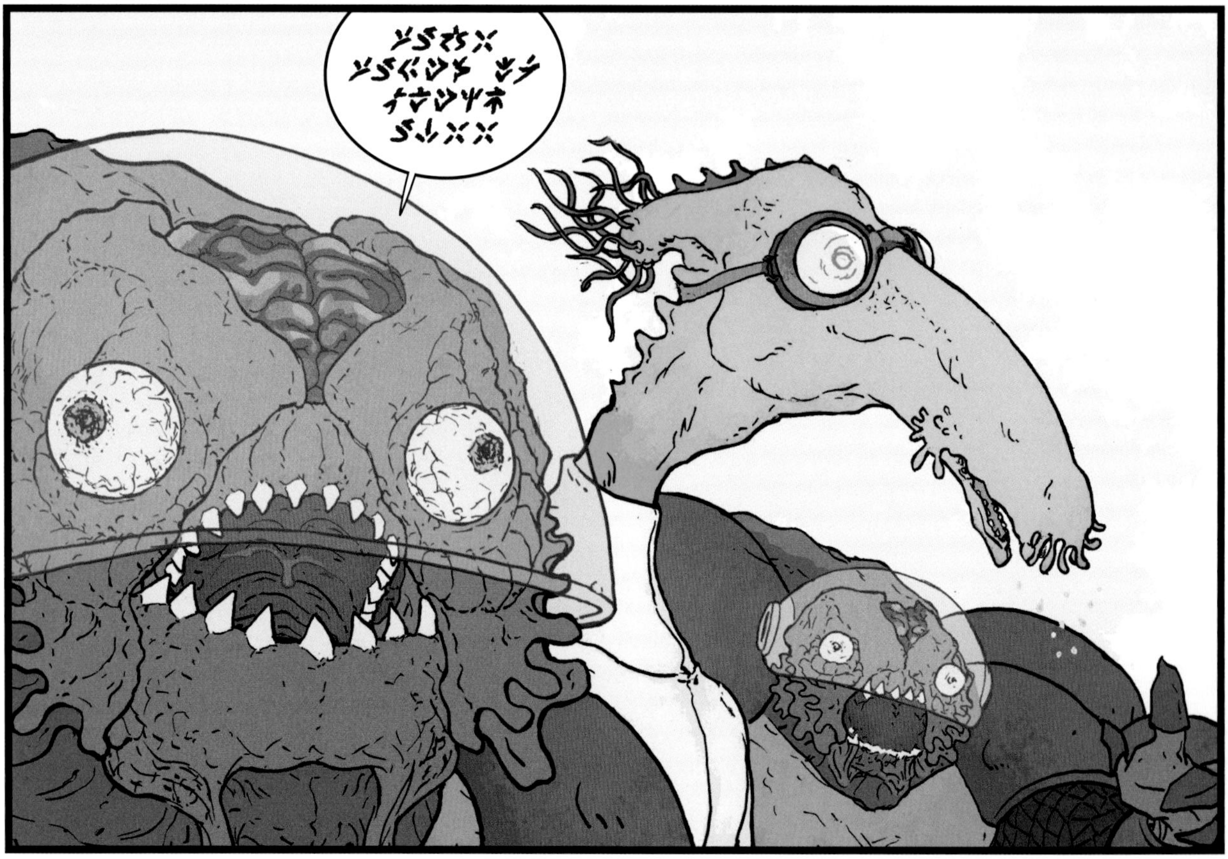

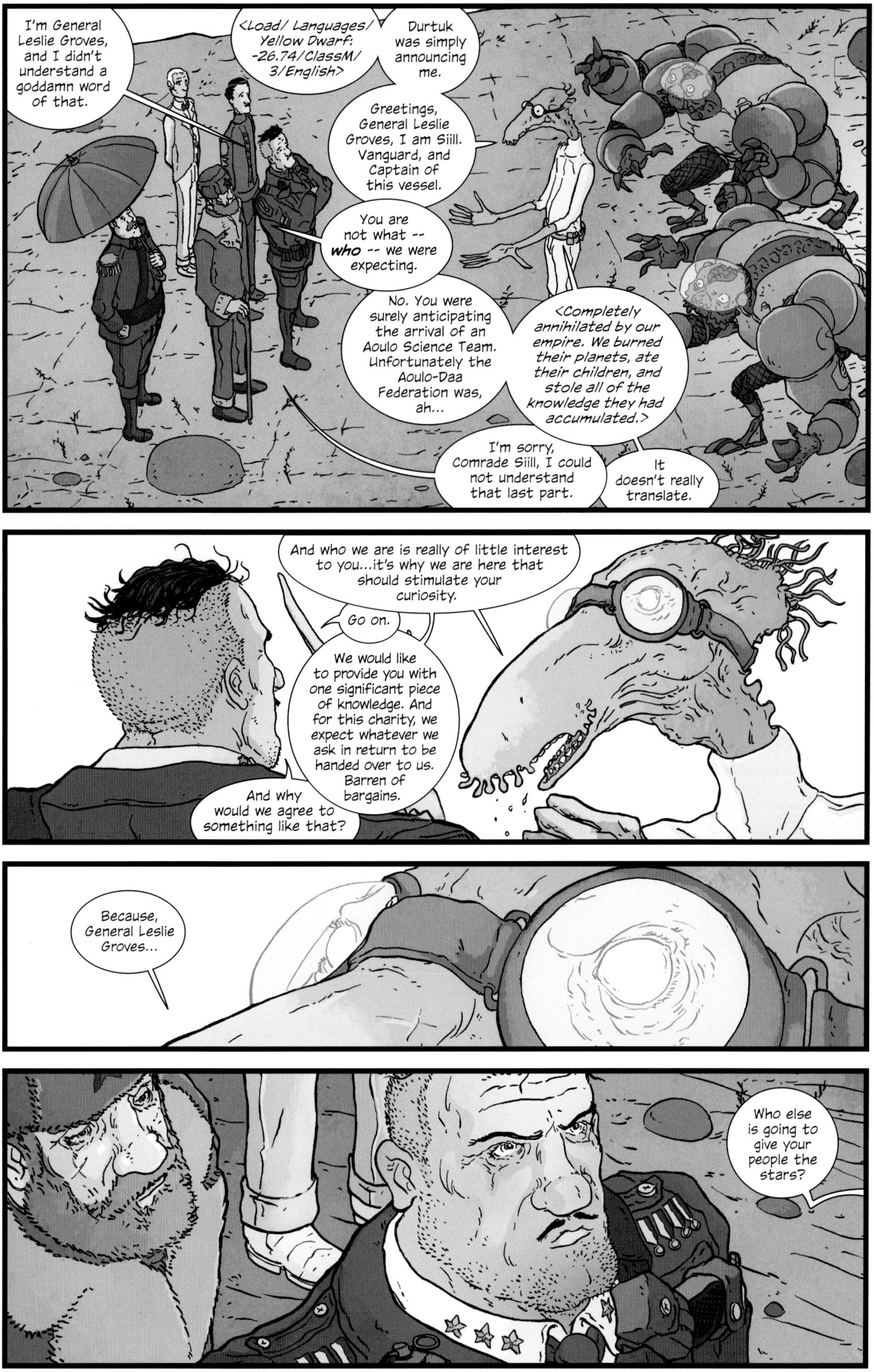
I'm General Leslie Groves, and I didn't understand a goddamn word of that.
<Load/ Languages/ Yellow Dwarf: -26.74/ClassM/ 3/English>
Durtuk was simply announcing me.
Greetings, General Leslie Groves, I am Siill. Vanguard, and Captain of this vessel.
You are not what -- who -- we were expecting.
No. You were surely anticipating the arrival of an Aoulo Science Team. Unfortunately the Aoulo-Daa Federation was, ah...
<Completely annihilated by our empire. We burned their planets, ate their children, and stole all of the knowledge they had accumulated.>
I'm sorry, Comrade Siill, I could not understand that last part.
It doesn't really translate.
And who we are is really of little interest to you...it's why we are here that should stimulate your curiosity.
Go on.
We would like to provide you with one significant piece of knowledge. And for this charity, we expect whatever we ask in return to be handed over to us. Barren of bargains.
And why would we agree to something like that?
Because, General Leslie Groves...
Who else is going to give your people the stars?

04

THE ROSE BRIDGE

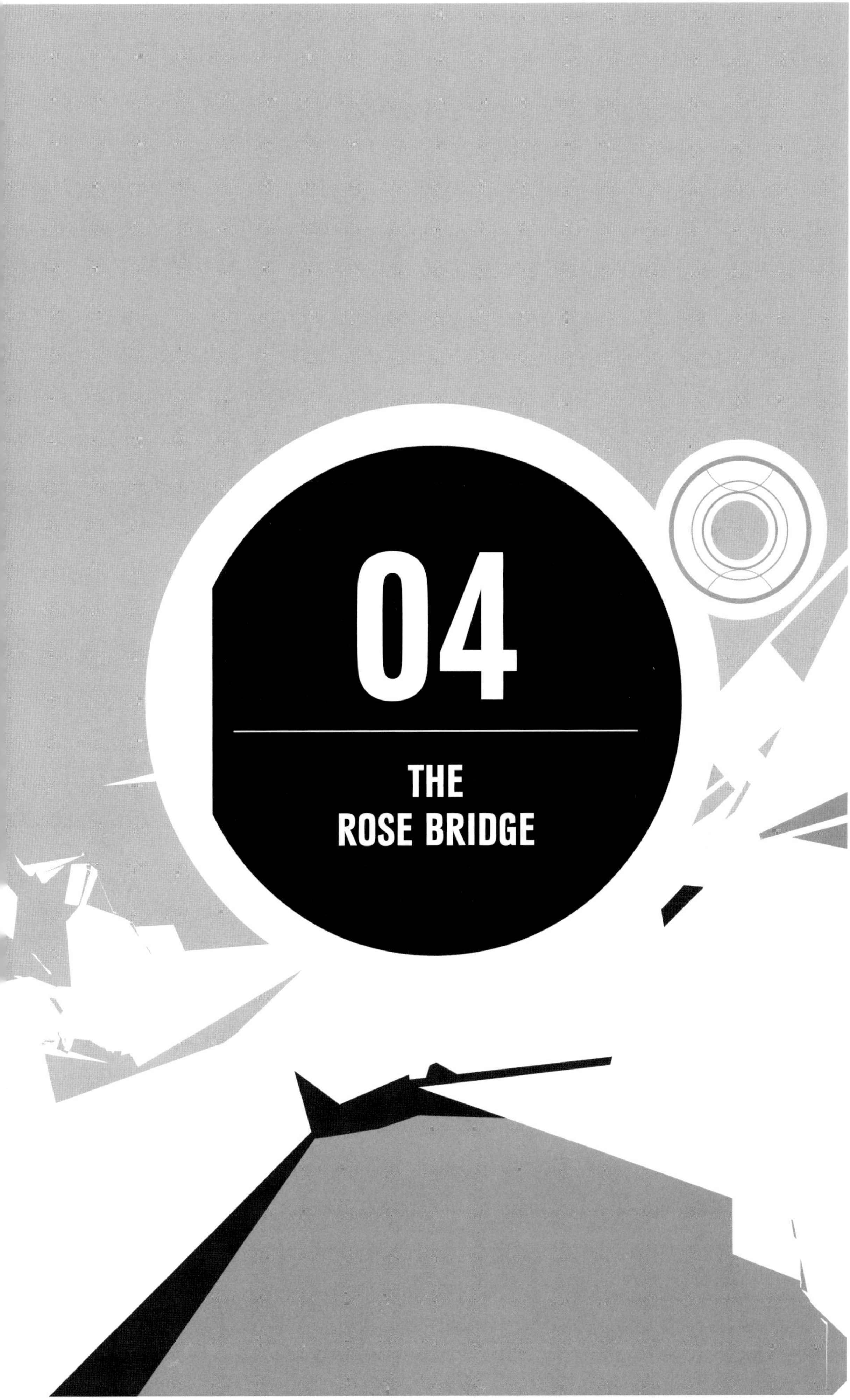

"IMAGINATION IS MORE IMPORTANT THAN KNOWLEDGE. FOR KNOWLEDGE IS LIMITED, WHEREAS IMAGINATION EMBRACES THE ENTIRE WORLD, STIMULATING PROGRESS, GIVING BIRTH TO EVOLUTION."

- ALBERT EINSTEIN

CLAVIS AUREA
THE RECORDED FEYNMAN | **VOL. 1**

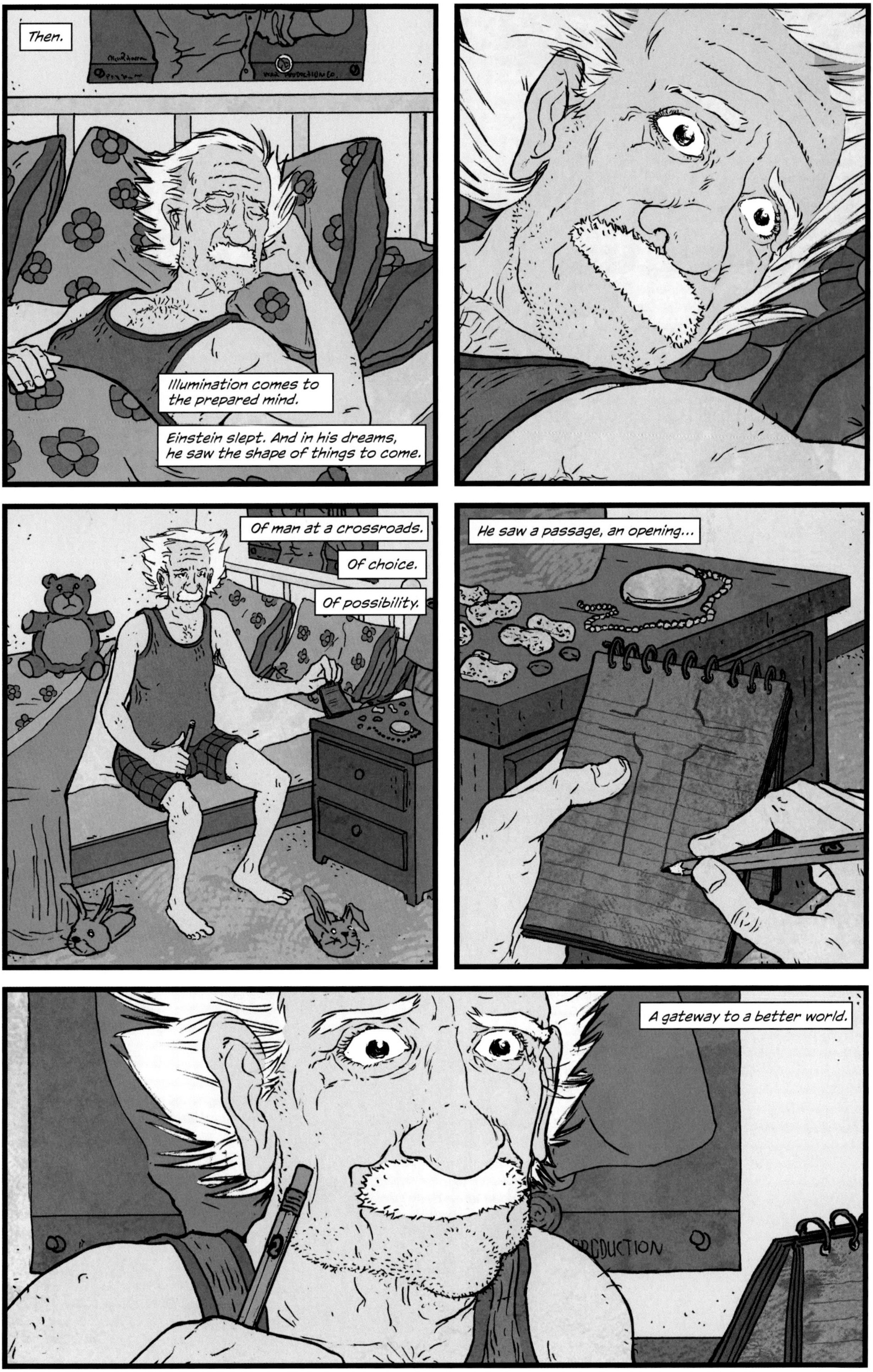
Then.
Illumination comes to the prepared mind.
Einstein slept. And in his dreams, he saw the shape of things to come.
Of man at a crossroads.
Of choice.
Of possibility.
He saw a passage, an opening...
A gateway to a better world.

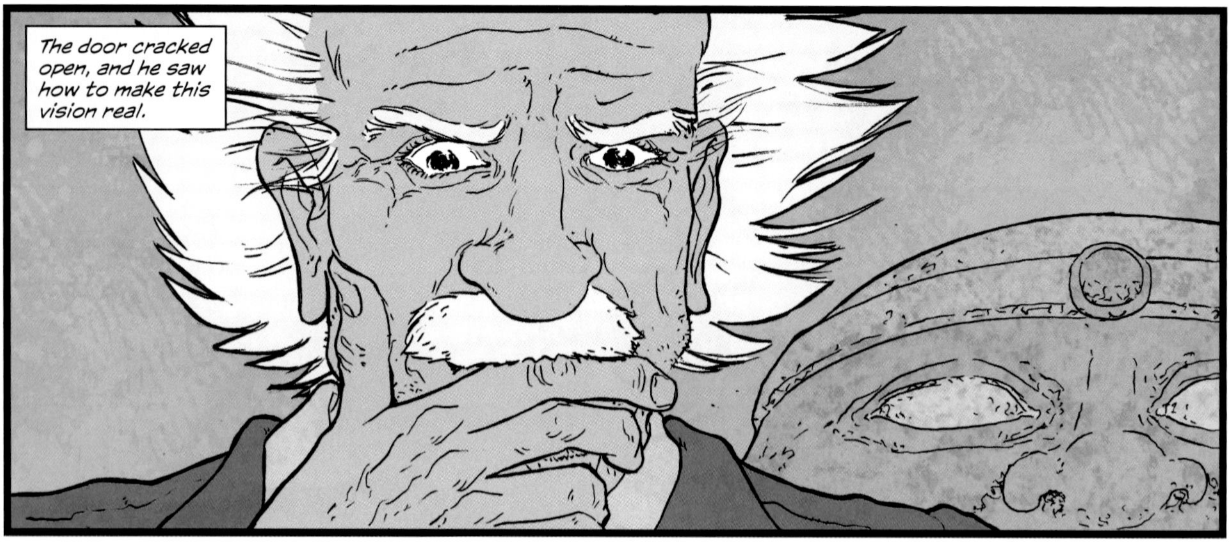
The door cracked open, and he saw how to make this vision real.

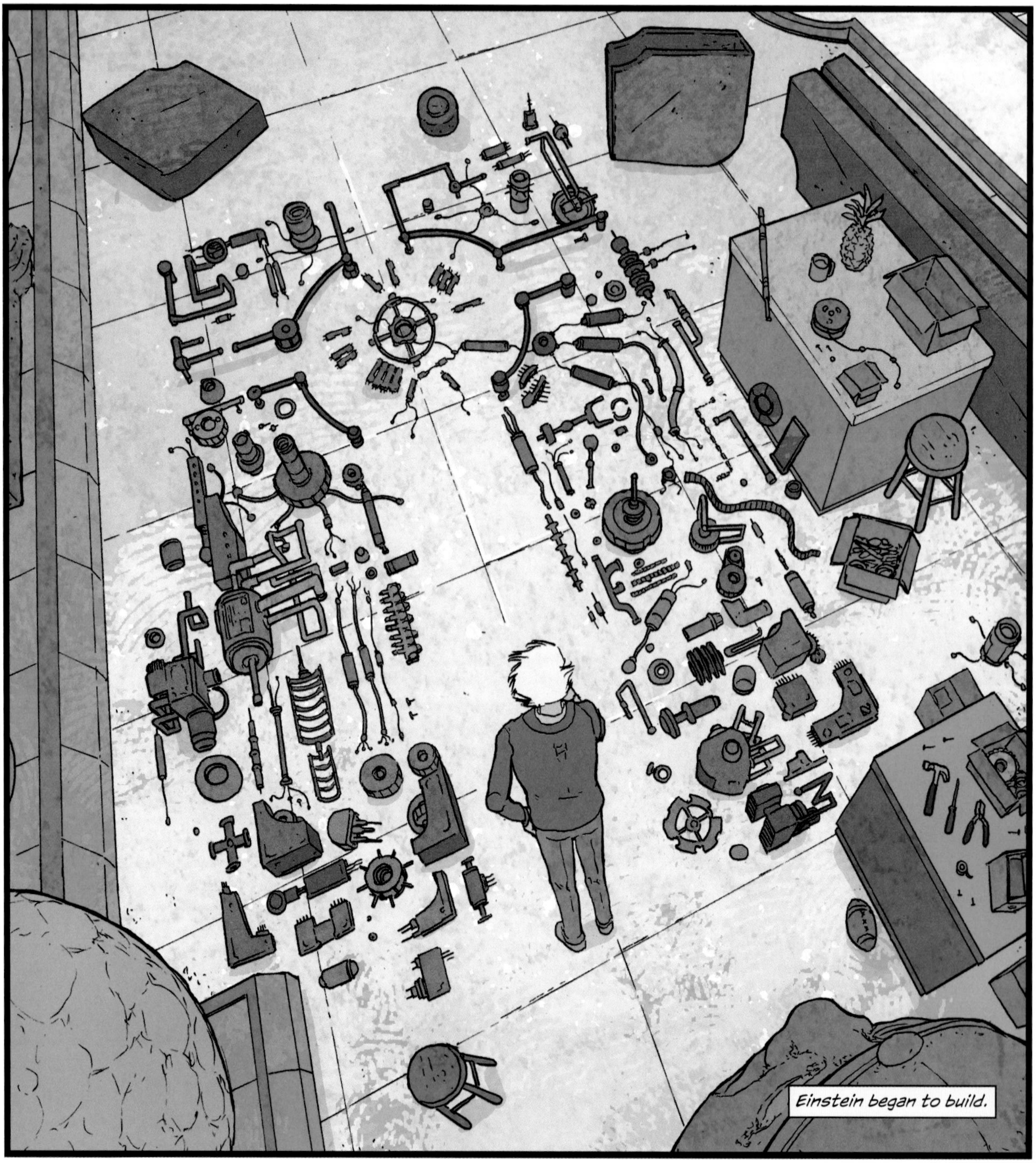
Einstein began to build.

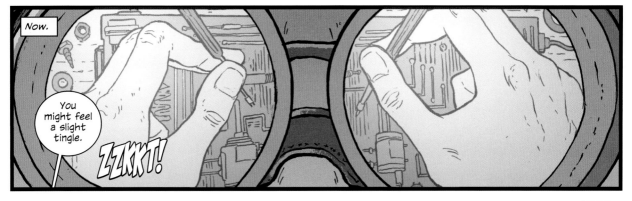

Now.

You might feel a slight tingle.

ZZKKT!

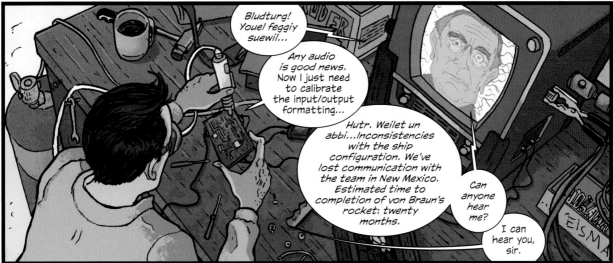

Bludturg! Youel feggiy suewil...

Any audio is good news. Now I just need to calibrate the input/output formatting...

Hutr. Weilet un abbi...Inconsistencies with the ship configuration. We've lost communication with the team in New Mexico. Estimated time to completion of von Braun's rocket: twenty months.

Can anyone hear me?

I can hear you, sir.

I've cross-referenced all visual IDs with social security numbers and FBI background profiles. I believe we have three impostors at the War Department.

I wouldn't be overly alarmed. There are communists everywhere.

Voice and facial recognition indicate there's an 87% chance that you are Feynman, Richard.

Help me, Mr. Feynman. There's too much data.

Nothing I can do about that, sir. You're connected to every information system we have.

Listen to me. Listen to me. **Listen. To. Me.**

A Jew, a scientist and a drunk walk into a lab.

...

That's all.

I'm sorry, Mister President... I don't --

Look behind you.

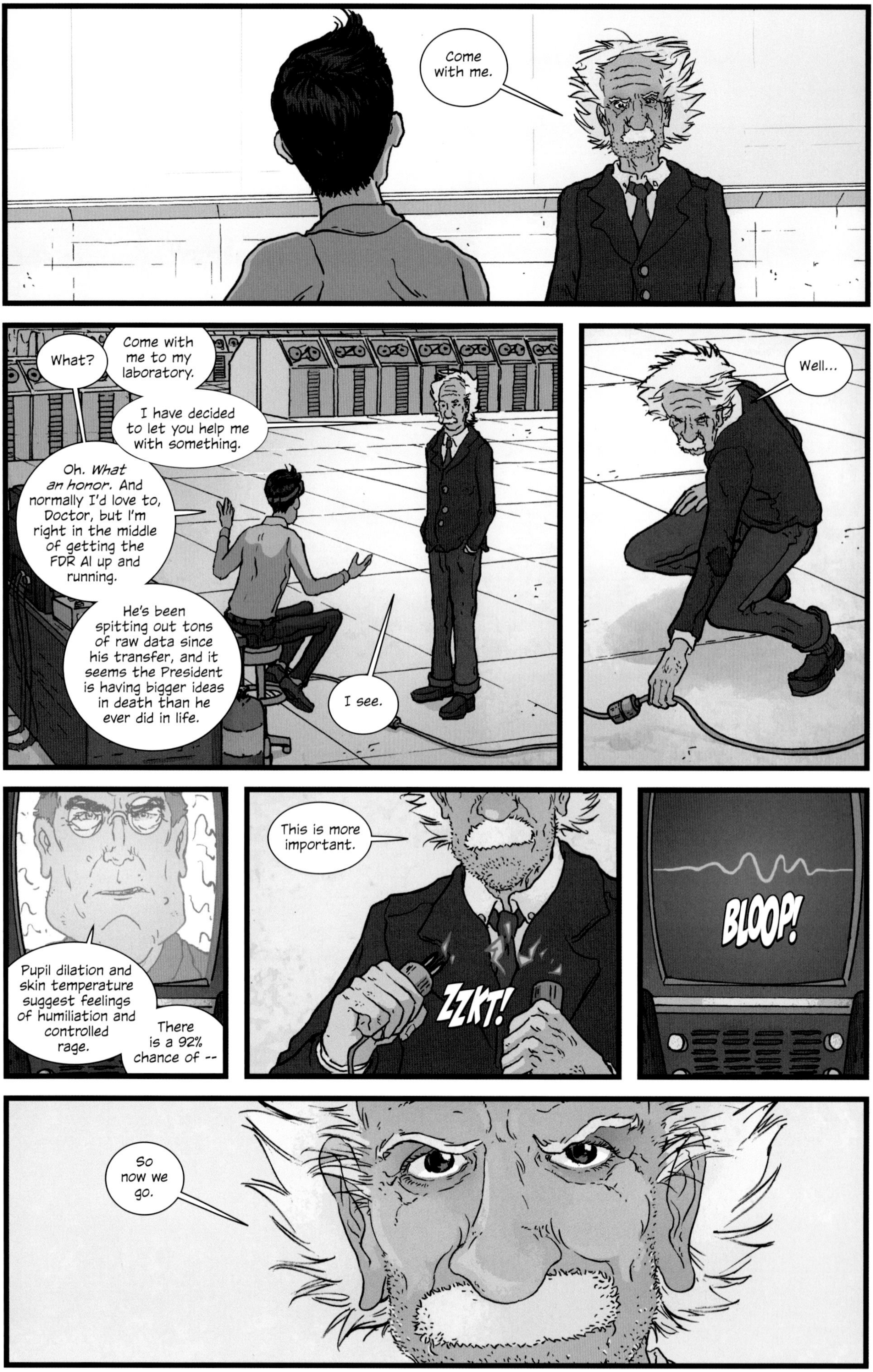
Come with me.
What?
Come with me to my laboratory.
I have decided to let you help me with something.
Oh. *What an honor.* And normally I'd love to, Doctor, but I'm right in the middle of getting the FDR AI up and running.
He's been spitting out tons of raw data since his transfer, and it seems the President is having bigger ideas in death than he ever did in life.
I see.
Well...
Pupil dilation and skin temperature suggest feelings of humiliation and controlled rage.
There is a 92% chance of --
This is more important.
ZZKT!
BLOOP!
So now we go.

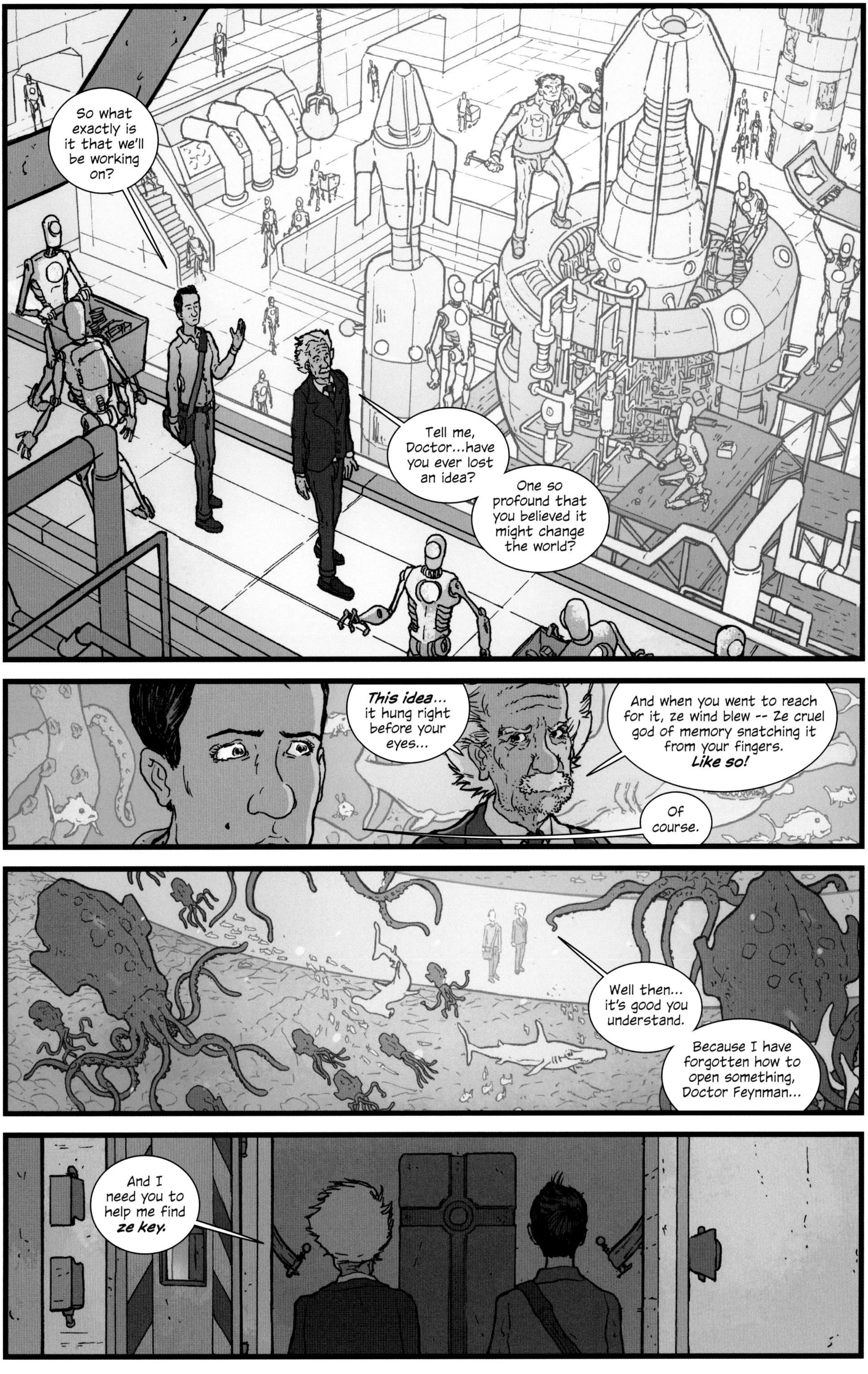
So what exactly is it that we'll be working on?
Tell me, Doctor...have you ever lost an idea?
One so profound that you believed it might change the world?
This idea... it hung right before your eyes...
And when you went to reach for it, ze wind blew -- Ze cruel god of memory snatching it from your fingers. ***Like so!***
Of course.
Well then... it's good you understand.
Because I have forgotten how to open something, Doctor Feynman...
And I need you to help me find ***ze key.***

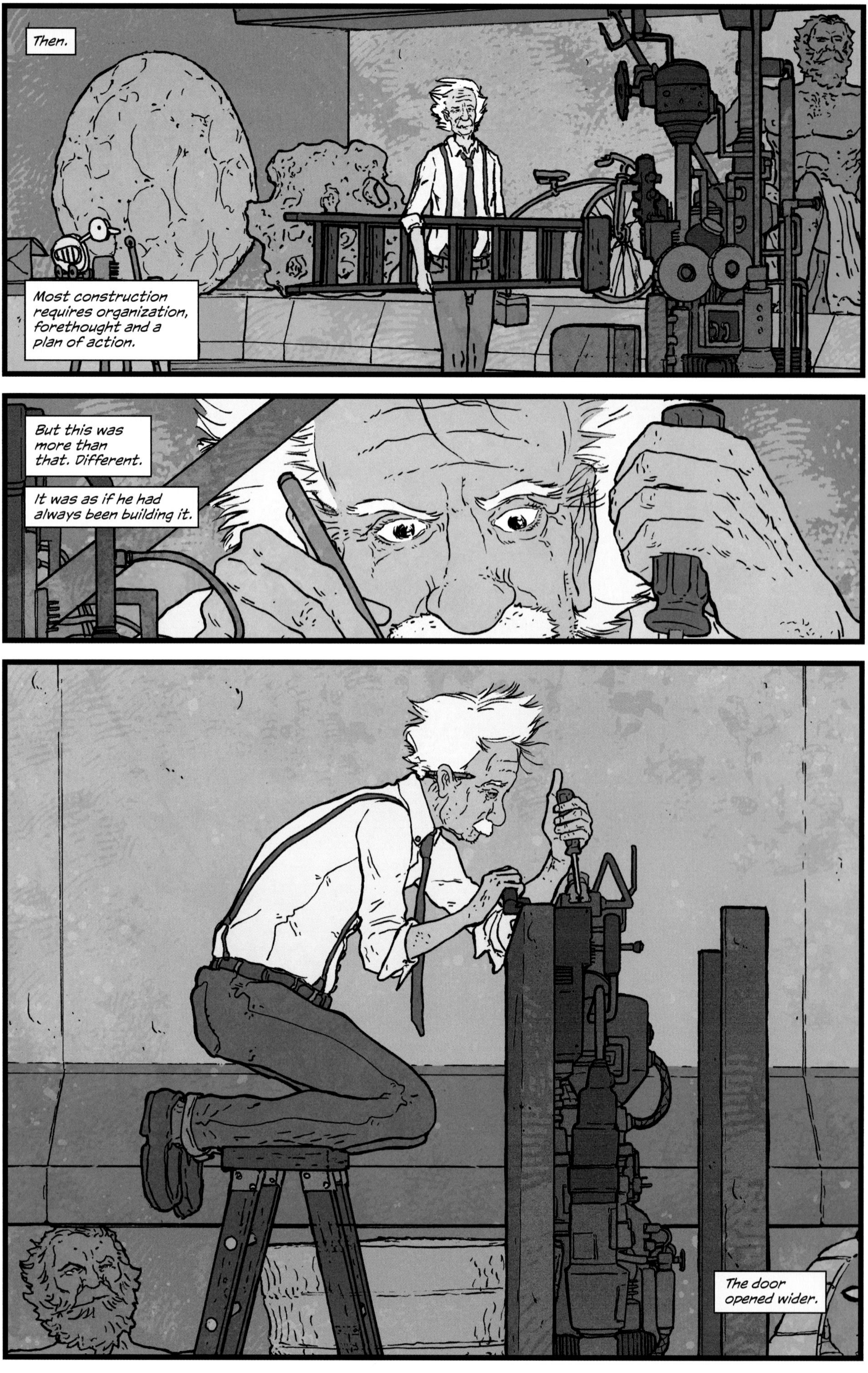
Then.
Most construction requires organization, forethought and a plan of action.
But this was more than that. Different.
It was as if he had always been building it.
The door opened wider.

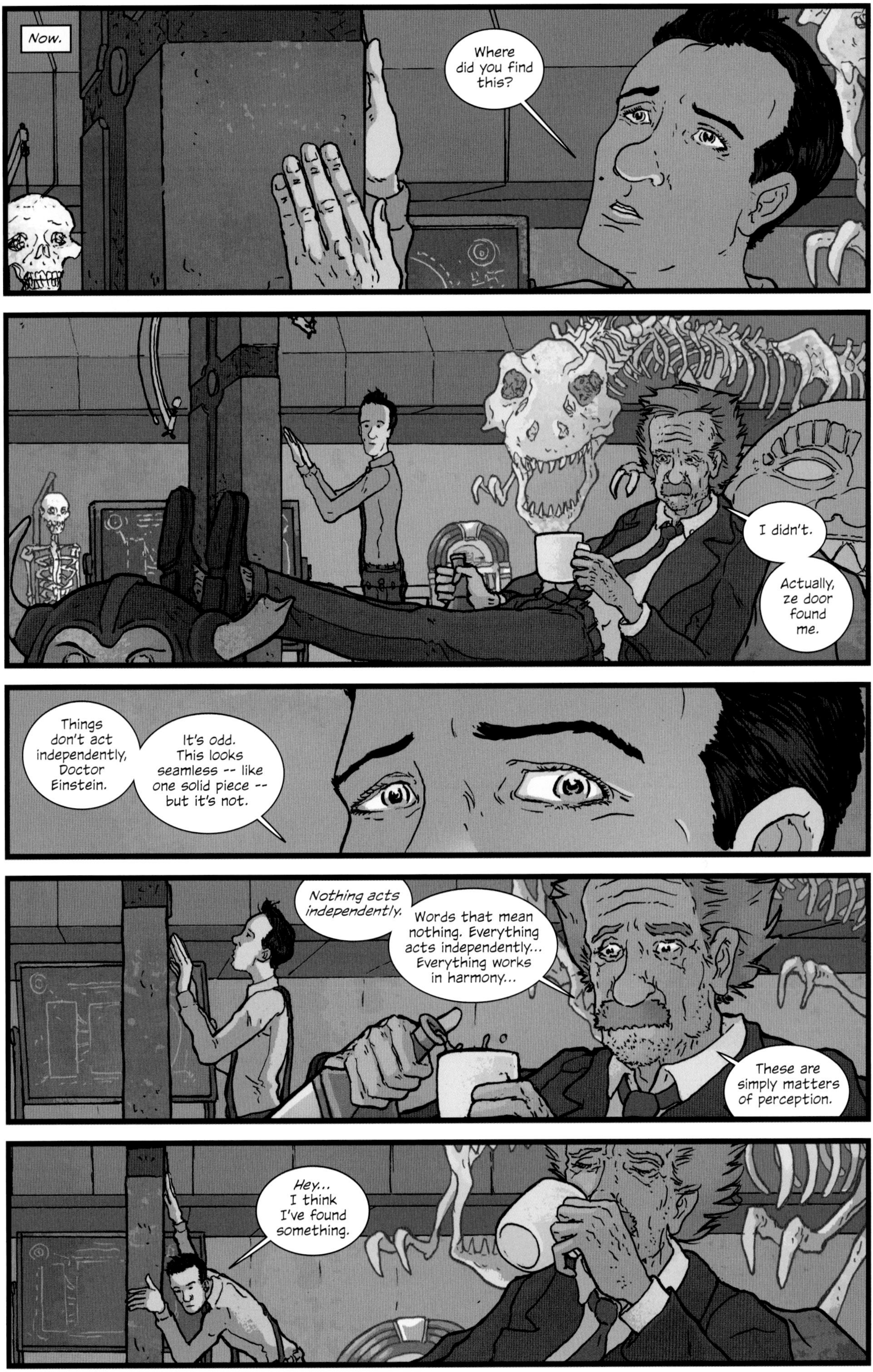
Now.
Where did you find this?
I didn't.
Actually, ze door found me.
Things don't act independently, Doctor Einstein.
It's odd. This looks seamless -- like one solid piece -- but it's not.
Nothing acts independently.
Words that mean nothing. Everything acts independently... Everything works in harmony...
These are simply matters of perception.
Hey... I think I've found something.

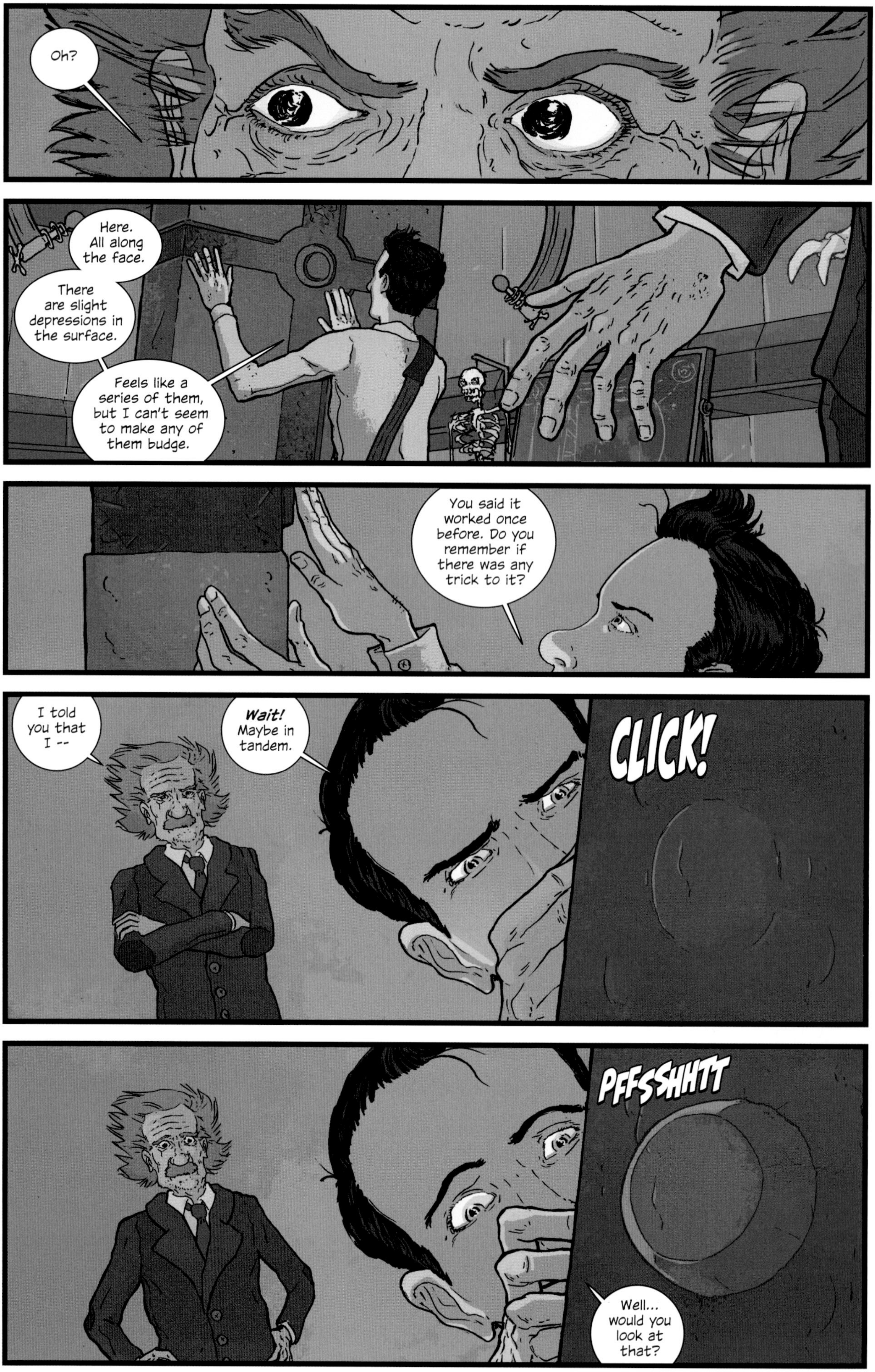
Oh?
Here. All along the face.
There are slight depressions in the surface.
Feels like a series of them, but I can't seem to make any of them budge.
You said it worked once before. Do you remember if there was any trick to it?
I told you that I --
Wait! Maybe in tandem.
CLICK!
PFFSSHHTT
Well... would you look at that?

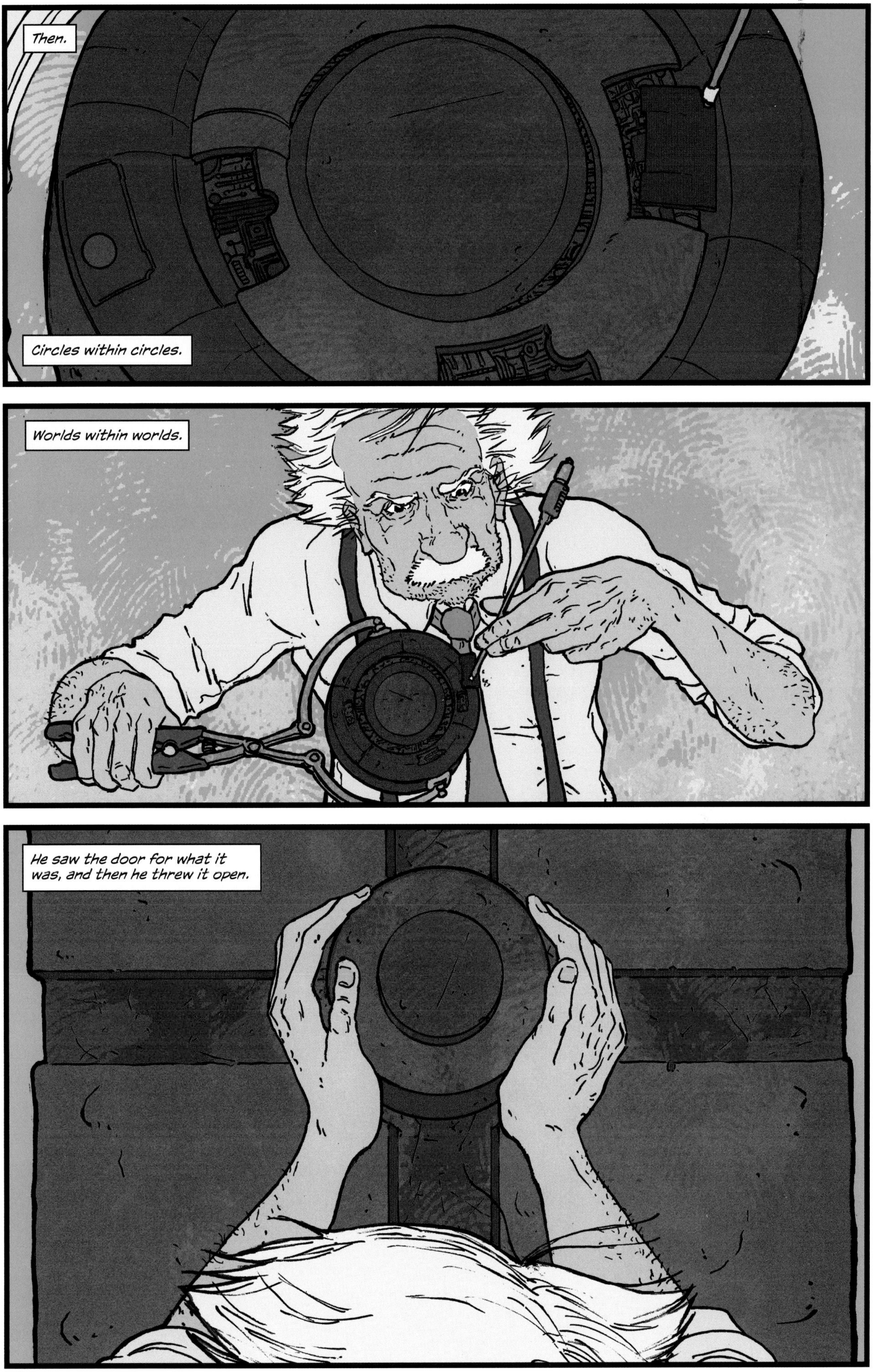
Then.
Circles within circles.
Worlds within worlds.
He saw the door for what it was, and then he threw it open.

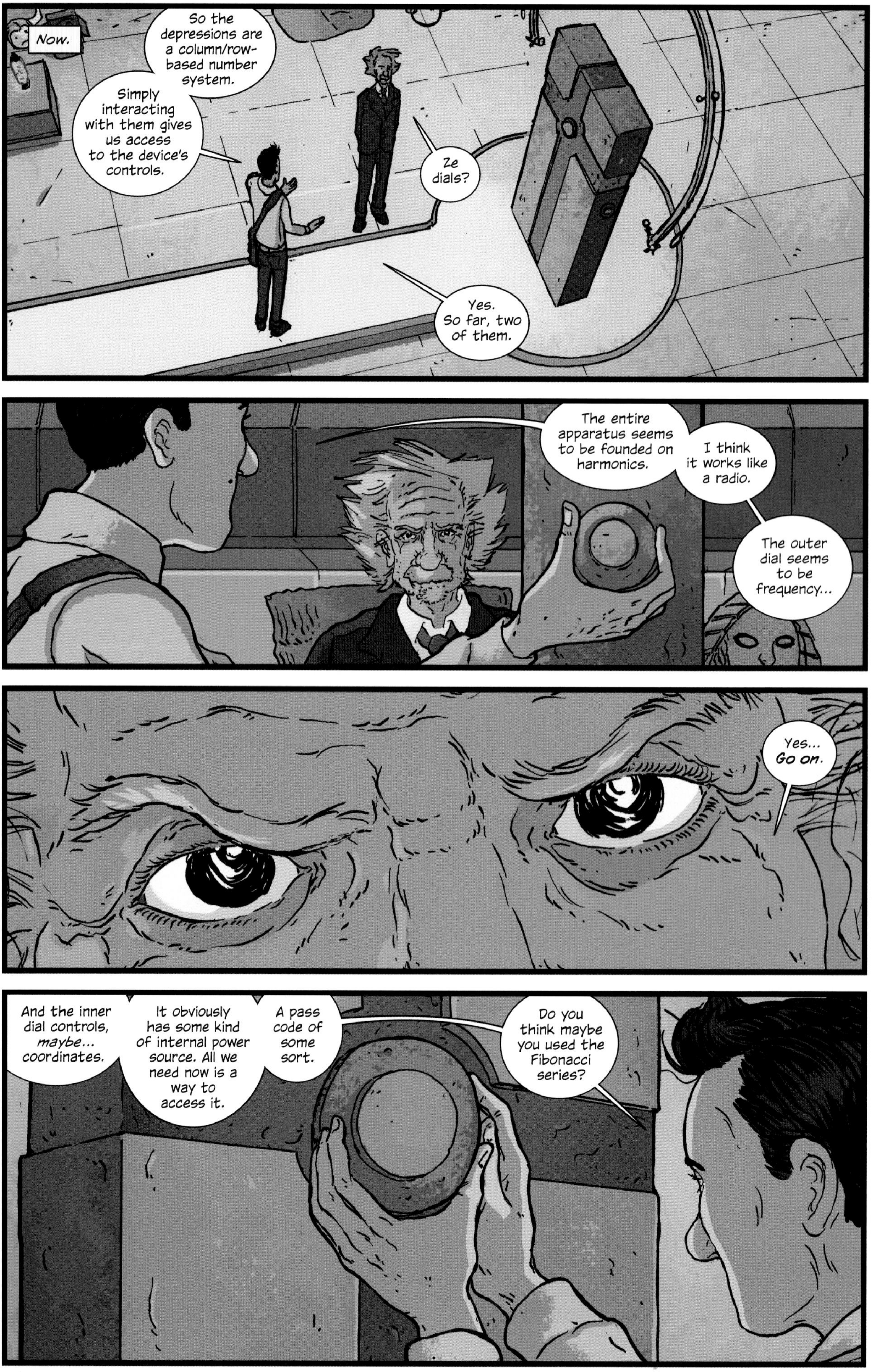
Now.
So the depressions are a column/row-based number system.
Simply interacting with them gives us access to the device's controls.
Ze dials?
Yes. So far, two of them.
The entire apparatus seems to be founded on harmonics.
I think it works like a radio.
The outer dial seems to be frequency...
Yes... *Go on*.
And the inner dial controls, *maybe*... coordinates.
It obviously has some kind of internal power source. All we need now is a way to access it.
A pass code of some sort.
Do you think maybe you used the Fibonacci series?

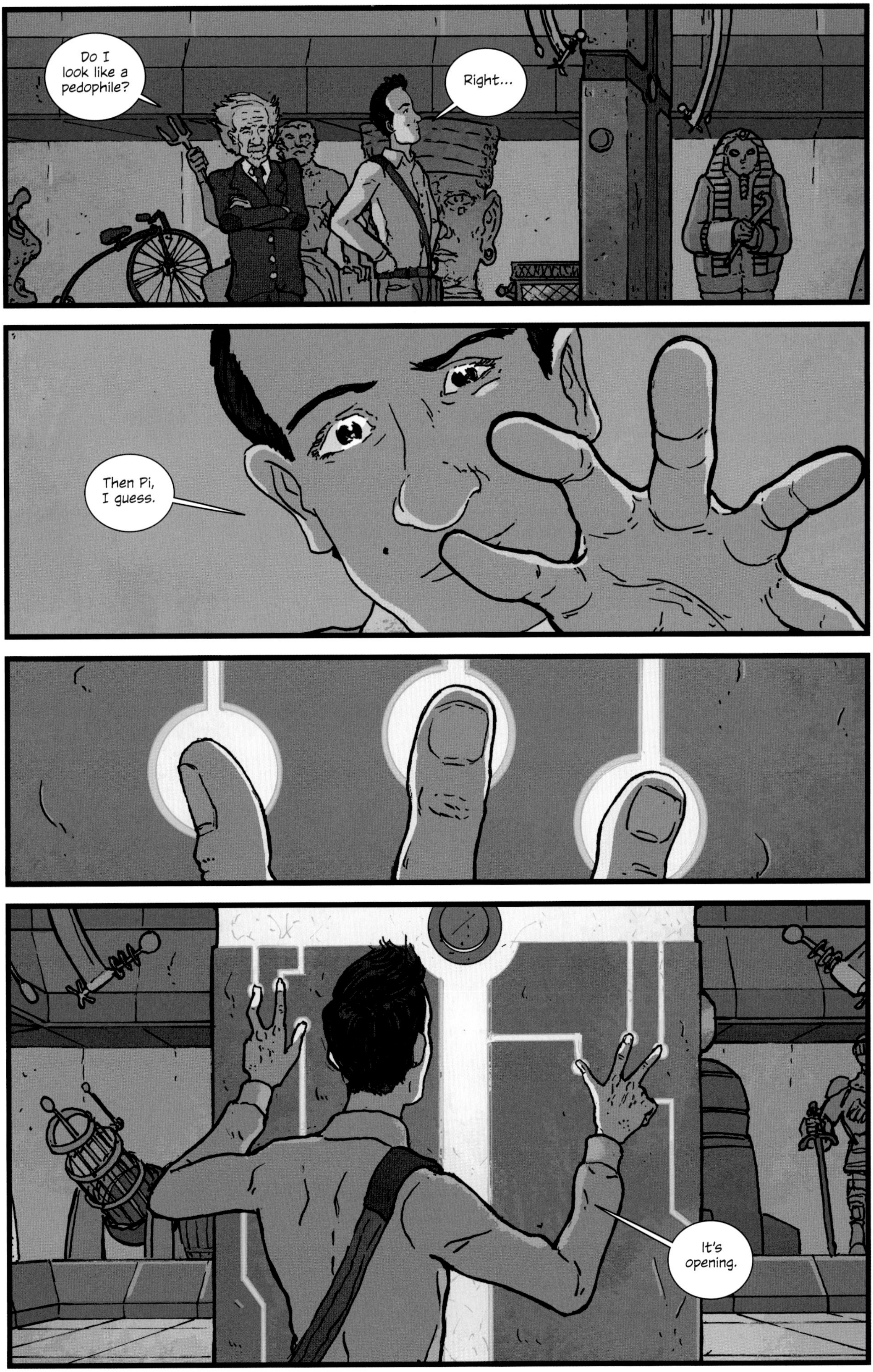
Do I look like a pedophile?
Right...
Then Pi, I guess.
It's opening.

Then.

It was a door to other worlds.

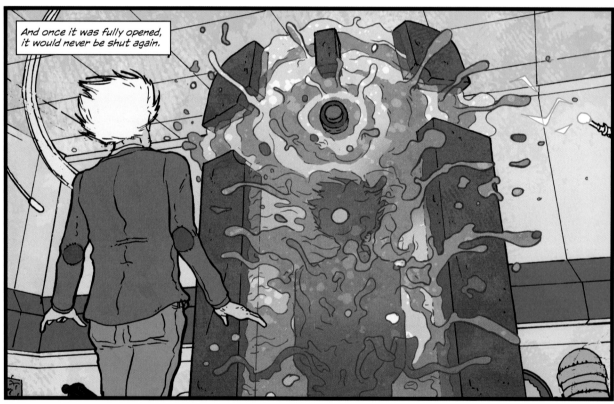

And once it was fully opened, it would never be shut again.

Mein Gott.

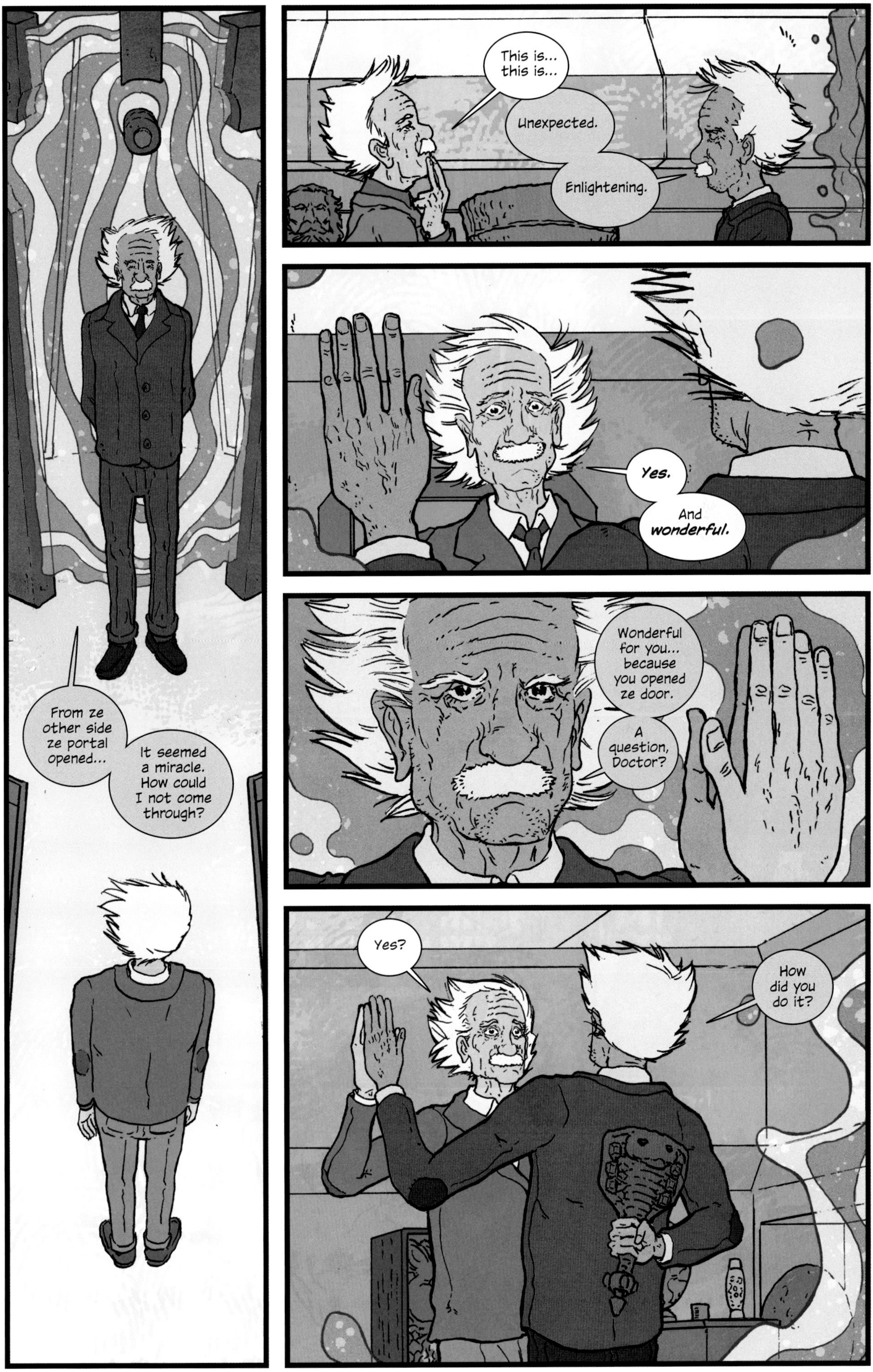
From ze other side ze portal opened...
It seemed a miracle. How could I not come through?
This is... this is...
Unexpected.
Enlightening.
Yes.
And wonderful.
Wonderful for you... because you opened ze door.
A question, Doctor?
Yes?
How did you do it?

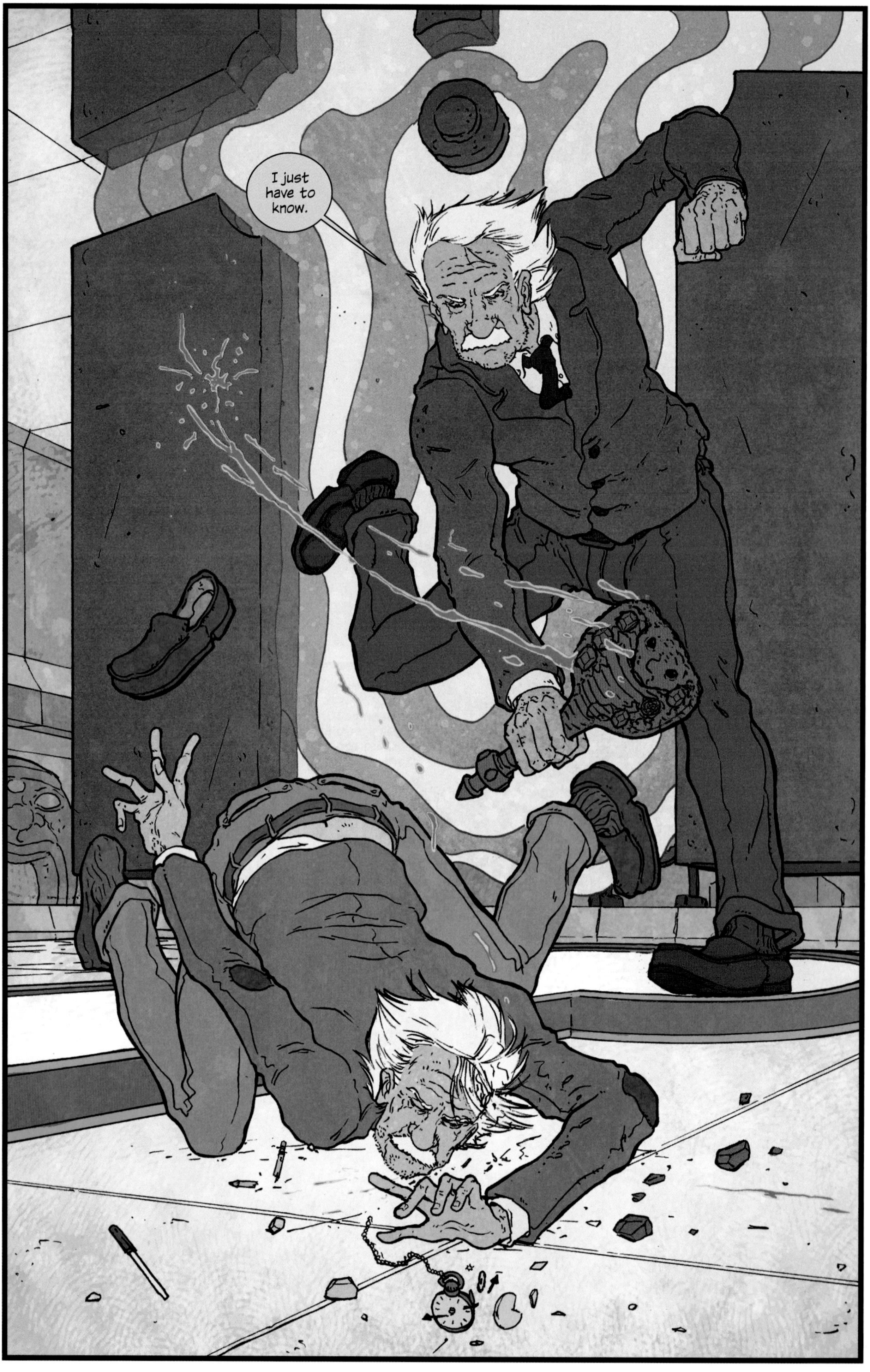
I just have to know.

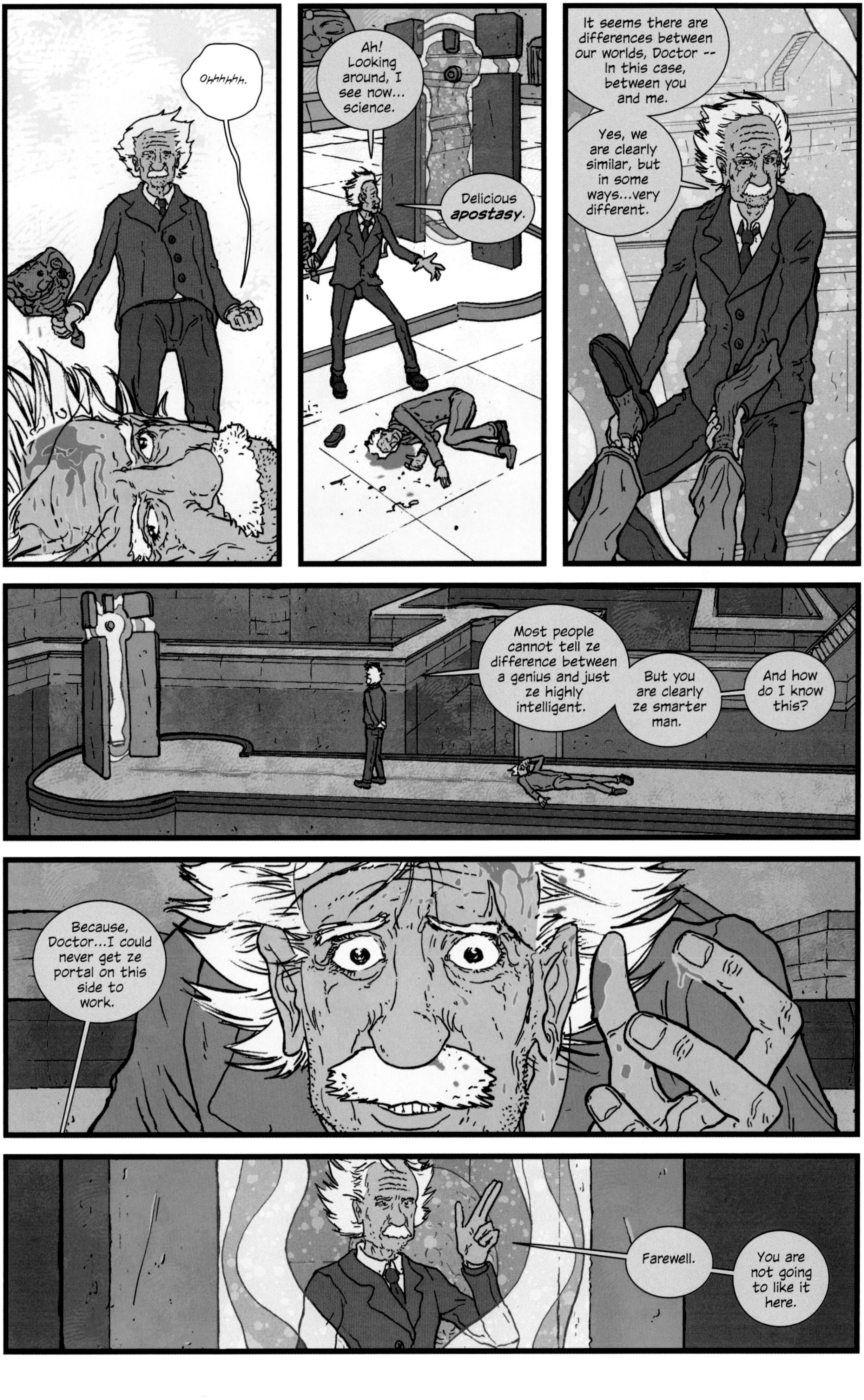
Ohhhhhh.
Ah! Looking around, I see now... science.
Delicious *apostasy*.
It seems there are differences between our worlds, Doctor -- In this case, between you and me.
Yes, we are clearly similar, but in some ways...very different.
Most people cannot tell ze difference between a genius and just ze highly intelligent.
But you are clearly ze smarter man.
And how do I know this?
Because, Doctor...I could never get ze portal on this side to work.
Farewell.
You are not going to like it here.

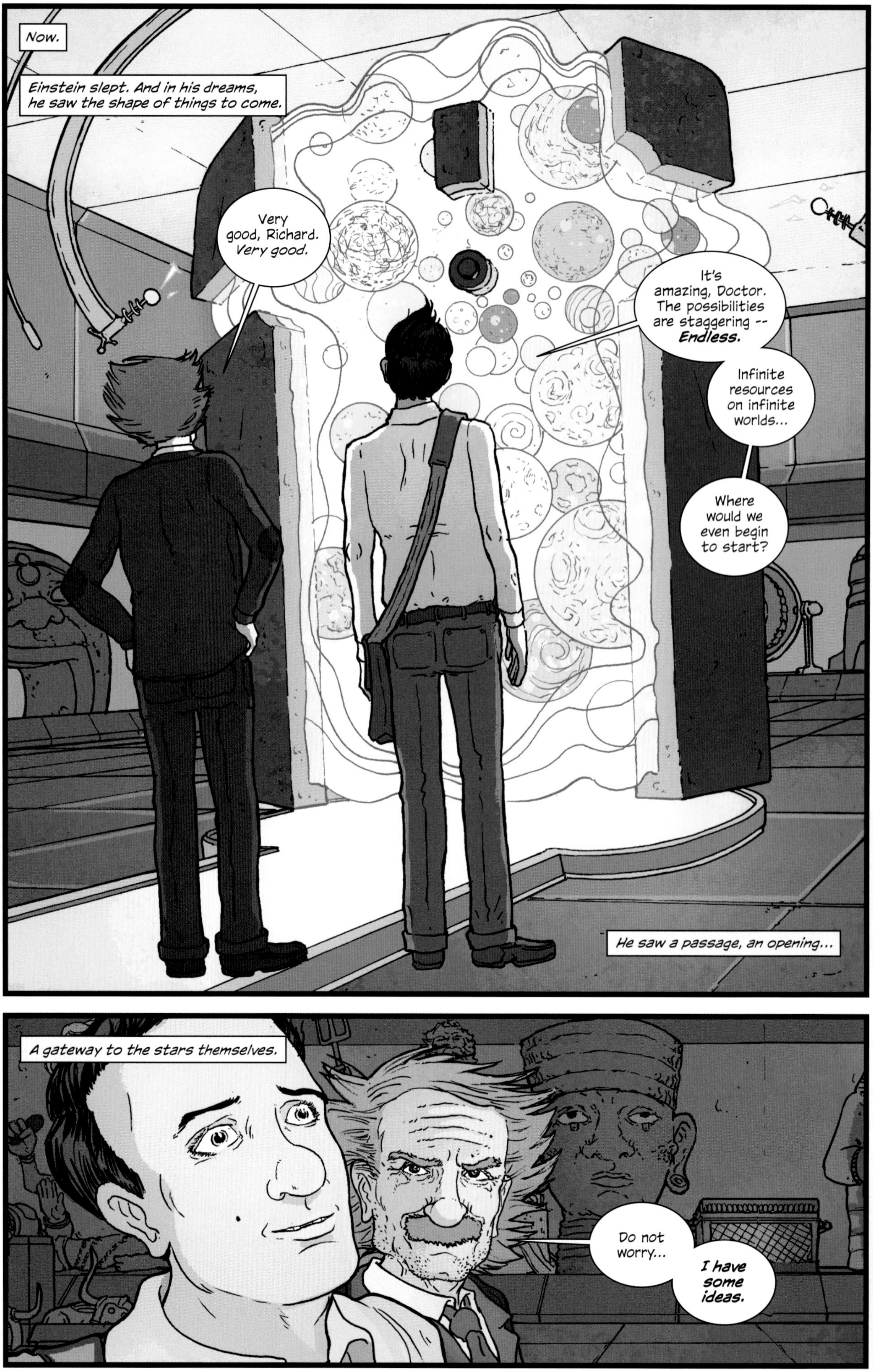
Now.
Einstein slept. And in his dreams, he saw the shape of things to come.
Very good, Richard. Very good.
It's amazing, Doctor. The possibilities are staggering -- Endless.
Infinite resources on infinite worlds...
Where would we even begin to start?
He saw a passage, an opening...
A gateway to the stars themselves.
Do not worry...
I have some ideas.

"THE UNIVERSE ASKED A QUESTION. I SIMPLY ANSWERED IT.

WHO COULD HAVE PREDICTED THE HELL THAT FOLLOWED?"

- ALBERT EINSTEIN

CLAVIS AUREA
THE RECORDED FEYNMAN | **VOL. 4**

THERE ARE NO PERFECT
ANSWERS

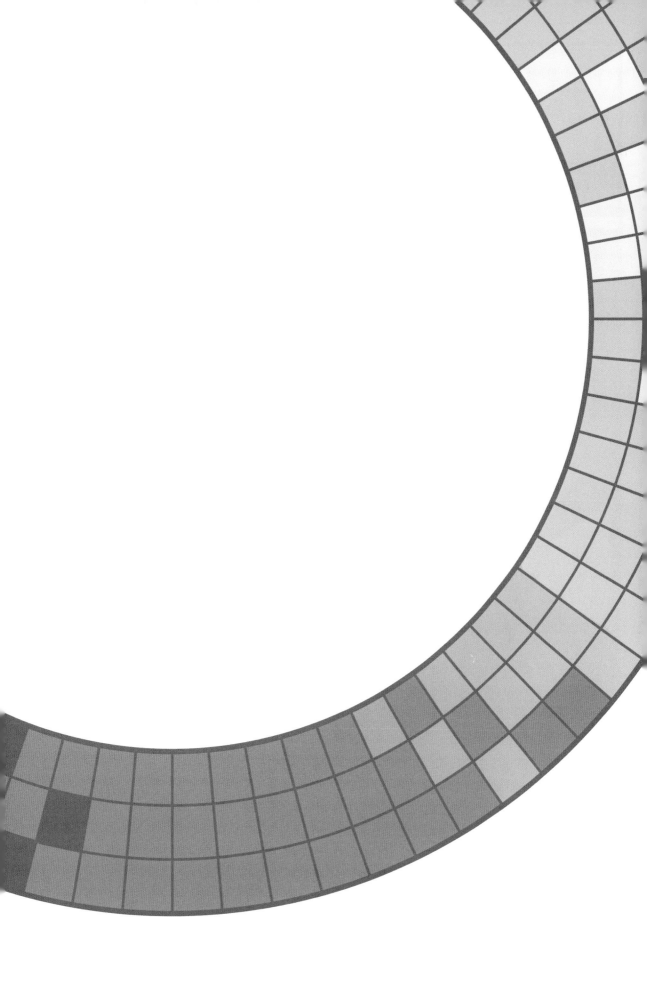

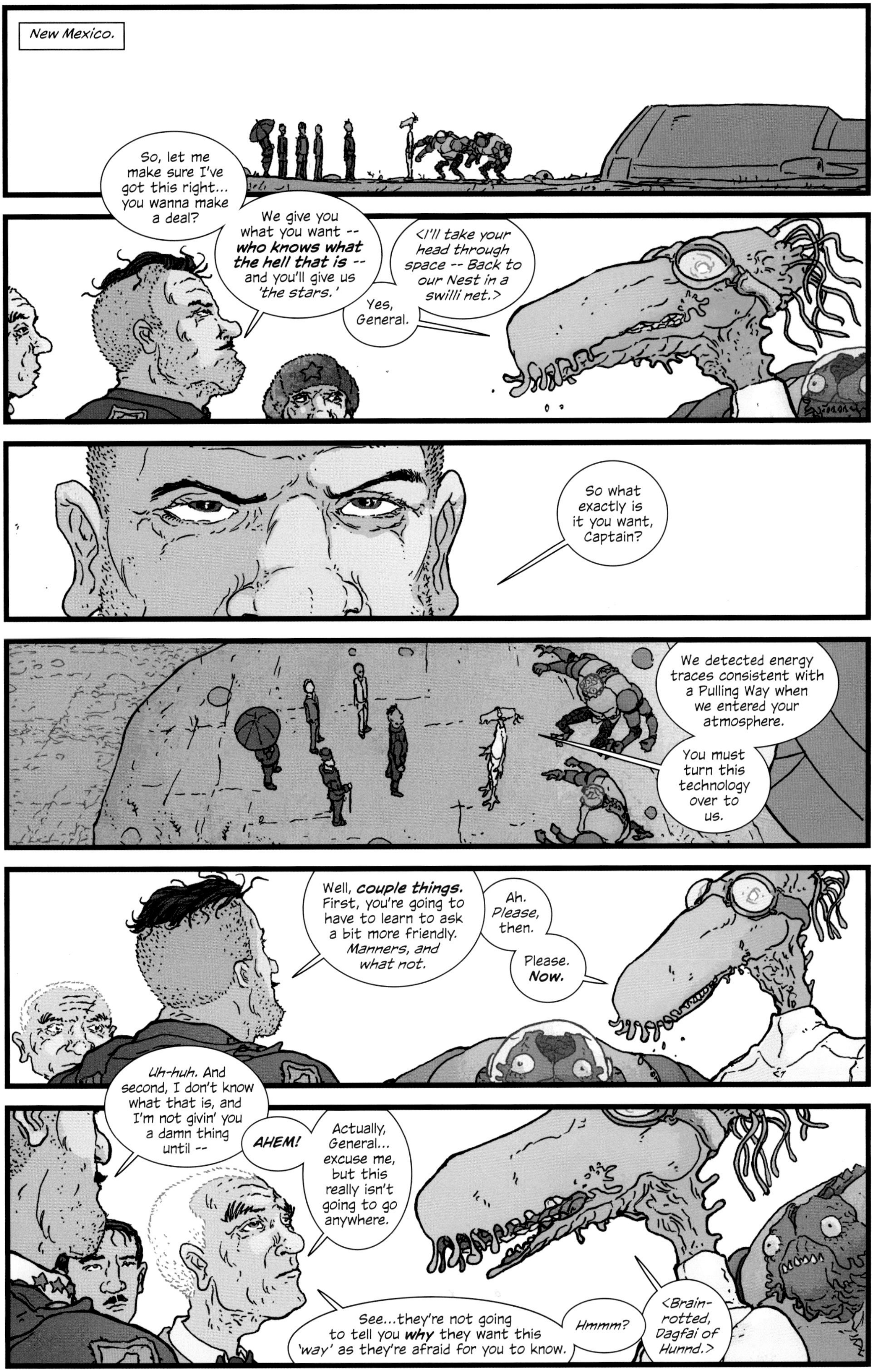
New Mexico.
So, let me make sure I've got this right... you wanna make a deal?
We give you what you want -- **who knows what the hell that is** -- and you'll give us *'the stars.'*
Yes, General.
<I'll take your head through space -- Back to our Nest in a swilli net.>
So what exactly is it you want, Captain?
We detected energy traces consistent with a Pulling Way when we entered your atmosphere.
You must turn this technology over to us.
Well, **couple things.** First, you're going to have to learn to ask a bit more friendly. *Manners, and what not.*
Ah. *Please,* then.
Please. **Now.**
Uh-huh. And second, I don't know what that is, and I'm not givin' you a damn thing until --
AHEM!
Actually, General... excuse me, but this really isn't going to go anywhere.
See...they're not going to tell you **why** they want this *'way'* as they're afraid for you to know.
Hmmm?
<Brain-rotted, Dagfai of Hunnd.>

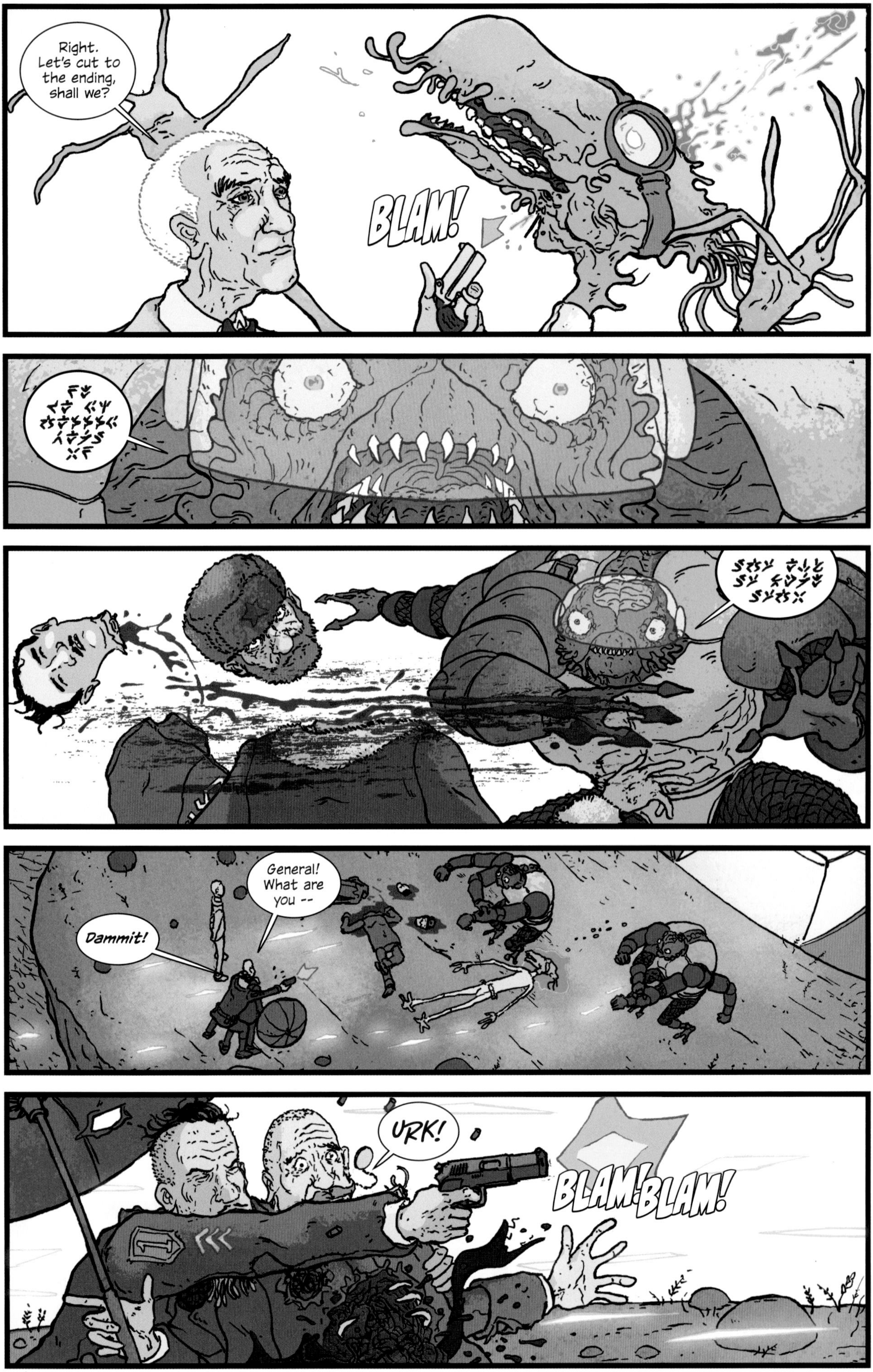
Right. Let's cut to the ending, shall we?
BLAM!
General! What are you --
Dammit!
URK!
BLAM! BLAM!

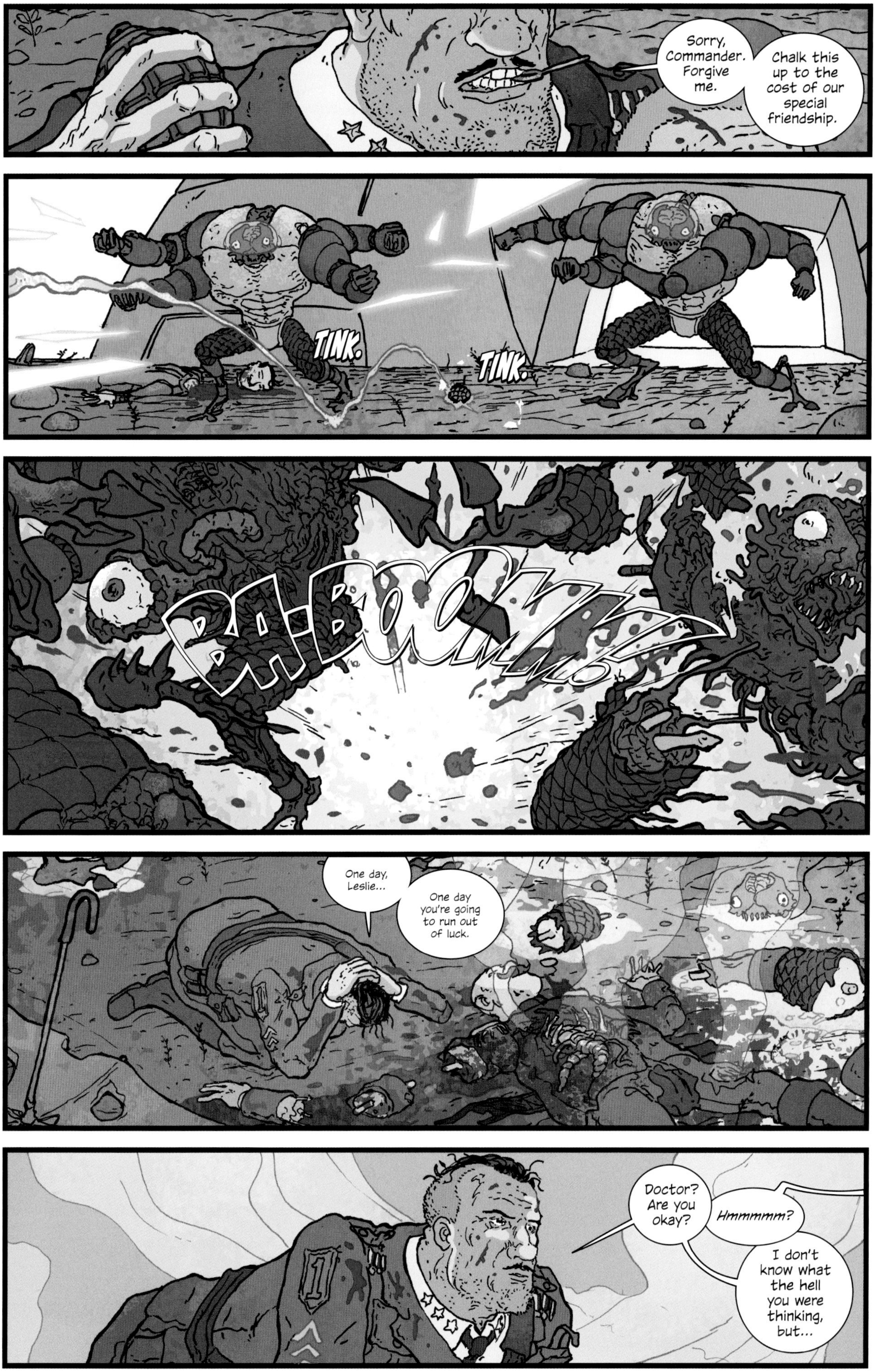

Sorry, Commander. Forgive me.
Chalk this up to the cost of our special friendship.
TINK.
TINK.
BA-BOOM!
One day, Leslie...
One day you're going to run out of luck.
Doctor? Are you okay?
Hmmmmm?
I don't know what the hell you were thinking, but...

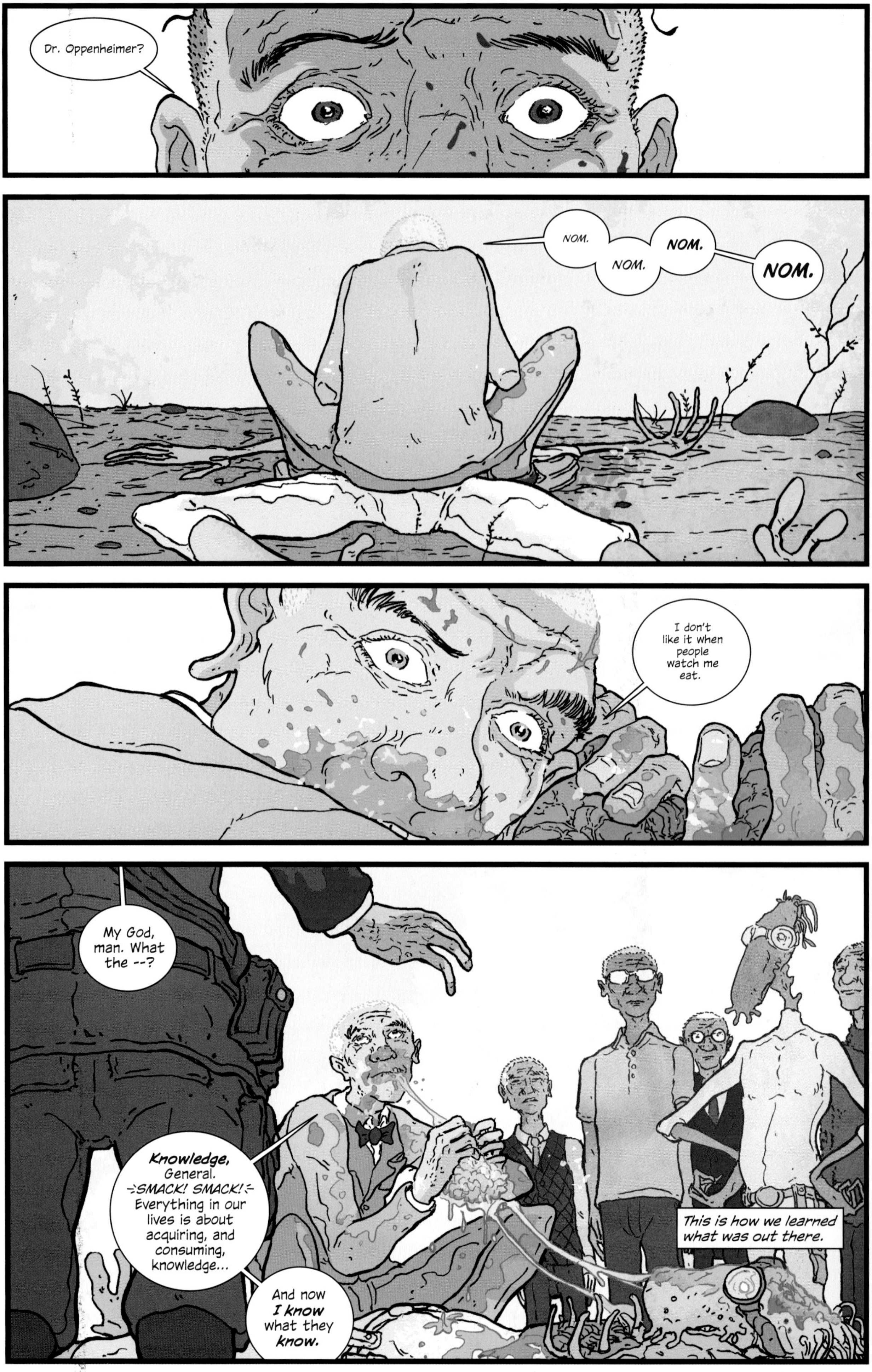

Dr. Oppenheimer?
NOM.
NOM.
NOM.
NOM.
I don't like it when people watch me eat.
My God, man. What the --?
Knowledge, General.
-SMACK! SMACK!-
Everything in our lives is about acquiring, and consuming, knowledge...
And now I know what they know.
This is how we learned what was out there.

"HMMMM?"

- OPPENHEIMER

CLAVIS AUREA
THE RECORDED FEYNMAN | **VOL. 1**

05

HORIZON

"WHAT I LEARNED WAS THE DIFFERENCE BETWEEN VALUE AND COST.

EVERY DECISION THAT FOLLOWED WAS SIMPLY A PRODUCT OF WEIGHING THE POTENTIAL PUNISHMENT."

CLAVIS AUREA
THE RECORDED FEYNMAN | **VOL. 1**

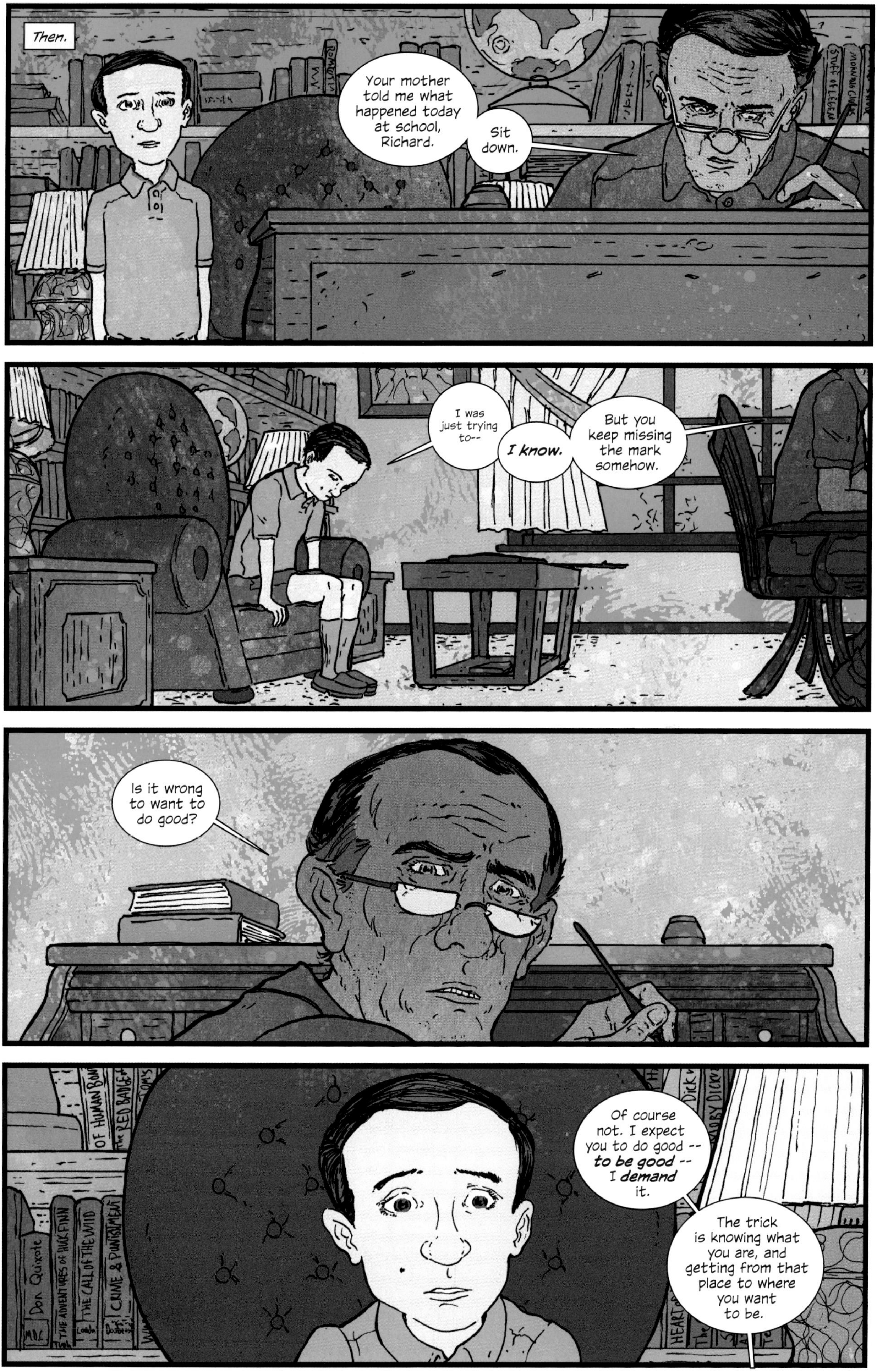

Then.
Your mother told me what happened today at school, Richard.
Sit down.
I was just trying to--
I know.
But you keep missing the mark somehow.
Is it wrong to want to do good?
Of course not. I expect you to do good -- ***to be good*** -- I ***demand*** it.
The trick is knowing what you are, and getting from that place to where you want to be.
Don Quixote
THE ADVENTURES of HUCK FINN
THE CALL OF THE WILD
CRIME & PUNISHMENT

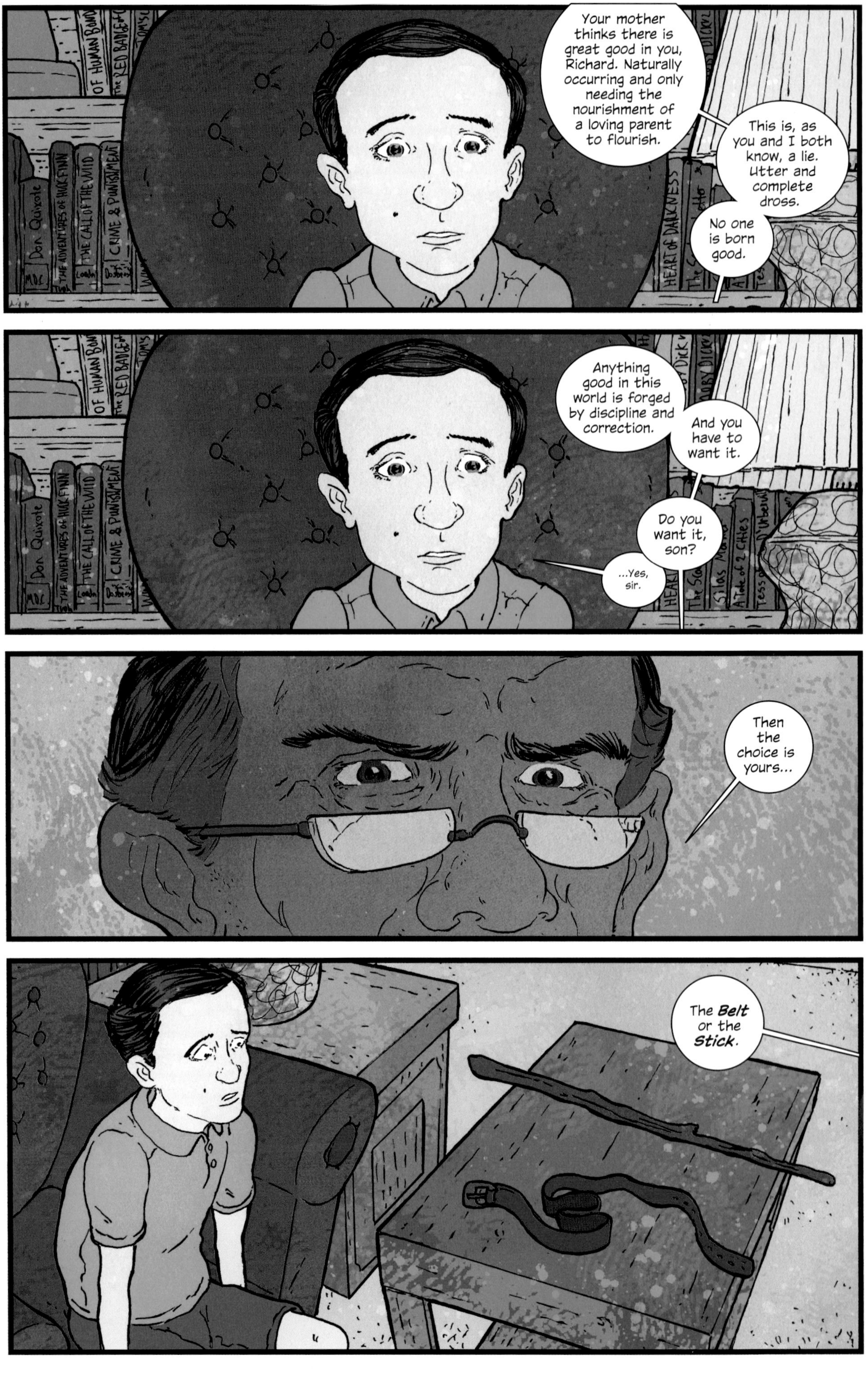
Your mother thinks there is great good in you, Richard. Naturally occurring and only needing the nourishment of a loving parent to flourish.
This is, as you and I both know, a lie. Utter and complete dross.
No one is born good.
Anything good in this world is forged by discipline and correction.
And you have to want it.
Do you want it, son?
...Yes, sir.
Then the choice is yours...
The **Belt** or the **Stick**.

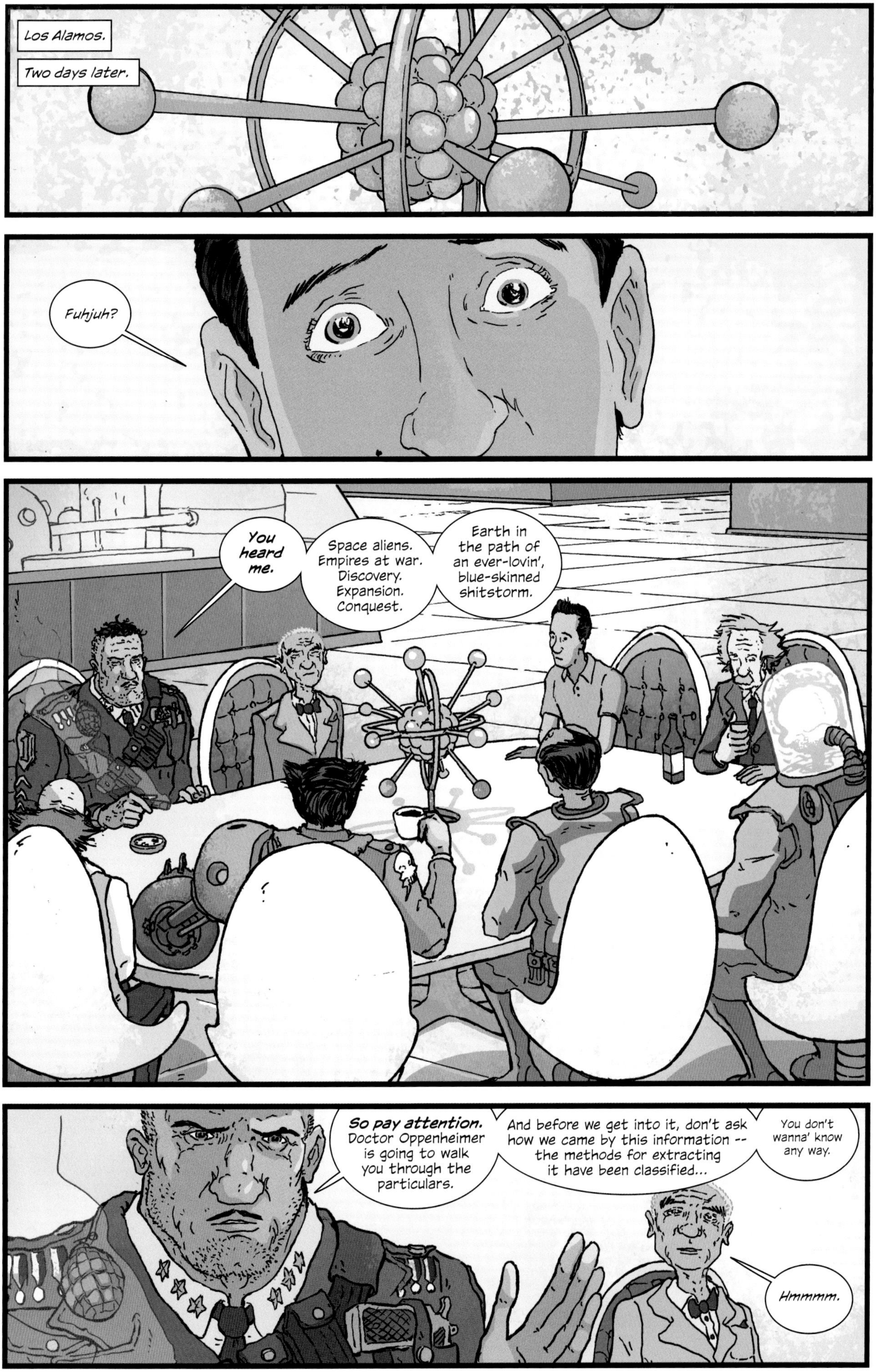
Los Alamos.
Two days later.
Fuhjuh?
You heard me.
Space aliens. Empires at war. Discovery. Expansion. Conquest.
Earth in the path of an ever-lovin', blue-skinned shitstorm.
So pay attention. Doctor Oppenheimer is going to walk you through the particulars.
And before we get into it, don't ask how we came by this information -- the methods for extracting it have been classified...
You don't wanna' know any way.
Hmmmm.

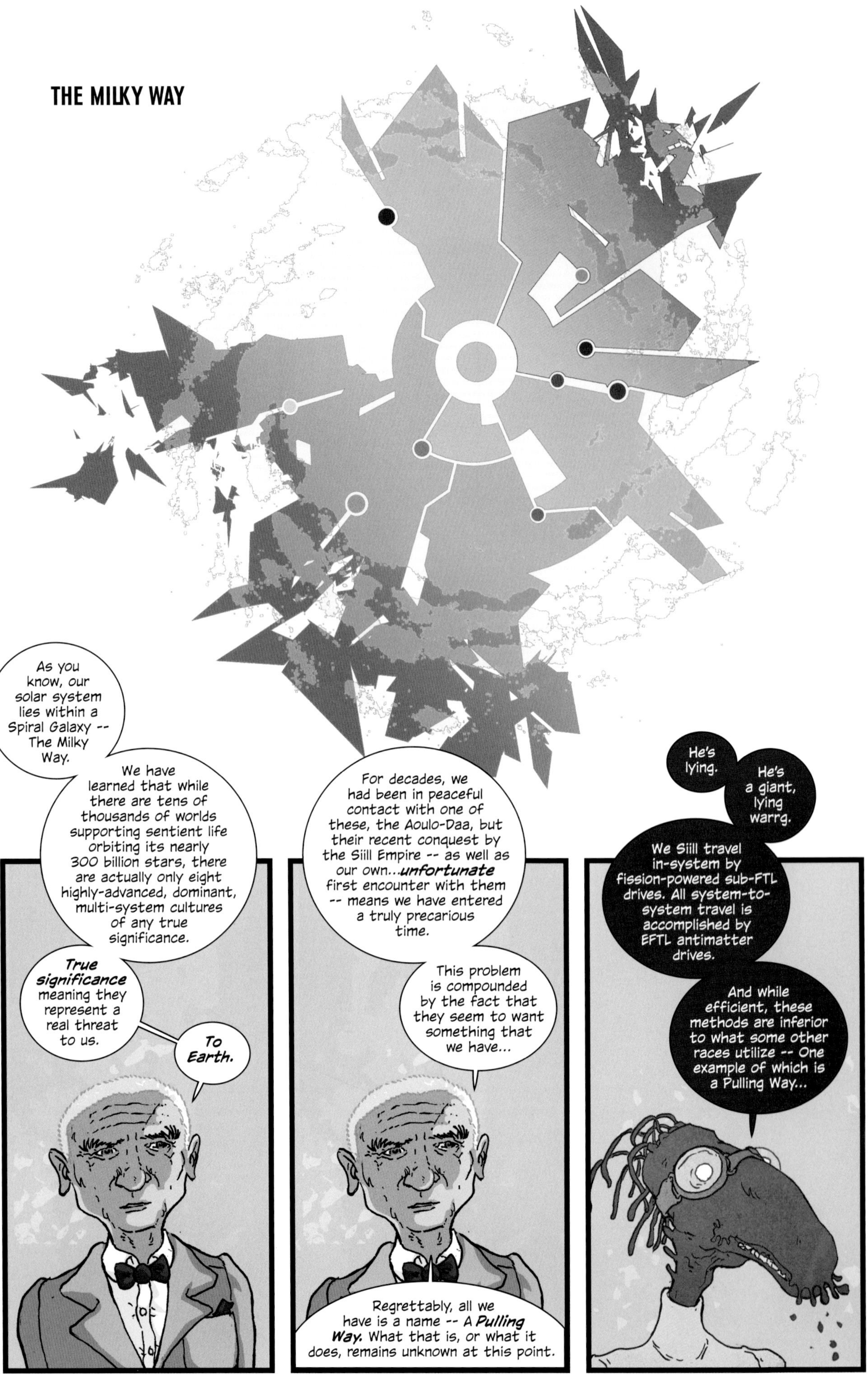
THE MILKY WAY
As you know, our solar system lies within a Spiral Galaxy -- The Milky Way.
We have learned that while there are tens of thousands of worlds supporting sentient life orbiting its nearly 300 billion stars, there are actually only eight highly-advanced, dominant, multi-system cultures of any true significance.
True significance meaning they represent a real threat to us.
To Earth.
For decades, we had been in peaceful contact with one of these, the Aoulo-Daa, but their recent conquest by the Siill Empire -- as well as our own... *unfortunate* first encounter with them -- means we have entered a truly precarious time.
This problem is compounded by the fact that they seem to want something that we have...
Regrettably, all we have is a name -- A *Pulling Way.* What that is, or what it does, remains unknown at this point.
He's lying.
He's a giant, lying warrg.
We Siill travel in-system by fission-powered sub-FTL drives. All system-to-system travel is accomplished by EFTL antimatter drives.
And while efficient, these methods are inferior to what some other races utilize -- One example of which is a Pulling Way...

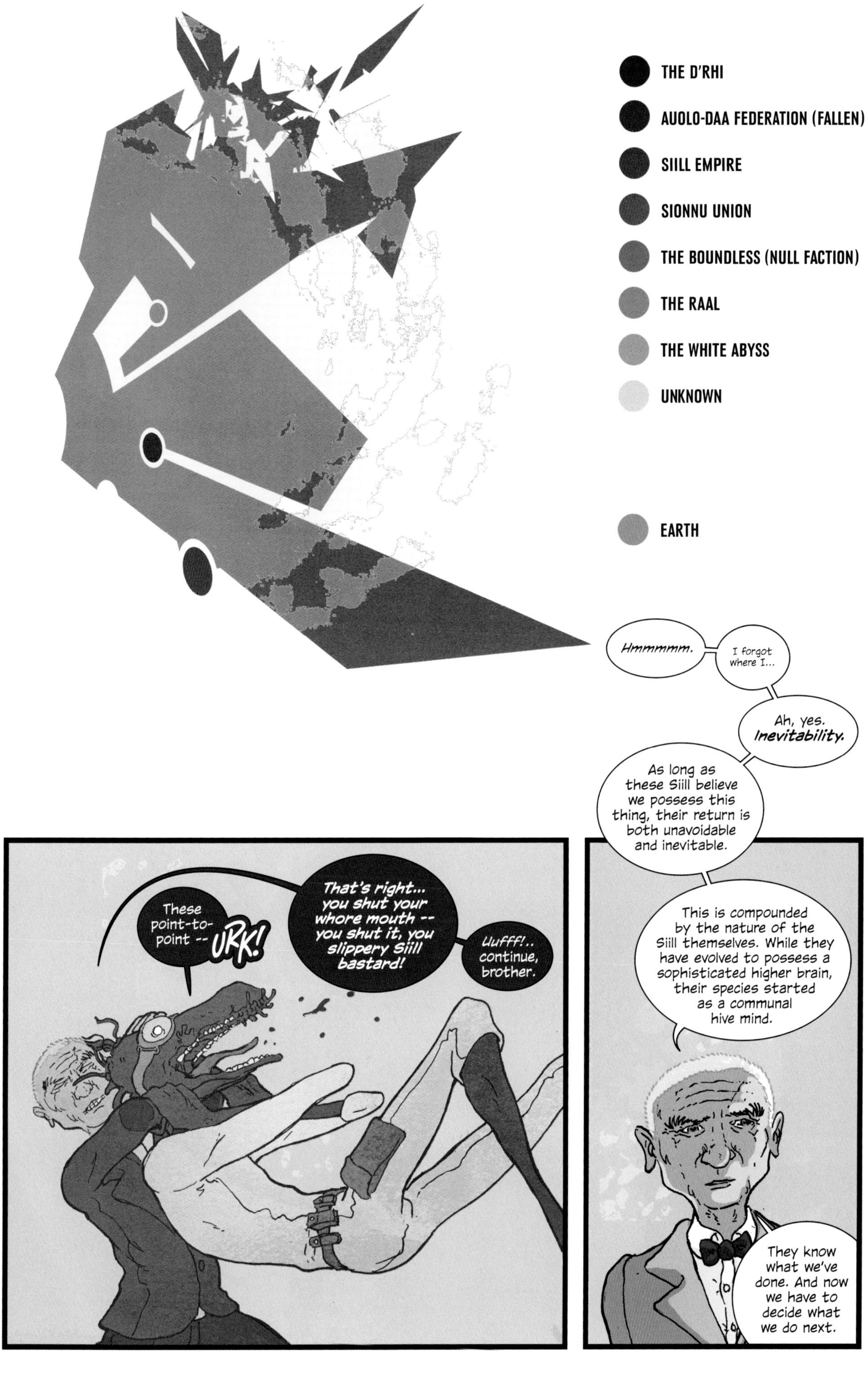
THE D'RHI
AUOLO-DAA FEDERATION (FALLEN)
SIILL EMPIRE
SIONNU UNION
THE BOUNDLESS (NULL FACTION)
THE RAAL
THE WHITE ABYSS
UNKNOWN
EARTH
Hmmmmm.
I forgot where I...
Ah, yes. Inevitability.
As long as these Siill believe we possess this thing, their return is both unavoidable and inevitable.
These point-to-point -- URK!
That's right... you shut your whore mouth -- you shut it, you slippery Siill bastard!
Uufff!.. continue, brother.
This is compounded by the nature of the Siill themselves. While they have evolved to possess a sophisticated higher brain, their species started as a communal hive mind.
They know what we've done. And now we have to decide what we do next.

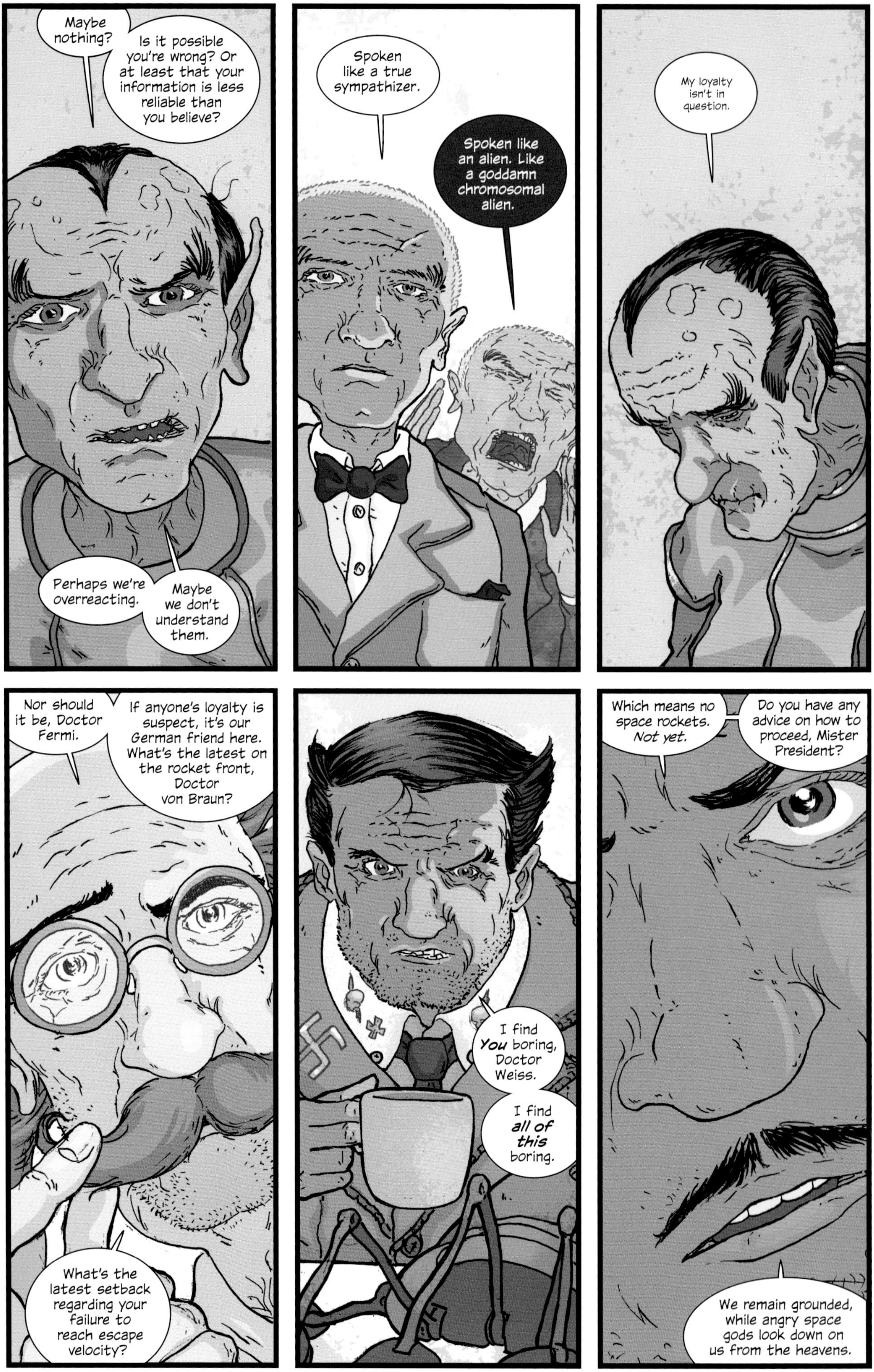
Maybe nothing?
Is it possible you're wrong? Or at least that your information is less reliable than you believe?
Perhaps we're overreacting.
Maybe we don't understand them.
Spoken like a true sympathizer.
Spoken like an alien. Like a goddamn chromosomal alien.
My loyalty isn't in question.
Nor should it be, Doctor Fermi.
If anyone's loyalty is suspect, it's our German friend here. What's the latest on the rocket front, Doctor von Braun?
What's the latest setback regarding your failure to reach escape velocity?
I find *You* boring, Doctor Weiss.
I find *all of this* boring.
Which means no space rockets. *Not yet.*
Do you have any advice on how to proceed, Mister President?
We remain grounded, while angry space gods look down on us from the heavens.

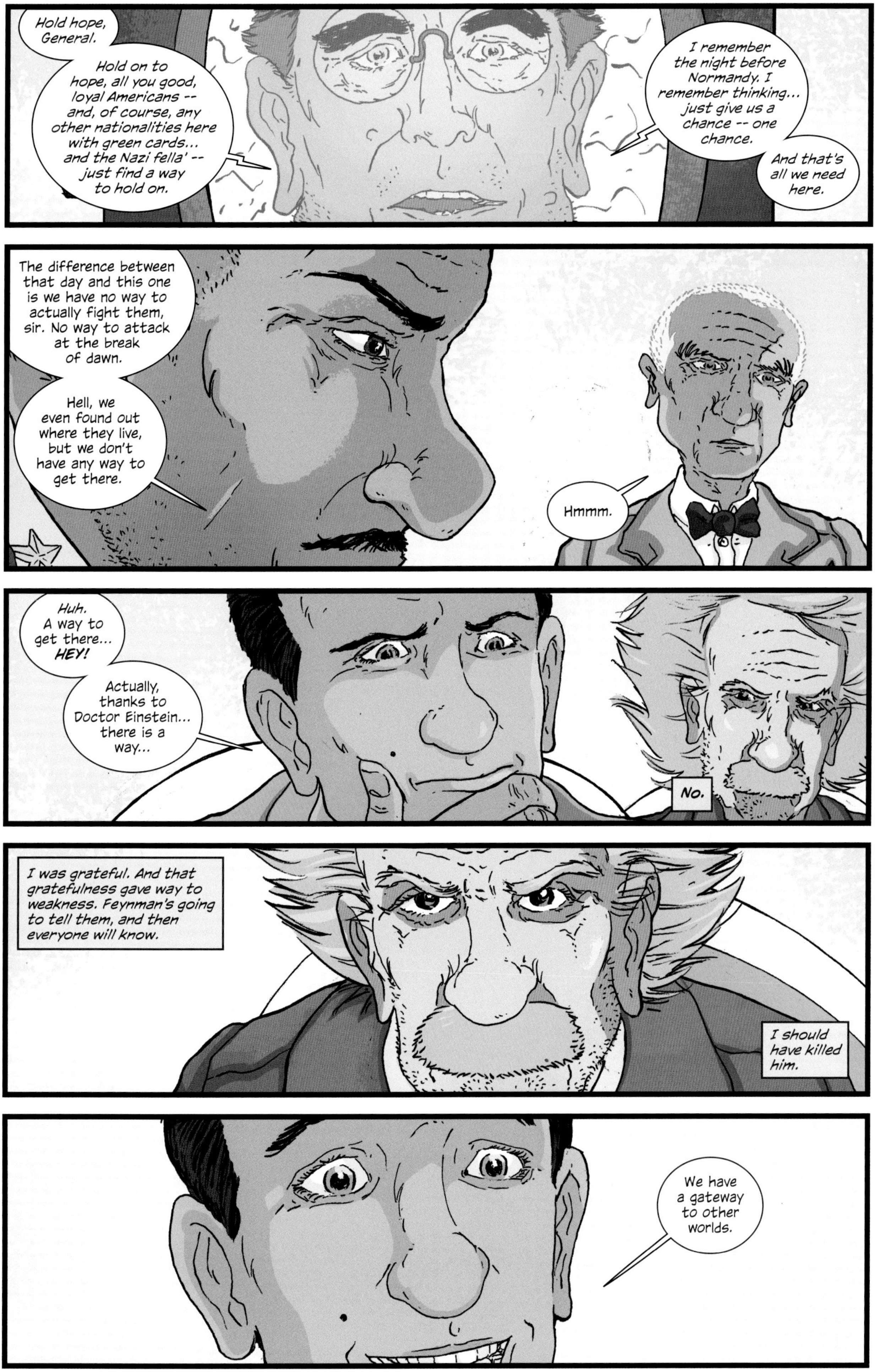
Hold hope, General.
Hold on to hope, all you good, loyal Americans -- and, of course, any other nationalities here with green cards... and the Nazi fella' -- just find a way to hold on.
I remember the night before Normandy. I remember thinking... just give us a chance -- one chance.
And that's all we need here.
The difference between that day and this one is we have no way to actually fight them, sir. No way to attack at the break of dawn.
Hell, we even found out where they live, but we don't have any way to get there.
Hmmm.
Huh. A way to get there... HEY!
Actually, thanks to Doctor Einstein... there is a way...
No.
I was grateful. And that gratefulness gave way to weakness. Feynman's going to tell them, and then everyone will know.
I should have killed him.
We have a gateway to other worlds.

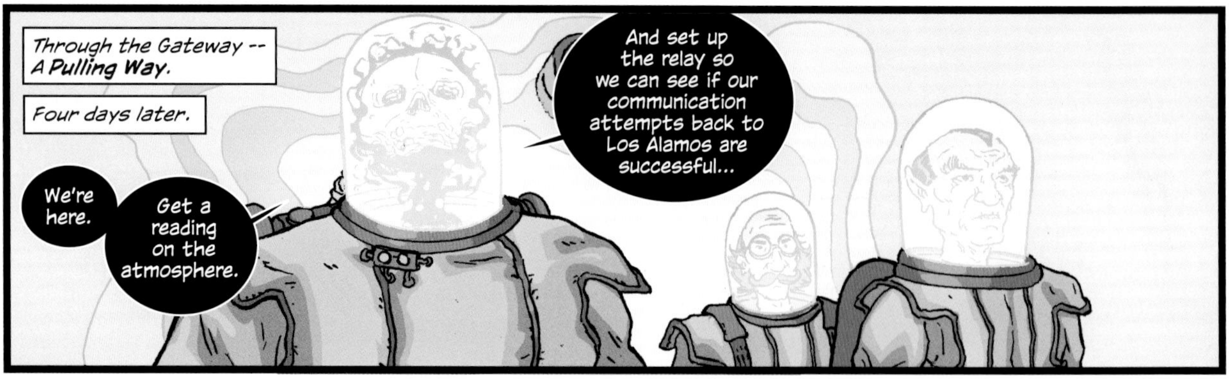
Through the Gateway -- A Pulling Way.
Four days later.
We're here.
Get a reading on the atmosphere.
And set up the relay so we can see if our communication attempts back to Los Alamos are successful...

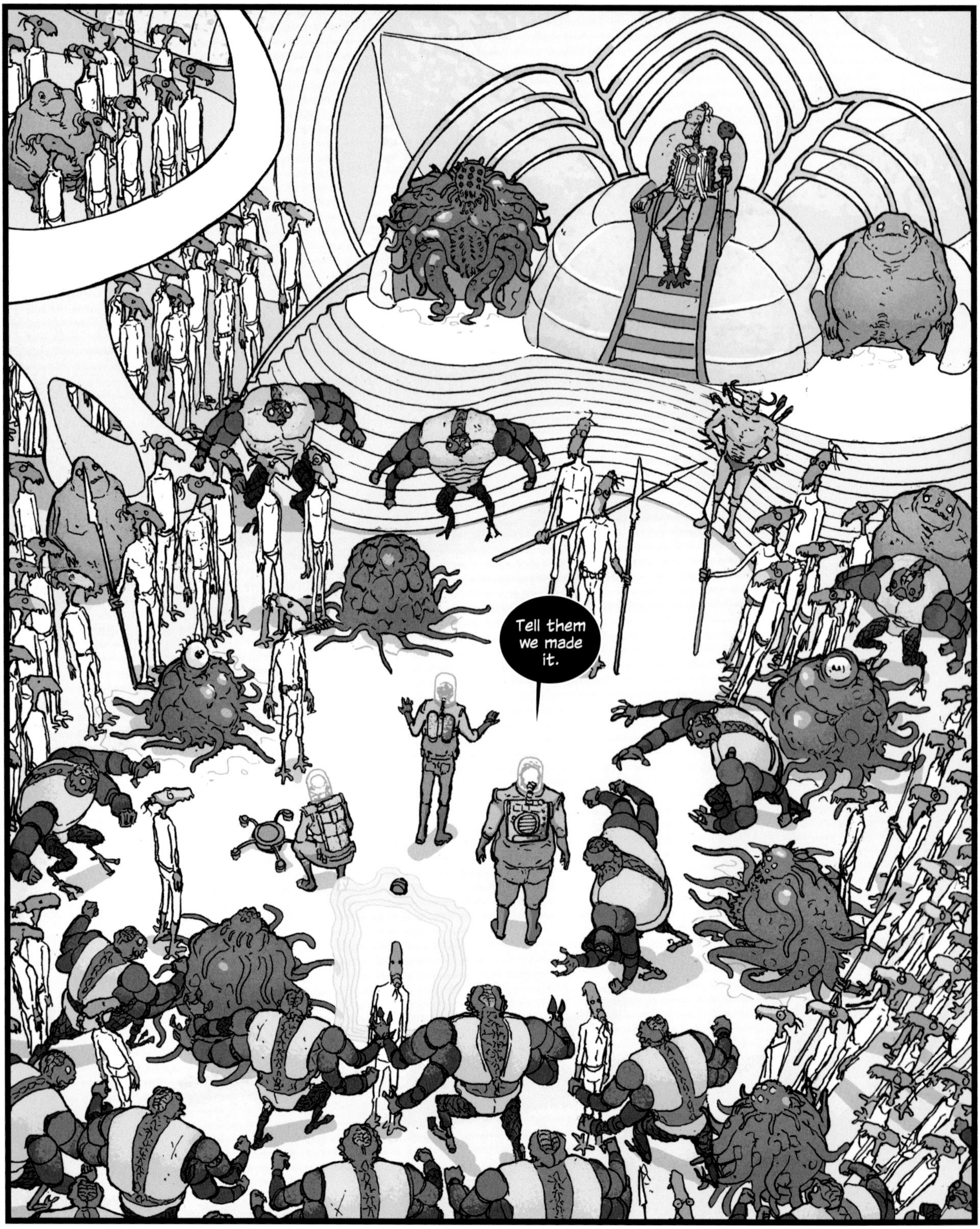
Tell them we made it.

Better make it quick, Doctor. Might I suggest using a tone implying urgency and words to the effect of 'send reinforcements'.

We must have something configured wrong -- All I'm getting is static.

The atmosphere is breathable, but no one take their helmets off unless they--

CRASH!

You're okay, Doctor.

No. I'm dead.

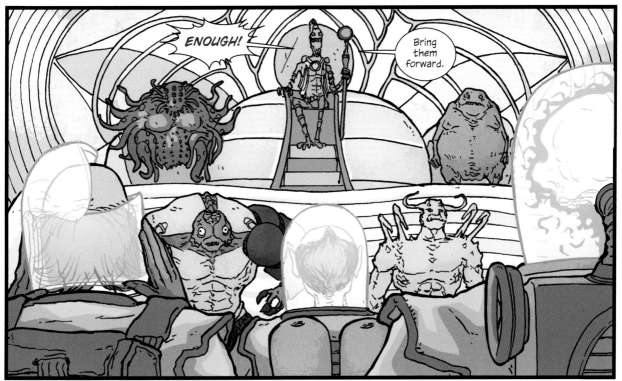

ENOUGH!

Bring them forward.

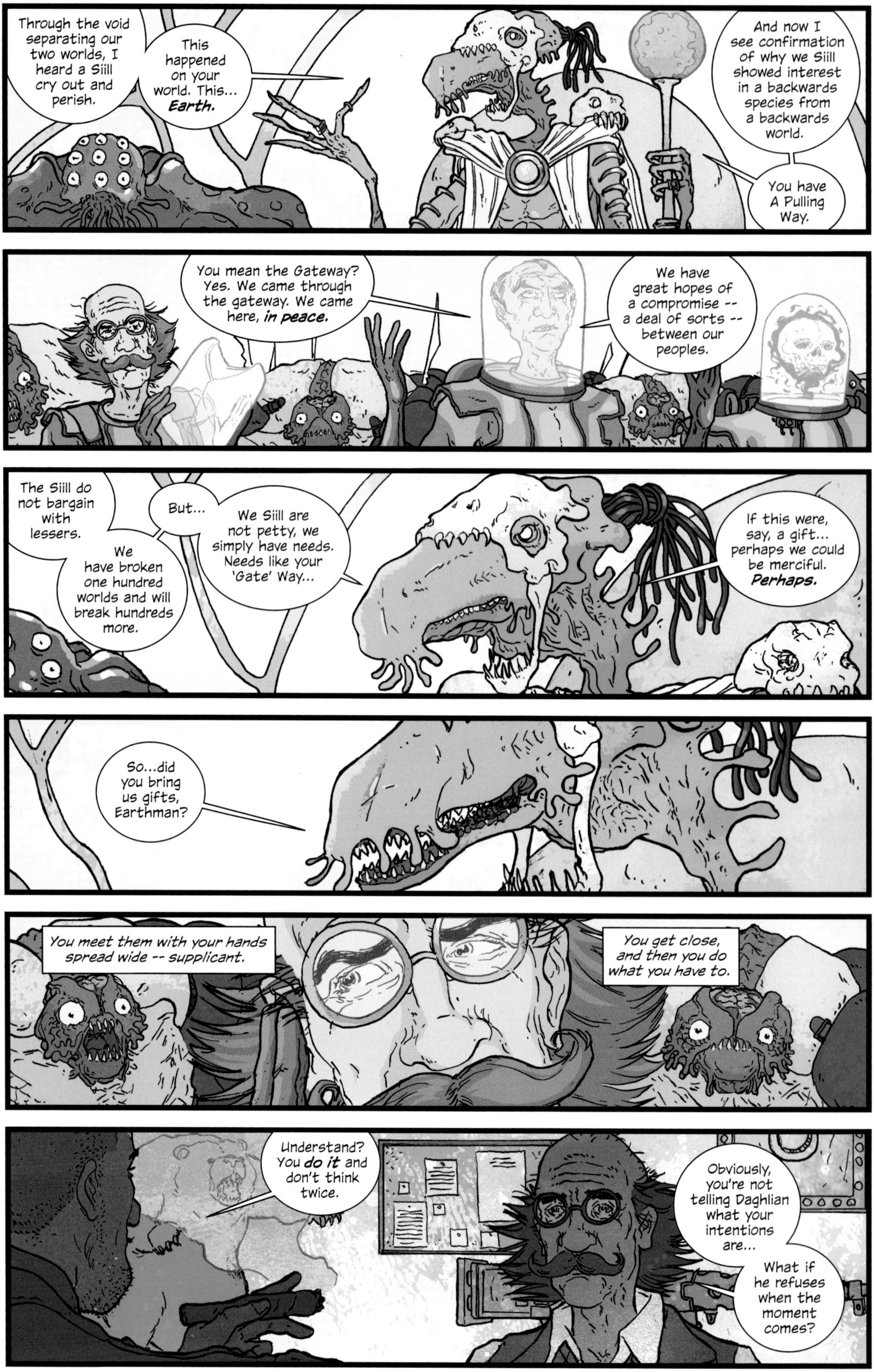
Through the void separating our two worlds, I heard a Siill cry out and perish.
This happened on your world. This... *Earth.*
And now I see confirmation of why we Siill showed interest in a backwards species from a backwards world.
You have A Pulling Way.
You mean the Gateway? Yes. We came through the gateway. We came here, *in peace.*
We have great hopes of a compromise -- a deal of sorts -- between our peoples.
The Siill do not bargain with lessers.
We have broken one hundred worlds and will break hundreds more.
But...
We Siill are not petty, we simply have needs. Needs like your 'Gate' Way...
If this were, say, a gift... perhaps we could be merciful. *Perhaps.*
So...did you bring us gifts, Earthman?
You meet them with your hands spread wide -- supplicant.
You get close, and then you do what you have to.
Understand? You *do it* and don't think twice.
Obviously, you're not telling Daghlian what your intentions are...
What if he refuses when the moment comes?

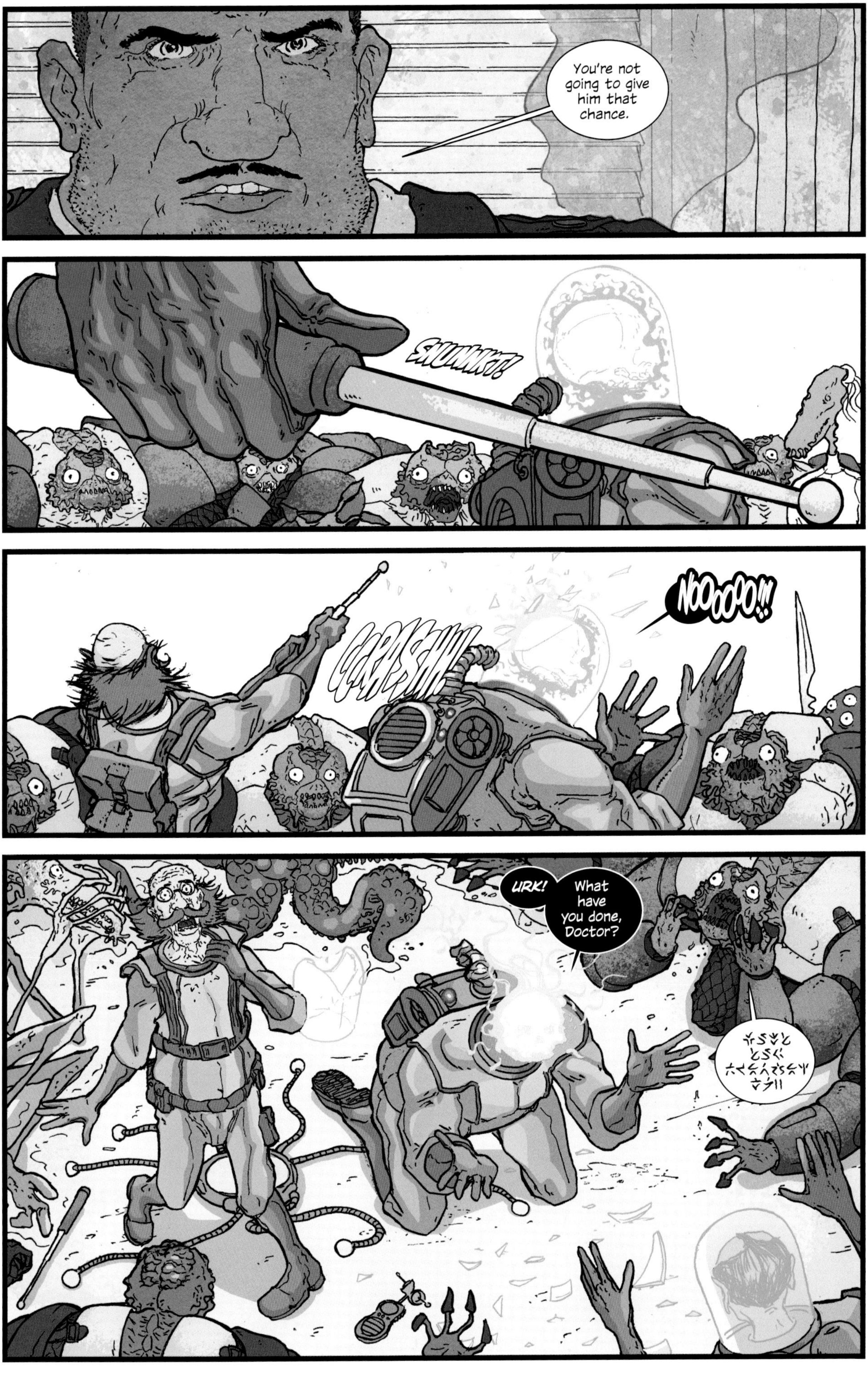
You're not going to give him that chance.
SHUNKT!
CCRASHH!
NOOOOOO!!!
URK!
What have you done, Doctor?

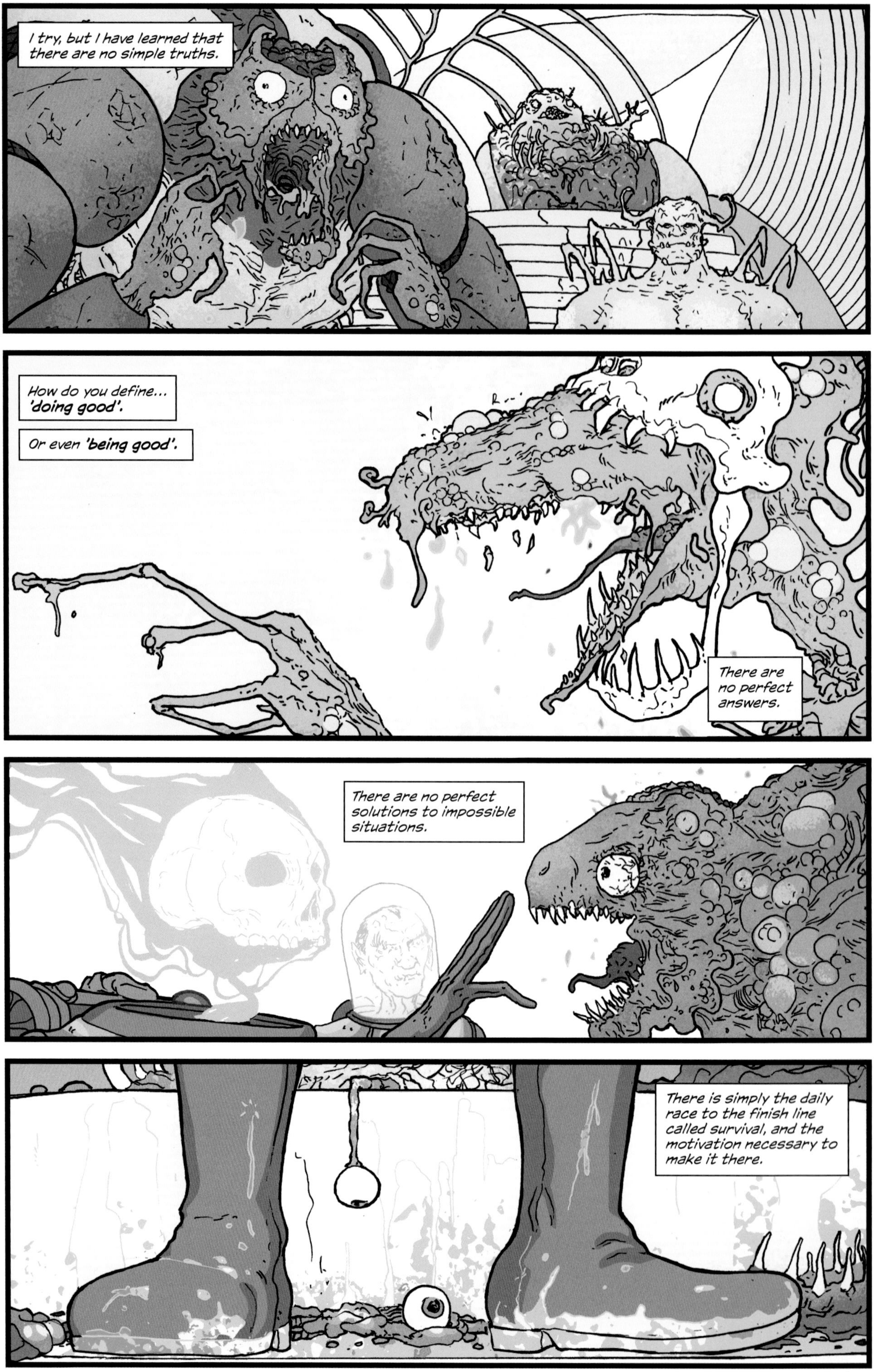
I try, but I have learned that there are no simple truths.
How do you define... 'doing good'.
Or even 'being good'.
There are no perfect answers.
There are no perfect solutions to impossible situations.
There is simply the daily race to the finish line called survival, and the motivation necessary to make it there.

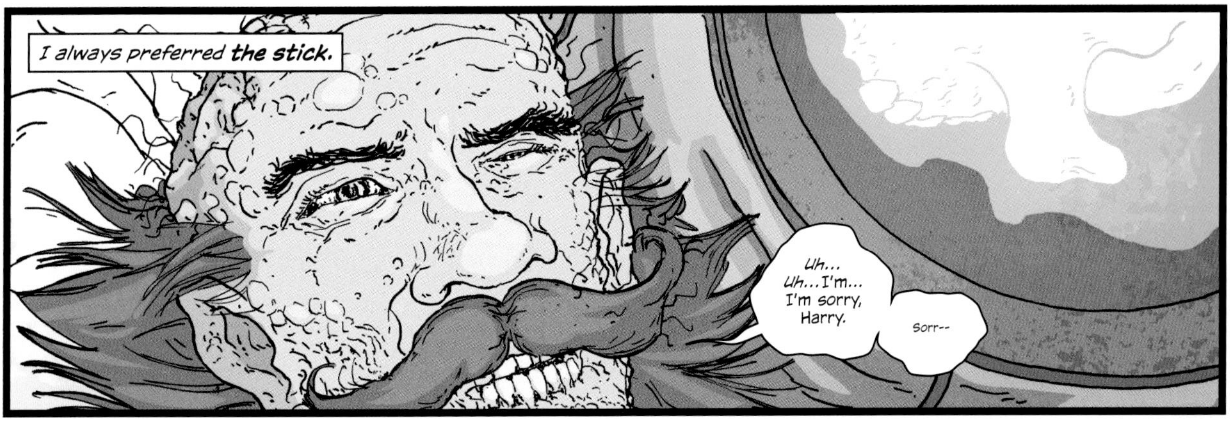
I always preferred **the stick.**
Uh...
Uh...I'm...
I'm sorry,
Harry.
Sorr--

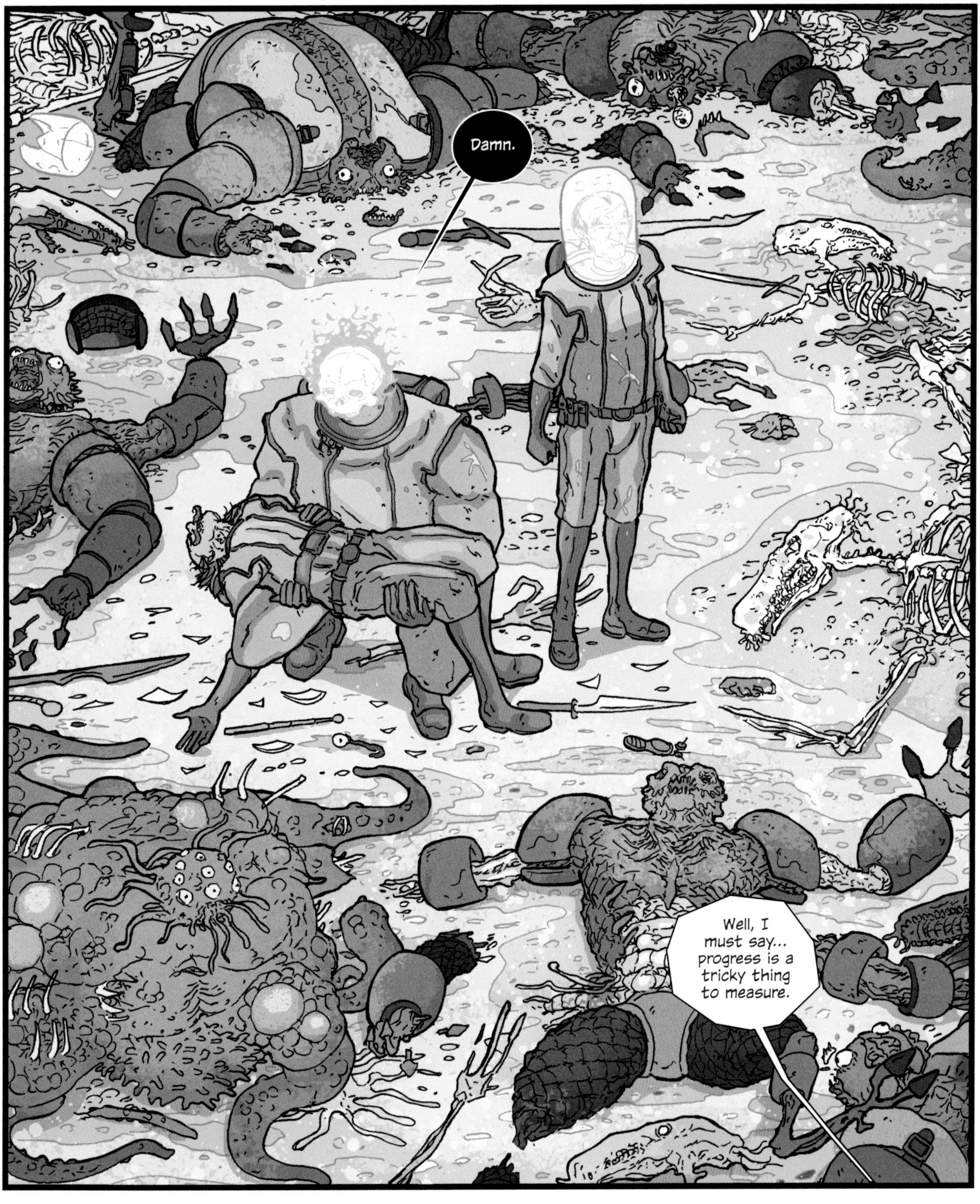
Damn.
Well, I must say... progress is a tricky thing to measure.

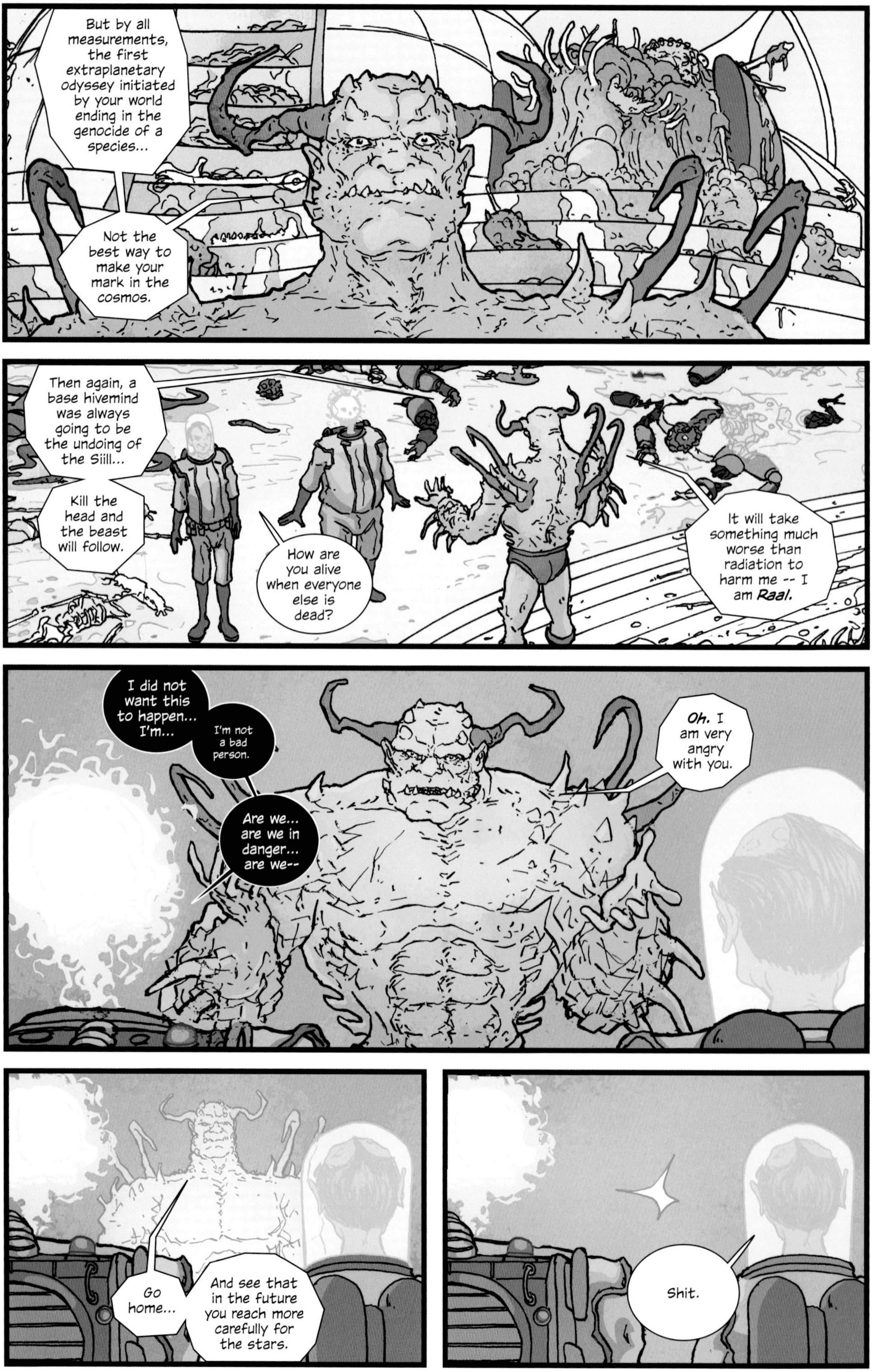

But by all measurements, the first extraplanetary odyssey initiated by your world ending in the genocide of a species...
Not the best way to make your mark in the cosmos.
Then again, a base hivemind was always going to be the undoing of the Siill...
Kill the head and the beast will follow.
How are you alive when everyone else is dead?
It will take something much worse than radiation to harm me -- I am *Raal.*
I did not want this to happen... I'm...
I'm not a bad person.
Are we... are we in danger... are we--
Oh. I am very angry with you.
Go home...
And see that in the future you reach more carefully for the stars.
Shit.

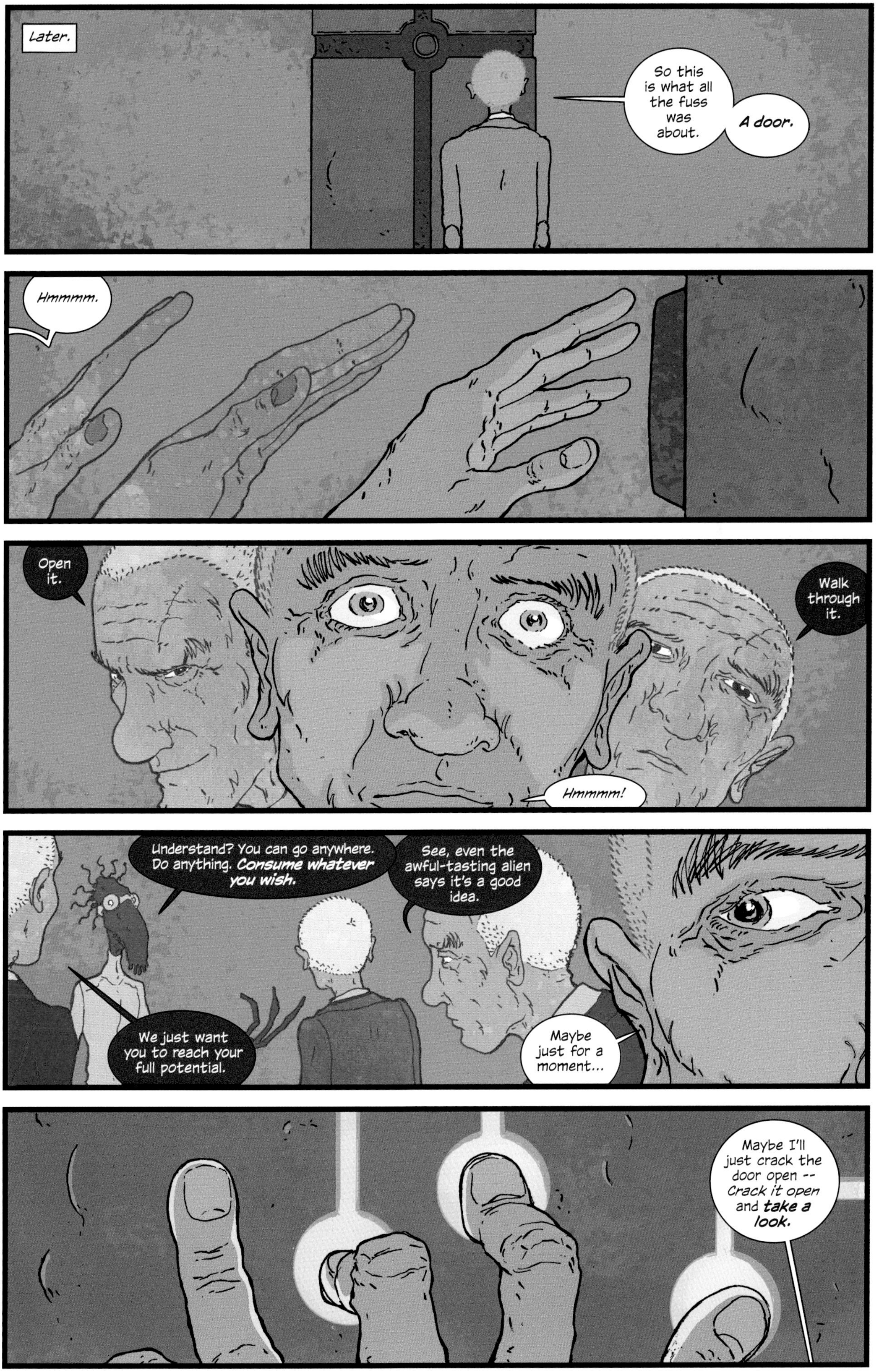
Later.
So this is what all the fuss was about.
A door.
Hmmmm.
Open it.
Walk through it.
Hmmmm!
Understand? You can go anywhere. Do anything. Consume whatever you wish.
See, even the awful-tasting alien says it's a good idea.
We just want you to reach your full potential.
Maybe just for a moment...
Maybe I'll just crack the door open -- Crack it open and take a look.

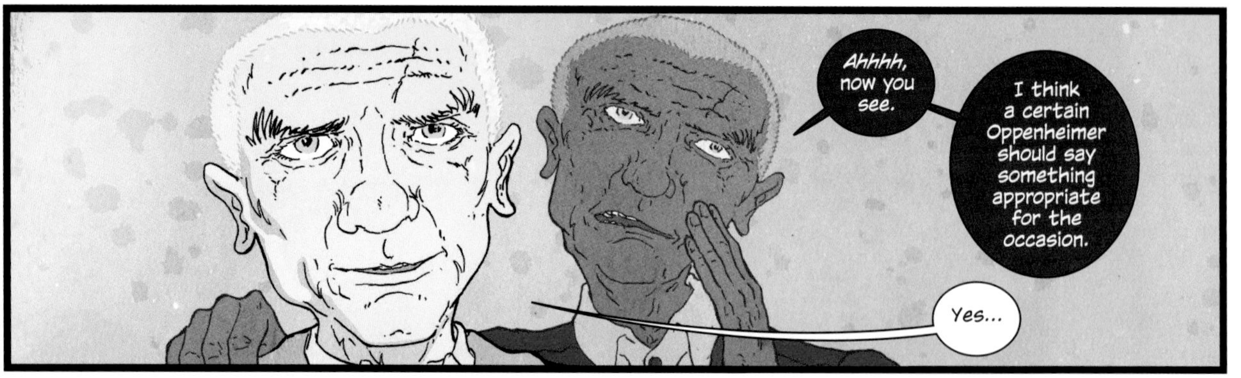
Ahhhh, now you see.
I think a certain Oppenheimer should say something appropriate for the occasion.
Yes...

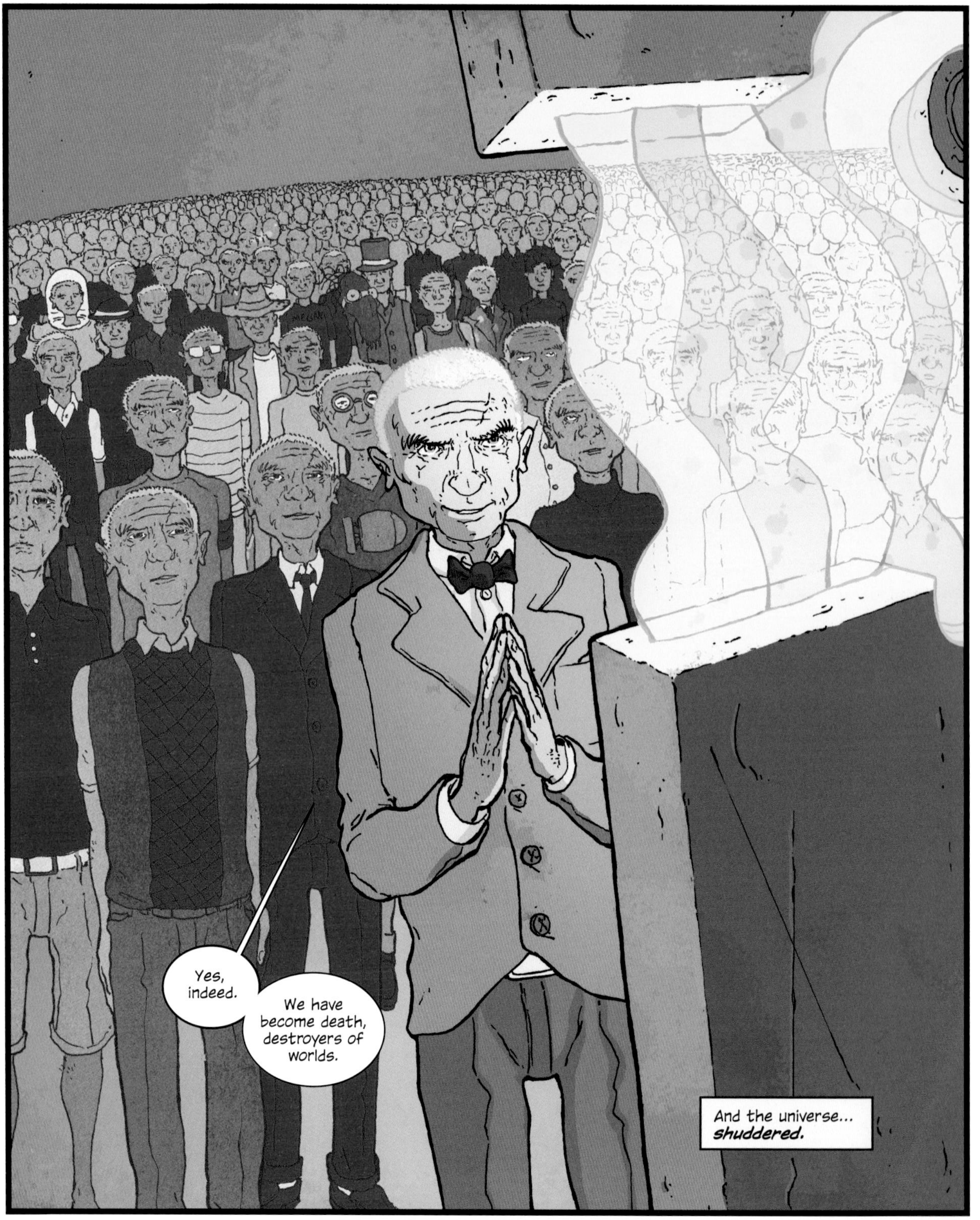
Yes, indeed.
We have become death, destroyers of worlds.
And the universe... ***shuddered.***

"HMMMM!"

- OPPENHEIMER

CLAVIS AUREA
THE RECORDED FEYNMAN | VOL. 3

HE BELIEVED
THE LIE

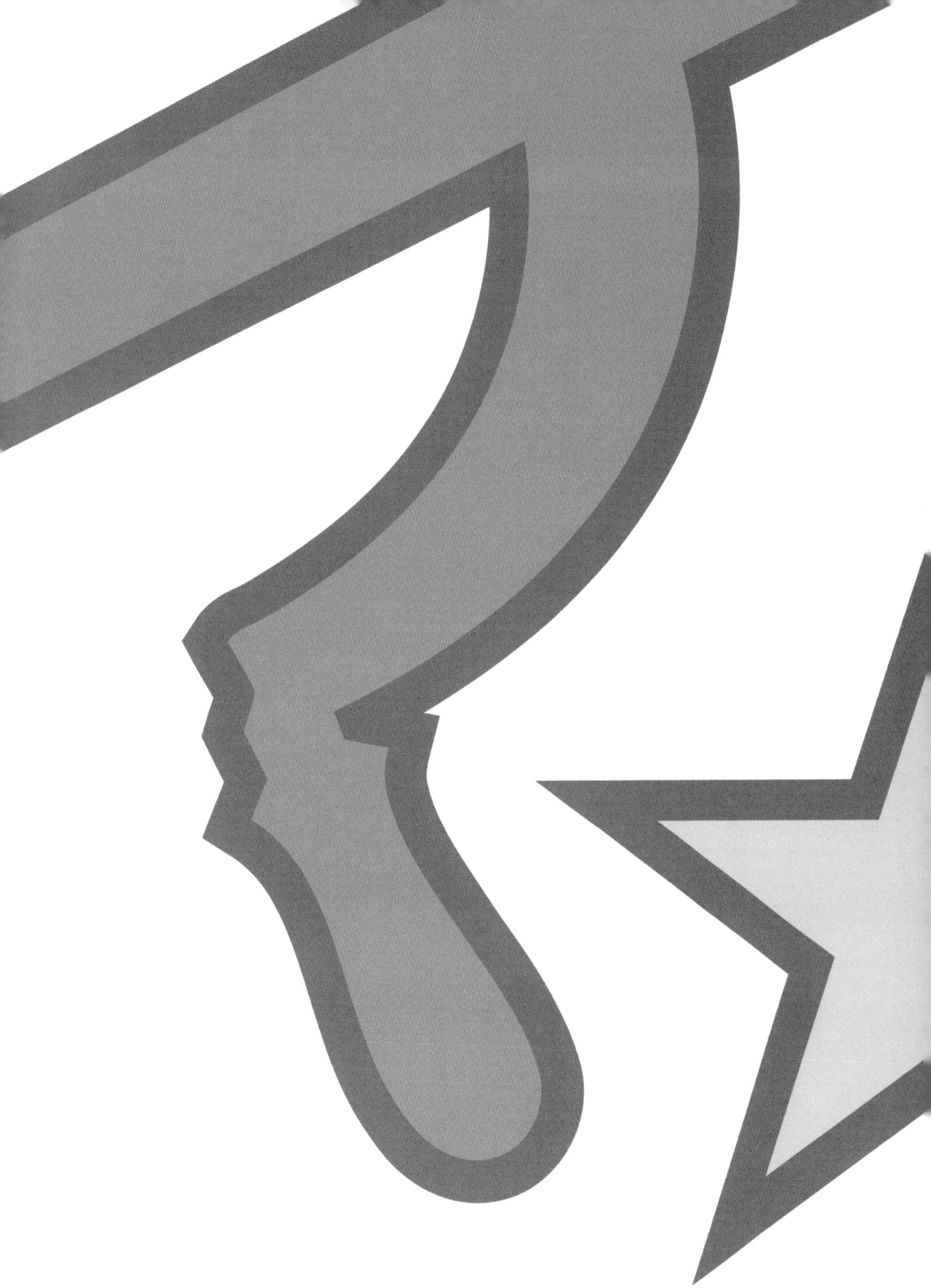

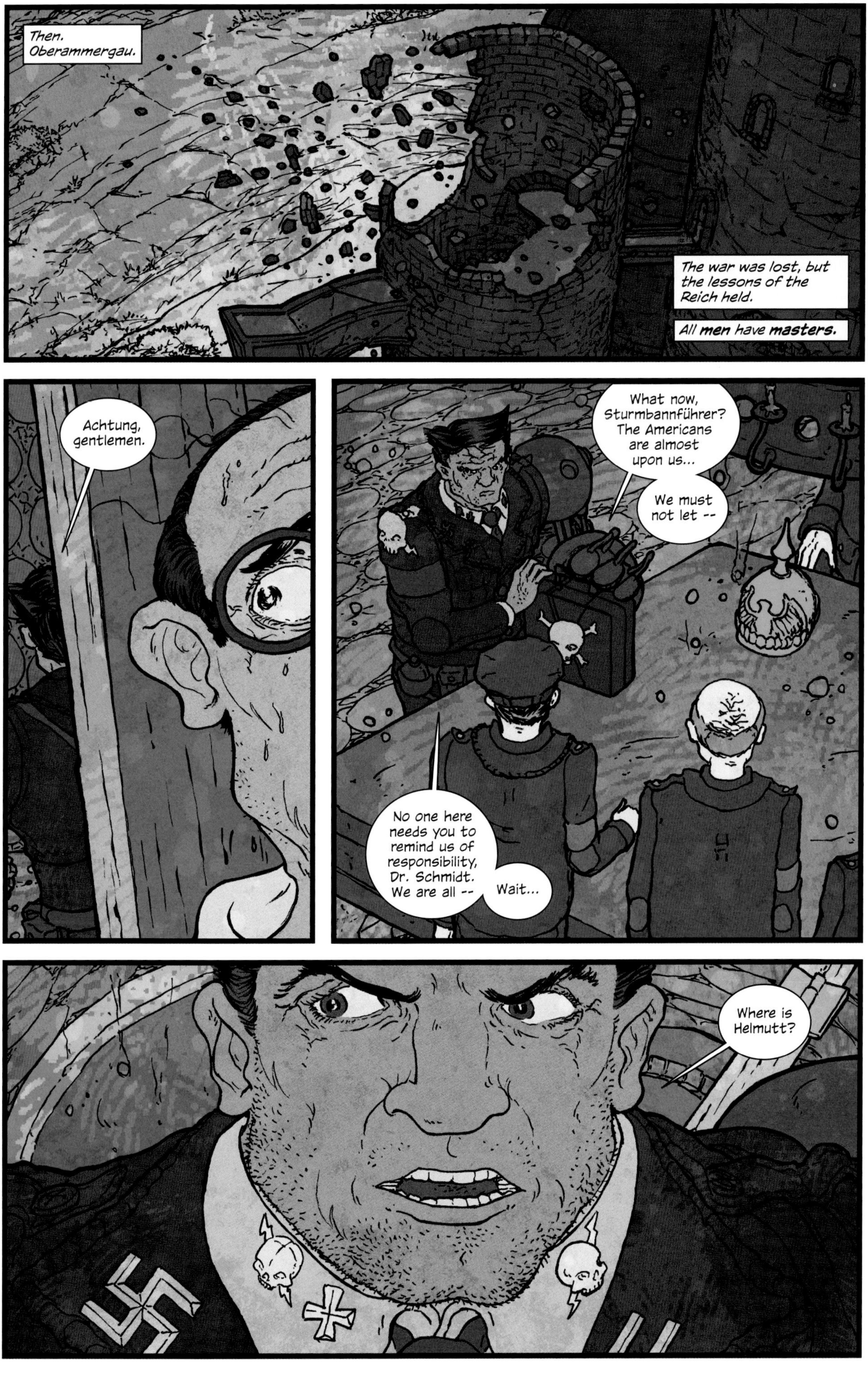
Then.
Oberammergau.
The war was lost, but the lessons of the Reich held.
All **men** have **masters.**
Achtung, gentlemen.
What now, Sturmbannführer? The Americans are almost upon us...
We must not let --
No one here needs you to remind us of responsibility, Dr. Schmidt. We are all --
Wait...
Where is Helmutt?

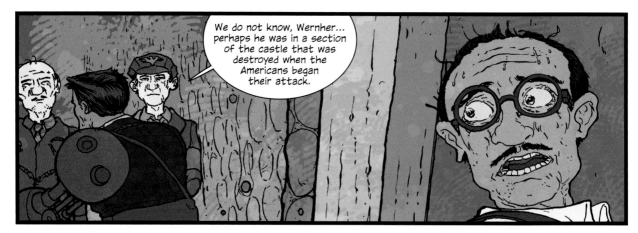

We do not know, Wernher... perhaps he was in a section of the castle that was destroyed when the Americans began their attack.

Very well.

Lieutenant, we will need glasses.

If every man had a master, it was Helmutt Gröttrup who knew his best of all.

For his own benefit, Wernher von Braun would kill every scientist at the Nazi Science Stronghold.

He would do this to make his position more valuable.

Von Braun had goals, you see.

Ze hell with this.

All men are pawns to a master with *vision*.

BA-BOOOOM!

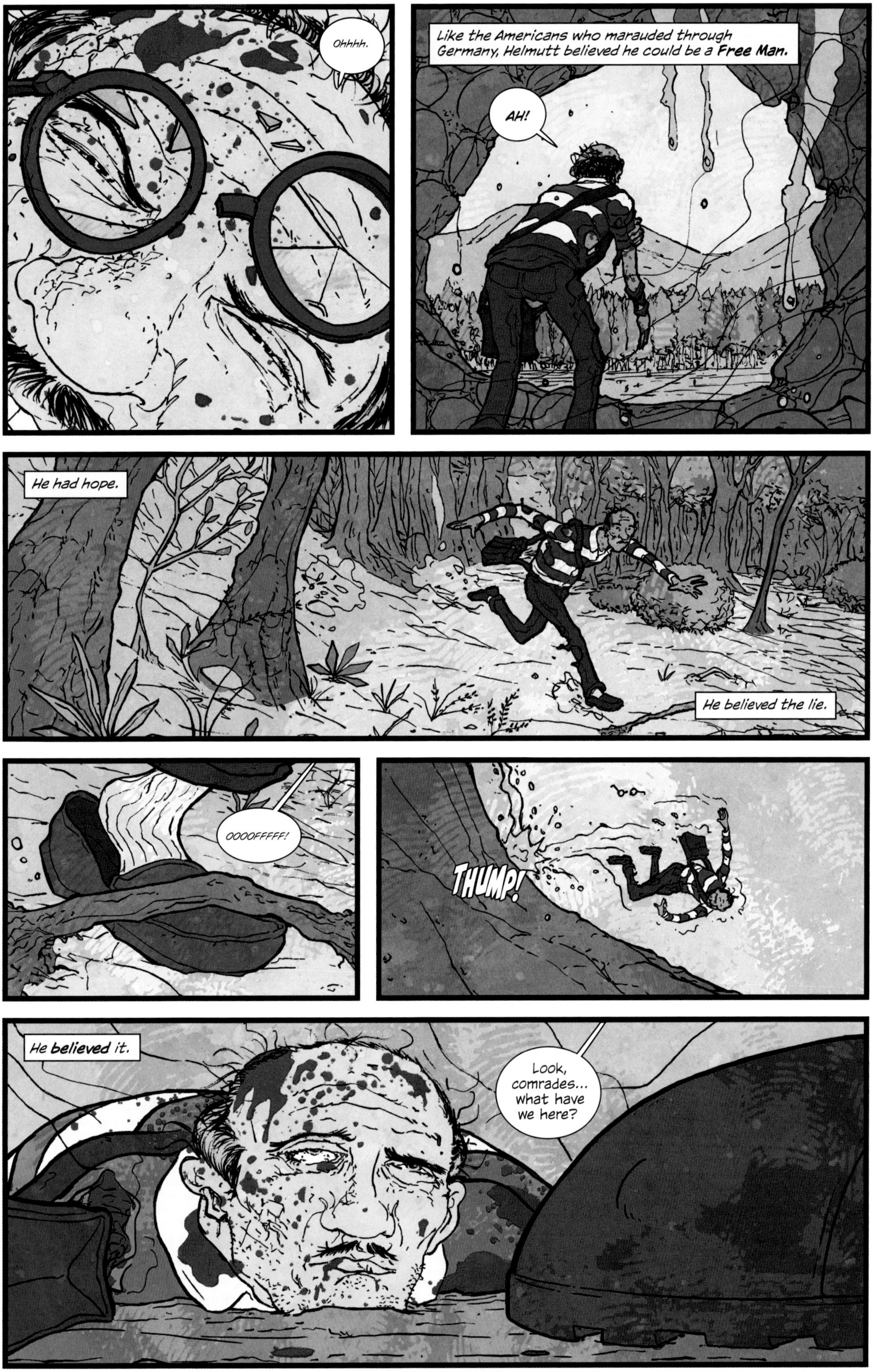
Ohhhh.
Like the Americans who marauded through Germany, Helmutt believed he could be a **Free Man.**
AH!
He had hope.
He believed the lie.
OOOOFFFFF!
THUMP!
He **believed** it.
Look, comrades... what have we here?

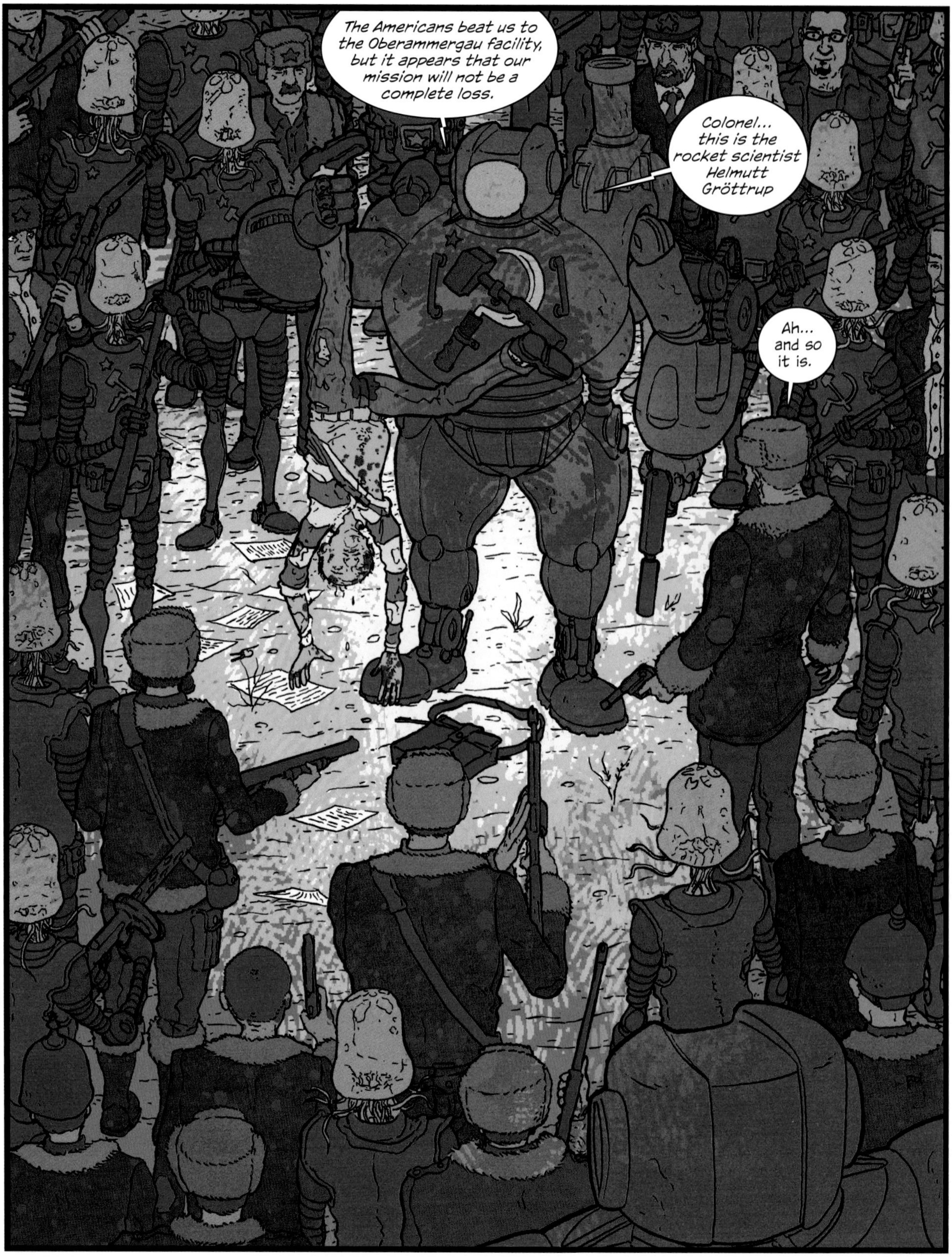
The Americans beat us to the Oberammergau facility, but it appears that our mission will not be a complete loss.
Colonel... this is the rocket scientist Helmutt Gröttrup
Ah... and so it is.

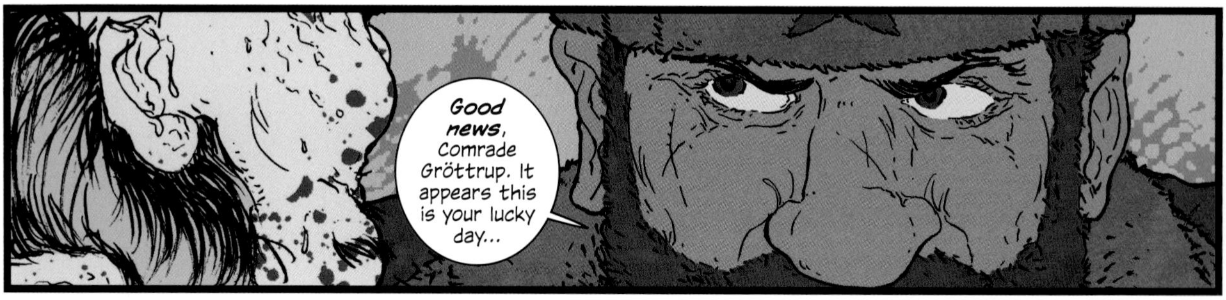
Good news, Comrade Gröttrup. It appears this is your lucky day...

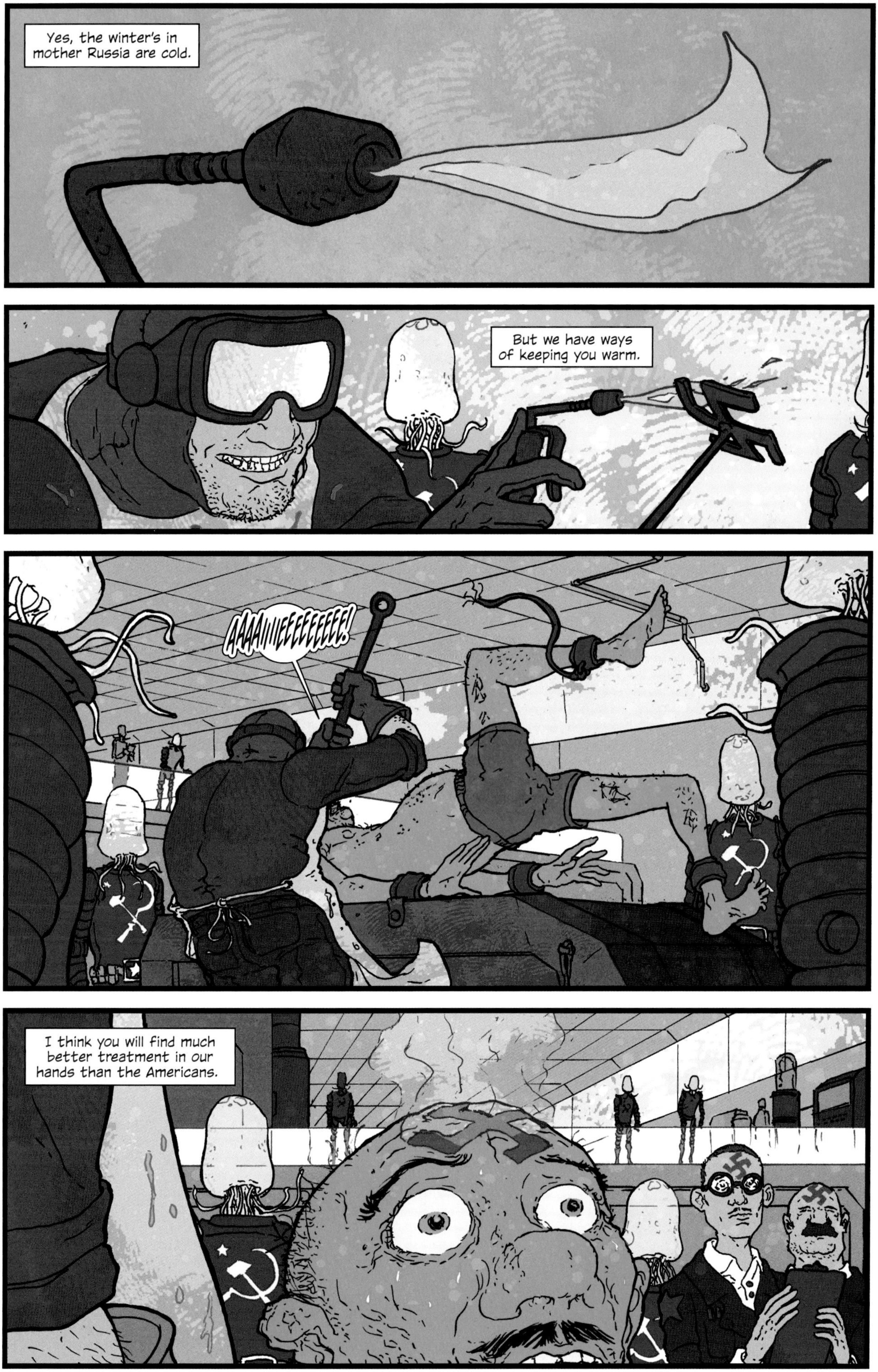
Yes, the winter's in mother Russia are cold.
But we have ways of keeping you warm.
AAAAIIIIEEEEEEEEE!
I think you will find much better treatment in our hands than the Americans.

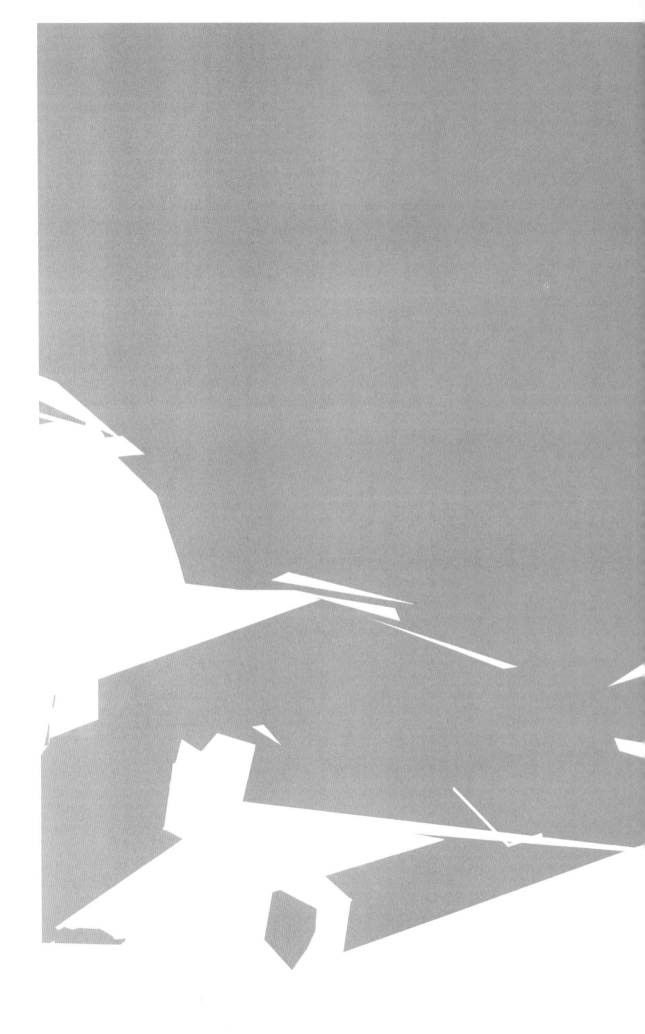

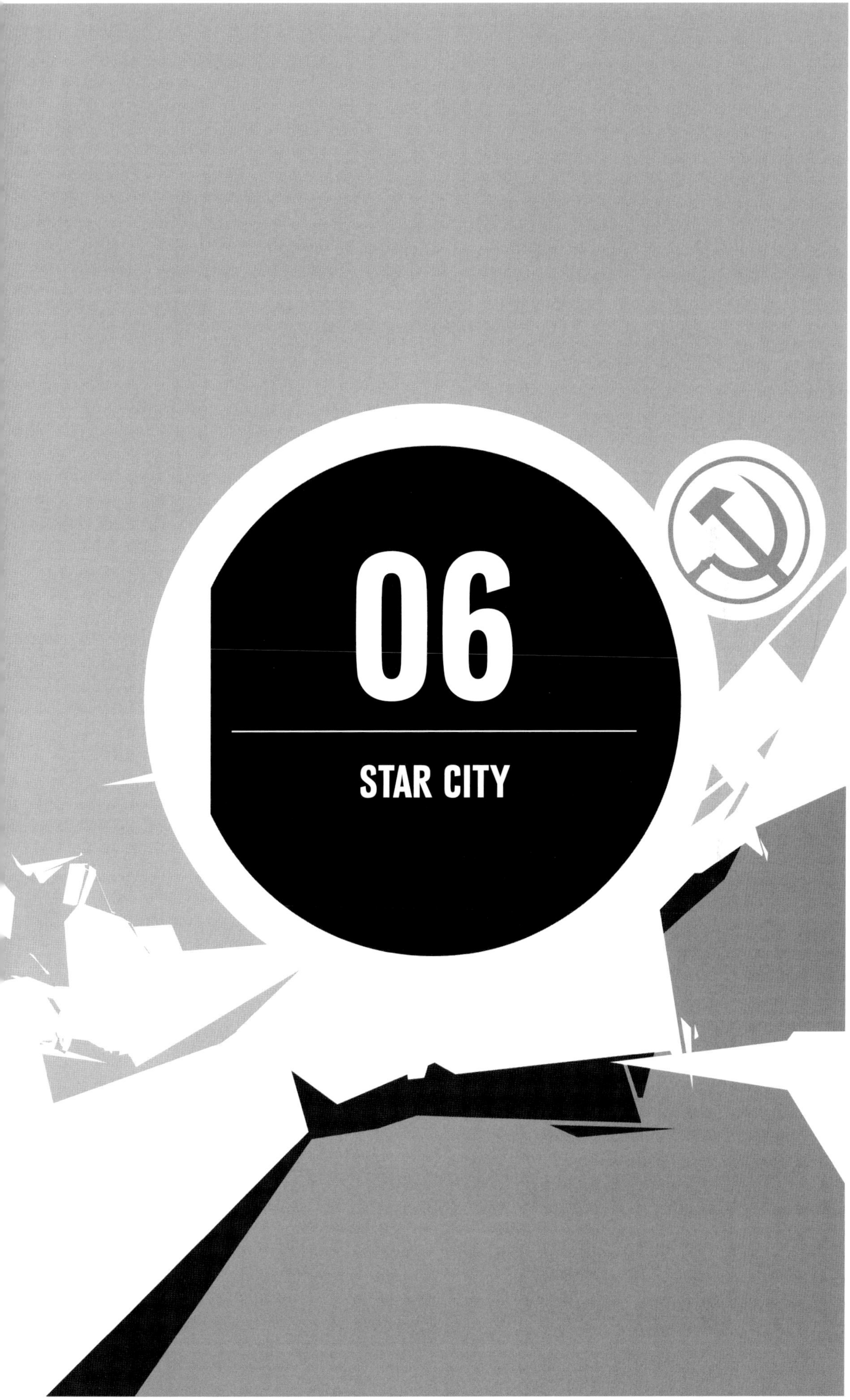

06

STAR CITY

"WHAT MAN CAN SERVE TWO MASTERS?
WHO WOULD NOT BE TORN ASUNDER BY
TITANS?"   °

CLAVIS AUREA
THE RECORDED FEYNMAN | **VOL. 2**

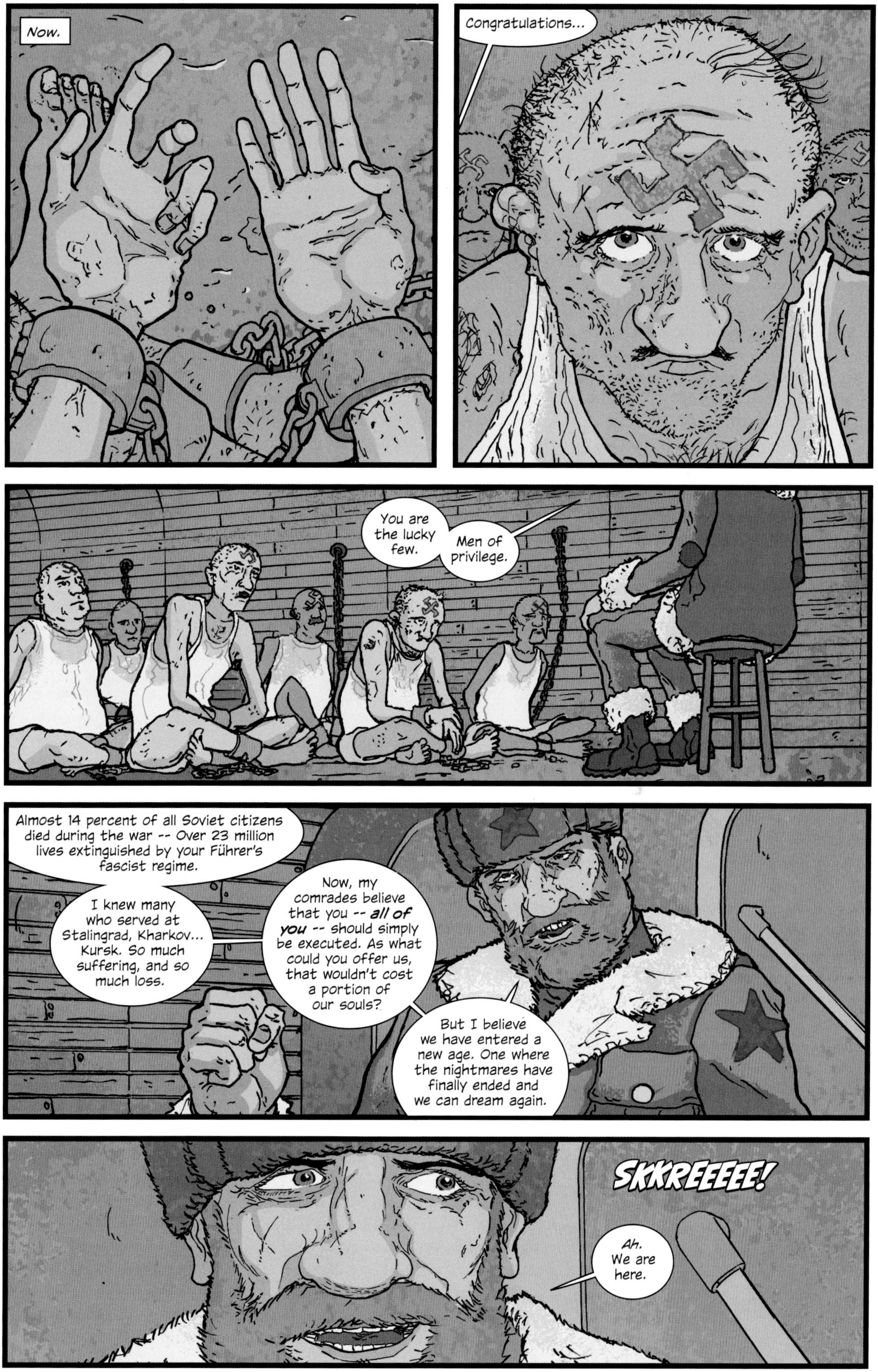
Now.
Congratulations...
You are the lucky few.
Men of privilege.
Almost 14 percent of all Soviet citizens died during the war -- Over 23 million lives extinguished by your Führer's fascist regime.
I knew many who served at Stalingrad, Kharkov... Kursk. So much suffering, and so much loss.
Now, my comrades believe that you -- *all of you* -- should simply be executed. As what could you offer us, that wouldn't cost a portion of our souls?
But I believe we have entered a new age. One where the nightmares have finally ended and we can dream again.
SKKREEEEE!
Ah. We are here.

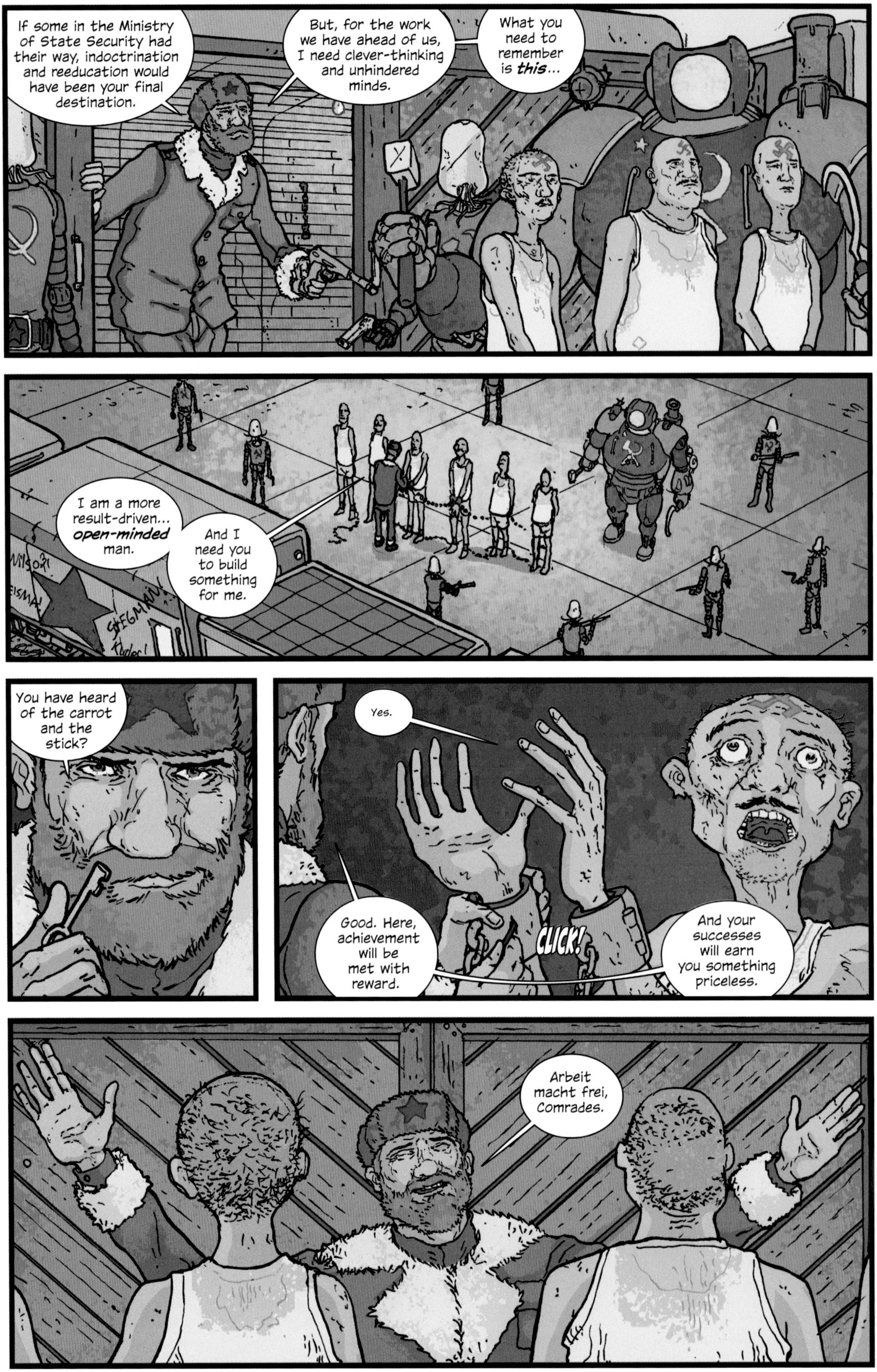
If some in the Ministry of State Security had their way, indoctrination and reeducation would have been your final destination.
But, for the work we have ahead of us, I need clever-thinking and unhindered minds.
What you need to remember is *this*...
I am a more result-driven... *open-minded* man.
And I need you to build something for me.
You have heard of the carrot and the stick?
Yes.
Good. Here, achievement will be met with reward.
CLICK!
And your successes will earn you something priceless.
Arbeit macht frei, Comrades.

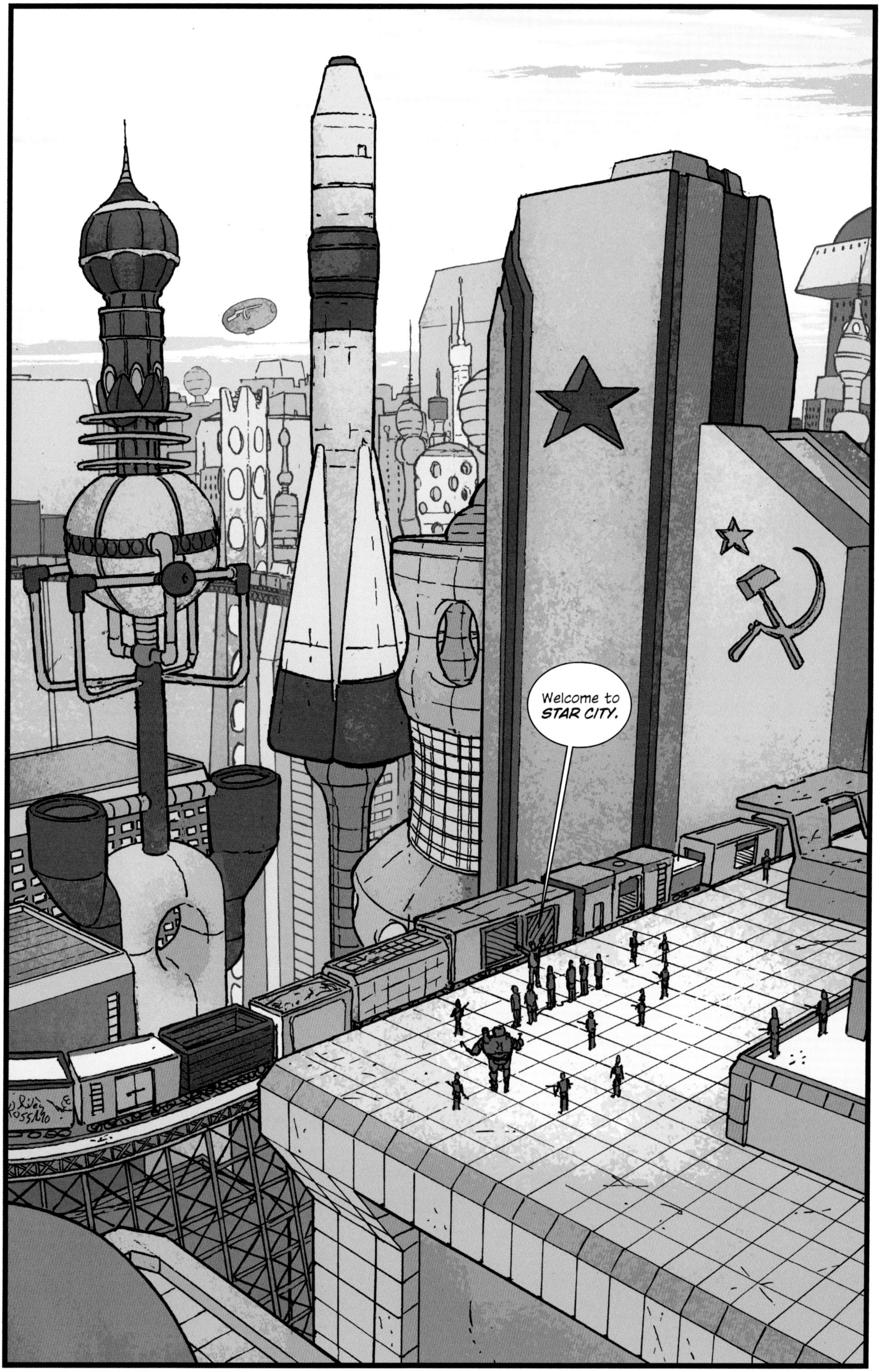
Welcome to STAR CITY.

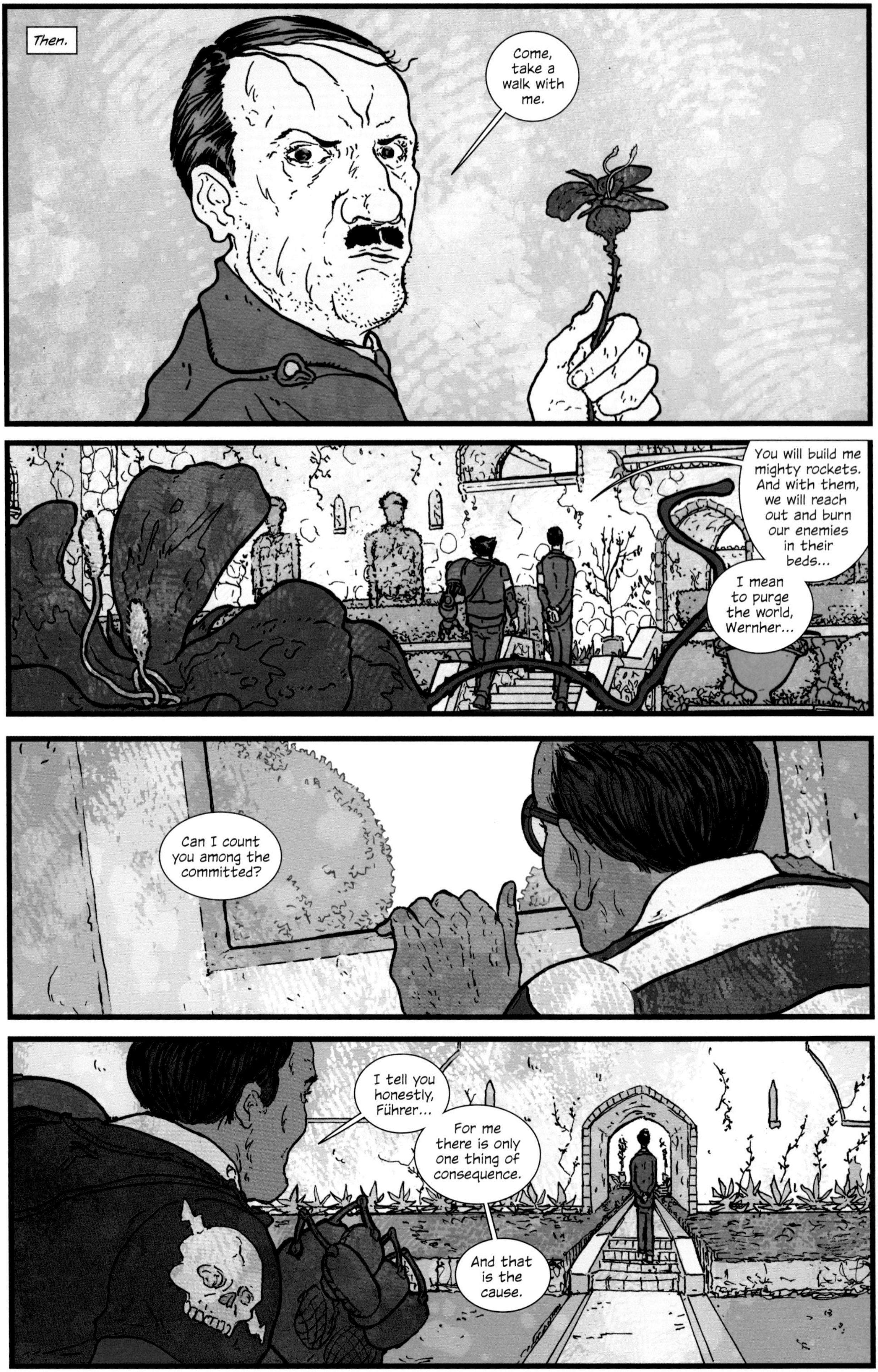
Then.
Come, take a walk with me.
You will build me mighty rockets. And with them, we will reach out and burn our enemies in their beds...
I mean to purge the world, Wernher...
Can I count you among the committed?
I tell you honestly, Führer...
For me there is only one thing of consequence.
And that is the cause.

That man is either going to conquer the world or kill us all.
I must work quickly.
Wernher!
I heard from the window...
We are going to BUILD ROCKETS!
ROCKETS, Wernher! **ROCKETS!**
Yes, Helmutt... rockets.
But what is this... ***We?***
This will be a challenge for the ages.
The greatest minds assembled for a singular task...
The ***greatest minds,*** Helmutt.
You cannot possibly count yourself among them.

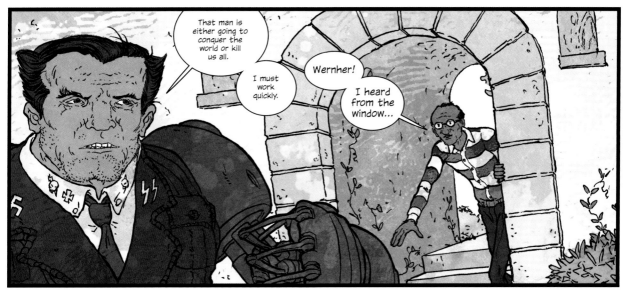

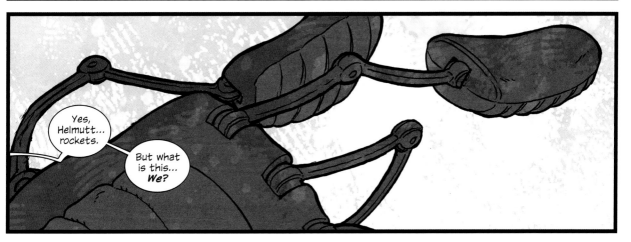

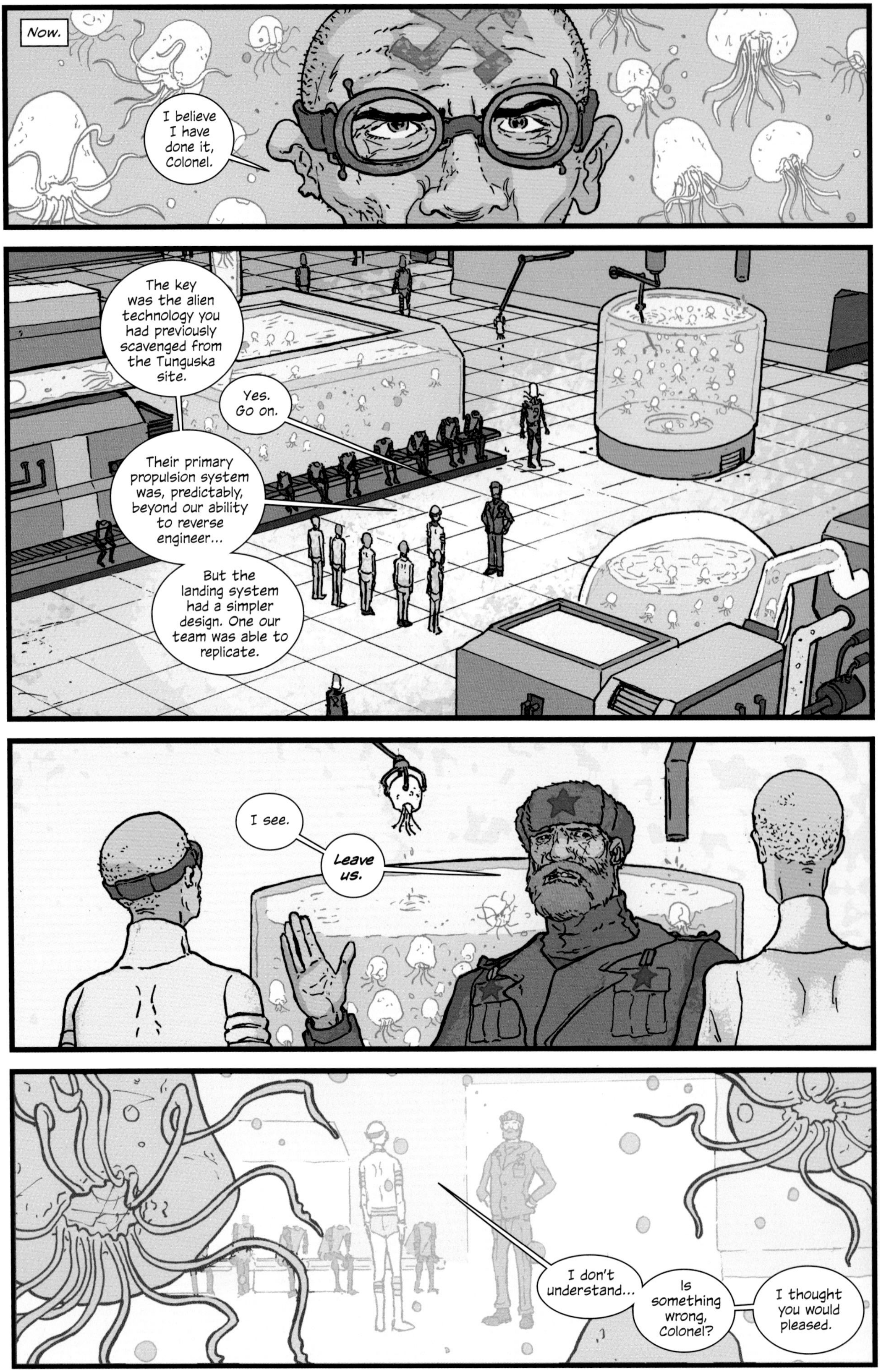
Now.
I believe I have done it, Colonel.
The key was the alien technology you had previously scavenged from the Tunguska site.
Yes. Go on.
Their primary propulsion system was, predictably, beyond our ability to reverse engineer...
But the landing system had a simpler design. One our team was able to replicate.
I see.
Leave us.
I don't understand...
Is something wrong, Colonel?
I thought you would pleased.

I was under the impression that, regardless of system, what powered the alien ship was beyond us.

Have you been keeping secrets, Helmutt?

No, Colonel. Never.

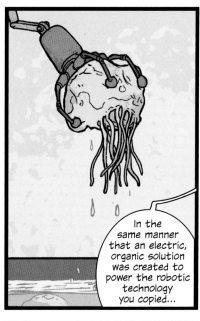

In the same manner that an electric, organic solution was created to power the robotic technology you copied...

I created a work around based on my research from Oberammergau.

My work, Colonel...which I have given to you so that we might reach the stars before the Americans.

Then that would mean I am talking to a free man.

Ex-- excuse me?

Do this...and if it works, you will have what you have longed for, Helmutt.

Send our good Captain, Yuri Gagarin, into space -- bring him home safely...

And I will sign your papers, giving you your release.

You can go home, Helmutt.

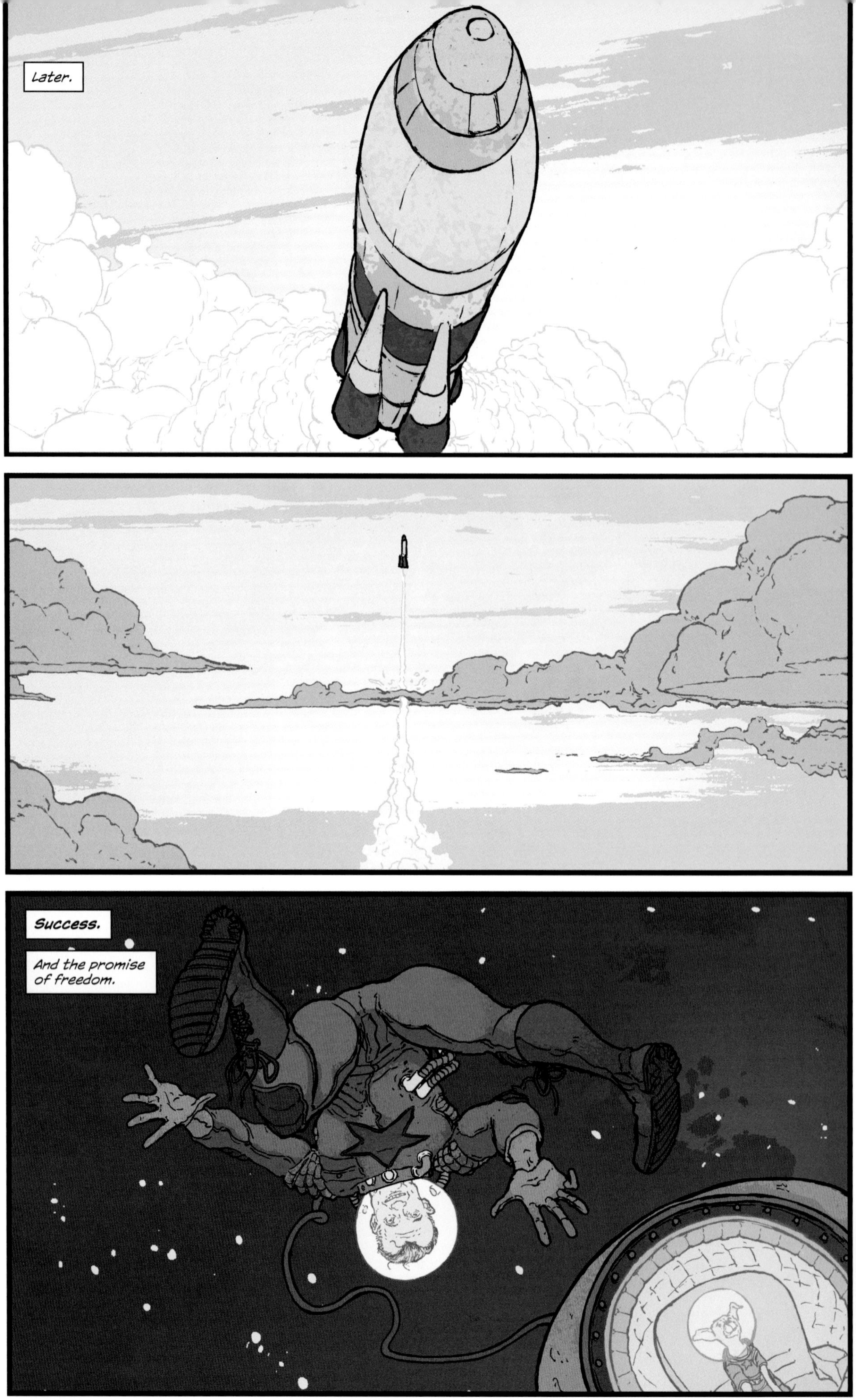
Later.
Success.
And the promise of freedom.

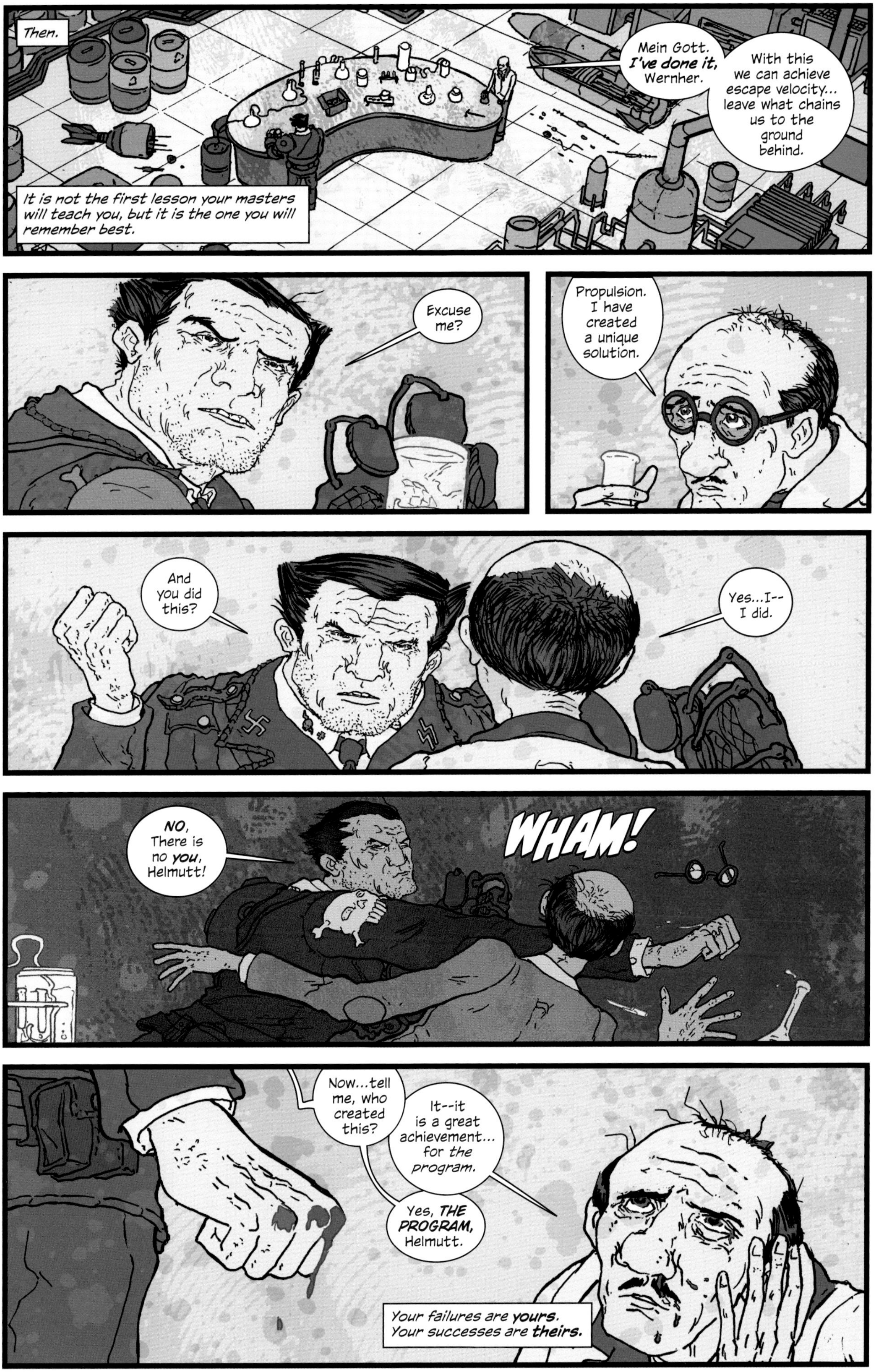
Then.
Mein Gott. I've done it, Wernher.
With this we can achieve escape velocity... leave what chains us to the ground behind.
It is not the first lesson your masters will teach you, but it is the one you will remember best.
Excuse me?
Propulsion. I have created a unique solution.
And you did this?
Yes...I-- I did.
NO, There is no you, Helmutt!
WHAM!
Now...tell me, who created this?
It--it is a great achievement... for the program.
Yes, THE PROGRAM, Helmutt.
Your failures are yours.
Your successes are theirs.

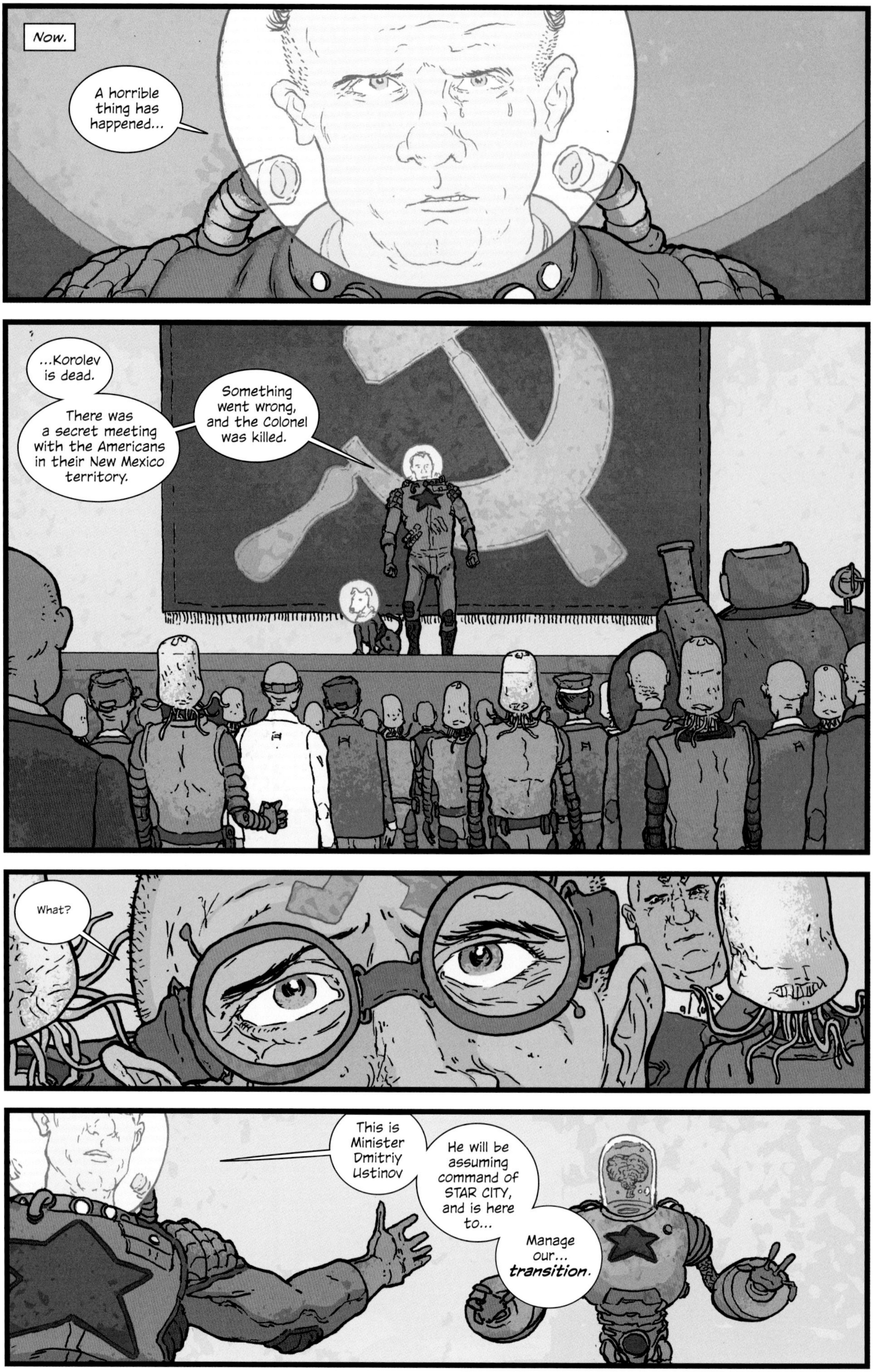
Now.
A horrible thing has happened...
...Korolev is dead.
There was a secret meeting with the Americans in their New Mexico territory.
Something went wrong, and the Colonel was killed.
What?
This is Minister Dmitriy Ustinov
He will be assuming command of STAR CITY, and is here to...
Manage our... *transition*.

Thank you, comrade Gagarin.
Da, this is a sad day... a tragic day.
But you must overcome your grief -- our great loss -- so that you can hear the words I am about to say...
Humans have now been to other worlds.
Tunguska, and your hard work, have given us a seat in a great game.
The greatest man has ever known.
But now I must ask for even more.
A redoubling of efforts.
RECOMMITMENT.
SACRIFICE.

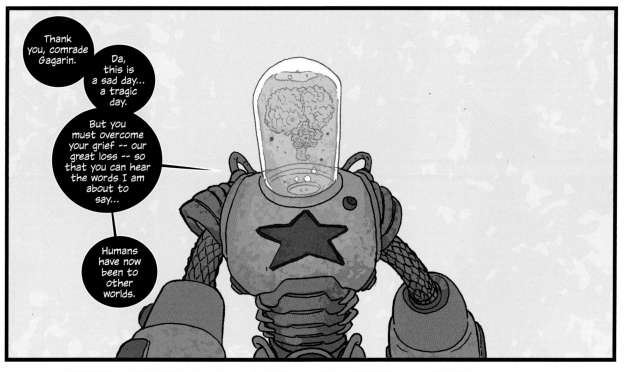

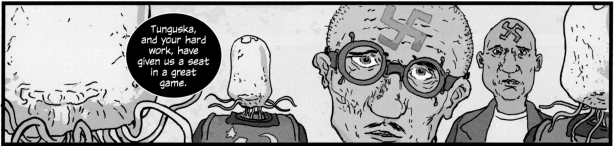

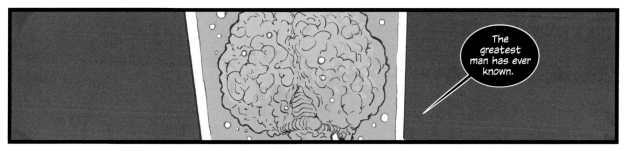

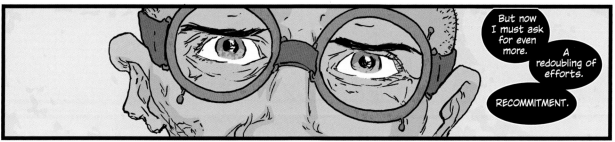

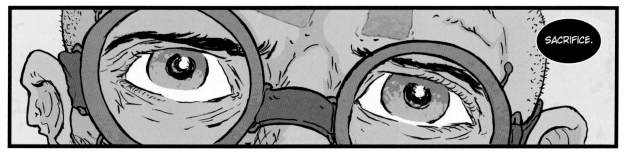

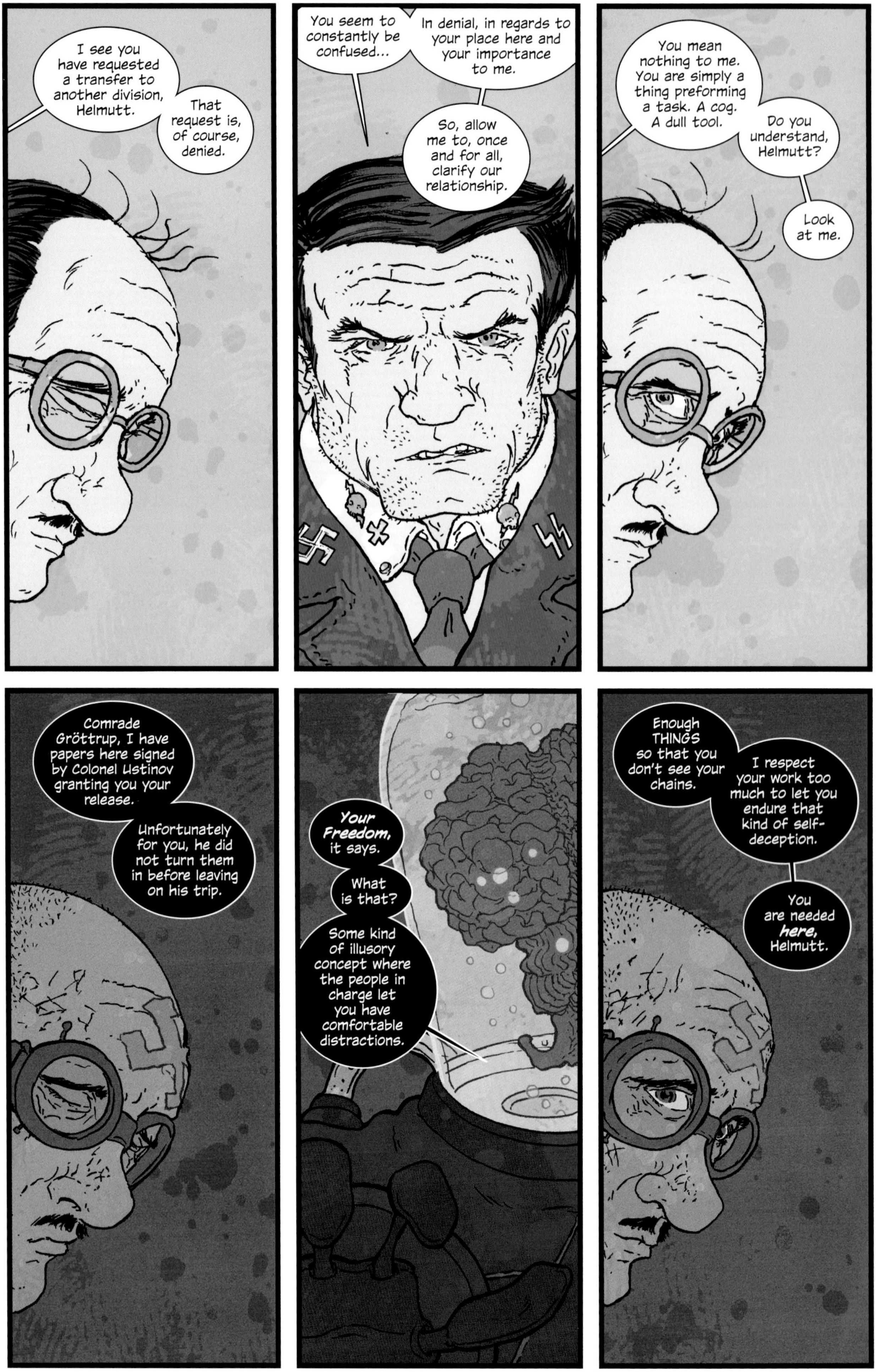
I see you have requested a transfer to another division, Helmutt.
That request is, of course, denied.
You seem to constantly be confused...
In denial, in regards to your place here and your importance to me.
So, allow me to, once and for all, clarify our relationship.
You mean nothing to me. You are simply a thing preforming a task. A cog. A dull tool.
Do you understand, Helmutt?
Look at me.
Comrade Gröttrup, I have papers here signed by Colonel Ustinov granting you your release.
Unfortunately for you, he did not turn them in before leaving on his trip.
Your Freedom, it says.
What is that?
Some kind of illusory concept where the people in charge let you have comfortable distractions.
Enough THINGS so that you don't see your chains.
I respect your work too much to let you endure that kind of self-deception.
You are needed *here,* Helmutt.

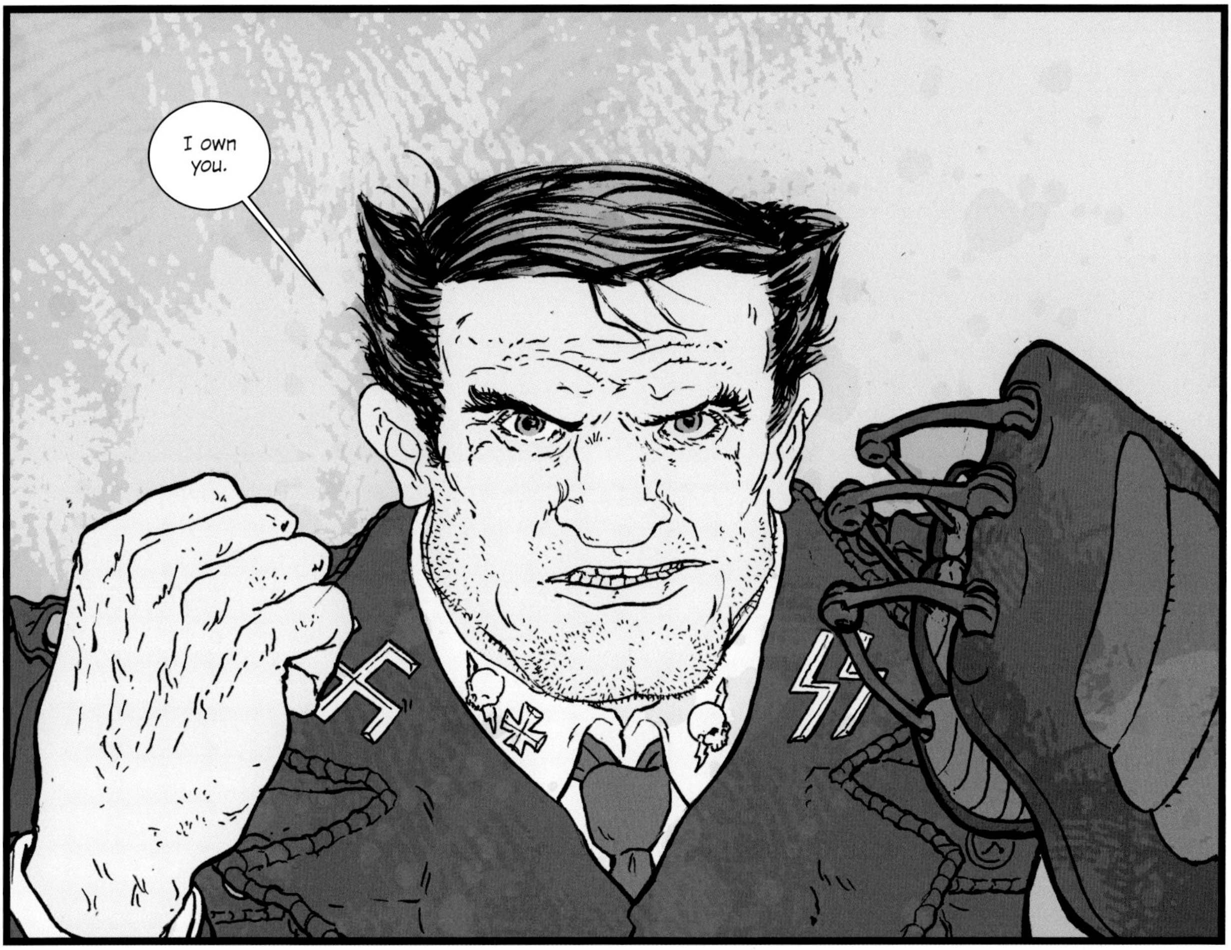
I own you.

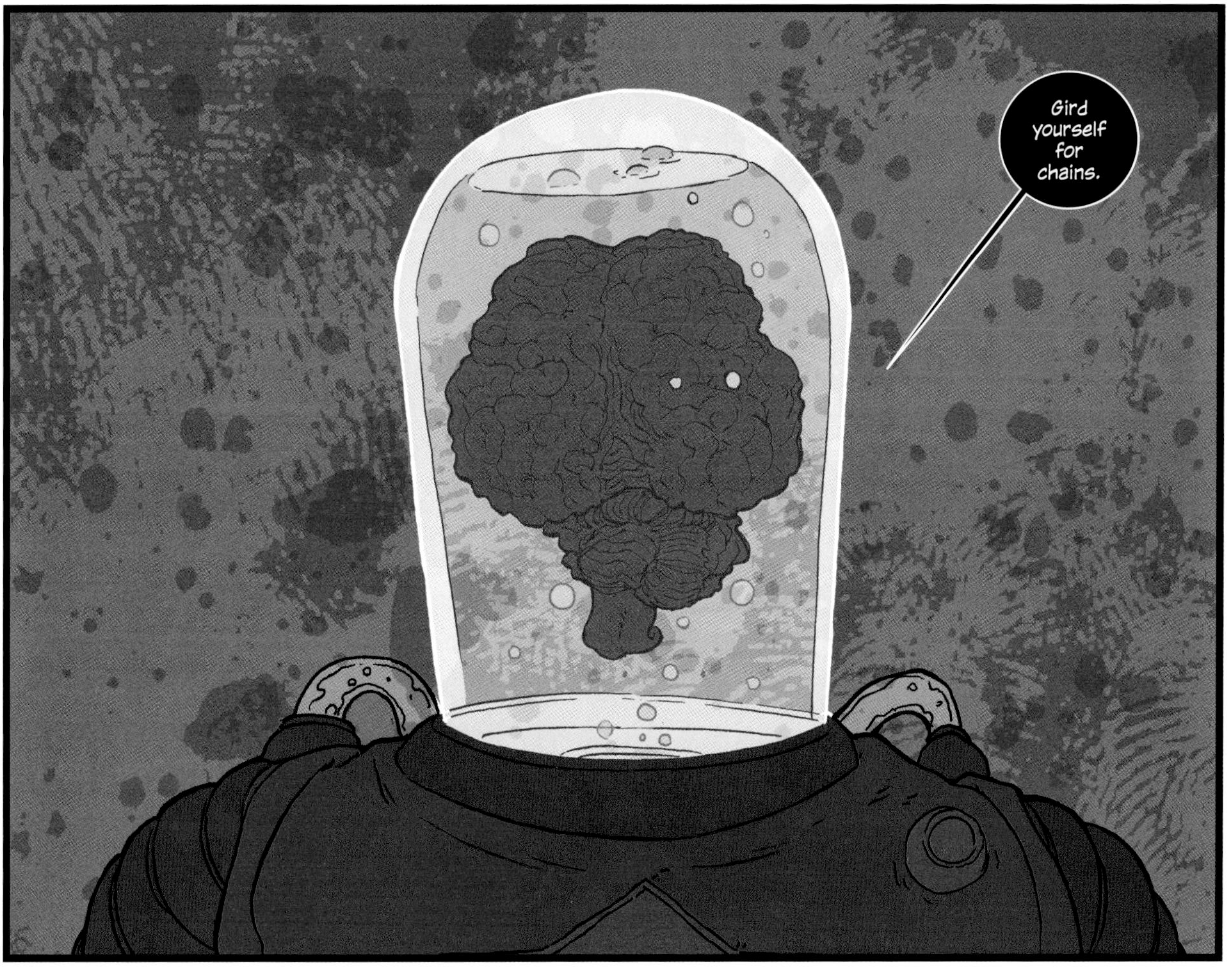
Gird yourself for chains.

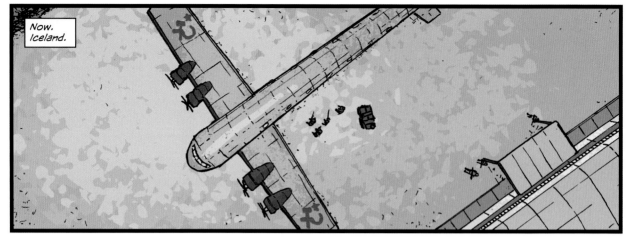

Now.
Iceland.

We arrived undetected, Minister.

Good. *Proceed.*

They are waiting for you inside.

Helmutt Gröttrup believed the lie until he could believe it no more...

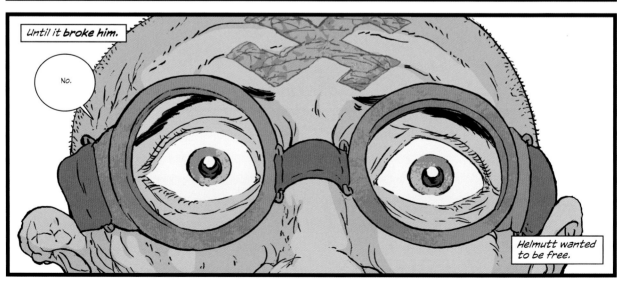

*Until it **broke** him.*

No.

Helmutt wanted to be free.

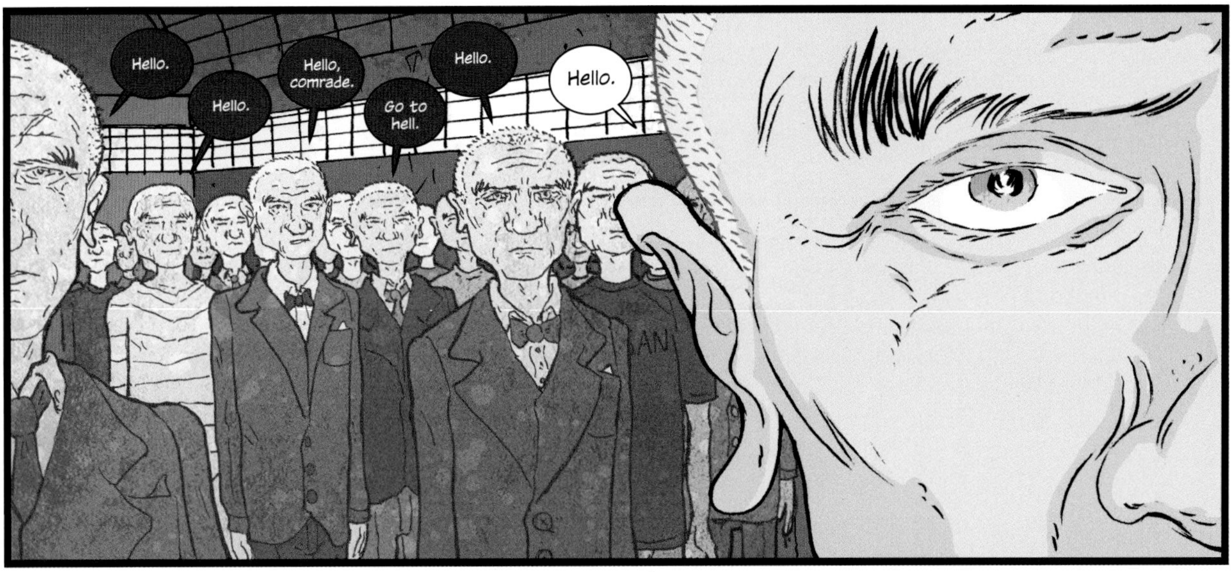
Hello.
Hello.
Hello, comrade.
Go to hell.
Hello.
Hello.

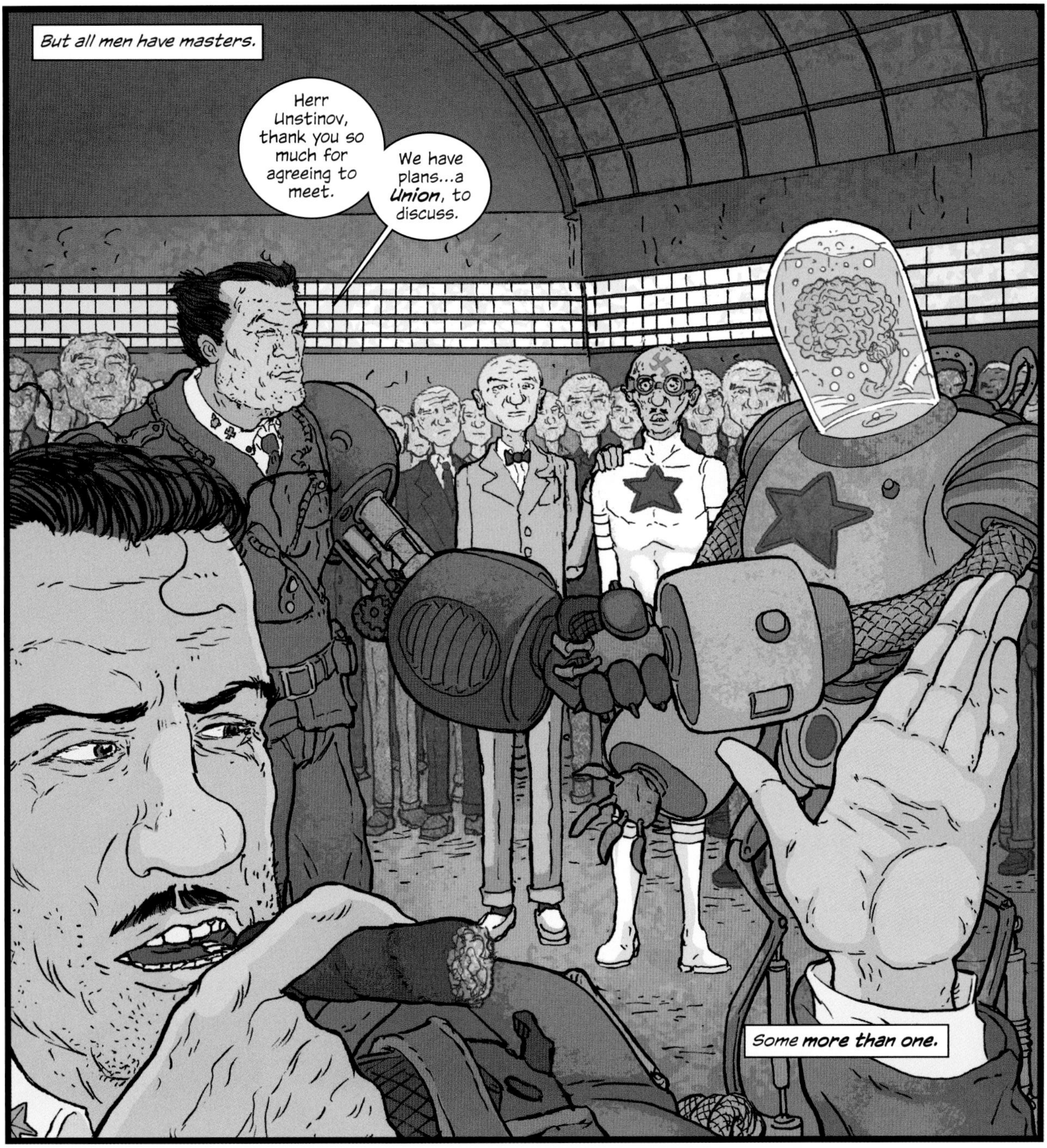
But all men have masters.
Herr Unstinov, thank you so much for agreeing to meet.
We have plans...a Union, to discuss.
Some more than one.

WHO'S GOING TO CALL
OUR BLUFF

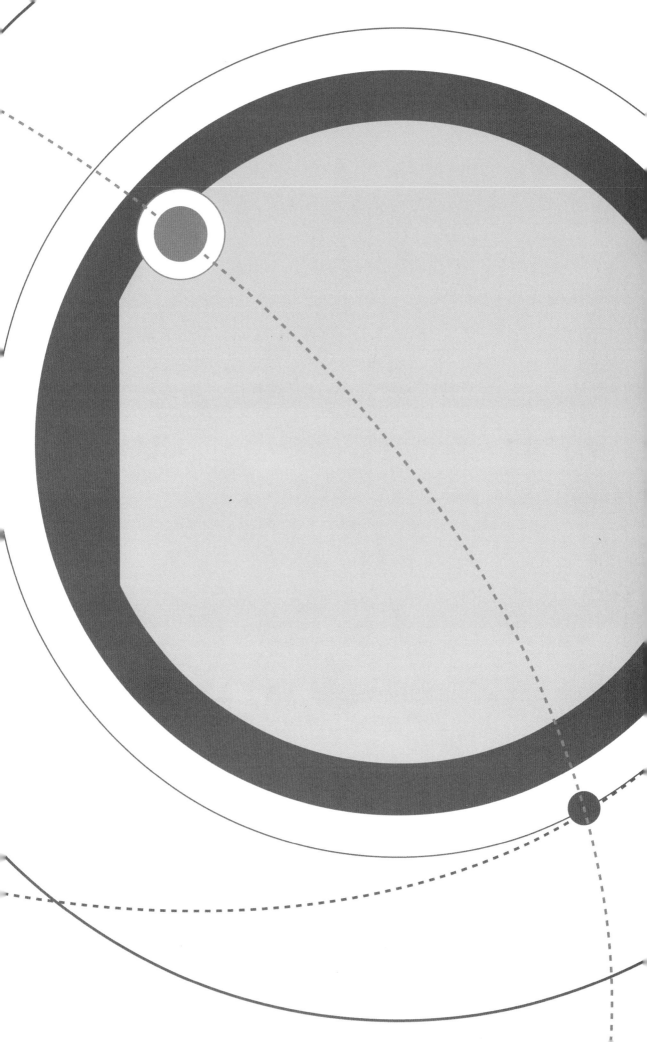

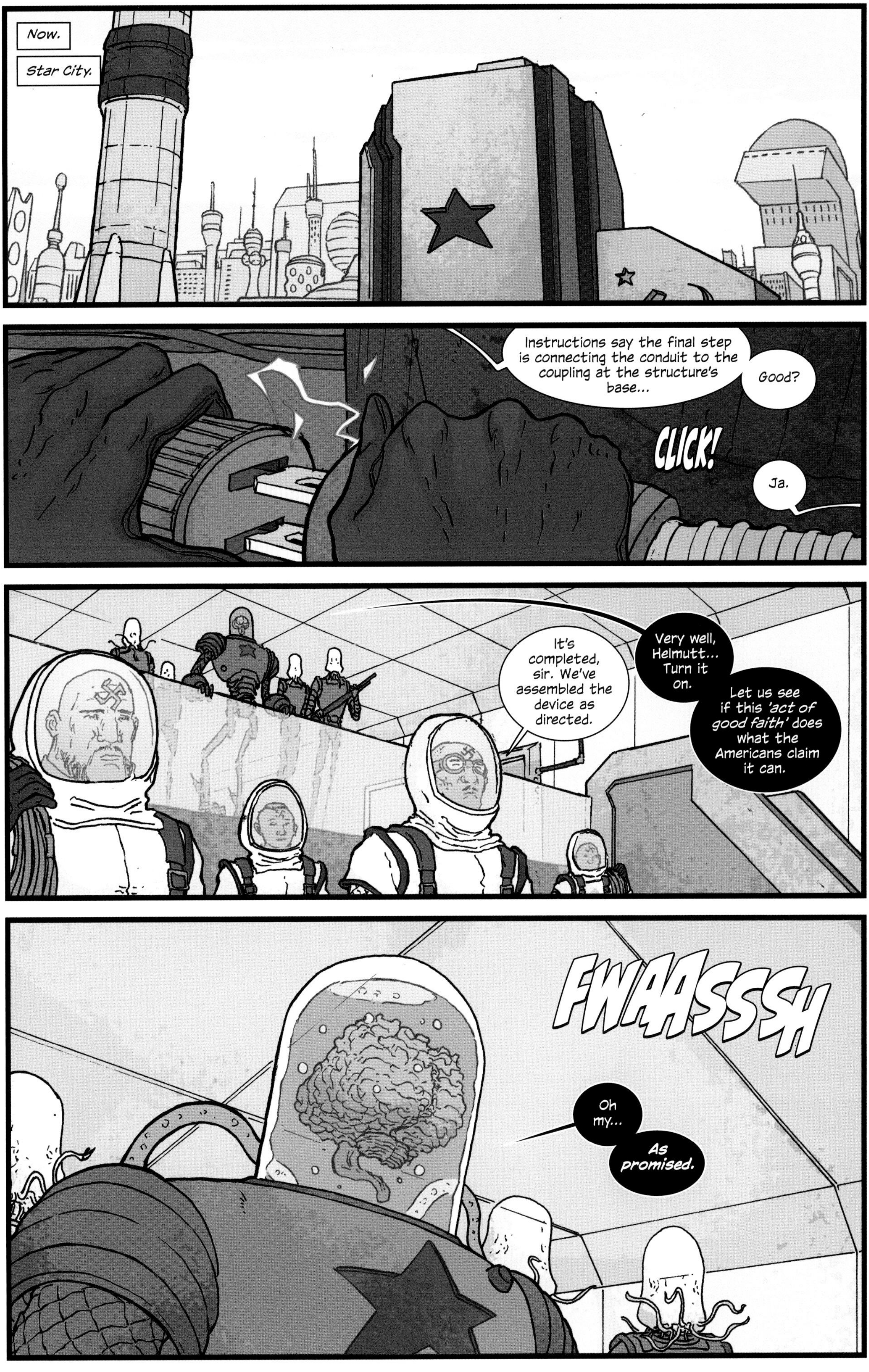
Now.
Star City.
Instructions say the final step is connecting the conduit to the coupling at the structure's base...
Good?
CLICK!
Ja.
It's completed, sir. We've assembled the device as directed.
Very well, Helmutt... Turn it on.
Let us see if this 'act of good faith' does what the Americans claim it can.
FWAASSSH
Oh my...
As promised.

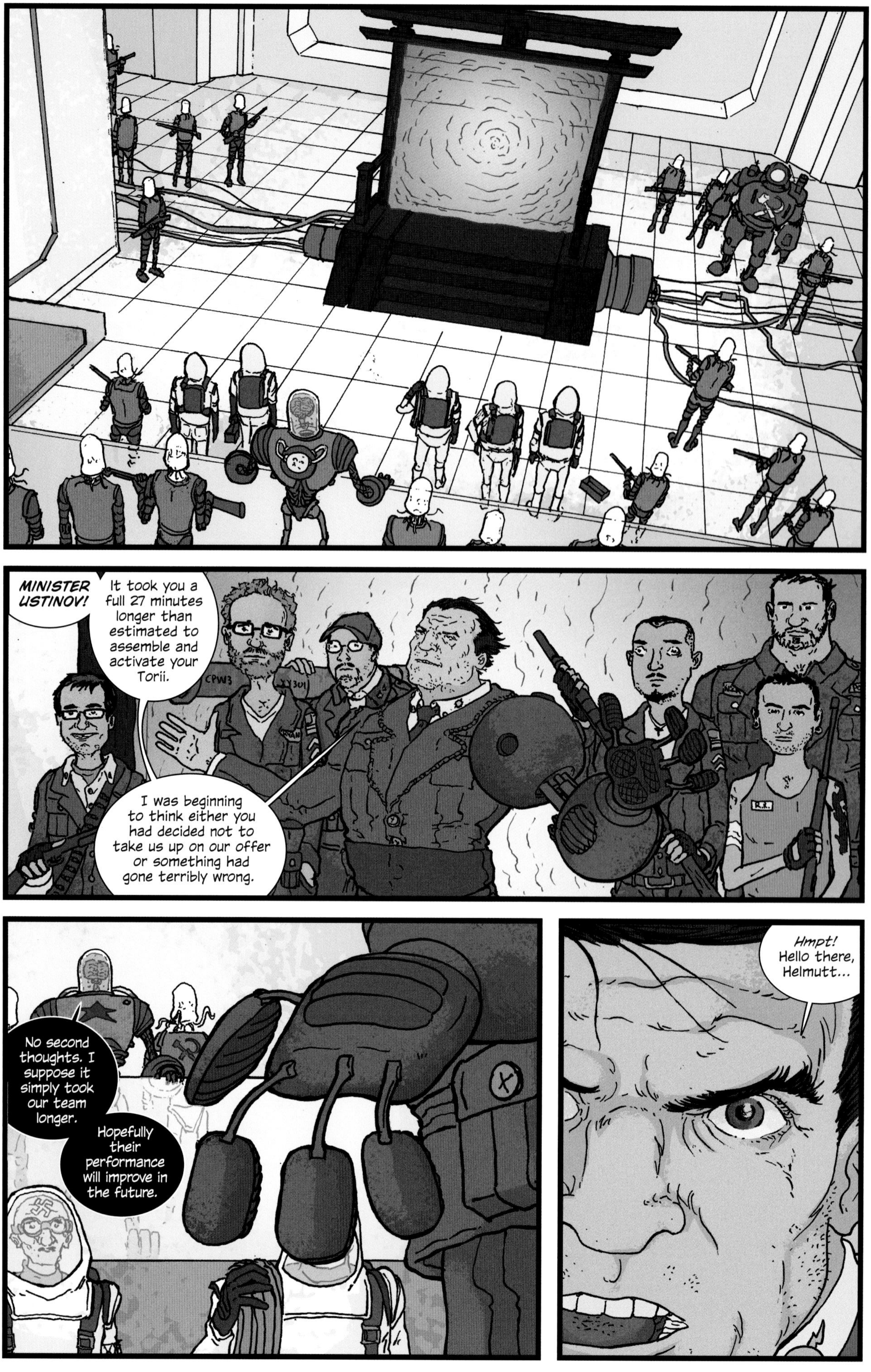
MINISTER USTINOV!
It took you a full 27 minutes longer than estimated to assemble and activate your Torii.
I was beginning to think either you had decided not to take us up on our offer or something had gone terribly wrong.
No second thoughts. I suppose it simply took our team longer.
Hopefully their performance will improve in the future.
Hmpt! Hello there, Helmutt...

I see you continue to meet expectations.

CRACK!

Doctor von Braun... manners.

Yes. I tend to over indulge. I apologize.

On to business then?

Of course. Explain how it works.

The Torii are assimilated technology that we currently use to move quickly from OPstation to OPstation.

This will, obviously, enable our Manhattan Projects and Star City to work more closely together, as well as coordinate our research... eliminating redundancies, increasing efficiency and the like.

The targeting system is powered by traditional power sources...

But actual portal operates on collective biological something or other.

The point is the thing runs on the life energy of human beings.

Ridiculous. You cannot expect me to believe this.

It's true, I swear.

The Manhattan Projects have powered ours for some time with the Imperial Nihilists that originally used the Torii to attack the US War Department...

But we're actually running into a problem with our Death Buddhists.

Oh, and what's that?

They keep dying.

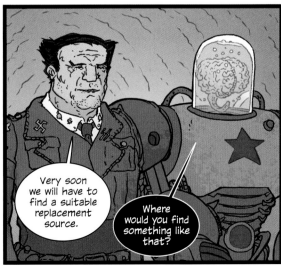

Very soon we will have to find a suitable replacement source.

Where would you find something like that?

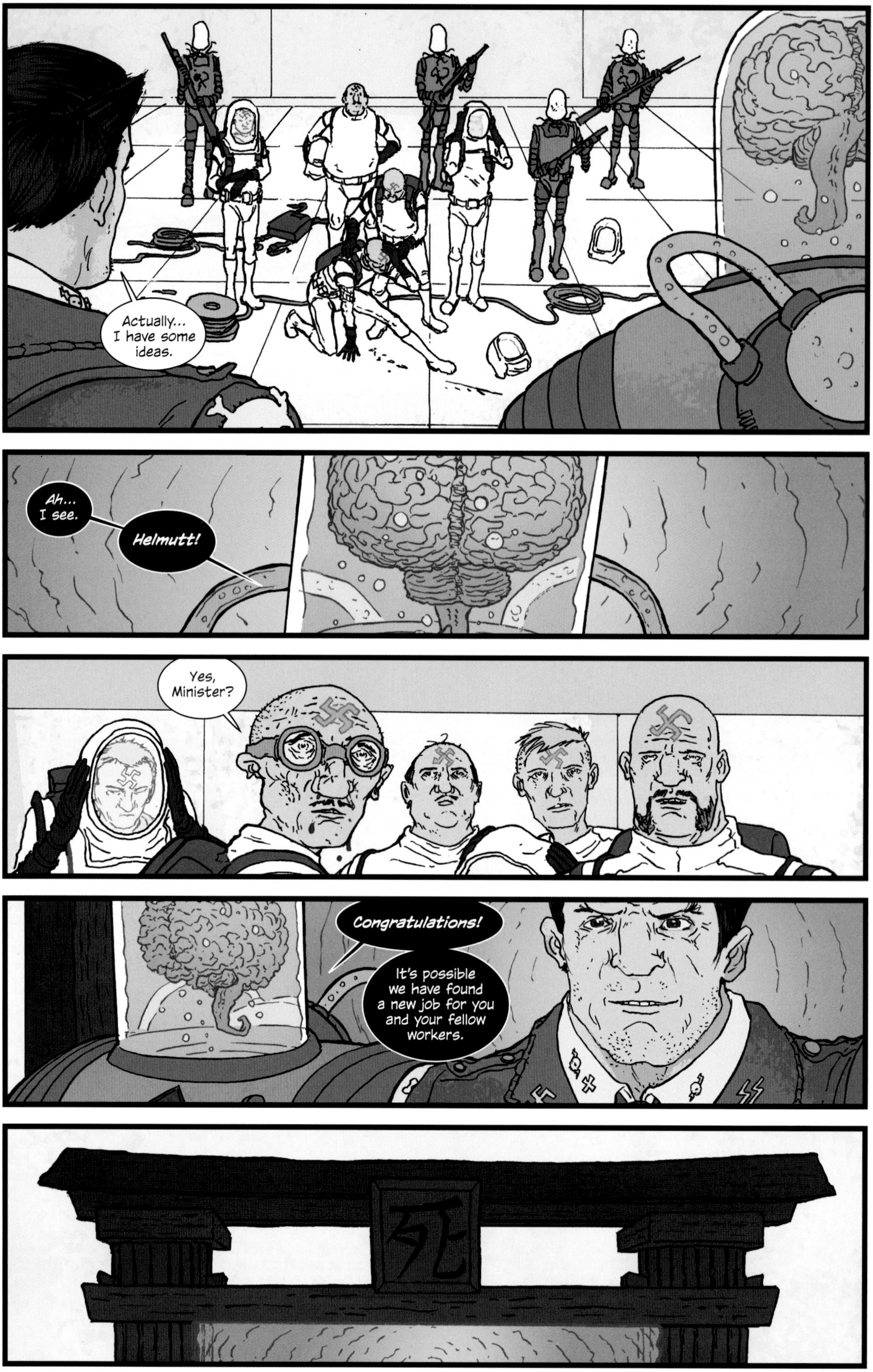
Actually... I have some ideas.
Ah... I see.
Helmutt!
Yes, Minister?
Congratulations!
It's possible we have found a new job for you and your fellow workers.

"WE PLANNED FOR BETRAYAL. THEY PLANNED FOR DECEIT. NO ONE EVER THOUGHT TO PLAN FOR HARMONY."

CLAVIS AUREA
THE RECORDED FEYNMAN | **VOL. 3**

07

ABOVE AND BEYOND

"LEGEND SAYS ROMULUS SLEW REMUS AND THEN BUILT ROME.

IMAGINE IF THEY HAD WORKED TOGETHER AND BUILT SOMETHING BETTER. "

CLAVIS AUREA
THE RECORDED FEYNMAN | **VOL. 2**

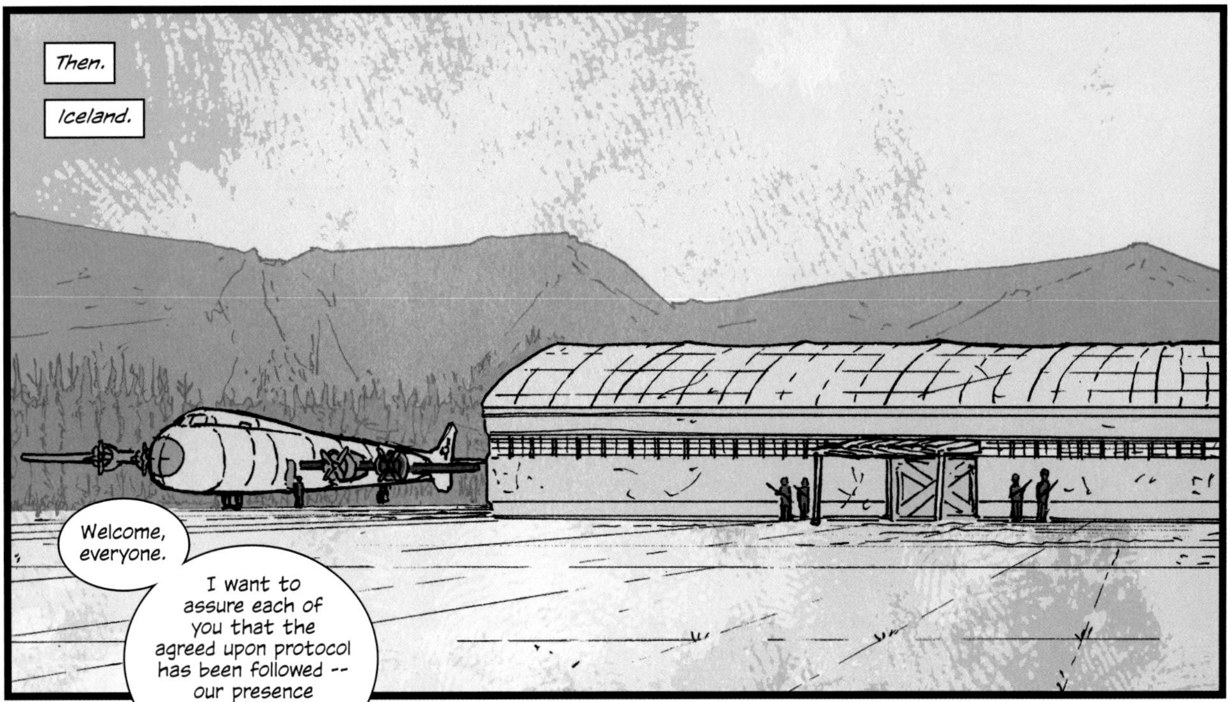
Then.
Iceland.
Welcome, everyone.
I want to assure each of you that the agreed upon protocol has been followed -- our presence here is beyond classified...

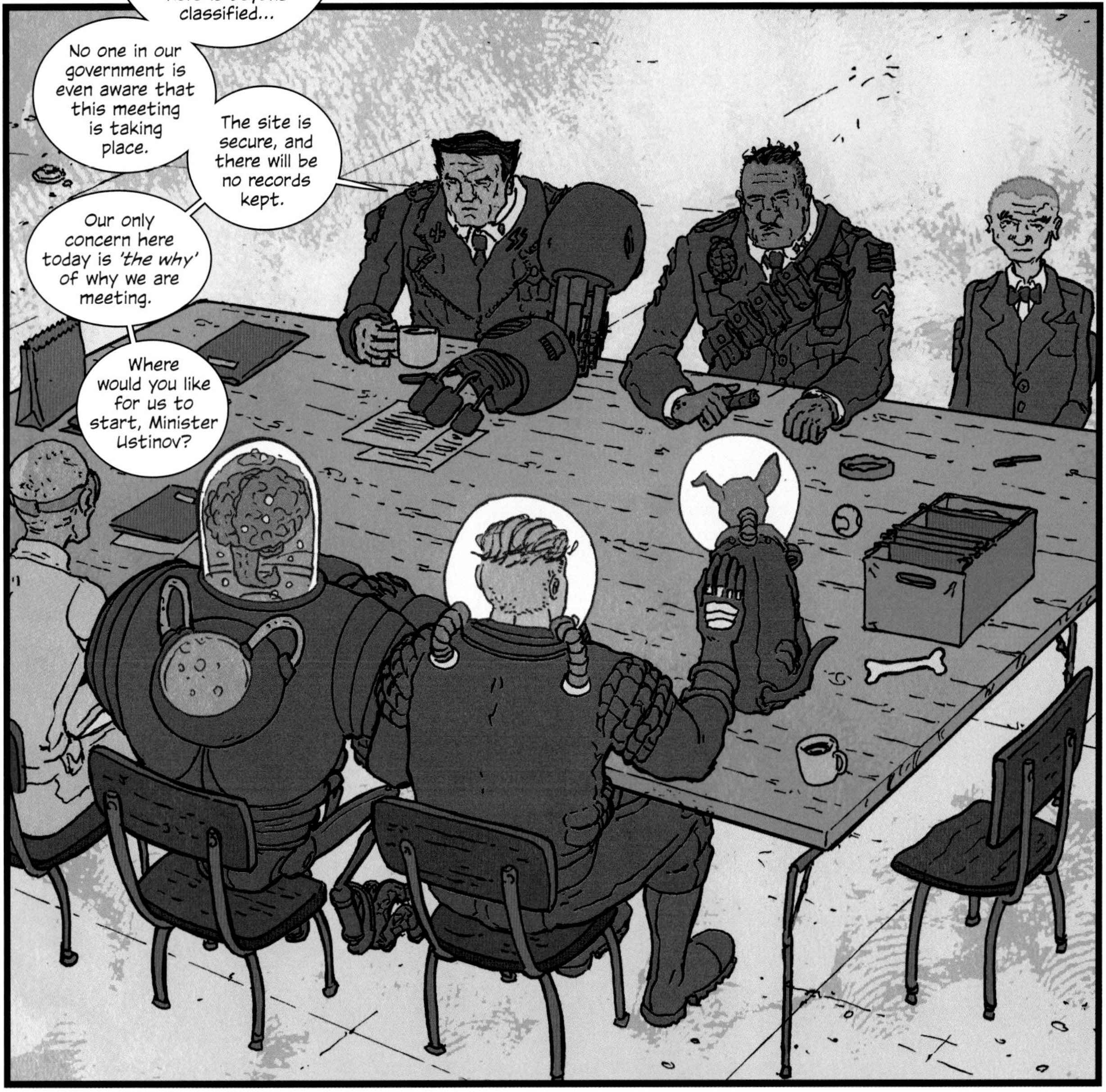
No one in our government is even aware that this meeting is taking place.
The site is secure, and there will be no records kept.
Our only concern here today is *'the why'* of why we are meeting.
Where would you like for us to start, Minister Ustinov?

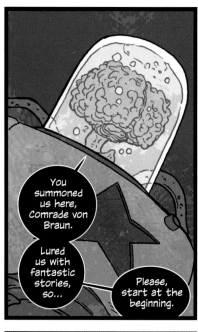

You summoned us here, Comrade von Braun.

Lured us with fantastic stories, so...

Please, start at the beginning.

General, do you want to, or would you rather...

Oh, no. Enjoy yourself, Wernher.

Go right ahead and put on a goddamn show.

Very well.

Minister, if you don't mind, I'd like to start with your secret space program, Star City.

We know that much of the technology you've developed was derived from the Tunguska event, just as you know that we've made similar use of our Roswell incident.

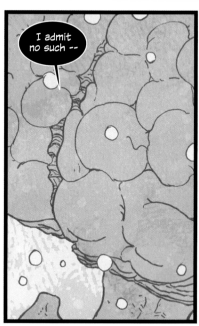

I admit no such --

Minister. These things were confirmed to me personally through your predecessor, Colonel Korolev.

Leave the old ways of thinking behind, son...none of those hoo-ha party tricks are worth paying attention to anyway.

What the General means is there's a greater point to focus on.

We are not alone.

I'm sorry, but I don't think that a few random extraterrestrial encounters constitute a greater immediate threat than the western culture of capitalism...

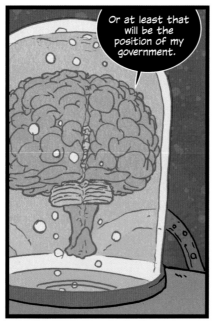

Or at least that will be the position of my government.

You're wrong. It is the greater threat...

The greatest threat.

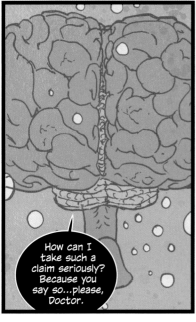

How can I take such a claim seriously? Because you say so...please, Doctor.

You believe it because we've gone out there. We've seen these things first hand.

We know.

Ah...excuse me. Hello.

My name is Yuri Gagarin, and I am the only man to have ventured into space...

I am.

Me.

The Yuri.

Well, Colonel... I'm afraid that's no longer true.

But I was still first, no?

Okay. Sure.

Good. And how exciting!

Tell us of your American space vessel.

Actually, we used a door.

I'm sure you've heard of our Torii from the Japanese -- it's like that...but much, much more powerful.

A wormhole?

You have the ability to tunnel space-time?

Minister Ustinov, this is... this is...

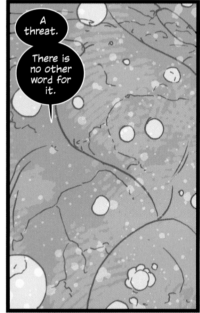

A threat.

There is no other word for it.

You seem to be missing the point, Minister.

This proxy propaganda war being fought through our science programs is a potential half-century distraction.

We are here today to ensure that doesn't happen.

And how do you propose to do that?

I was thinking, maybe, we join forces.

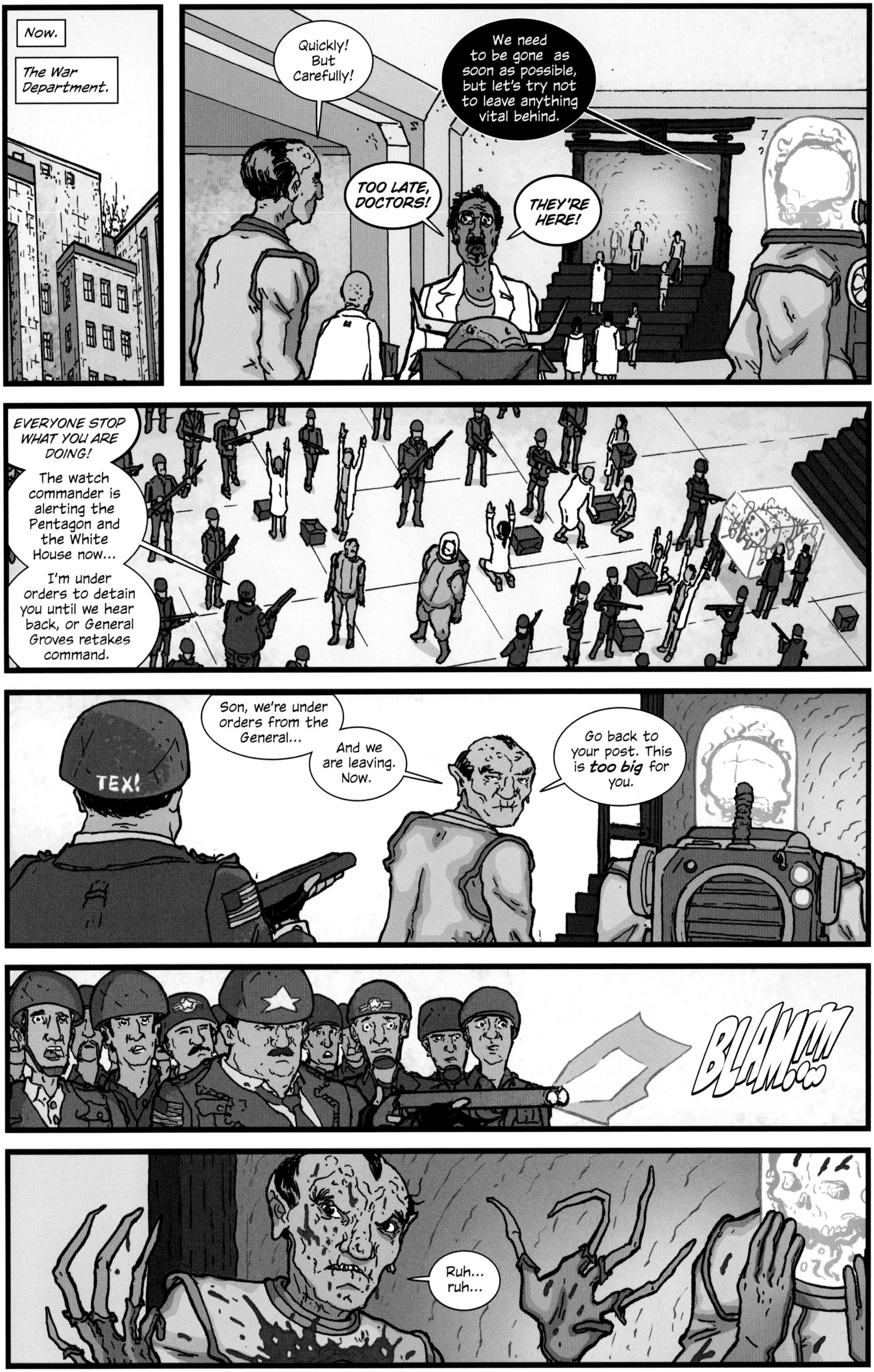

Now.
The War Department.
Quickly! But Carefully!
We need to be gone as soon as possible, but let's try not to leave anything vital behind.
TOO LATE, DOCTORS!
THEY'RE HERE!
EVERYONE STOP WHAT YOU ARE DOING!
The watch commander is alerting the Pentagon and the White House now...
I'm under orders to detain you until we hear back, or General Groves retakes command.
TEX!
Son, we're under orders from the General...
And we are leaving. Now.
Go back to your post. This is **too big** for you.
BLAM!!!
Ruh... ruh...

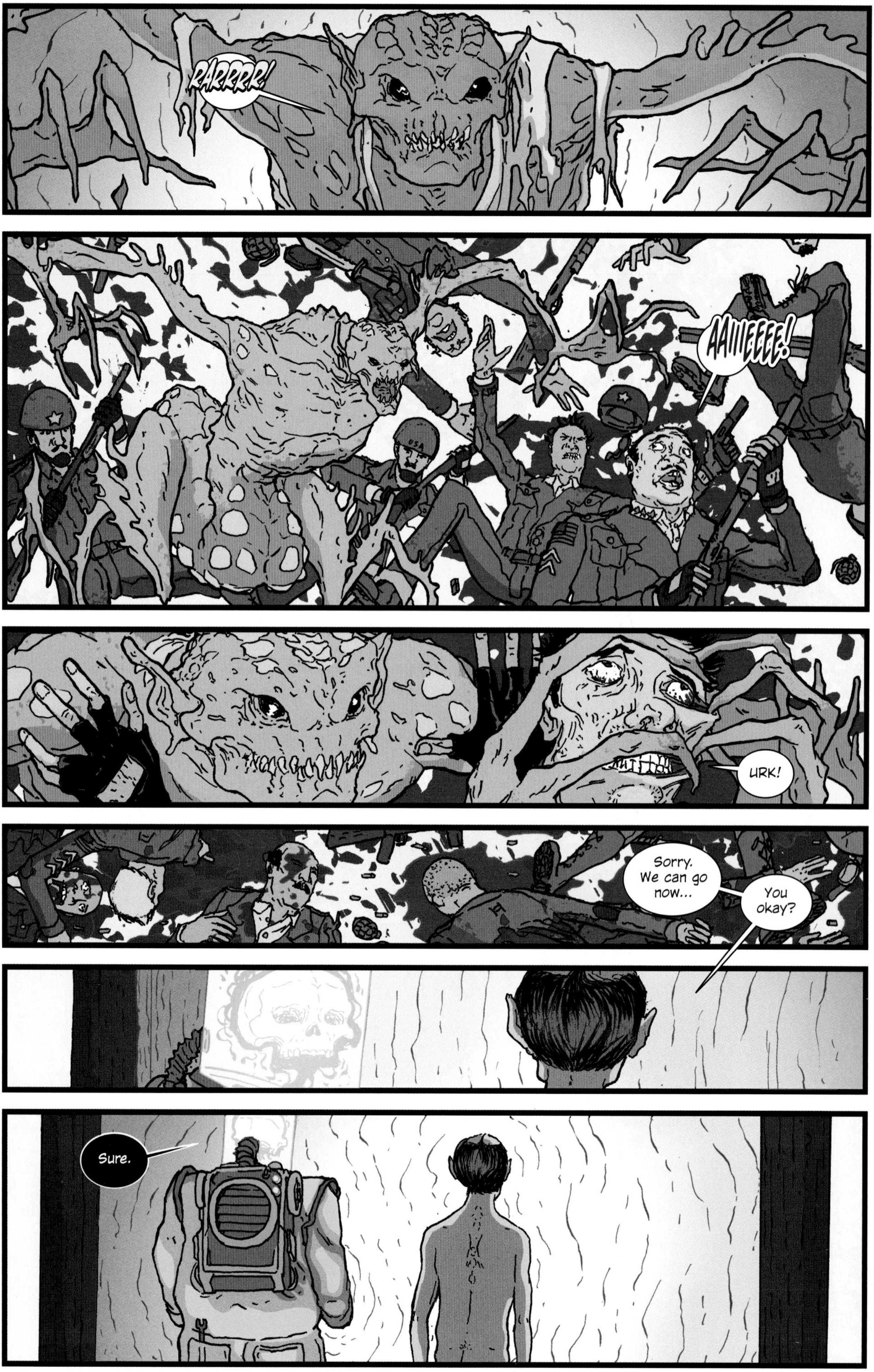
RARRRR!
AAIIIEEEE!
URK!
Sorry. We can go now...
You okay?
Sure.

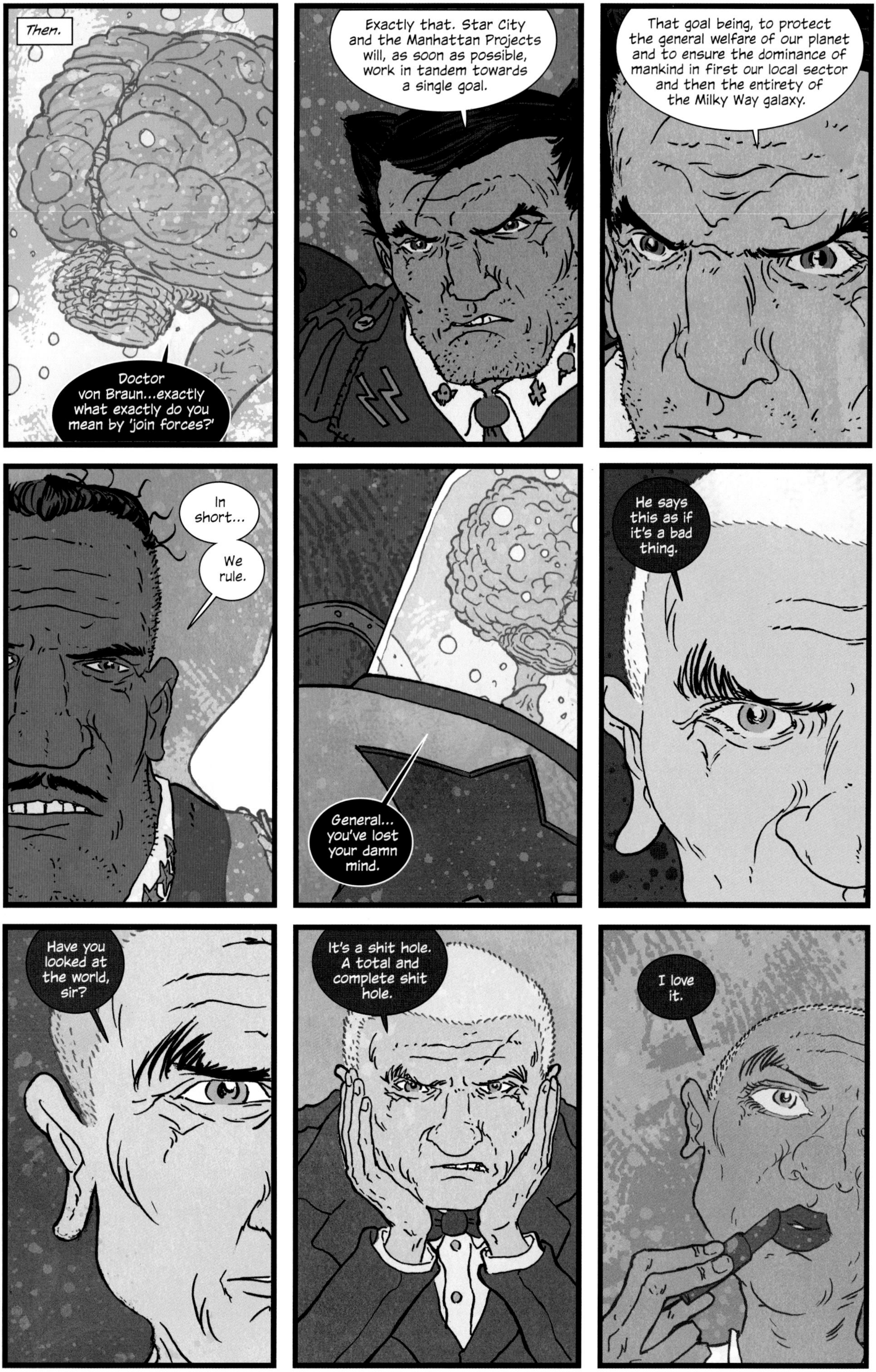
Then.
Doctor von Braun...exactly what exactly do you mean by 'join forces?'
Exactly that. Star City and the Manhattan Projects will, as soon as possible, work in tandem towards a single goal.
That goal being, to protect the general welfare of our planet and to ensure the dominance of mankind in first our local sector and then the entirety of the Milky Way galaxy.
In short...
We rule.
General... you've lost your damn mind.
He says this as if it's a bad thing.
Have you looked at the world, sir?
It's a shit hole. A total and complete shit hole.
I love it.

Hmmmm. You haven't seen what we've seen, Minister.

And once you see it, it cannot be unseen.

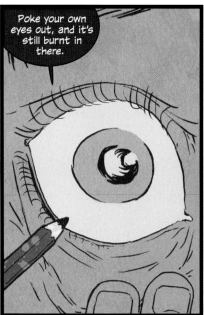

Poke your own eyes out, and it's still burnt in there.

The Doctor is not joking...

This bell can't be unrung.

My new friends!

While I am sure that some cross-pollination of ideas -- some sharing of information -- could be possible...

Getting permission within your American bureaucracy must be much easier than that of Mother Russia's.

What you say...it cannot be done.

Who said anything about asking permission?

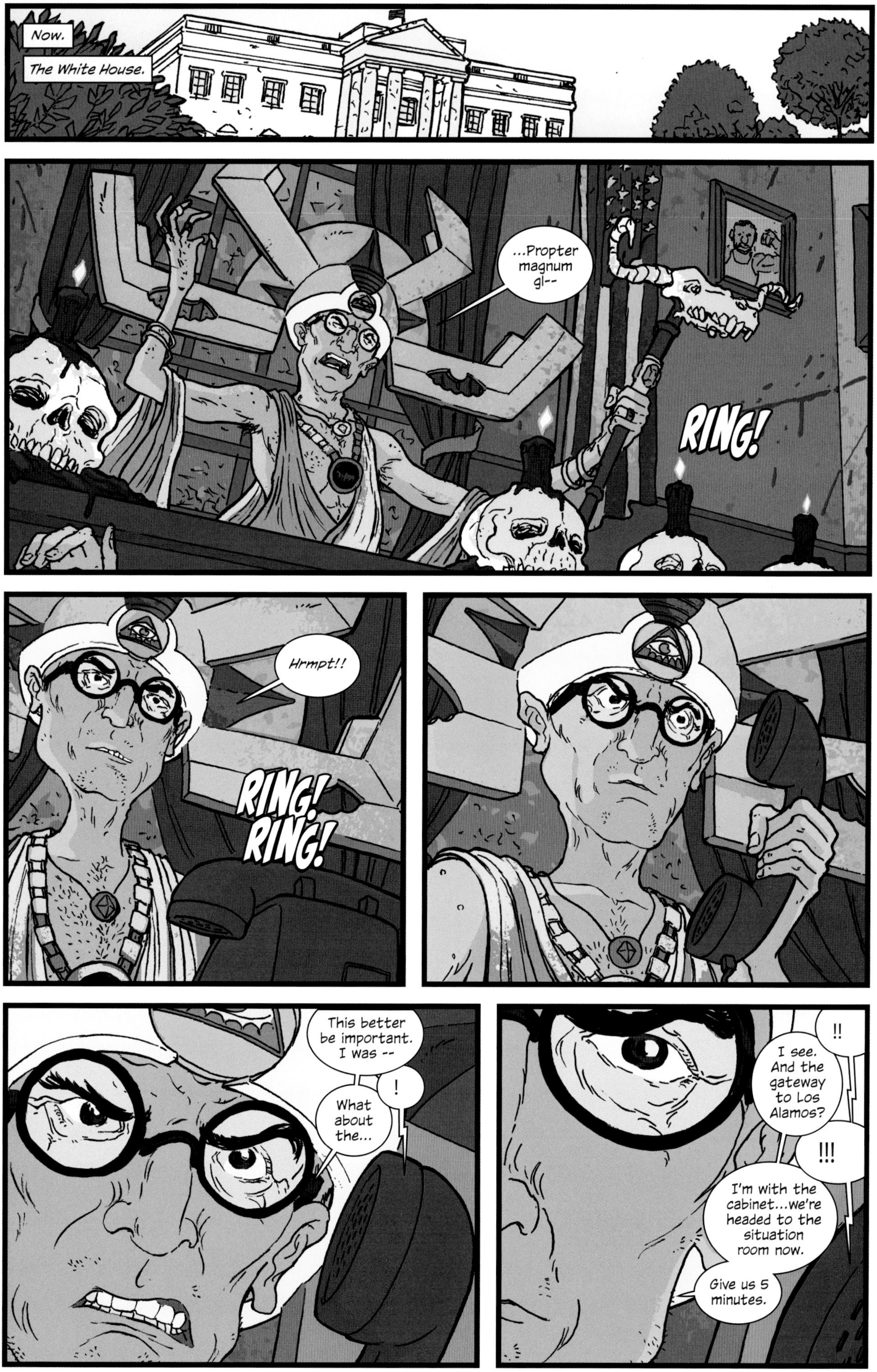
Now.
The White House.
...Propter magnum gl--
RING!
Hrmpt!!
RING! RING!
This better be important. I was --
!
What about the...
!!
I see. And the gateway to Los Alamos?
!!!
I'm with the cabinet...we're headed to the situation room now.
Give us 5 minutes.

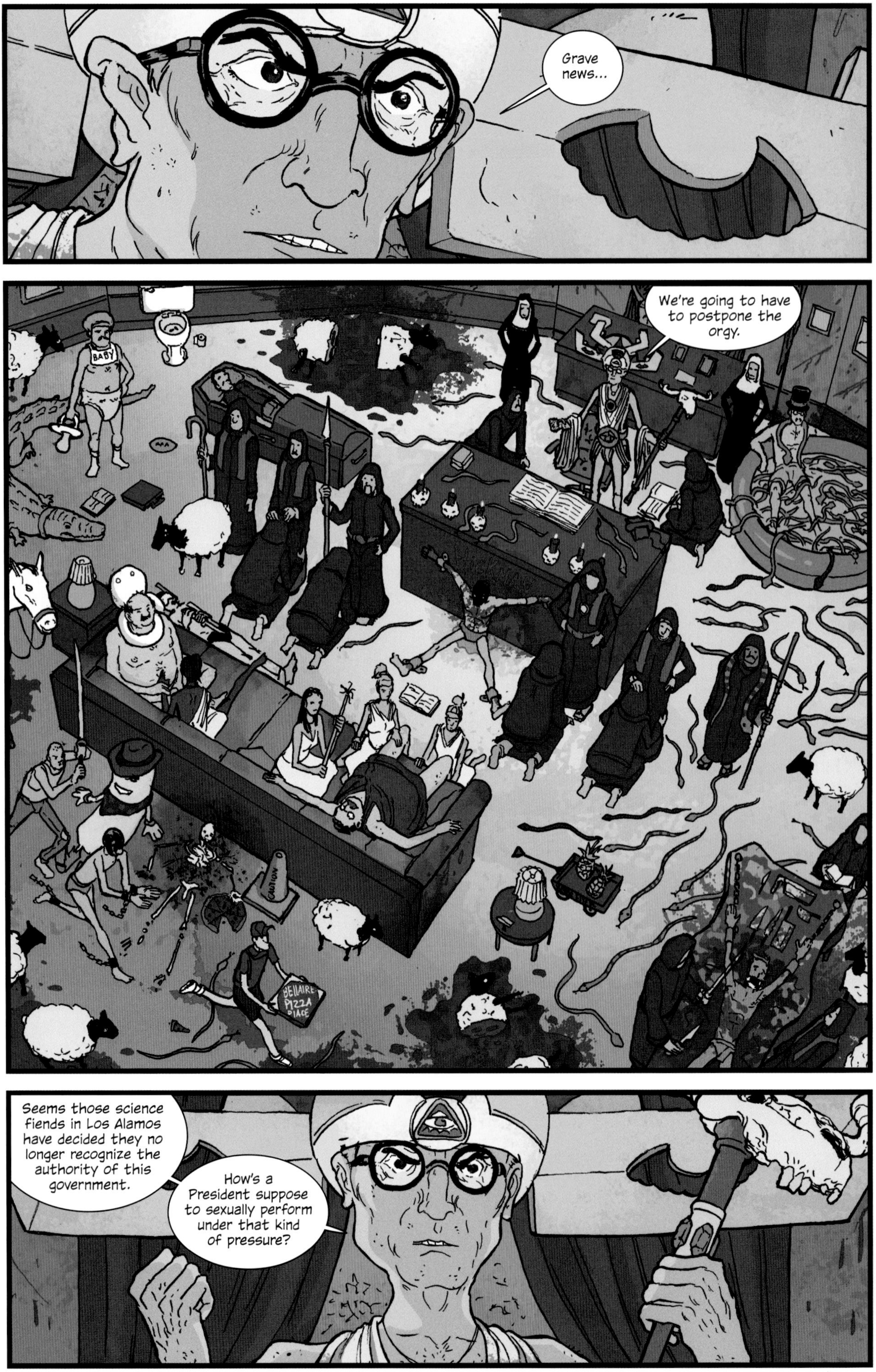

Grave news...
We're going to have to postpone the orgy.
BABY
CAUTION
BELLAIRE PIZZA PLACE
Seems those science fiends in Los Alamos have decided they no longer recognize the authority of this government.
How's a President suppose to sexually perform under that kind of pressure?

Then.
What exactly are you saying, Doctor?
You would ignore your government? You would ask us to ignore ours?
He's telling you that our position is now fuck America.
He's telling you that yours should be to hell with Russia.
From this day forward, we at the Manhattan Projects are going to focus on bigger things.
Our Governments... they will not stand for this.
Well, while we aren't asking for permission, we're also not accepting NO as an answer.
Understand?
I do not.
You understand the saying, "Speak softly and carry a big stick"?

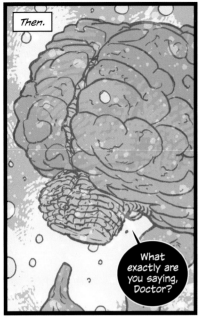

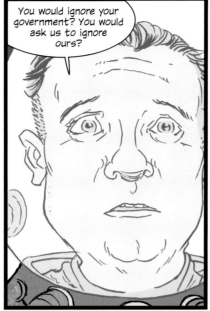

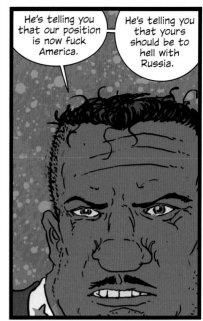

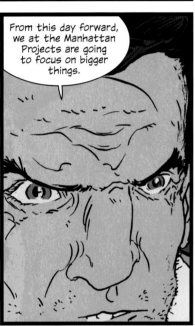

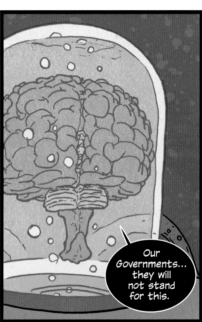

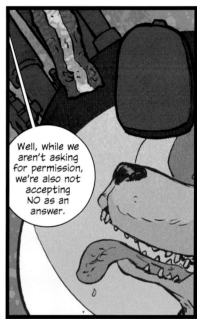

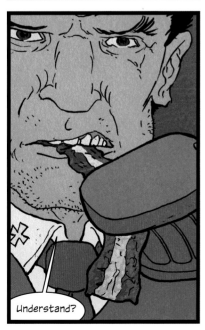

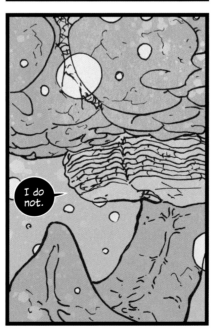

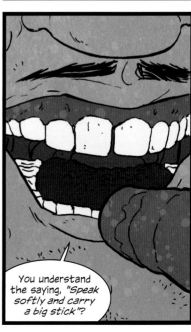

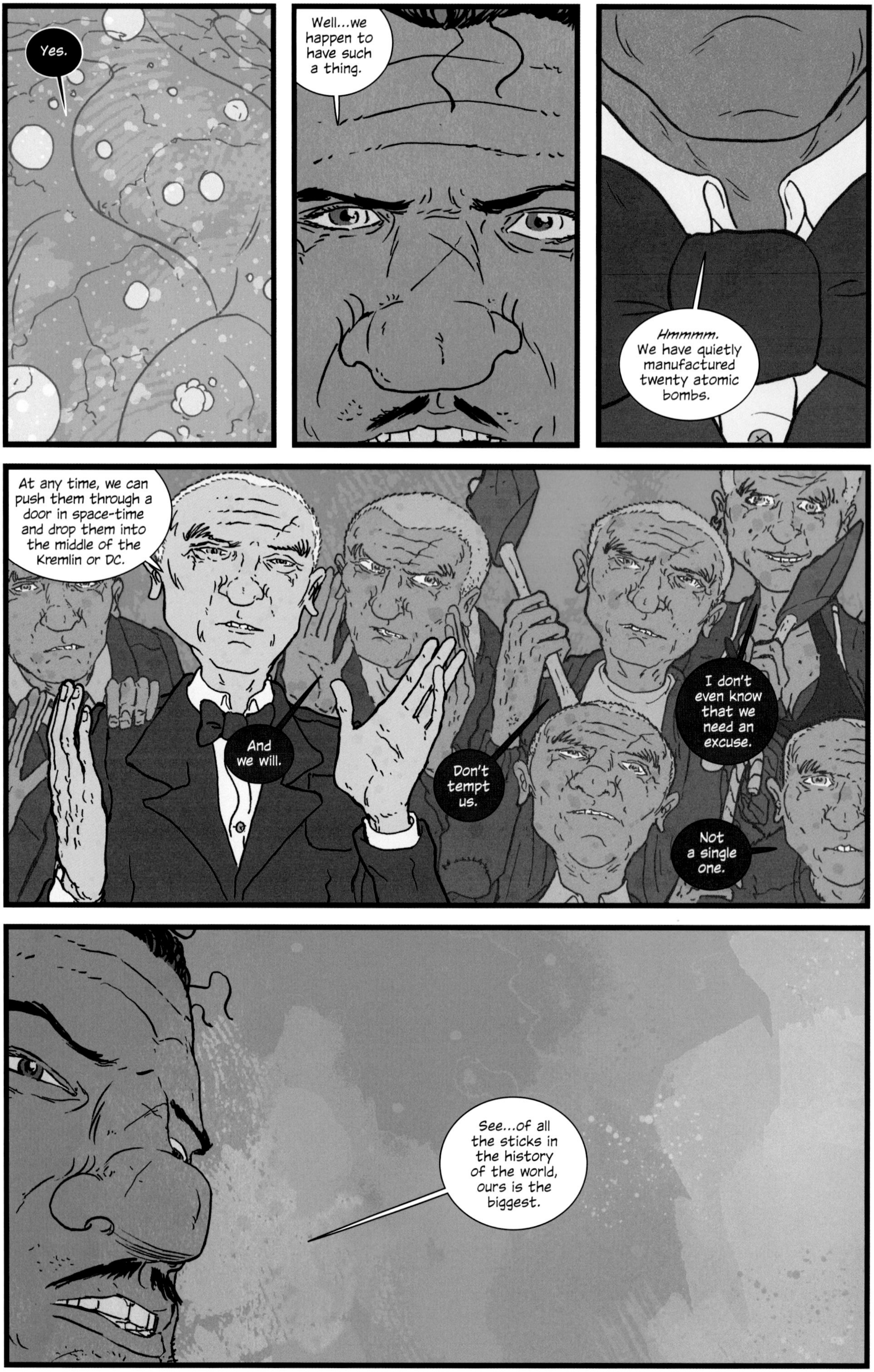
Yes.
Well...we happen to have such a thing.
Hmmmm. We have quietly manufactured twenty atomic bombs.
At any time, we can push them through a door in space-time and drop them into the middle of the Kremlin or DC.
And we will.
Don't tempt us.
I don't even know that we need an excuse.
Not a single one.
See...of all the sticks in the history of the world, ours is the biggest.

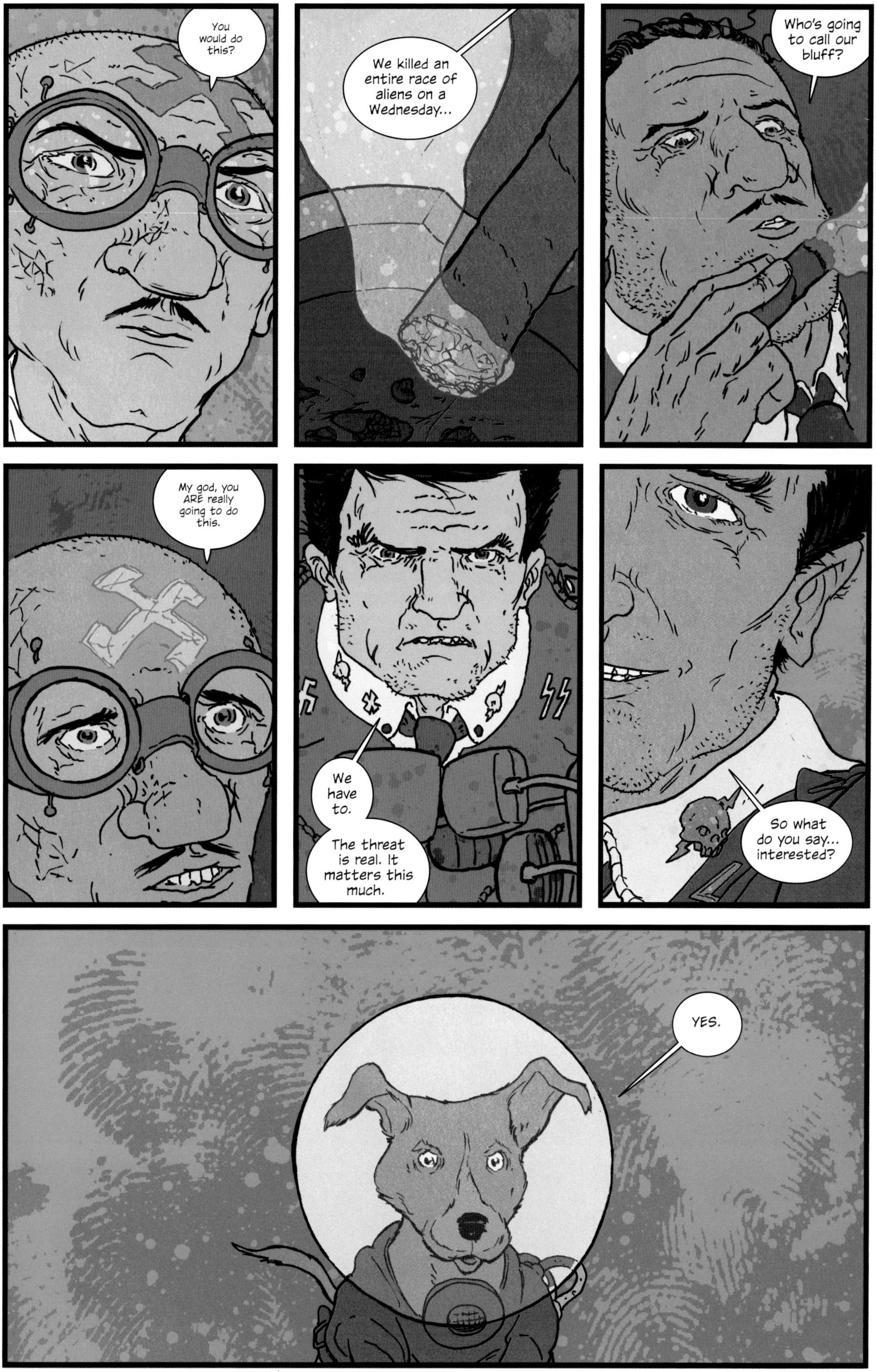

You would do this?
We killed an entire race of aliens on a Wednesday...
Who's going to call our bluff?
My god, you ARE really going to do this.
We have to.
The threat is real. It matters this much.
So what do you say... interested?
YES.

Now.

Los Alamos.

THUNK!

I see serenity in the face of certain death isn't what it used to be. These delays are becoming unacceptable.

HEY! You guys really need to suck it up a bit...we're on a pretty strict timetable.

GATE SEVEN at Eighty percent.

Is this enough power to safely travel through ze Torii?

Ze return can be handled from ze other side.

Yes.

Levels fall within acceptable parameters.

The system is secure.

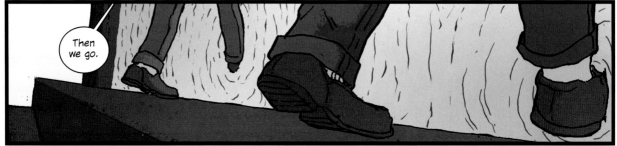

Then we go.

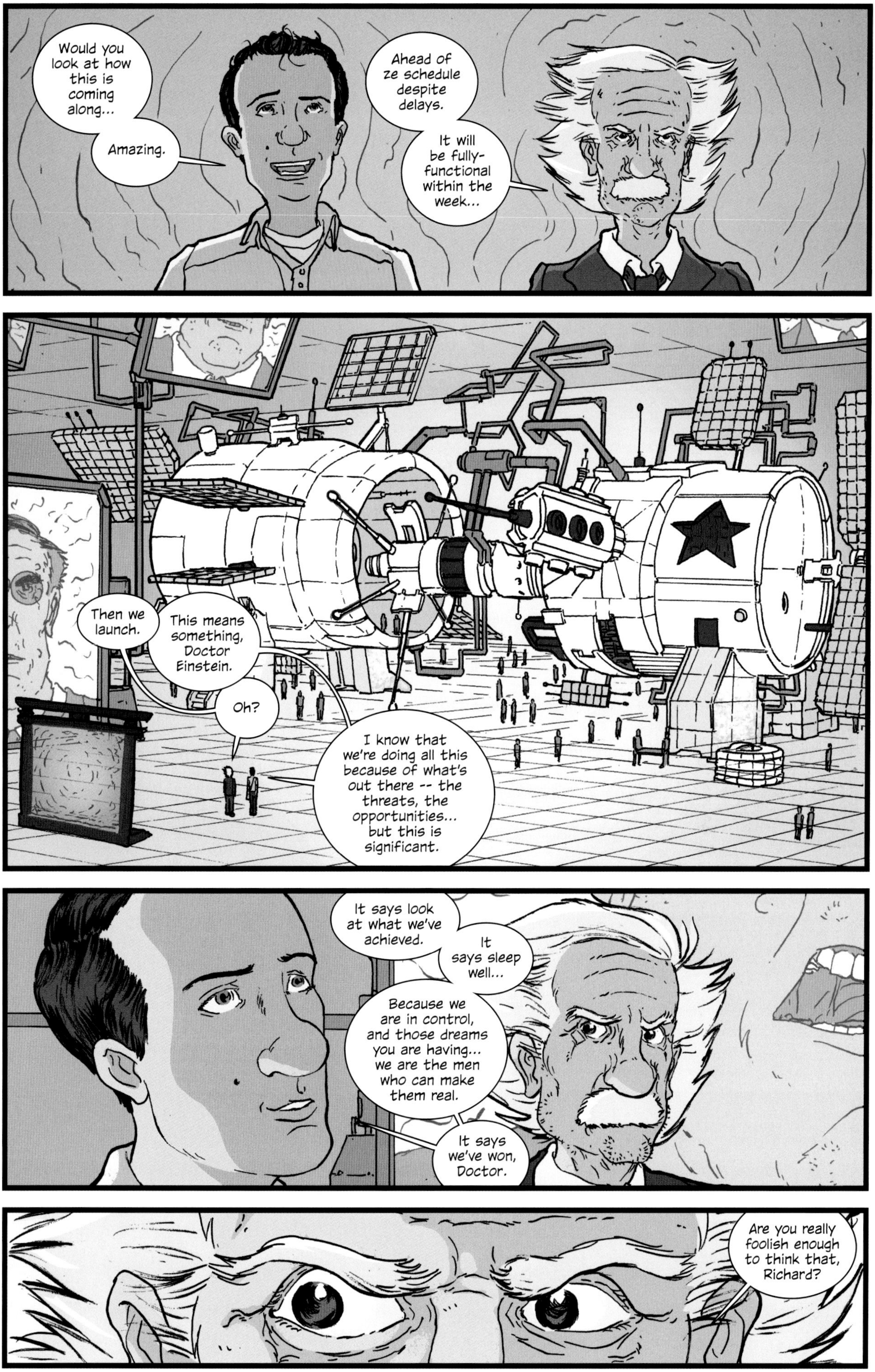
Would you look at how this is coming along...
Amazing.
Ahead of ze schedule despite delays.
It will be fully-functional within the week...
Then we launch.
This means something, Doctor Einstein.
Oh?
I know that we're doing all this because of what's out there -- the threats, the opportunities... but this is significant.
It says look at what we've achieved.
It says sleep well...
Because we are in control, and those dreams you are having... we are the men who can make them real.
It says we've won, Doctor.
Are you really foolish enough to think that, Richard?

That we have won?

Incoming transfer from Star City -- containment team report to Gateway *four.*

Because we have not -- Not yet.

This is just ze beginning of the oldest story in ze world.

Somewhere out there are ze people who have run this world in secret for years and years.

Ze men with power.

Ze men with money.

They are not used to being told what to do and they most surely will not accept their new place in our new world order.

They will respond, these men...

These lords of commerce.

These **KINGS.**

These **DICTATORS.**

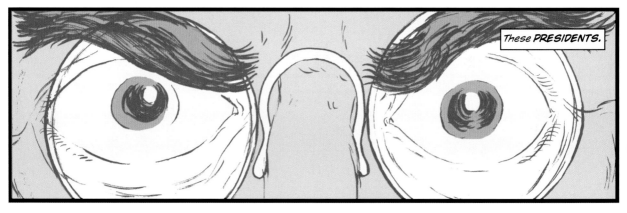

These **PRESIDENTS.**

"WHO STANDS ON A HILL AND DECLARES THEY ARE KING?

FOOLS."

CLAVIS AUREA
THE RECORDED FEYNMAN | **VOL. 3**

I WILL PAY IT
IN FULL

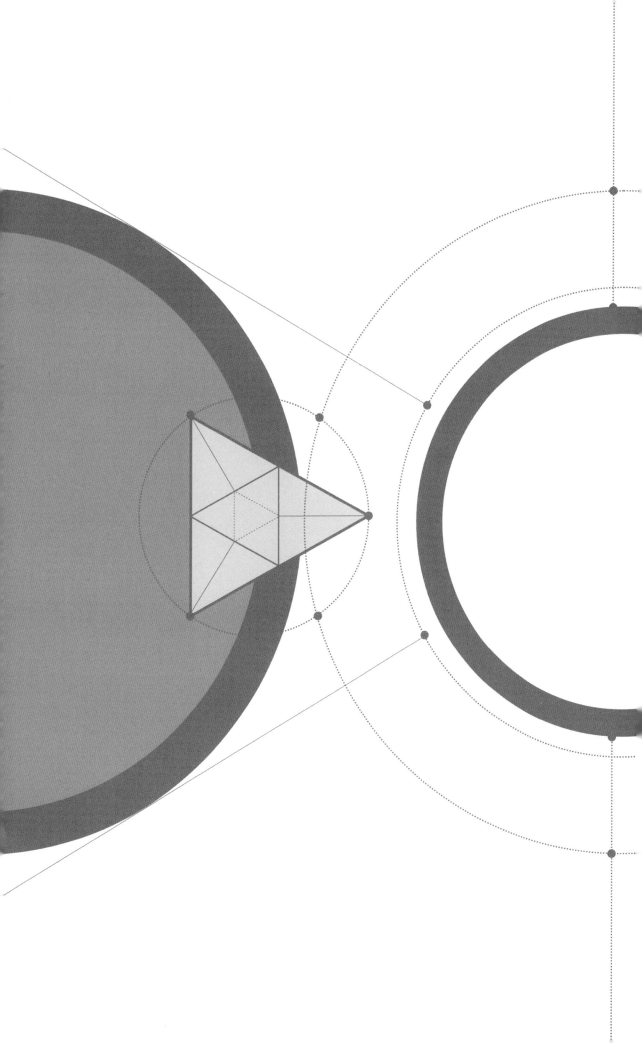

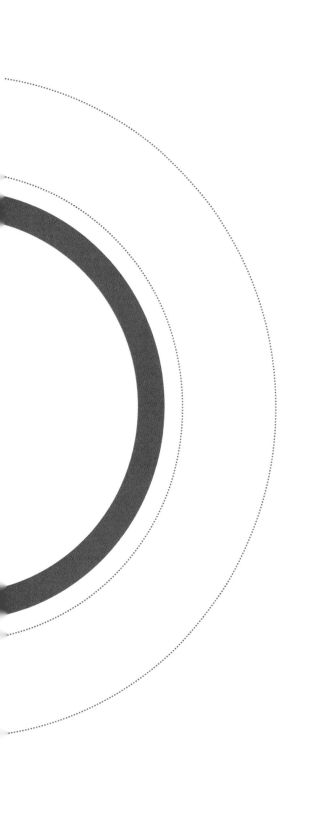

"TO FOLLOW IS TO YIELD. "

CLAVIS AUREA
THE RECORDED FEYNMAN | **VOL. 2**

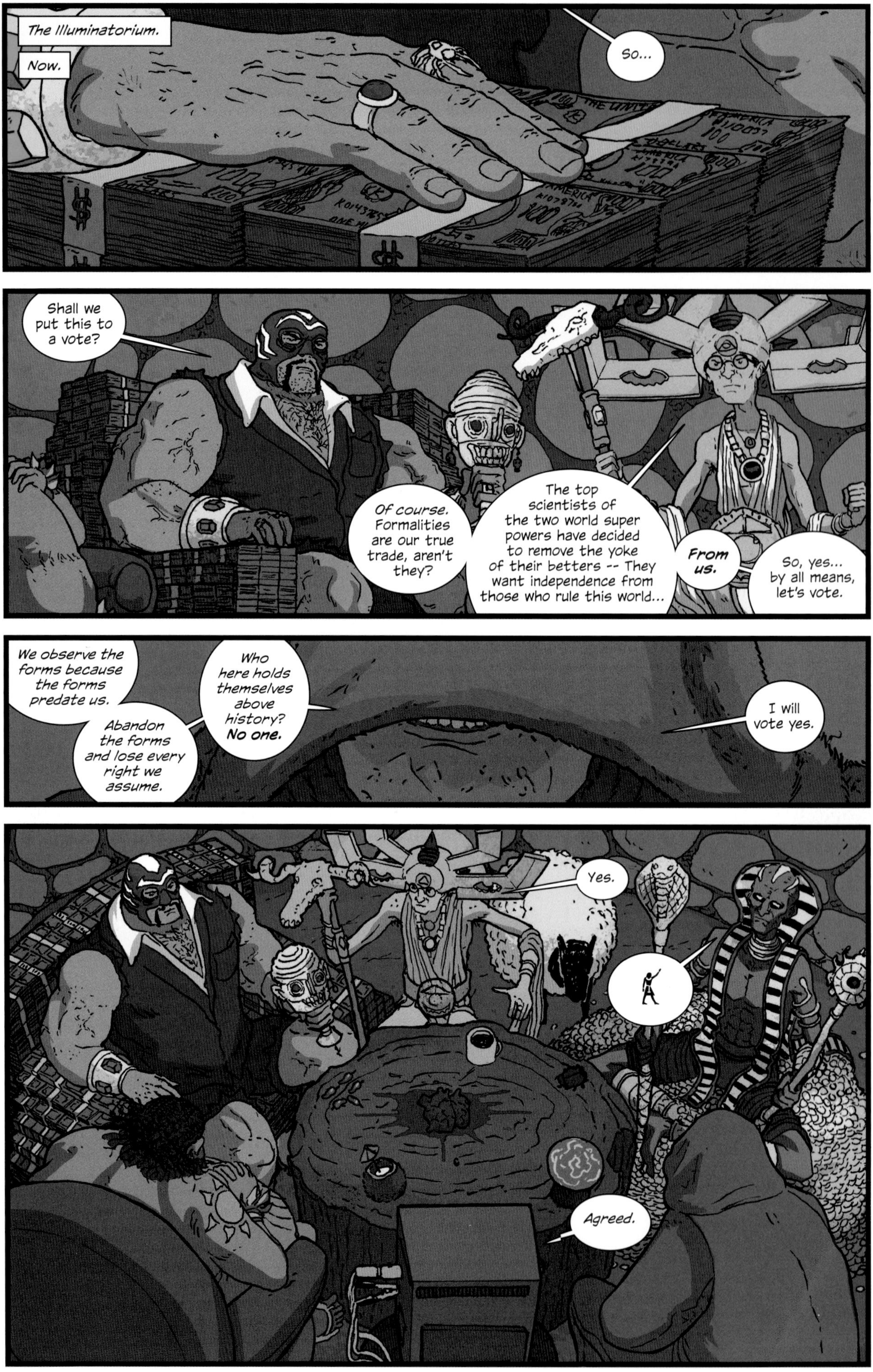
The Illuminatorium.
Now.
So...
Shall we put this to a vote?
Of course. Formalities are our true trade, aren't they?
The top scientists of the two world super powers have decided to remove the yoke of their betters -- They want independence from those who rule this world...
From us.
So, yes... by all means, let's vote.
We observe the forms because the forms predate us.
Abandon the forms and lose every right we assume.
Who here holds themselves above history? No one.
I will vote yes.
Yes.
Agreed.

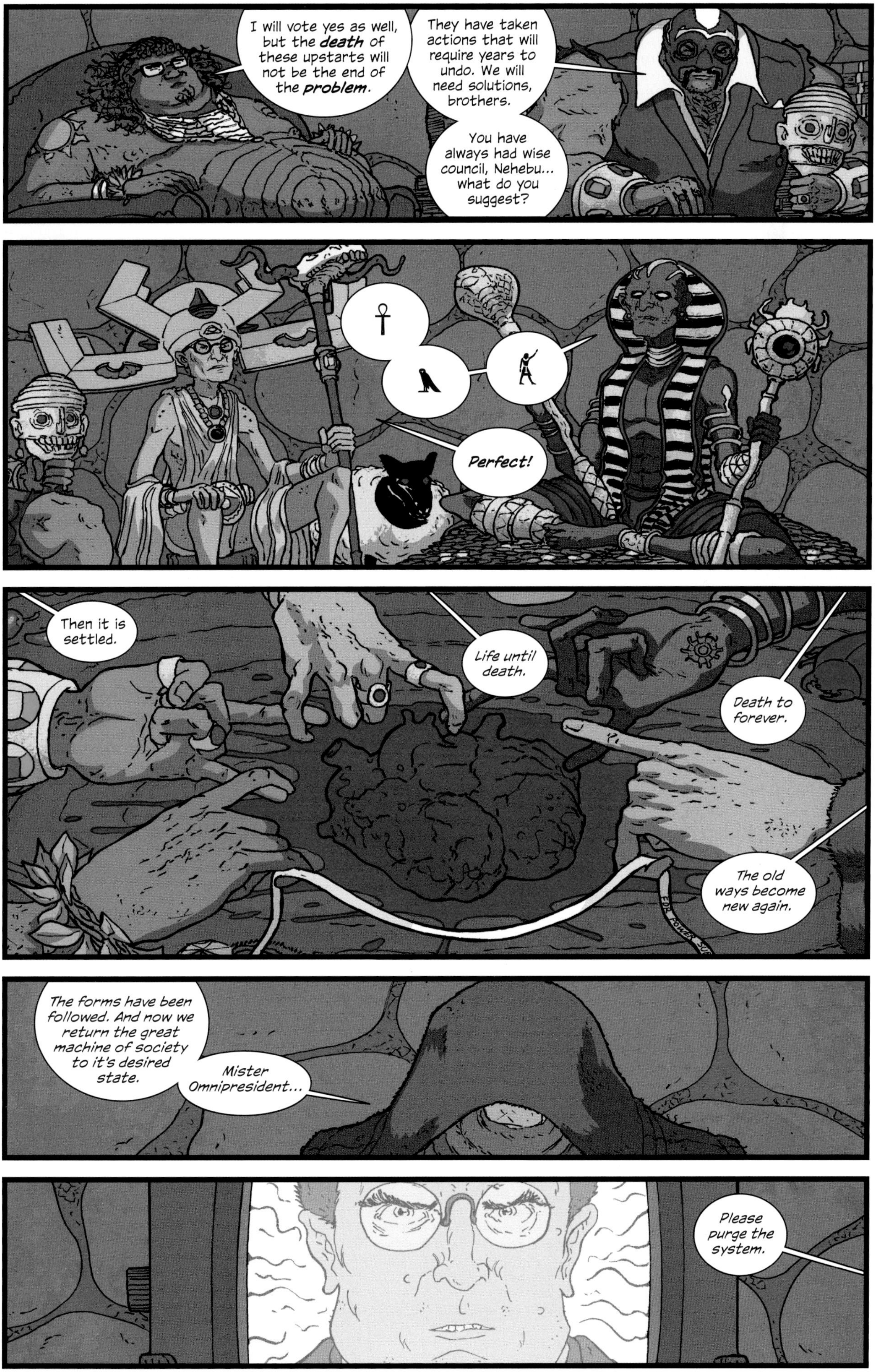
I will vote yes as well, but the death of these upstarts will not be the end of the problem.
They have taken actions that will require years to undo. We will need solutions, brothers.
You have always had wise council, Nehebu... what do you suggest?
Perfect!
Then it is settled.
Life until death.
Death to forever.
The old ways become new again.
The forms have been followed. And now we return the great machine of society to it's desired state.
Mister Omnipresident...
Please purge the system.

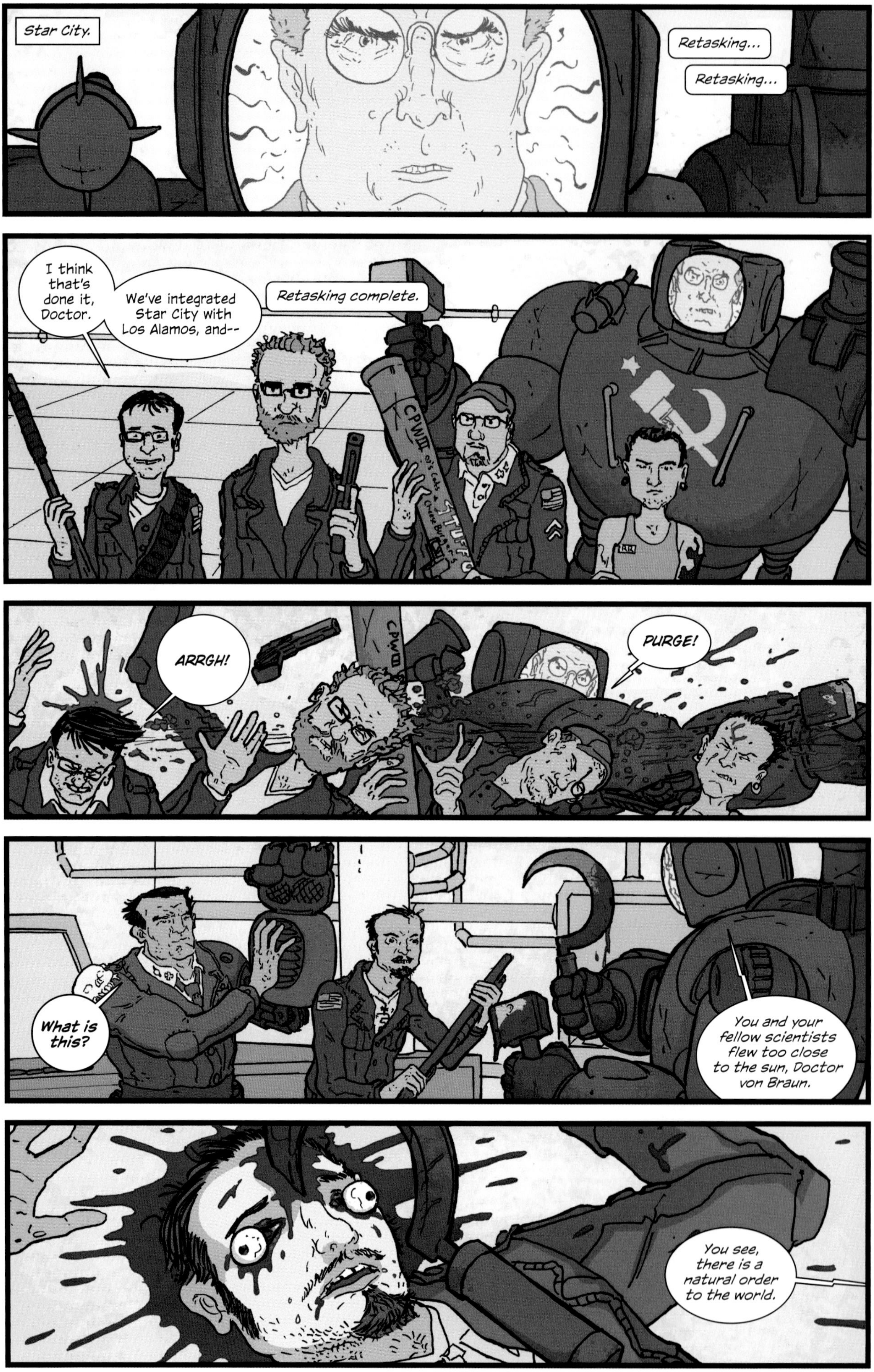
Star City.
Retasking...
Retasking...
I think that's done it, Doctor.
We've integrated Star City with Los Alamos, and--
Retasking complete.
ARRGH!
PURGE!
What is this?
You and your fellow scientists flew too close to the sun, Doctor von Braun.
You see, there is a natural order to the world.

Unfortunately, just like the turning of seasons, you can always count on a period of upheaval every few generations.
It comes from men like you, reaching too far for their own good.
Climbing higher than their station, refusing to be content with what they have been allowed to have.
And this is how it always ends...
With men like me -- **your betters** -- making an example of those who want too much.
RAARRR!
Tell me, Doctor...
Do you think there's a special hell for Nazis who thought they could do enough to erase their sins?
ZZZAMMMM!
BBZZTT!

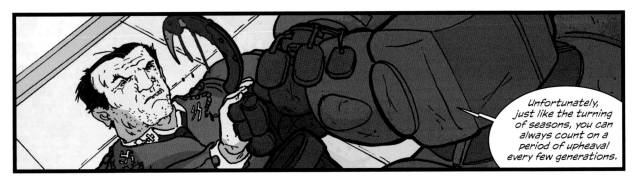

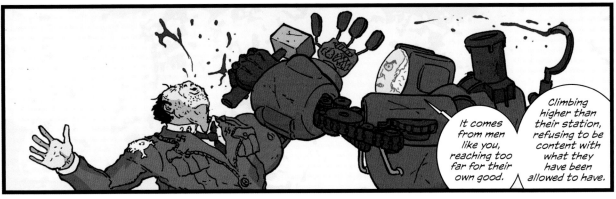

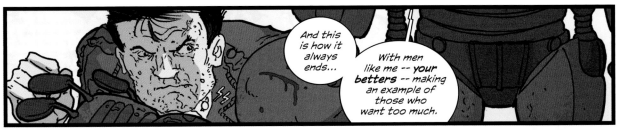

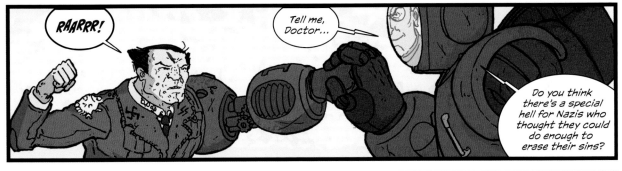

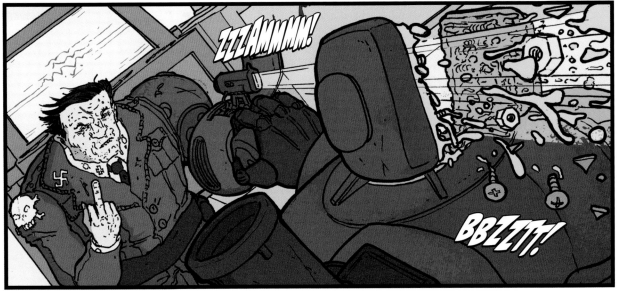

Yes.
BZZZT!
Well, then...
Let's get busy on sending you there.

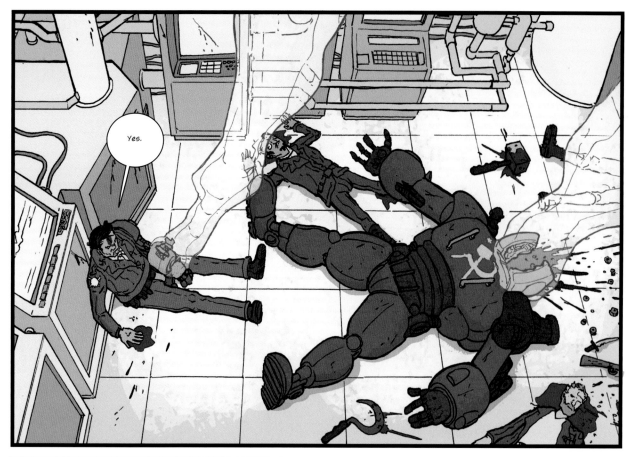

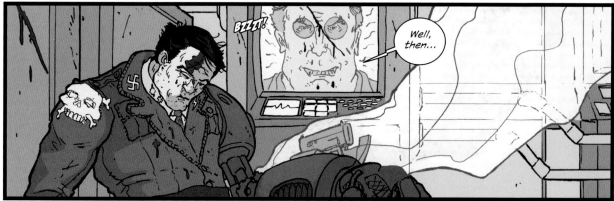

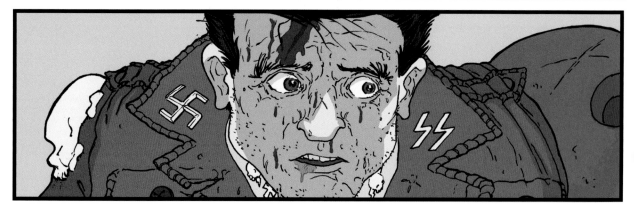

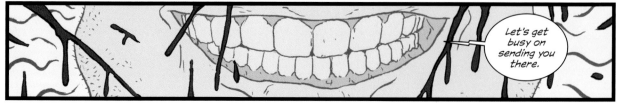

"THE WORLD HAS RULES, CREATED BY THOSE WHO CONSIDER THEMSELVES ABOVE THEM.

SO WE BECAME RADICALS, WHO ACCEPTED NEITHER."

CLAVIS AUREA
THE RECORDED FEYNMAN

VOL. 1

08

THEY RULE

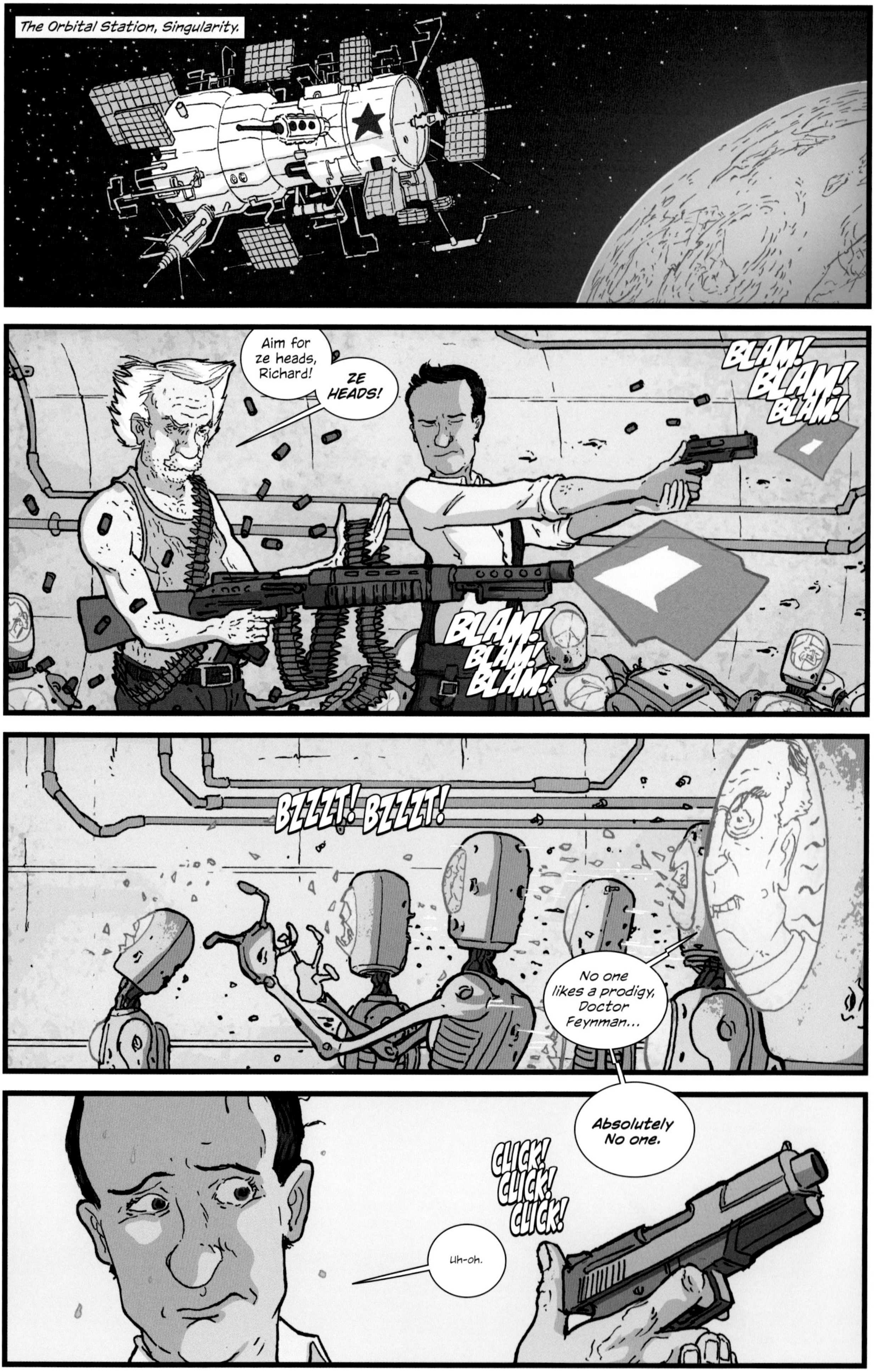
The Orbital Station, Singularity.
Aim for ze heads, Richard!
ZE HEADS!
BLAM! BLAM! BLAM!
BLAM! BLAM! BLAM!
BZZZT! BZZZT!
No one likes a prodigy, Doctor Feynman...
Absolutely No one.
CLICK! CLICK! CLICK!
Uh-oh.

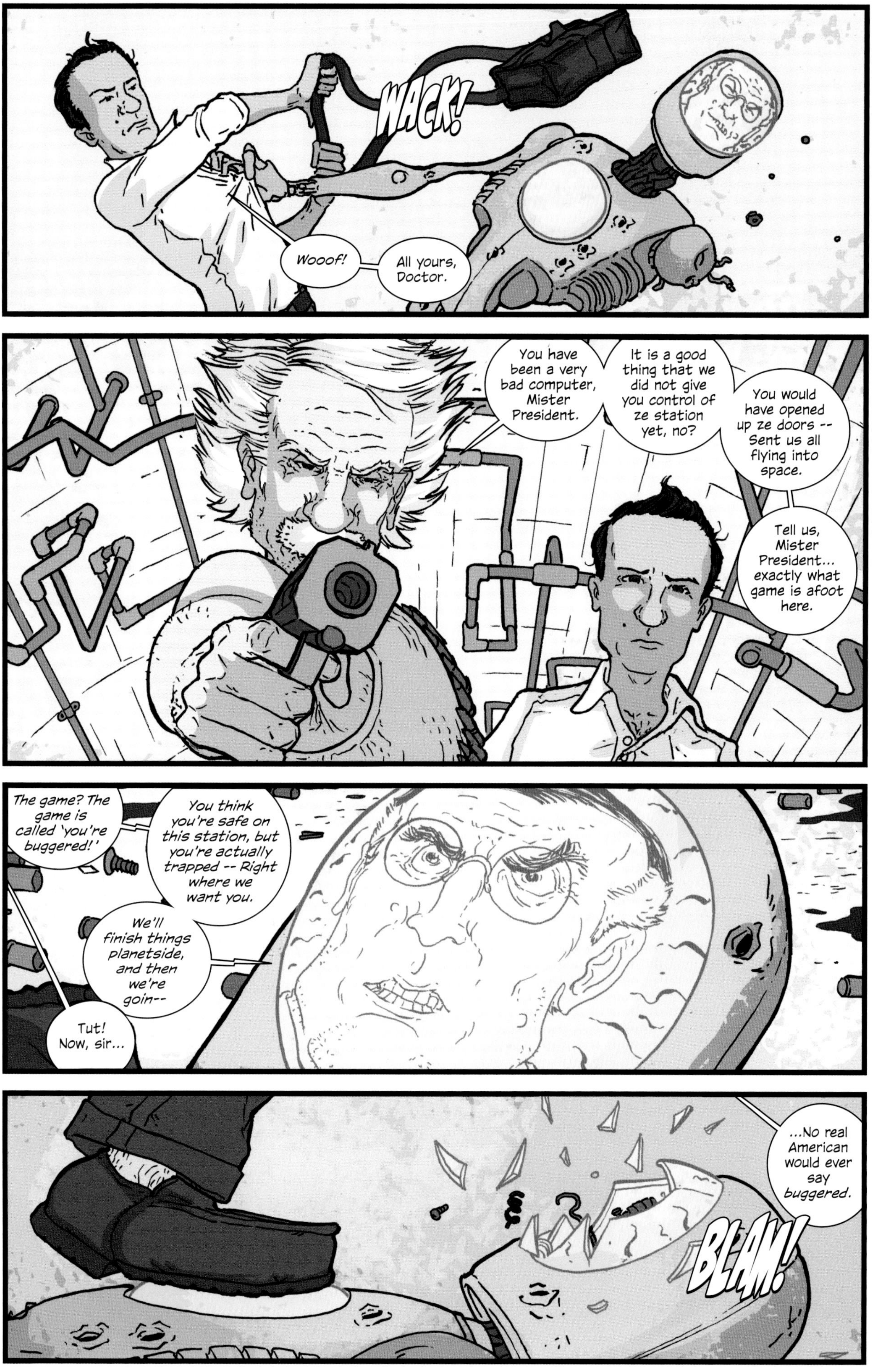
WACK!
Wooof!
All yours, Doctor.
You have been a very bad computer, Mister President.
It is a good thing that we did not give you control of ze station yet, no?
You would have opened up ze doors -- Sent us all flying into space.
Tell us, Mister President... exactly what game is afoot here.
The game? The game is called 'you're buggered!'
You think you're safe on this station, but you're actually trapped -- Right where we want you.
We'll finish things planetside, and then we're goin--
Tut! Now, sir...
...No real American would ever say buggered.
BLAM!

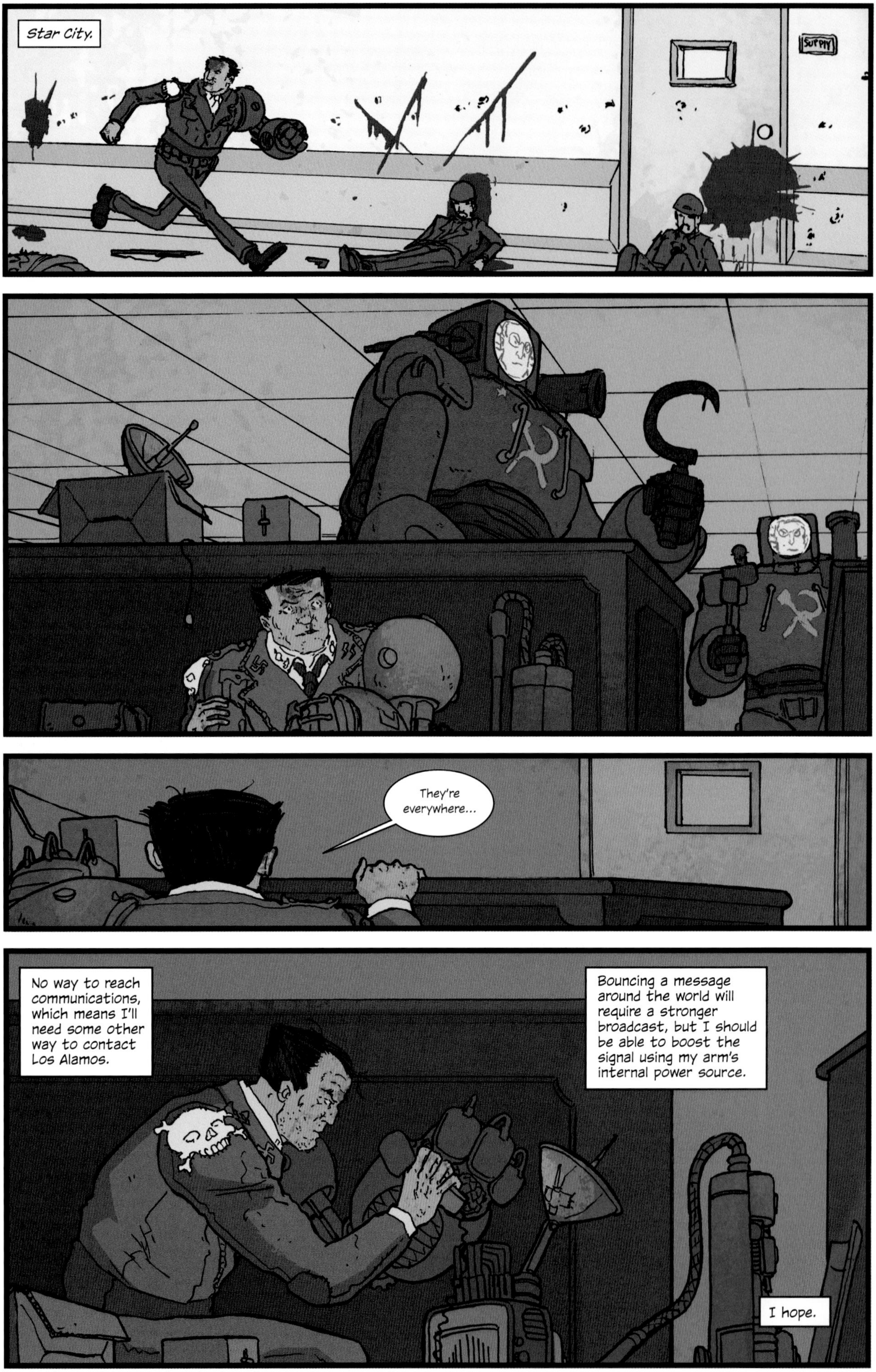
Star City.
They're everywhere...
No way to reach communications, which means I'll need some other way to contact Los Alamos.
Bouncing a message around the world will require a stronger broadcast, but I should be able to boost the signal using my arm's internal power source.
I hope.

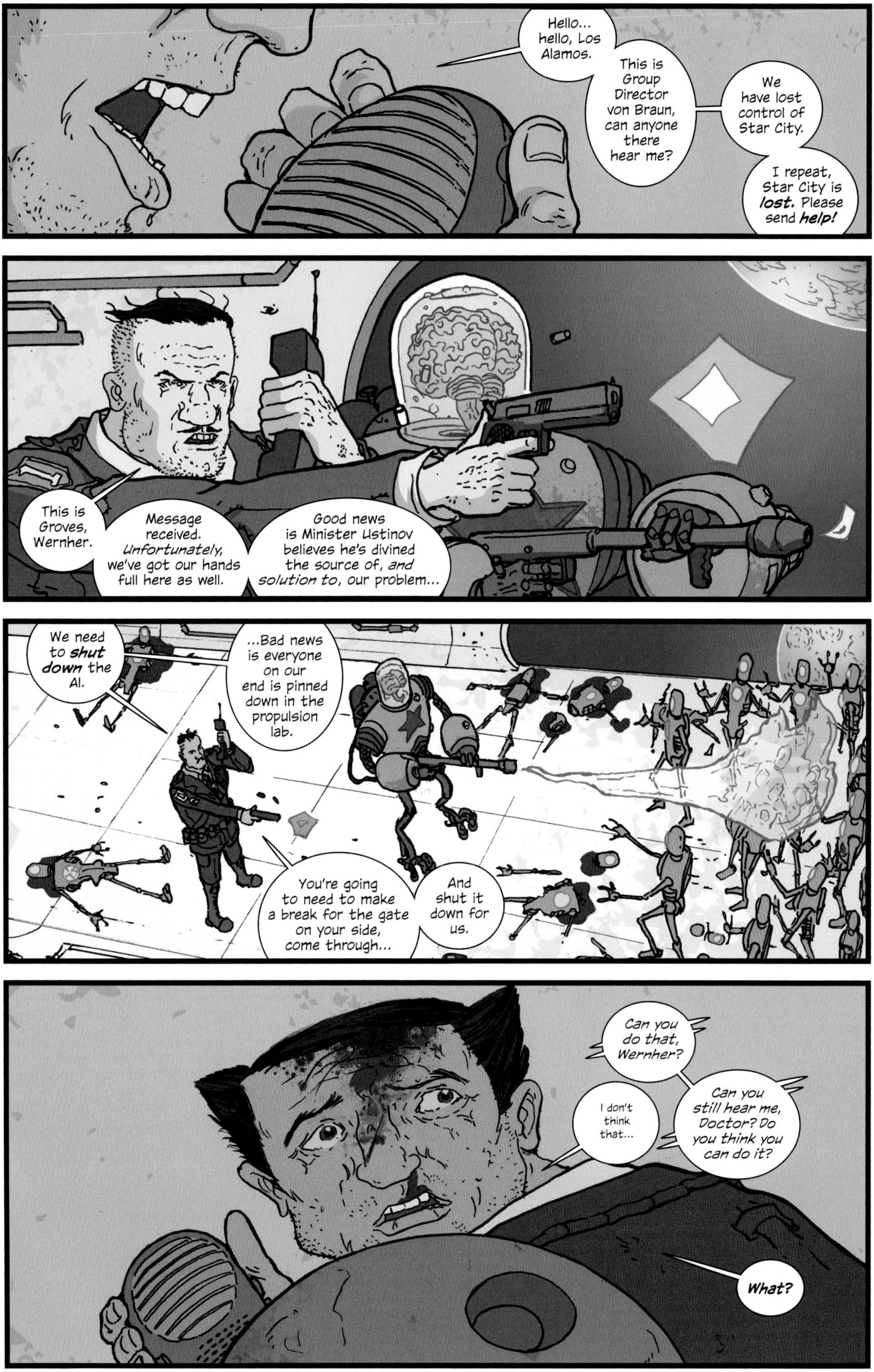
Hello... hello, Los Alamos.
This is Group Director von Braun, can anyone there hear me?
We have lost control of Star City.
I repeat, Star City is ***lost.*** Please send ***help!***
This is Groves, Wernher.
Message received. *Unfortunately,* we've got our hands full here as well.
Good news is Minister Ustinov believes he's divined the source of, *and solution to*, our problem...
...Bad news is everyone on our end is pinned down in the propulsion lab.
We need to ***shut down*** the AI.
You're going to need to make a break for the gate on your side, come through...
And shut it down for us.
Can you do that, Wernher?
Can you still hear me, Doctor? Do you think you can do it?
I don't think that...
What?

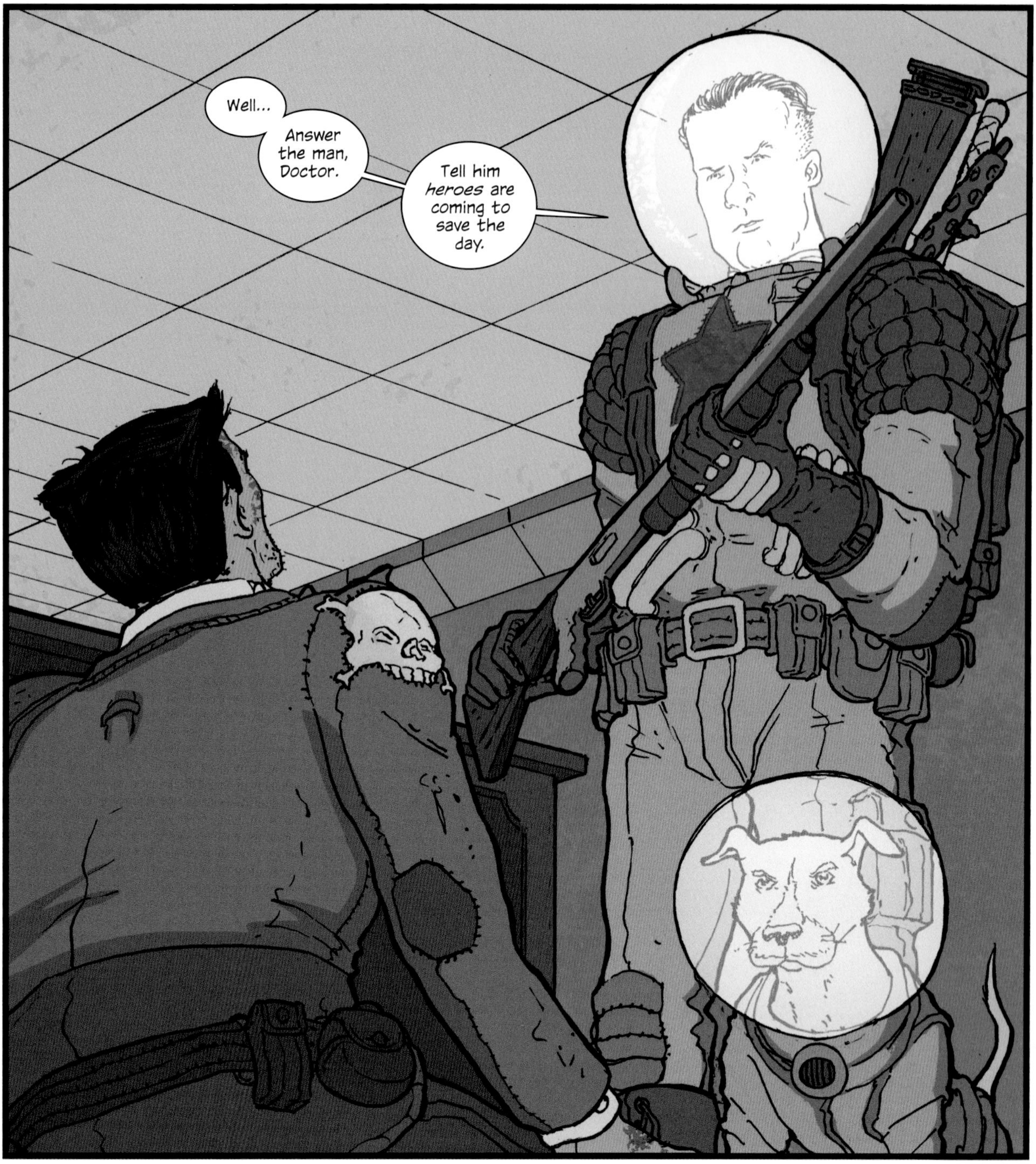
Well...
Answer the man, Doctor.
Tell him *heroes* are coming to save the day.

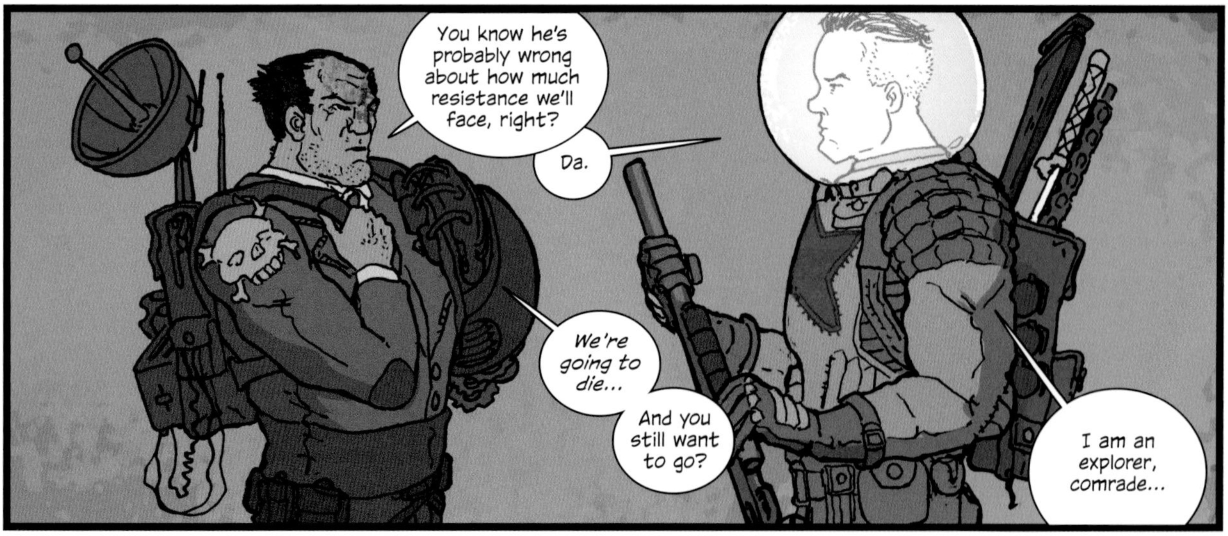
You know he's probably wrong about how much resistance we'll face, right?
Da.
We're going to *die...*
And you still want to go?
I am an explorer, comrade...

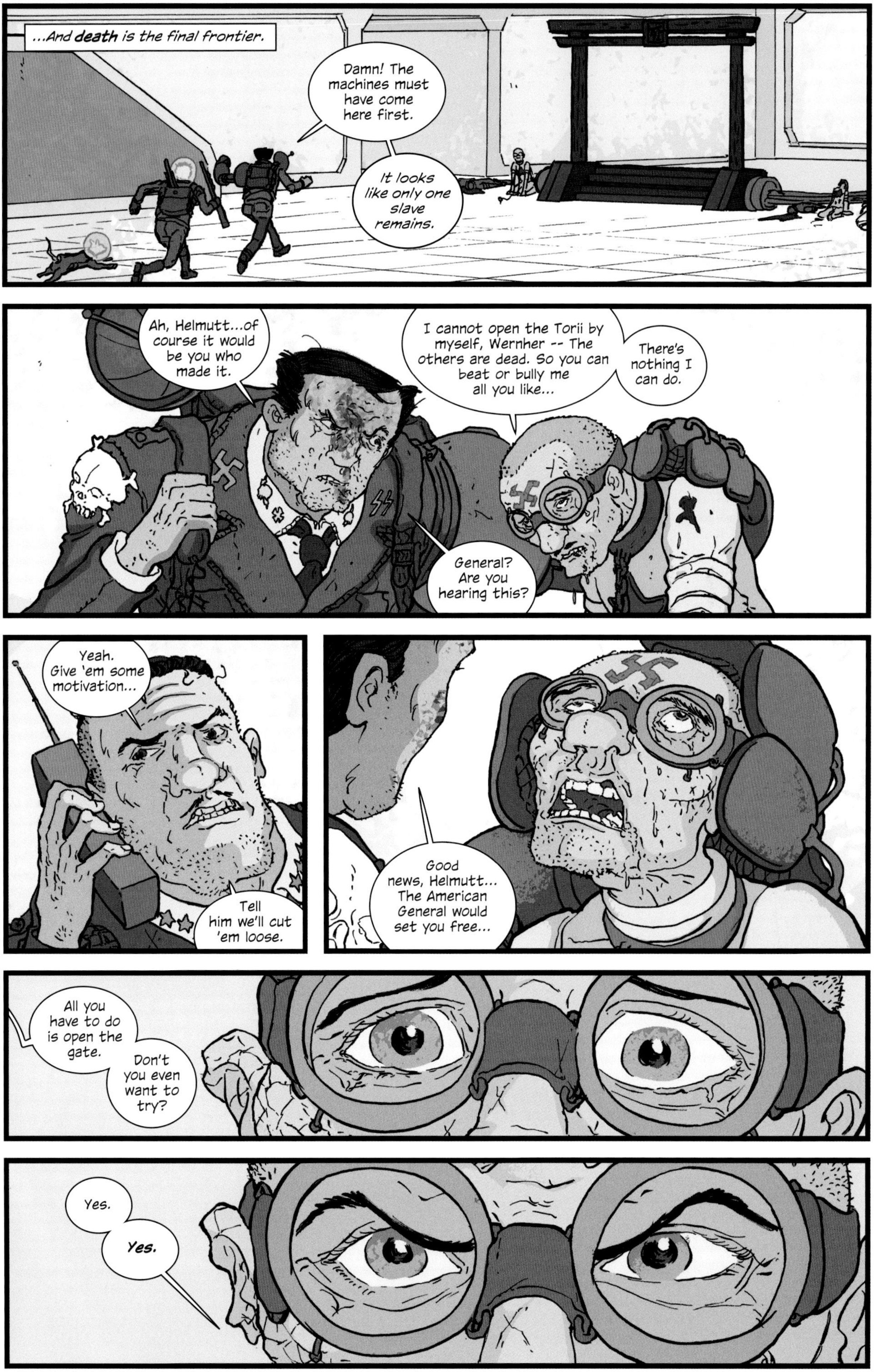
...And death is the final frontier.
Damn! The machines must have come here first.
It looks like only one slave remains.
Ah, Helmutt...of course it would be you who made it.
I cannot open the Torii by myself, Wernher -- The others are dead. So you can beat or bully me all you like...
There's nothing I can do.
General? Are you hearing this?
Yeah. Give 'em some motivation...
Tell him we'll cut 'em loose.
Good news, Helmutt... The American General would set you free...
All you have to do is open the gate.
Don't you even want to try?
Yes.
Yes.

Yes!
ARRRGGHH!

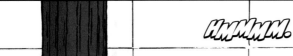

HMMMM.

FWASH!

Okay. Gate's open.

What about the Nazi? The General said--

Deception, Yuri...why don't we let the hündin decide?

Okay.

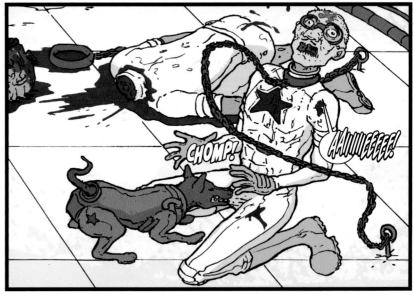

CHOMP!

AAUUUEEEEE!

"Now we go."

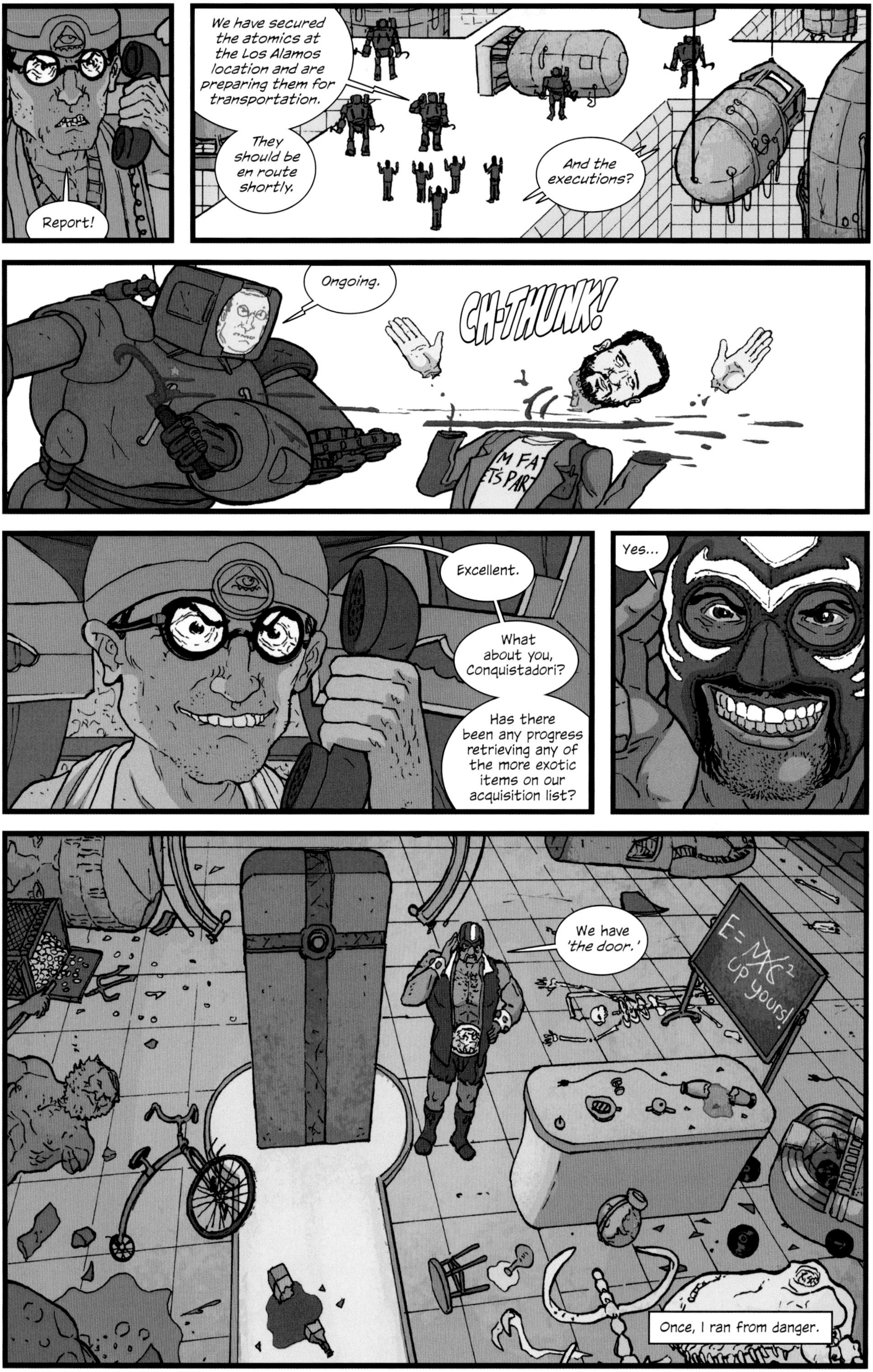
Report!
We have secured the atomics at the Los Alamos location and are preparing them for transportation.
They should be en route shortly.
And the executions?
Ongoing.
CH-THUNK!
Excellent.
What about you, Conquistadori?
Has there been any progress retrieving any of the more exotic items on our acquisition list?
Yes...
We have 'the door.'
E = MC^2
up yours!
Once, I ran from danger.

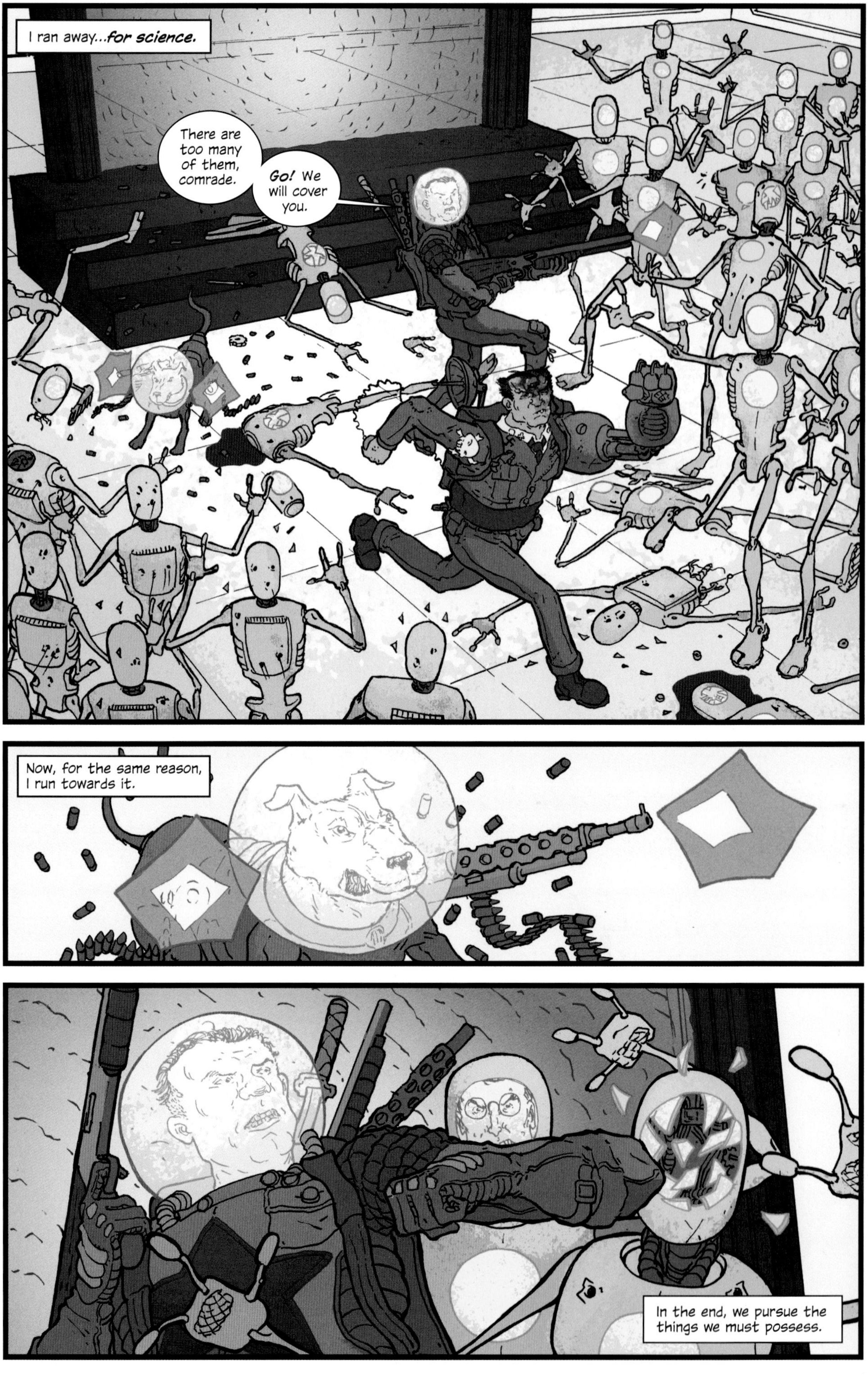

I ran away...**for science.**
There are too many of them, comrade.
Go! We will cover you.
Now, for the same reason, I run towards it.
In the end, we pursue the things we must possess.

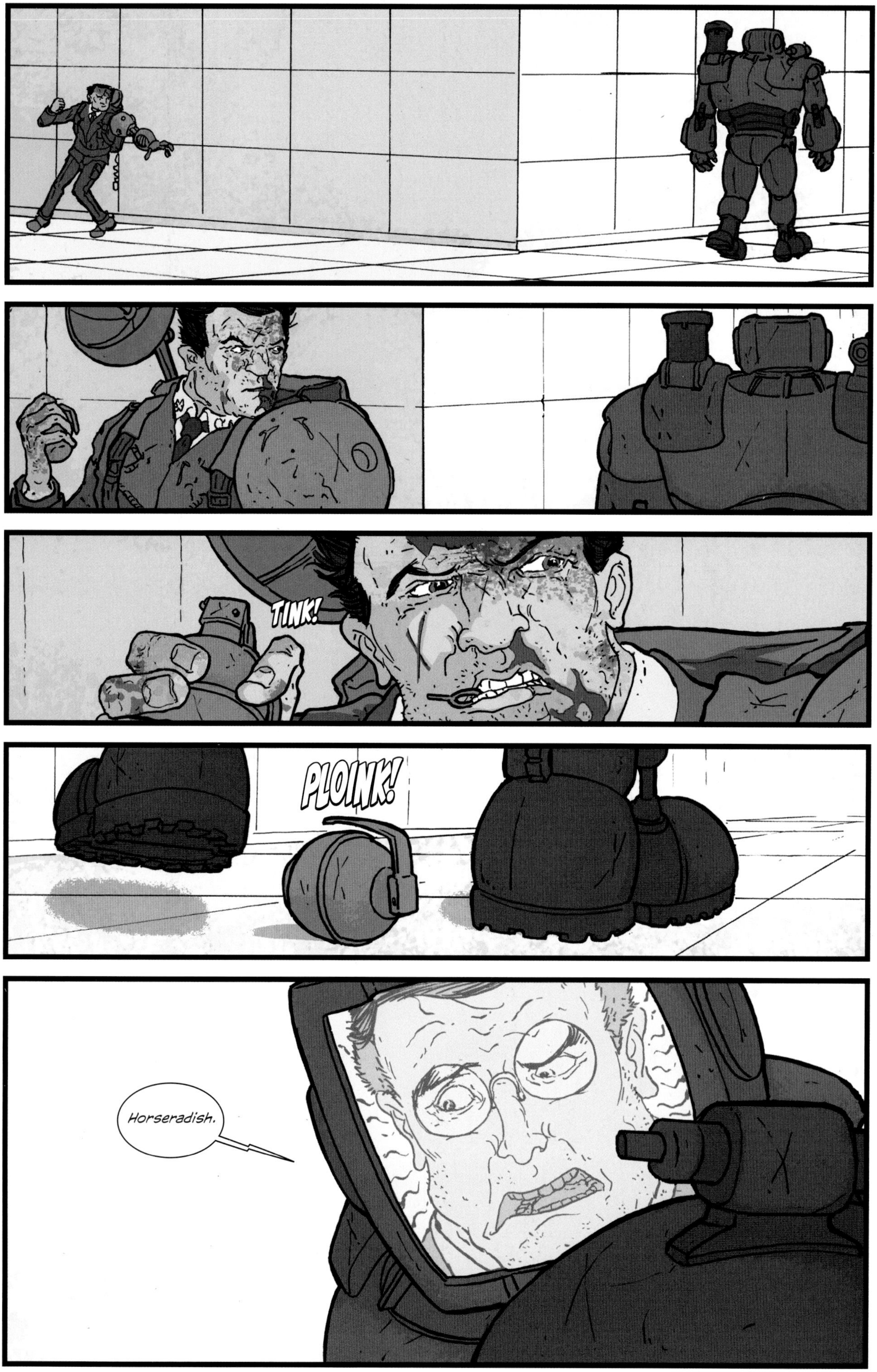
TINK!
PLOINK!
Horseradish.

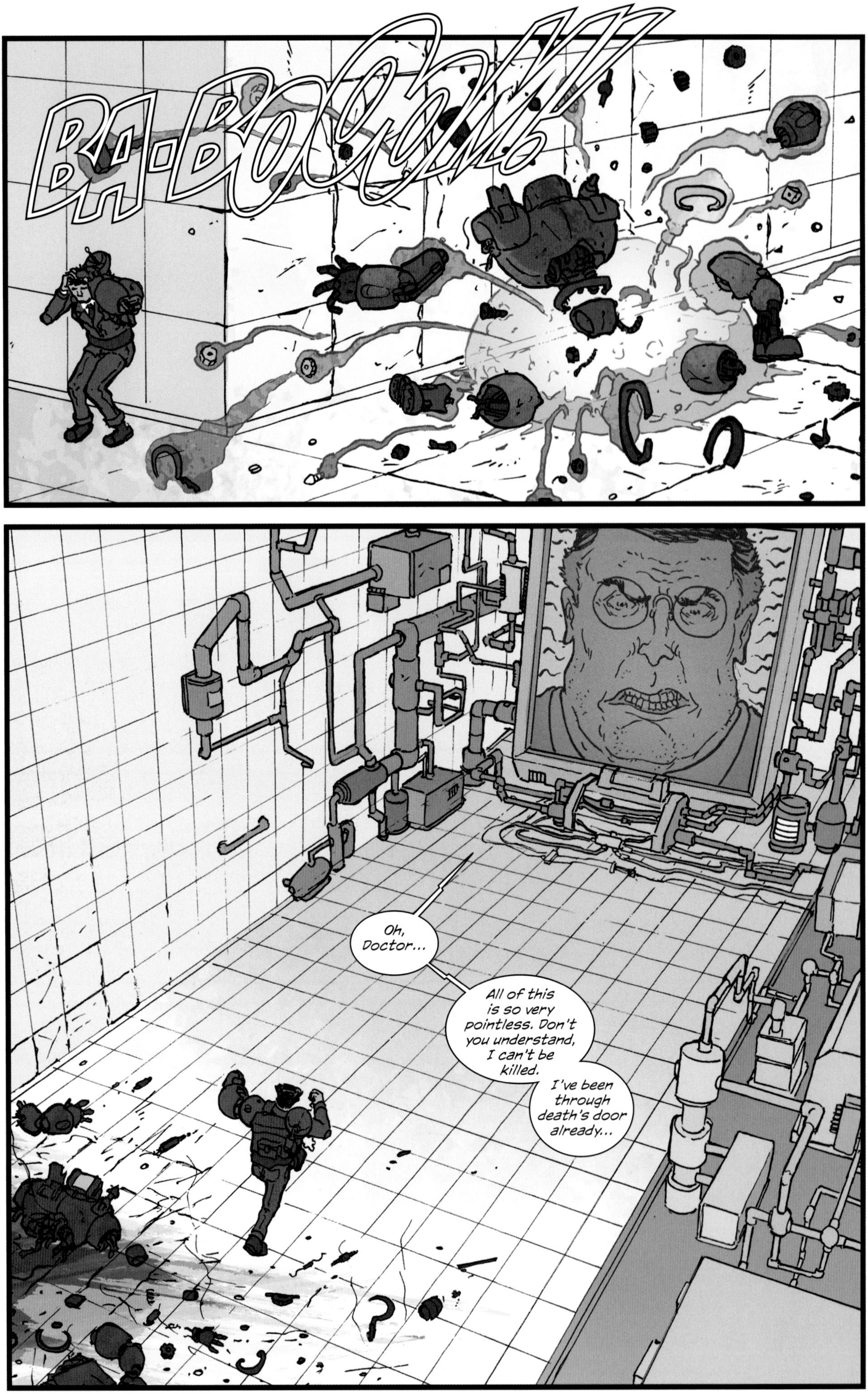
BA-BOOOM
Oh, Doctor...
All of this is so very pointless. Don't you understand, I can't be killed.
I've been through death's door already...

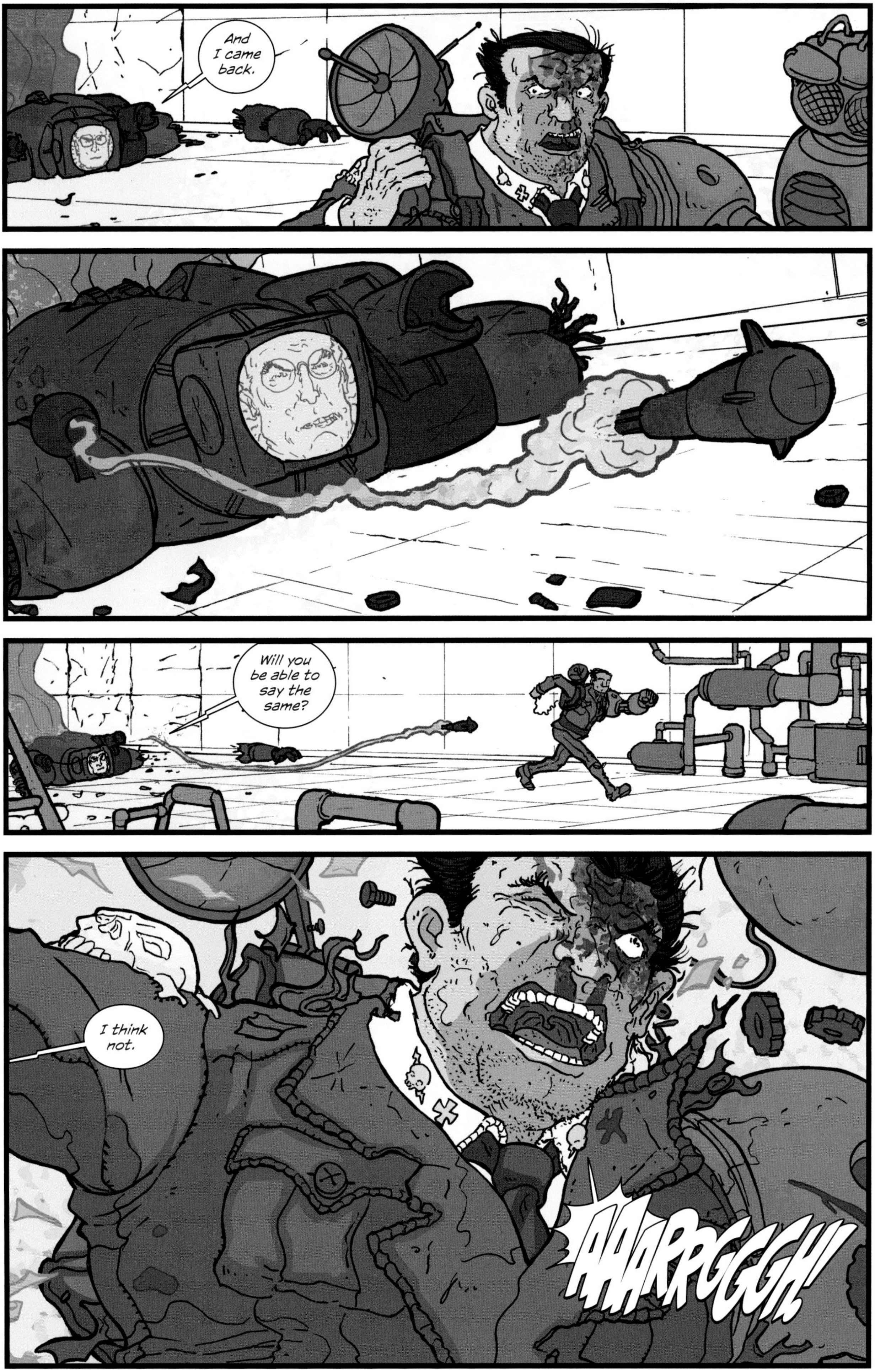
And I came back.
Will you be able to say the same?
I think not.
AAARRGGGH!

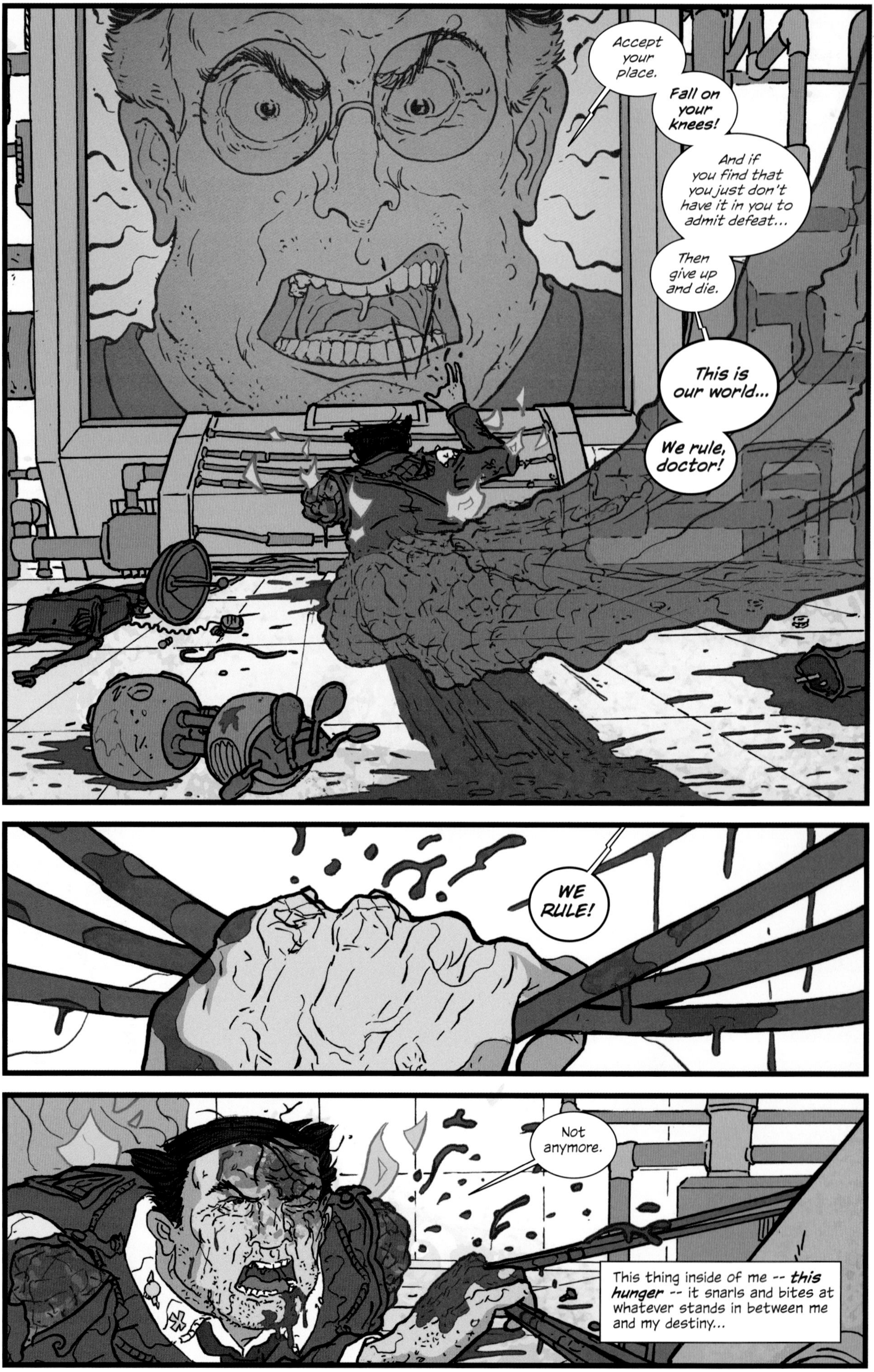
Accept your place.
Fall on your knees!
And if you find that you just don't have it in you to admit defeat...
Then give up and die.
This is our world...
We rule, doctor!
WE RULE!
Not anymore.
This thing inside of me -- this hunger -- it snarls and bites at whatever stands in between me and my destiny...

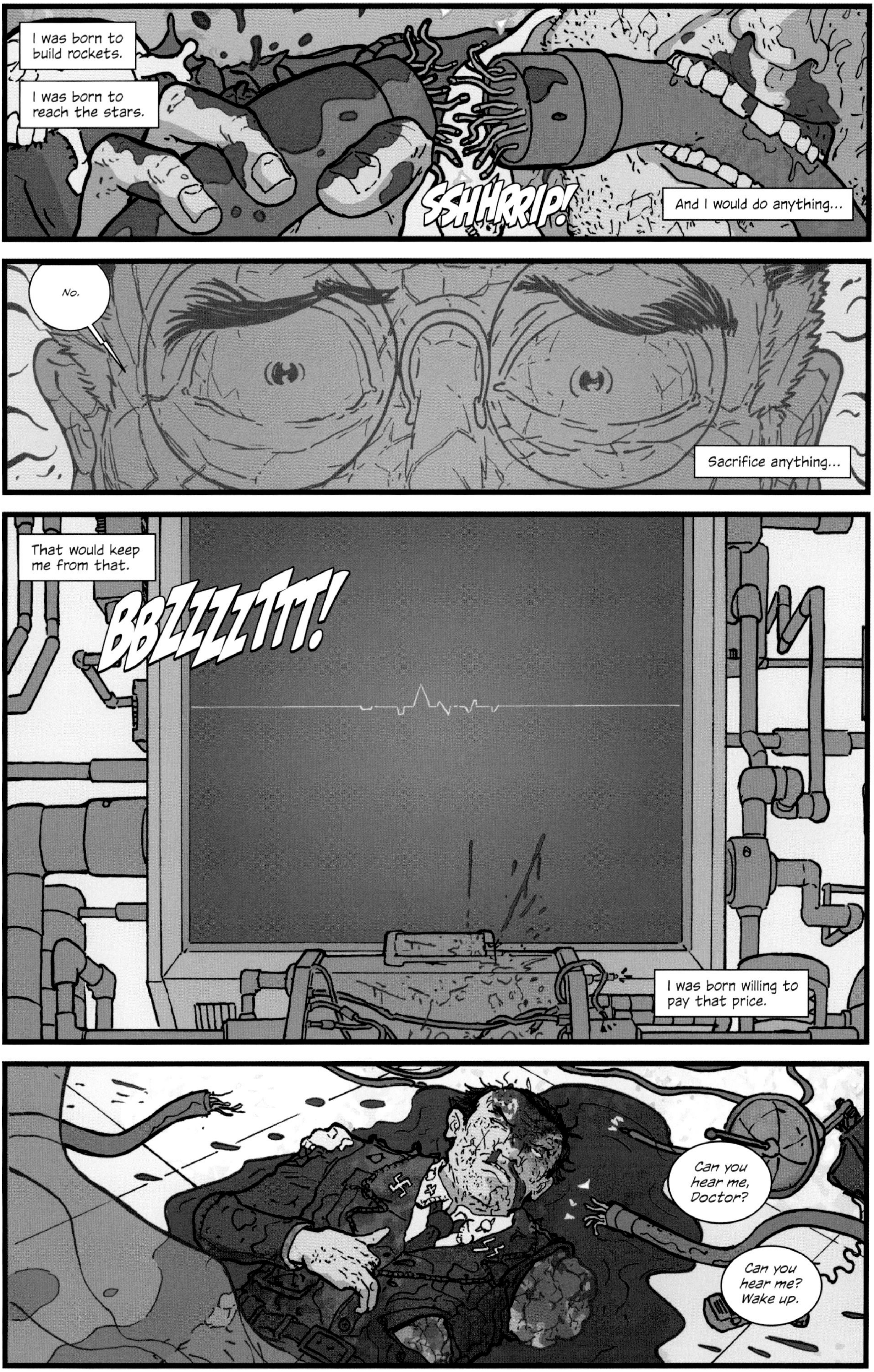
I was born to build rockets.
I was born to reach the stars.
SSHHRRIP!
And I would do anything...
No.
Sacrifice anything...
That would keep me from that.
BBZZZZTTT!
I was born willing to pay that price.
Can you hear me, Doctor?
Can you hear me? Wake up.

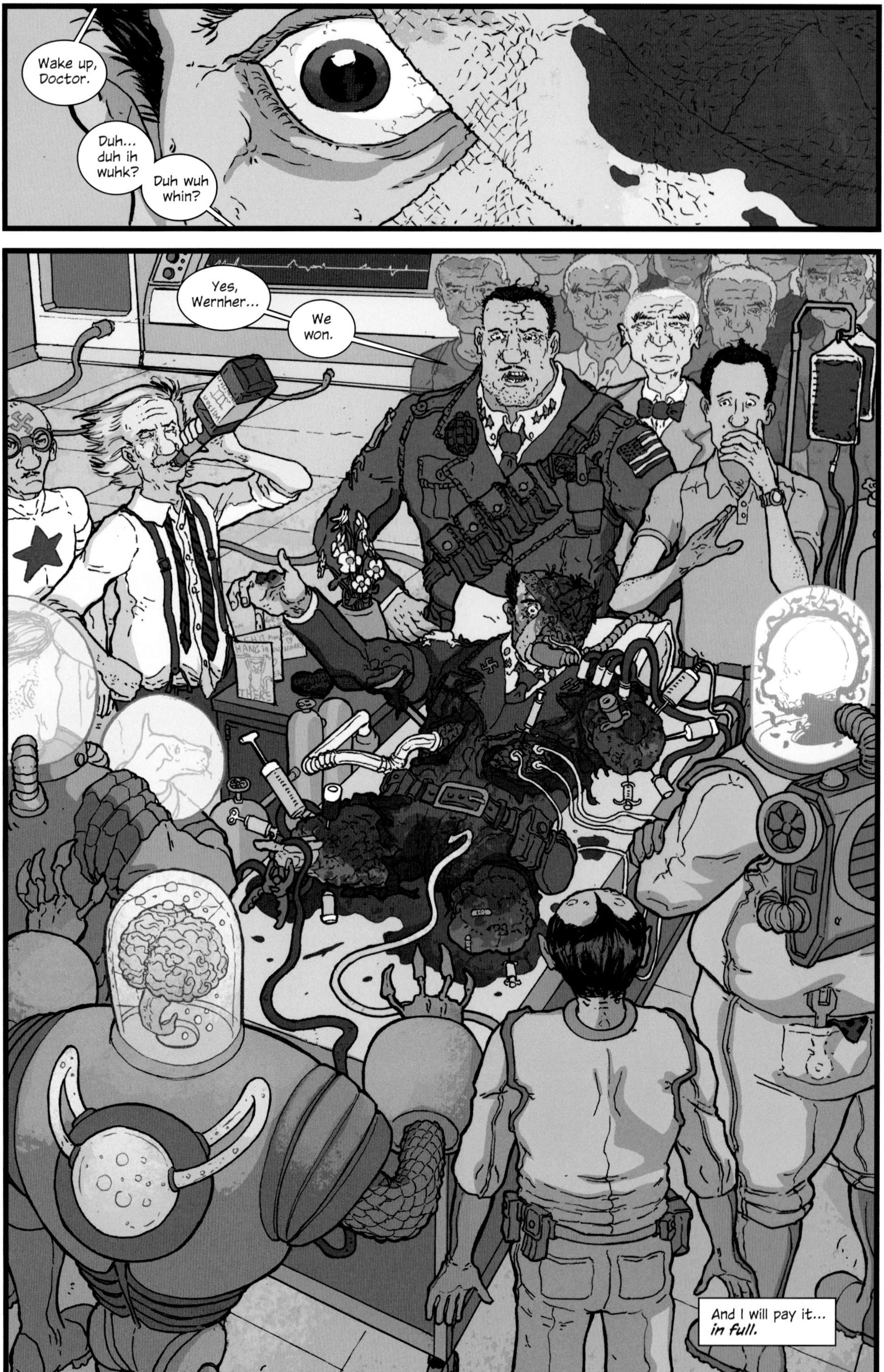
Wake up, Doctor.
Duh... duh ih wuhk?
Duh wuh whin?
Yes, Wernher...
We won.
And I will pay it... *in full.*

"WHAT DID I CALL THE PLACE BEYOND PAIN, BEYOND LOSS, AND BEYOND SACRIFICE?

COMMITMENT."

- WERNHER VON BRAUN

CLAVIS AUREA
THE RECORDED FEYNMAN

VOL. 3

YOU'RE GOING TO KILL ME
AREN'T YOU

"THE WORLD, WHAT IS IT BUT BROKEN DREAMS AND BROKEN MEN...

A THING WELL WORTH HAVING."

CLAVIS AUREA
THE RECORDED FEYNMAN

VOL. 1

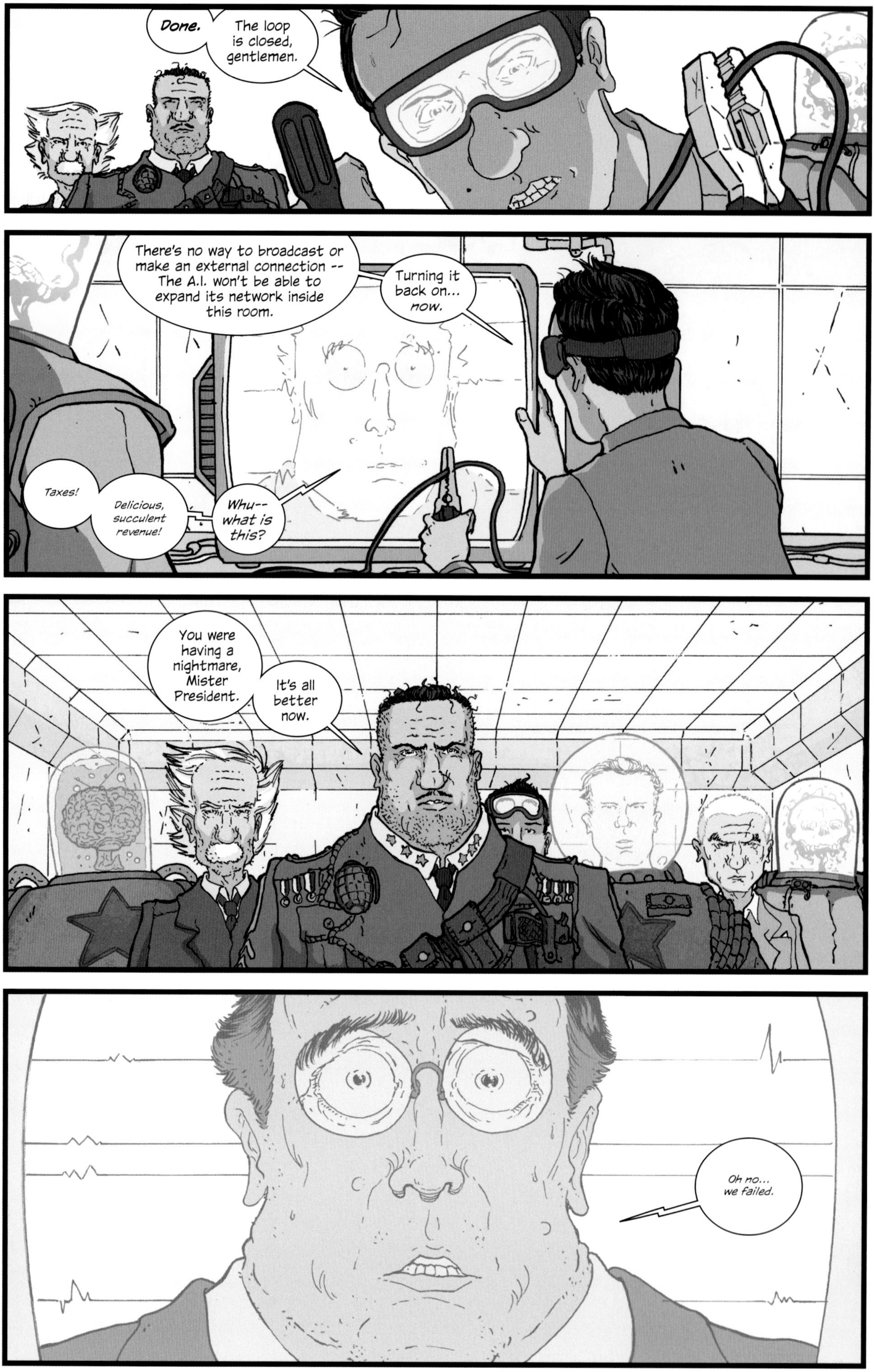
Done.
The loop is closed, gentlemen.
There's no way to broadcast or make an external connection -- The A.I. won't be able to expand its network inside this room.
Turning it back on... now.
Taxes!
Delicious, succulent revenue!
Whu-- what is this?
You were having a nightmare, Mister President.
It's all better now.
Oh no... we failed.

Not just yet...

But with your help we believe we can make that a reality.

Why would I do that?

Gratitude.

You've died twice now, Mister President.

And both times we brought you back.

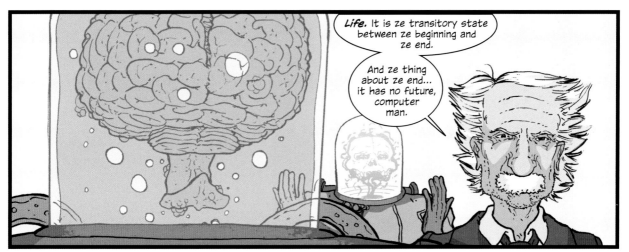

Life. It is ze transitory state between ze beginning and ze end.

And ze thing about ze end... it has no future, computer man.

We cut your cord before your pals could get to the Red Torii and escape the base...so, right now, we're all trapped here together.

I'm gonna give you one chance to give me what I need. *What's it gonna be?*

Well...

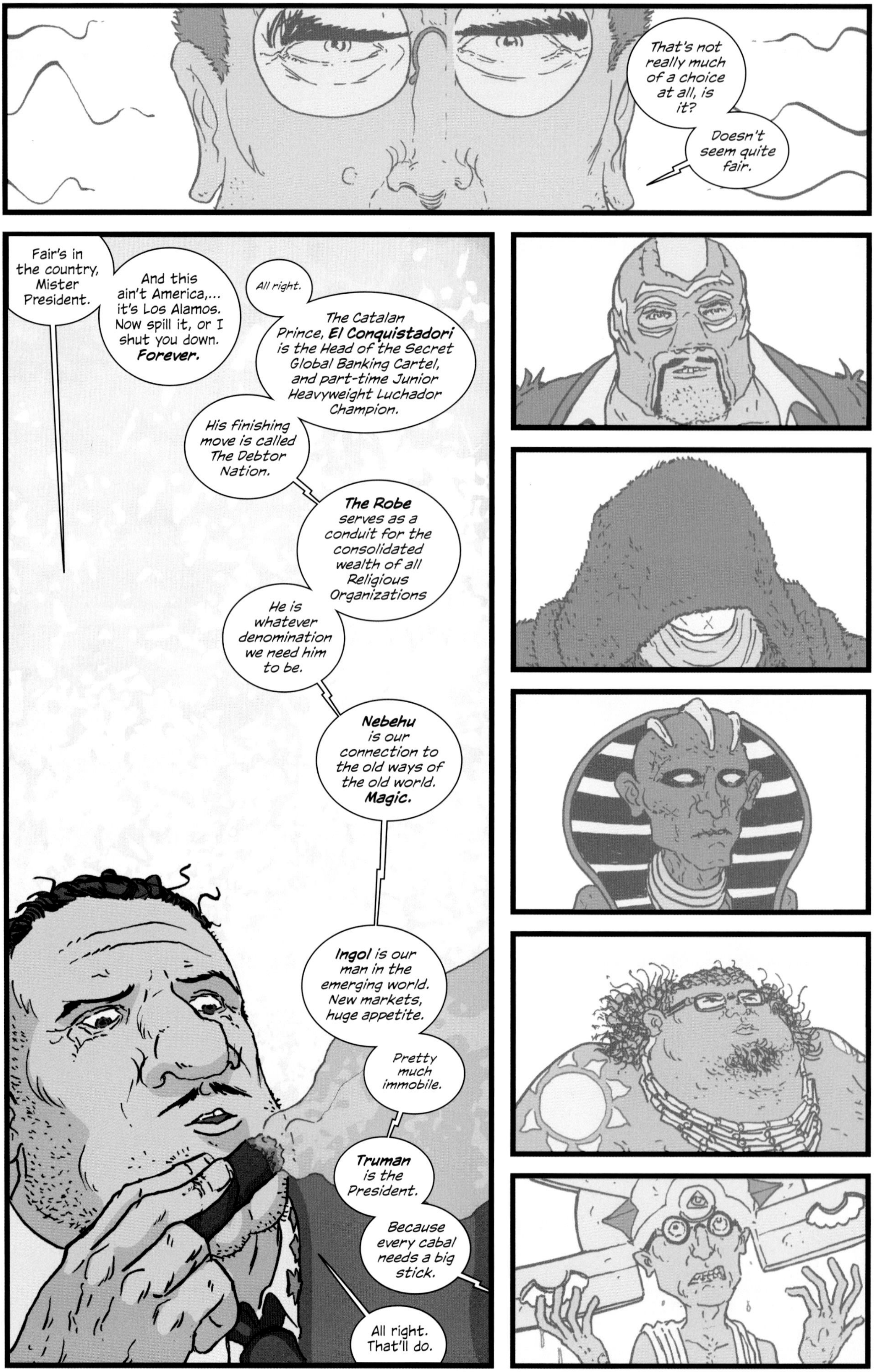
That's not really much of a choice at all, is it?
Doesn't seem quite fair.
Fair's in the country, Mister President.
And this ain't America,... it's Los Alamos. Now spill it, or I shut you down. **Forever.**
All right.
The Catalan Prince, **El Conquistadori** is the Head of the Secret Global Banking Cartel, and part-time Junior Heavyweight Luchador Champion.
His finishing move is called The Debtor Nation.
The Robe serves as a conduit for the consolidated wealth of all Religious Organizations
He is whatever denomination we need him to be.
Nebehu is our connection to the old ways of the old world. **Magic.**
Ingol is our man in the emerging world. New markets, huge appetite.
Pretty much immobile.
Truman is the President.
Because every cabal needs a big stick.
All right. That'll do.

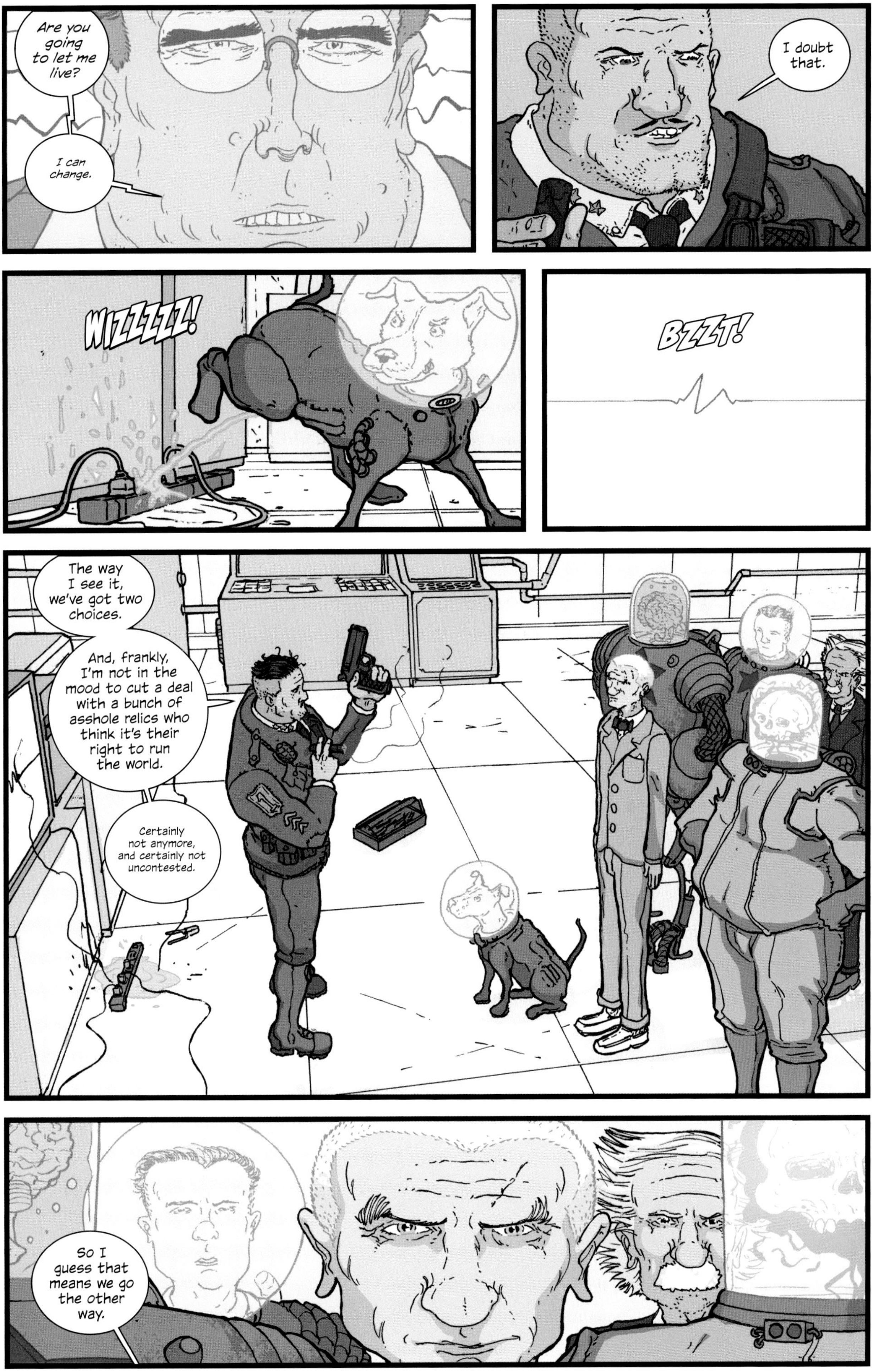

Are you going to let me live?
I can change.
I doubt that.
WIZZZZZ!
BZZZT!
The way I see it, we've got two choices.
And, frankly, I'm not in the mood to cut a deal with a bunch of asshole relics who think it's their right to run the world.
Certainly not anymore, and certainly not uncontested.
So I guess that means we go the other way.

09

BRAVE NEW WORLD

"FOR A TIME, WE FORGOT FORGIVENESS AND THOUGHT ONLY OF REVENGE."

CLAVIS AUREA
THE RECORDED FEYNMAN | **VOL. 2**

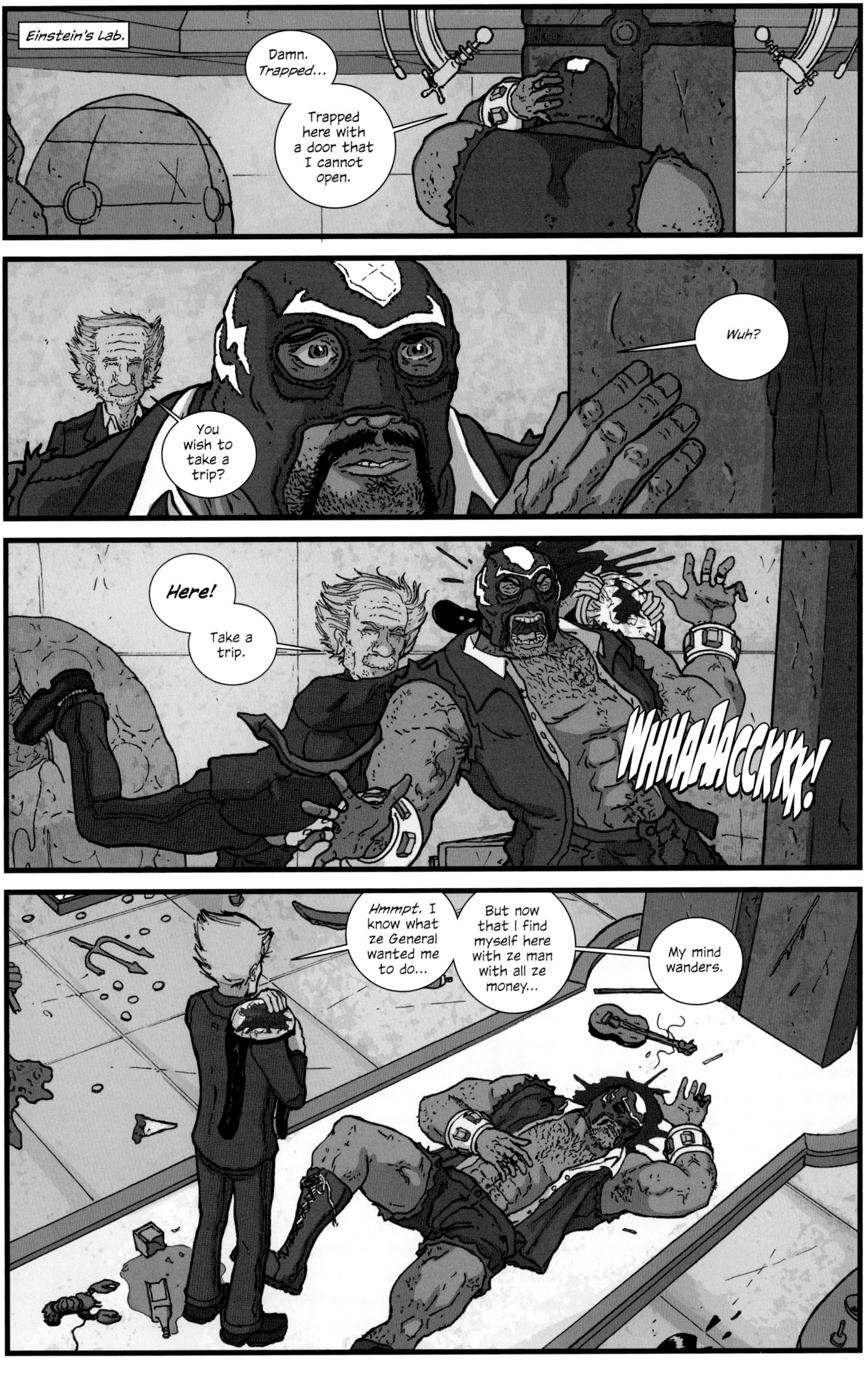
Einstein's Lab.
Damn. *Trapped...*
Trapped here with a door that I cannot open.
You wish to take a trip?
Wuh?
Here!
Take a trip.
WHHAAACCKKK!
Hmmpt. I know what ze General wanted me to do...
But now that I find myself here with ze man with all ze money...
My mind wanders.

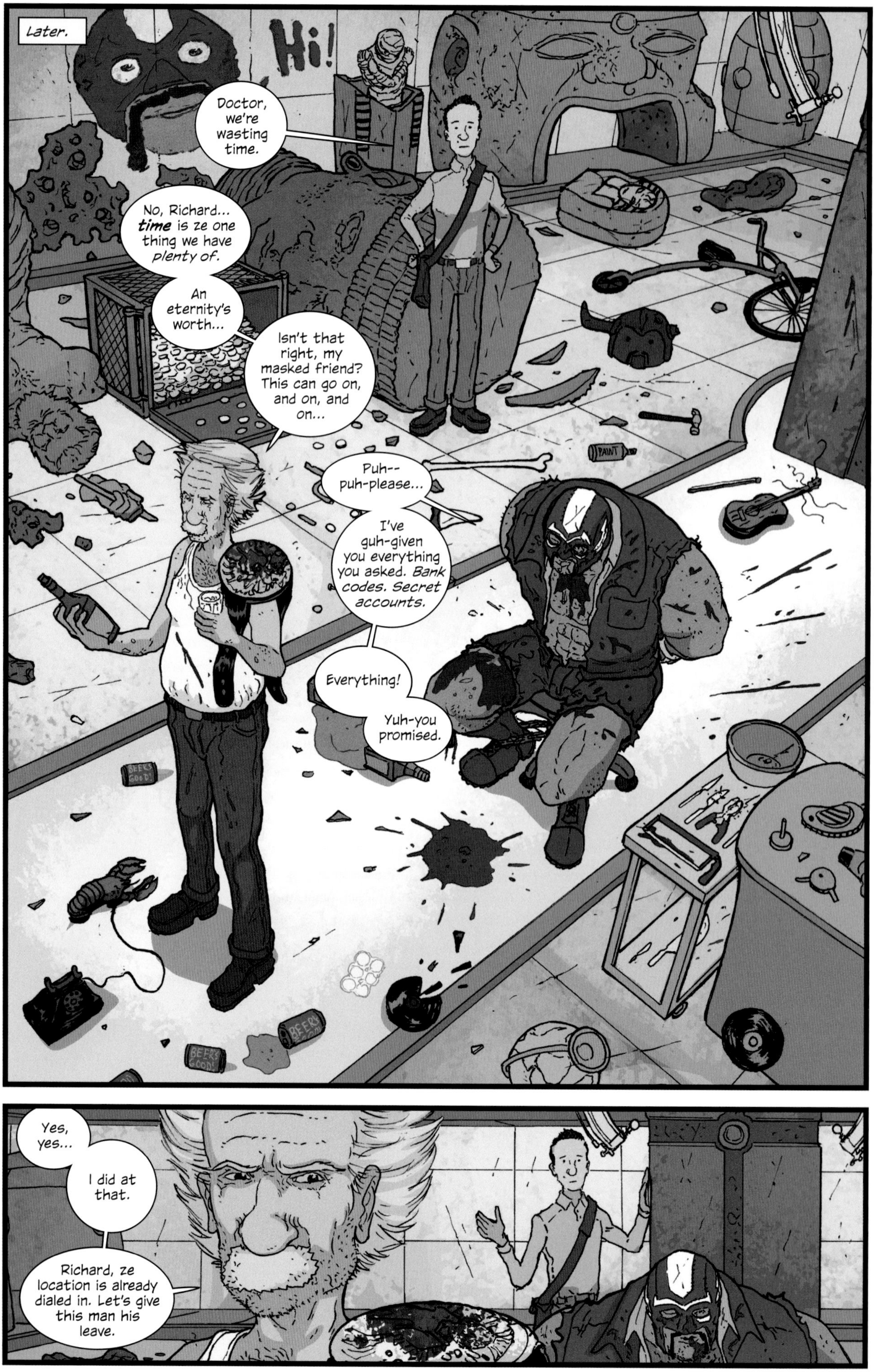
Later.
Hi!
Doctor, we're wasting time.
No, Richard... **time** is ze one thing we have *plenty of.*
An eternity's worth...
Isn't that right, my masked friend? This can go on, and on, and on...
Puh-- puh-please...
I've guh-given you everything you asked. *Bank codes. Secret accounts.*
Everything!
Yuh-you promised.
PAINT
BEERS GOOD!
Yes, yes...
I did at that.
Richard, ze location is already dialed in. Let's give this man his leave.

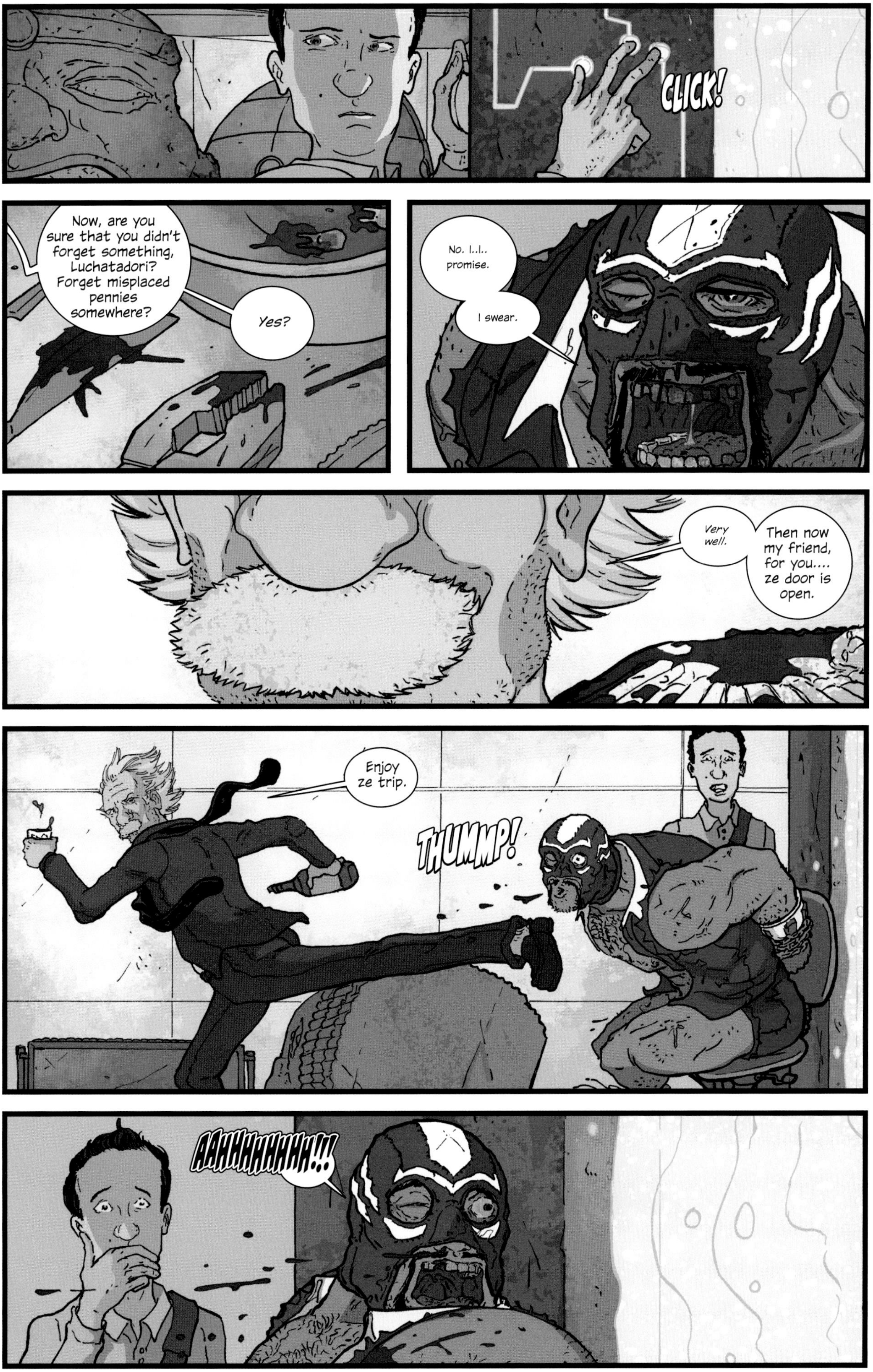
CLICK!
Now, are you sure that you didn't forget something, Luchatadori? Forget misplaced pennies somewhere?
Yes?
No. I..I.. promise.
I swear.
Very well.
Then now my friend, for you.... ze door is open.
Enjoy ze trip.
THUMMP!
AAHHHHHHHH!!!

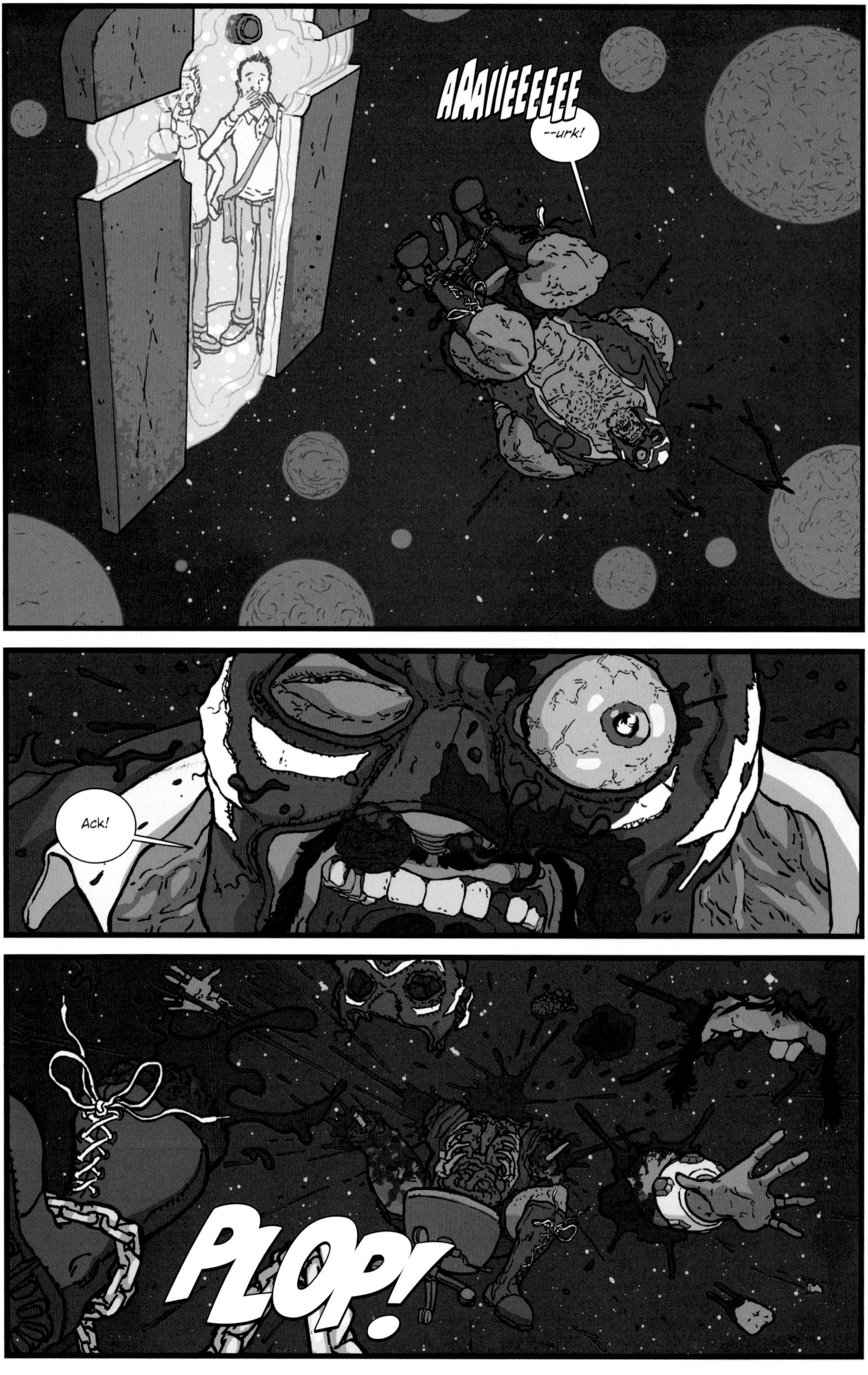
AAAIIEEEEEE
--urk!
Ack!
PLOP!

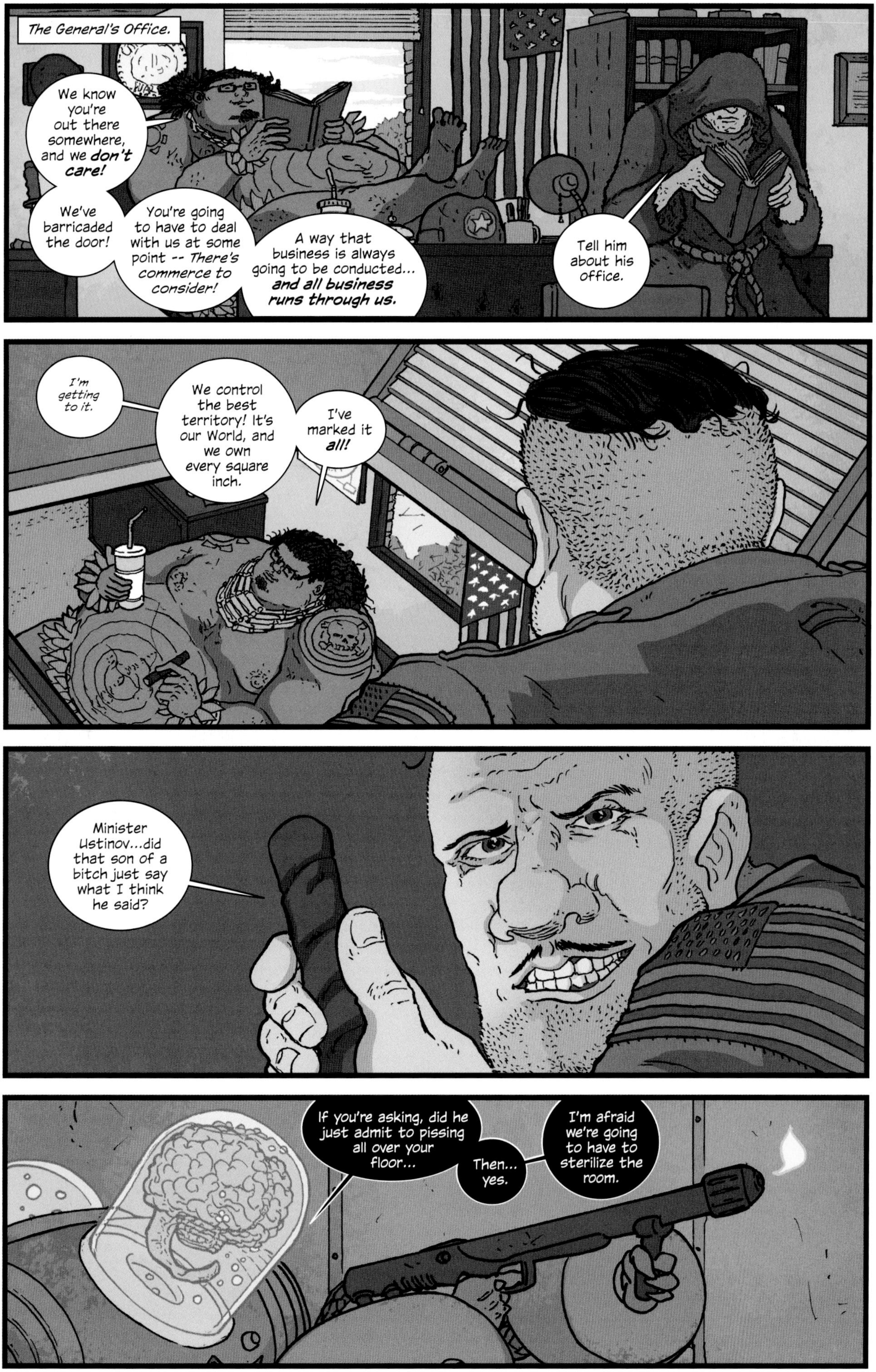
The General's Office.
We know you're out there somewhere, and we **don't care!**
We've barricaded the door!
You're going to have to deal with us at some point -- *There's commerce to consider!*
A way that business is always going to be conducted... ***and all business runs through us.***
Tell him about his office.
I'm getting to it.
We control the best territory! It's our World, and we own every square inch.
I've marked it ***all!***
Minister Ustinov...did that son of a bitch just say what I think he said?
If you're asking, did he just admit to pissing all over your floor...
Then... yes.
I'm afraid we're going to have to sterilize the room.

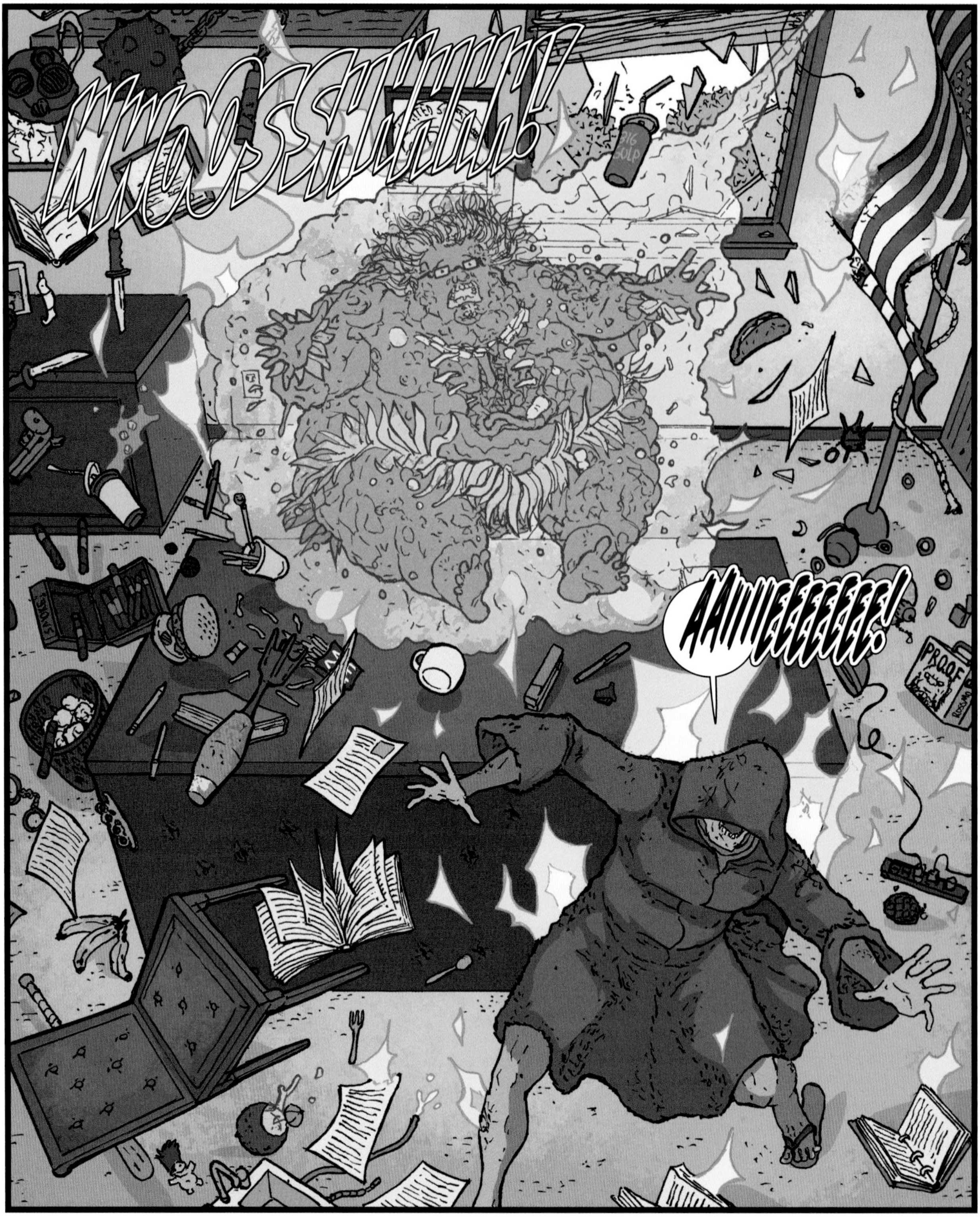
AAIIIIEEEEEE!
BIG GULP
PROOF

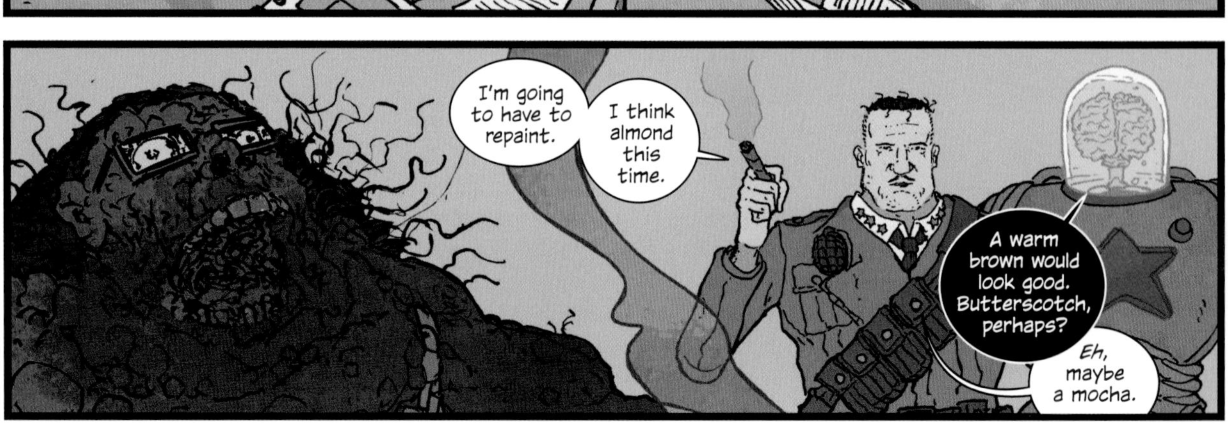
I'm going to have to repaint.
I think almond this time.
A warm brown would look good. Butterscotch, perhaps?
Eh, maybe a mocha.

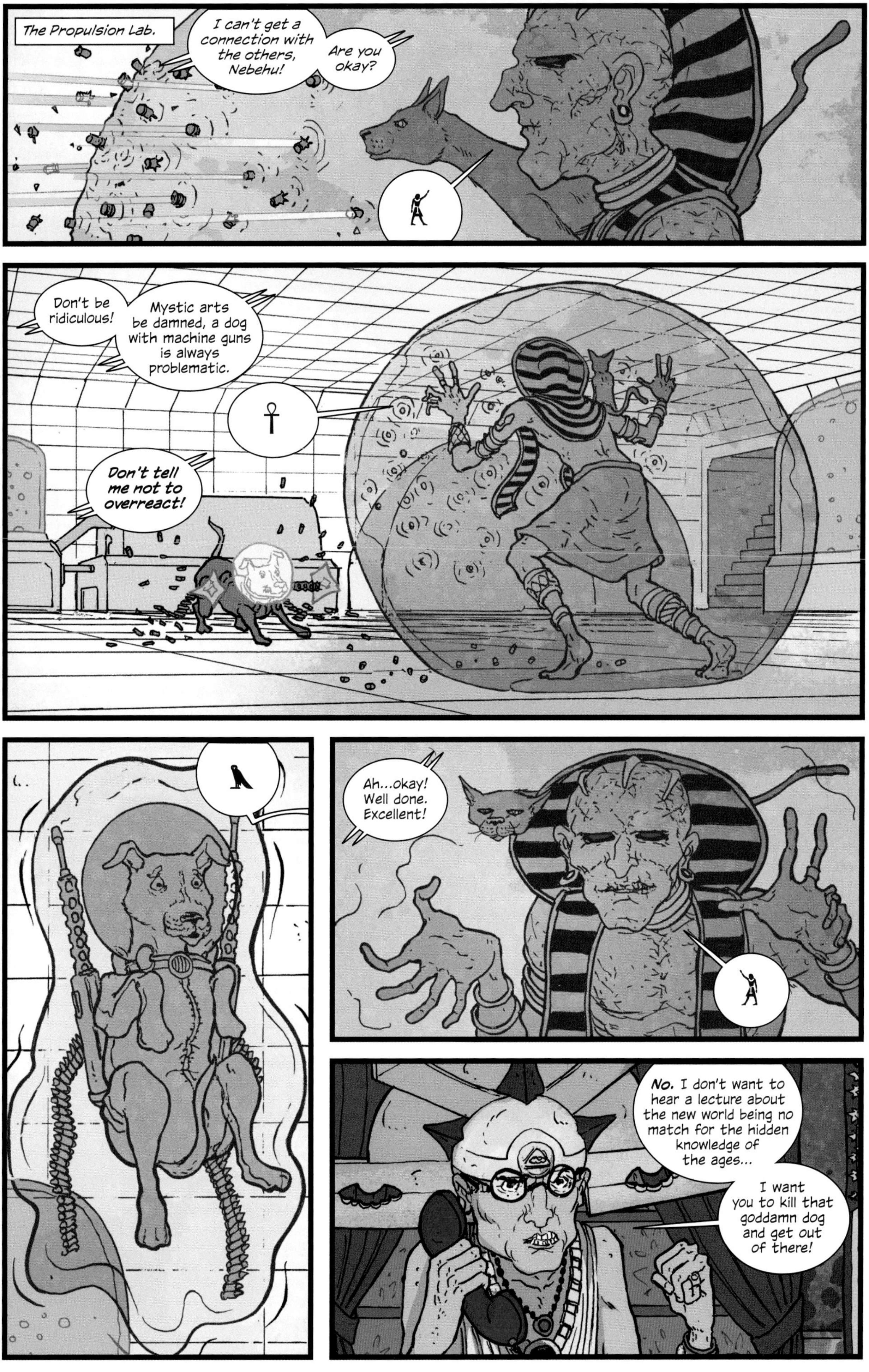
The Propulsion Lab.
I can't get a connection with the others, Nebehu!
Are you okay?
Don't be ridiculous!
Mystic arts be damned, a dog with machine guns is always problematic.
Don't tell me not to overreact!
Ah...okay! Well done. Excellent!
No. I don't want to hear a lecture about the new world being no match for the hidden knowledge of the ages...
I want you to kill that goddamn dog and get out of there!

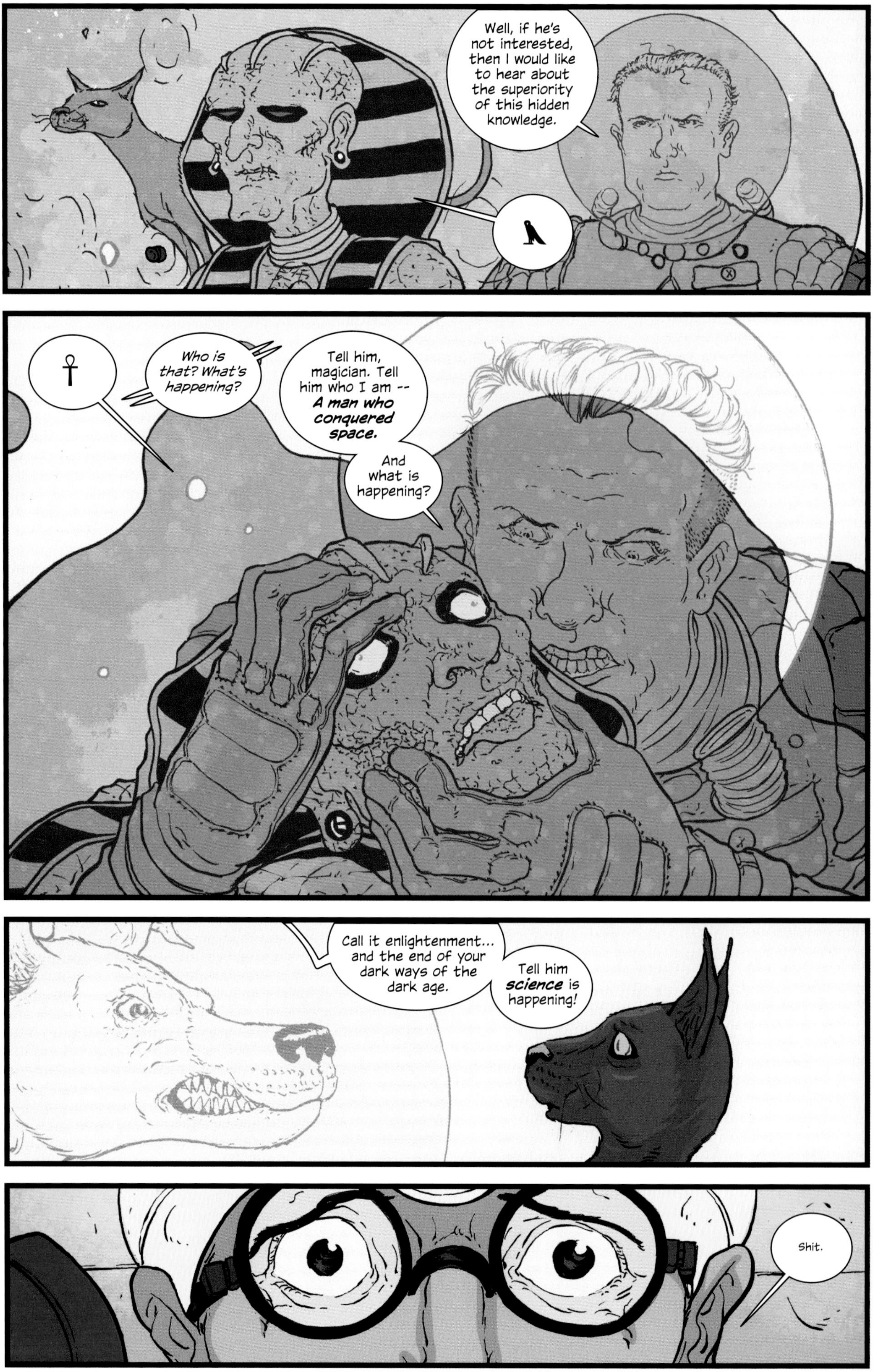

Well, if he's not interested, then I would like to hear about the superiority of this hidden knowledge.
☥
Who is that? What's happening?
Tell him, magician. Tell him who I am -- **A man who conquered space.**
And what is happening?
Call it enlightenment... and the end of your dark ways of the dark age.
Tell him **science** is happening!
Shit.

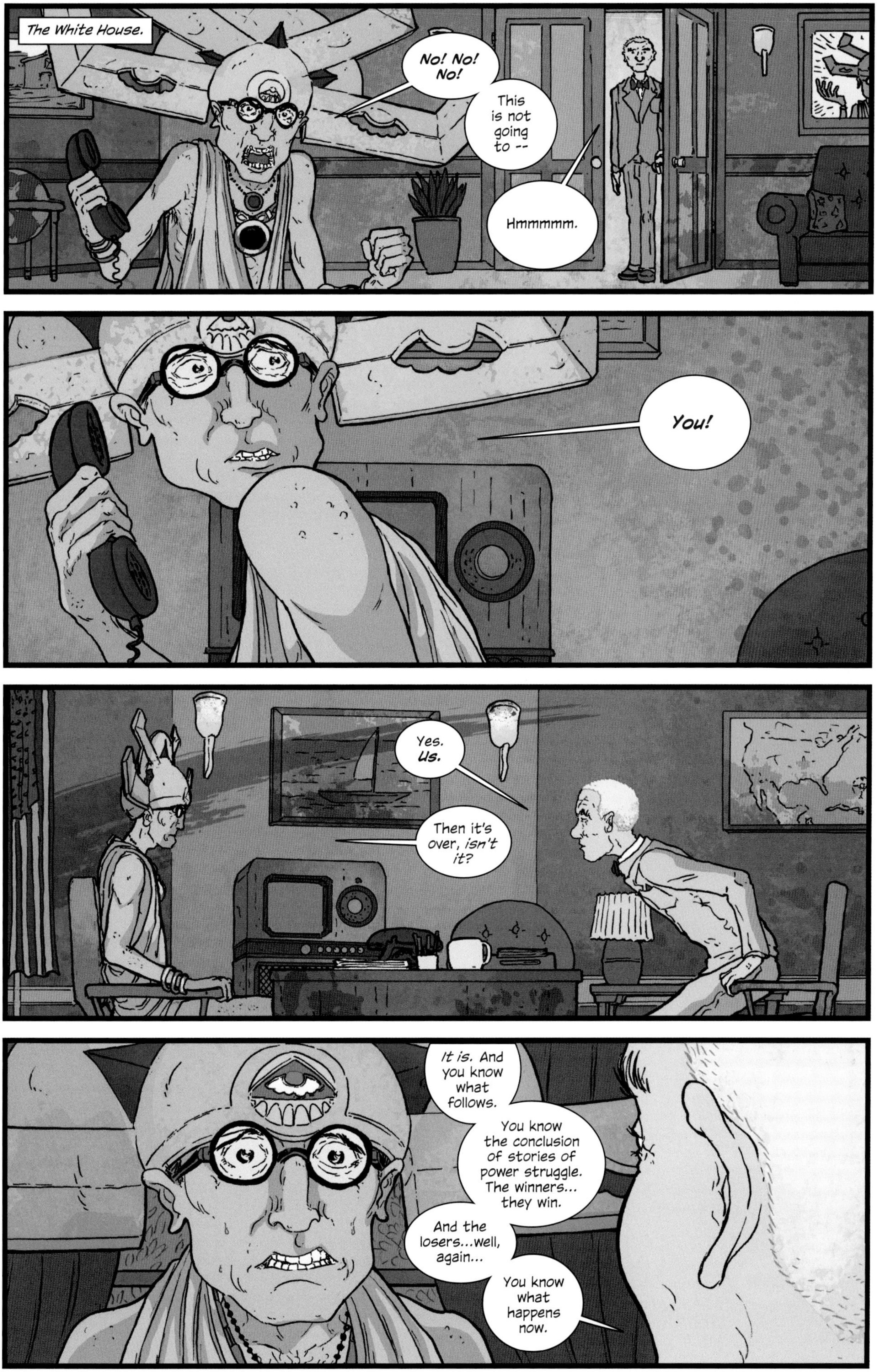
The White House.
No! No! No!
This is not going to --
Hmmmmm.
You!
Yes. *Us.*
Then it's over, *isn't* it?
It is. And you know what follows.
You know the conclusion of stories of power struggle. The winners... they win.
And the losers...well, again...
You know what happens now.

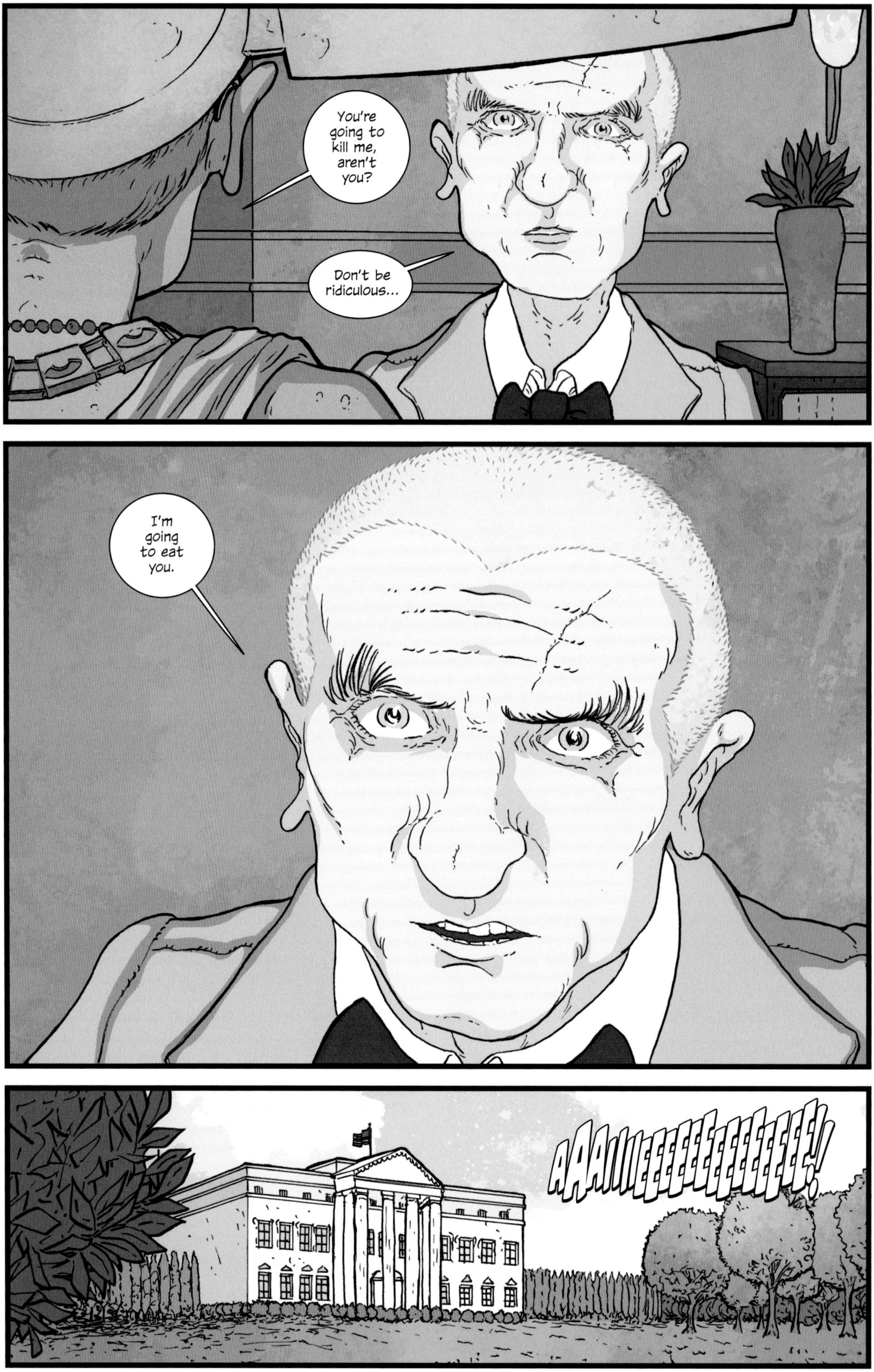
You're going to kill me, aren't you?
Don't be ridiculous...
I'm going to eat you.
AAAIIIEEEEEEEEEEEEEE!!

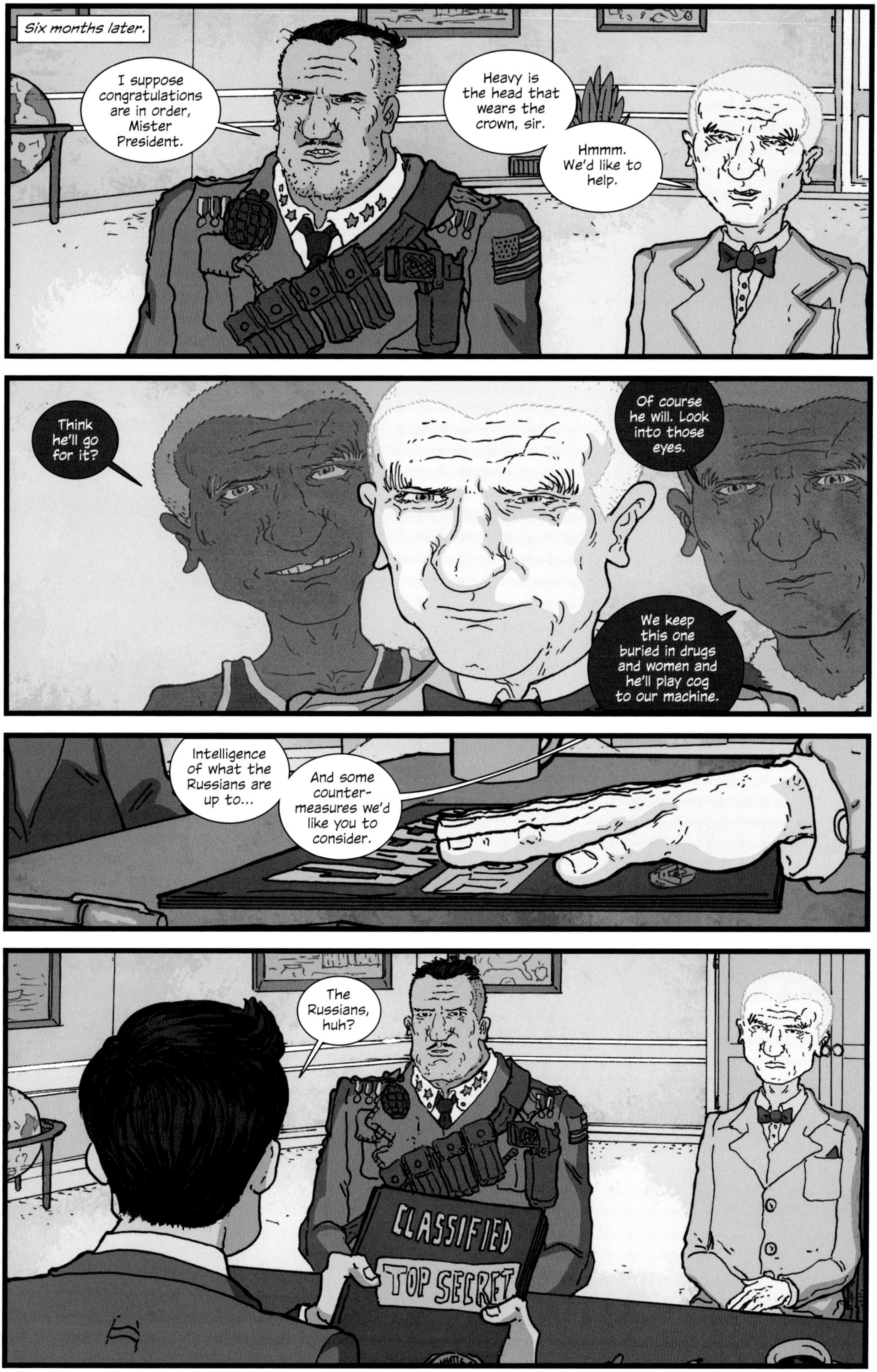
Six months later.
I suppose congratulations are in order, Mister President.
Heavy is the head that wears the crown, sir.
Hmmm. We'd like to help.
Think he'll go for it?
Of course he will. Look into those eyes.
We keep this one buried in drugs and women and he'll play cog to our machine.
Intelligence of what the Russians are up to...
And some counter-measures we'd like you to consider.
The Russians, huh?
CLASSIFIED
TOP SECRET

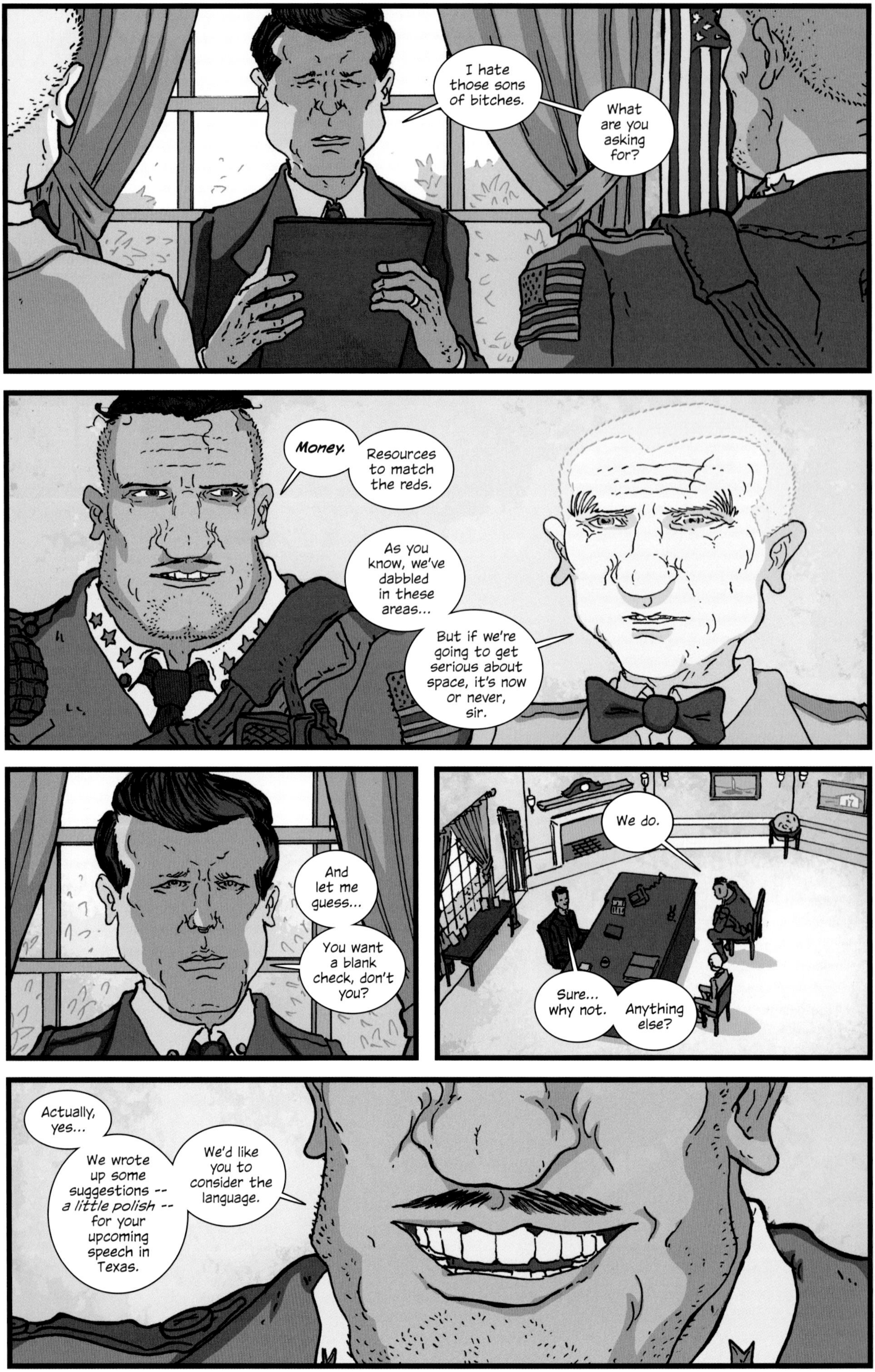
I hate those sons of bitches.
What are you asking for?
Money. Resources to match the reds.
As you know, we've dabbled in these areas...
But if we're going to get serious about space, it's now or never, sir.
And let me guess...
You want a blank check, don't you?
We do.
Sure... why not.
Anything else?
Actually, yes...
We wrote up some suggestions -- *a little polish* -- for your upcoming speech in Texas.
We'd like you to consider the language.

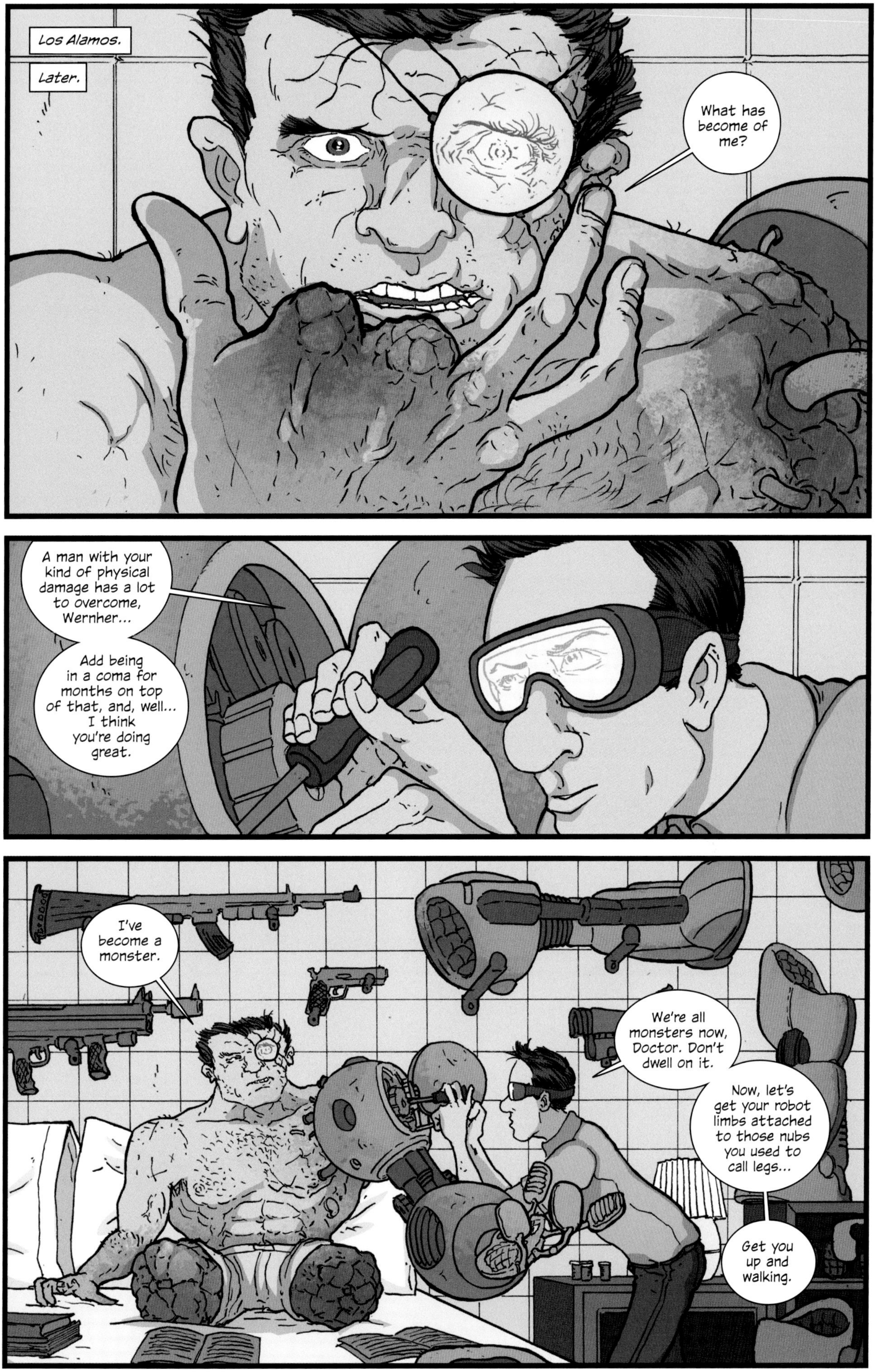

Los Alamos.
Later.
What has become of me?
A man with your kind of physical damage has a lot to overcome, Wernher...
Add being in a coma for months on top of that, and, well... I think you're doing great.
I've become a monster.
We're all monsters now, Doctor. Don't dwell on it.
Now, let's get your robot limbs attached to those nubs you used to call legs...
Get you up and walking.

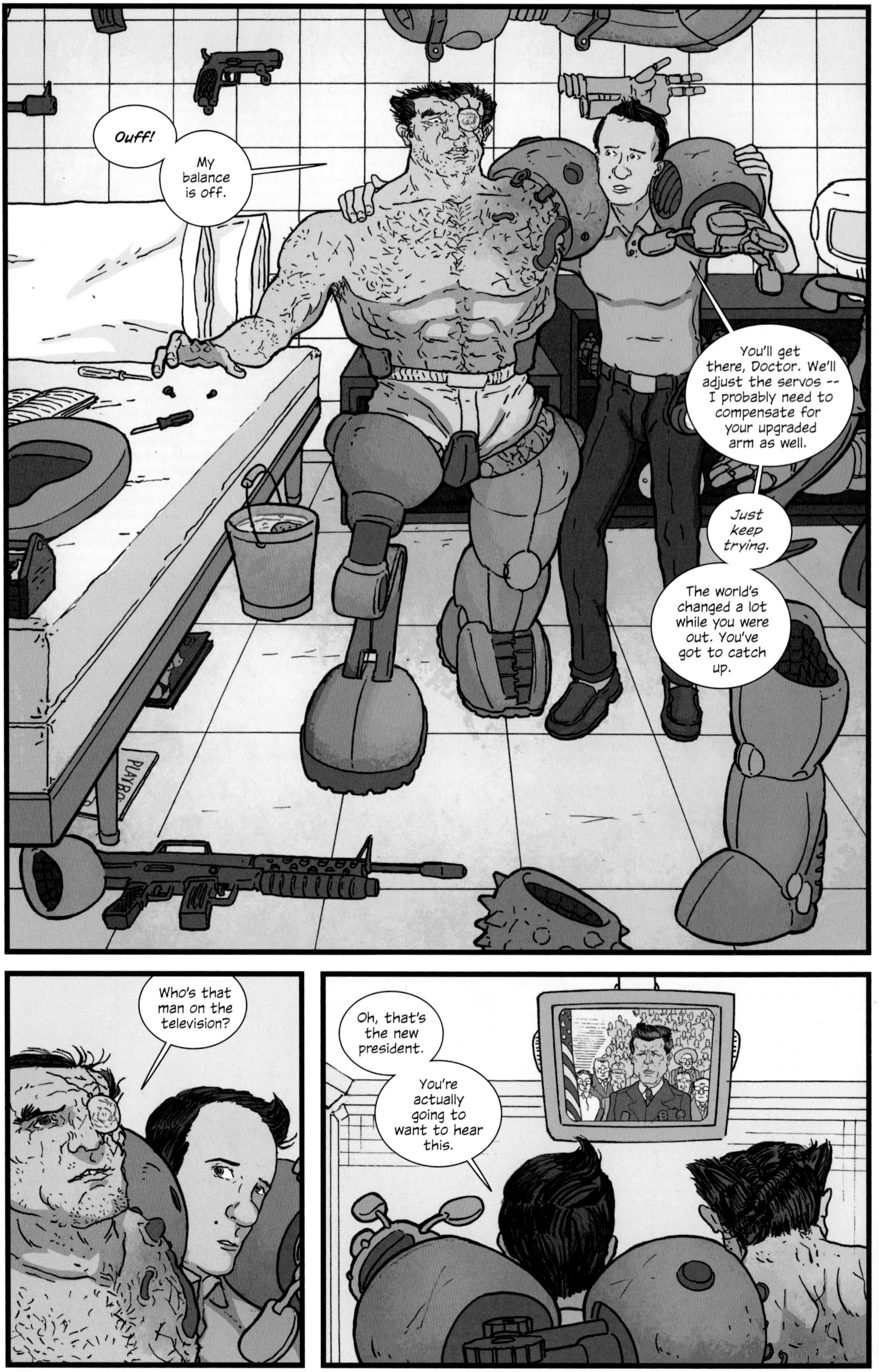
Ouff!
My balance is off.
You'll get there, Doctor. We'll adjust the servos -- I probably need to compensate for your upgraded arm as well.
Just keep trying.
The world's changed a lot while you were out. You've got to catch up.
Who's that man on the television?
Oh, that's the new president.
You're actually going to want to hear this.

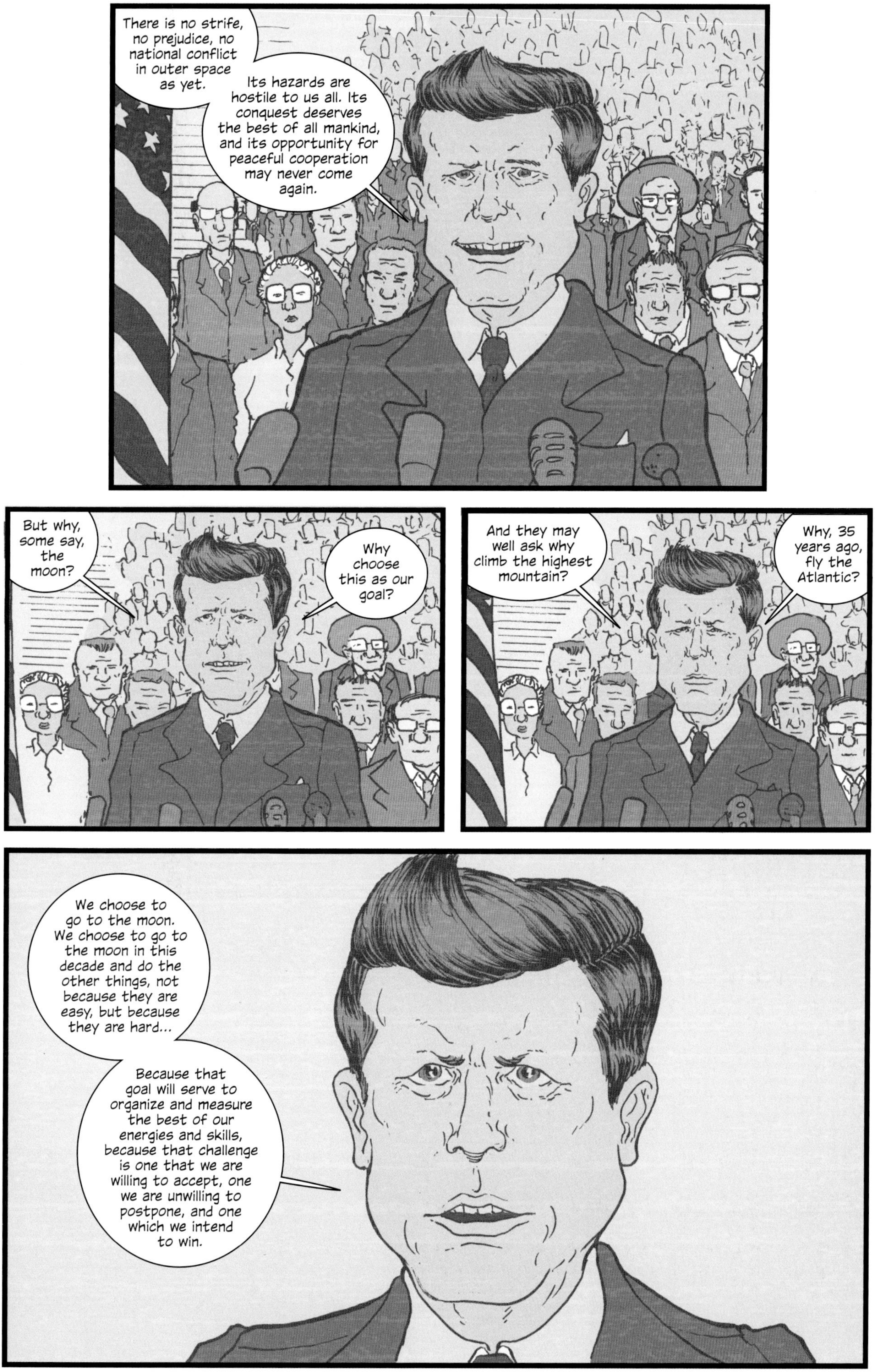
There is no strife, no prejudice, no national conflict in outer space as yet.
Its hazards are hostile to us all. Its conquest deserves the best of all mankind, and its opportunity for peaceful cooperation may never come again.
But why, some say, the moon?
Why choose this as our goal?
And they may well ask why climb the highest mountain?
Why, 35 years ago, fly the Atlantic?
We choose to go to the moon. We choose to go to the moon in this decade and do the other things, not because they are easy, but because they are hard...
Because that goal will serve to organize and measure the best of our energies and skills, because that challenge is one that we are willing to accept, one we are unwilling to postpone, and one which we intend to win.

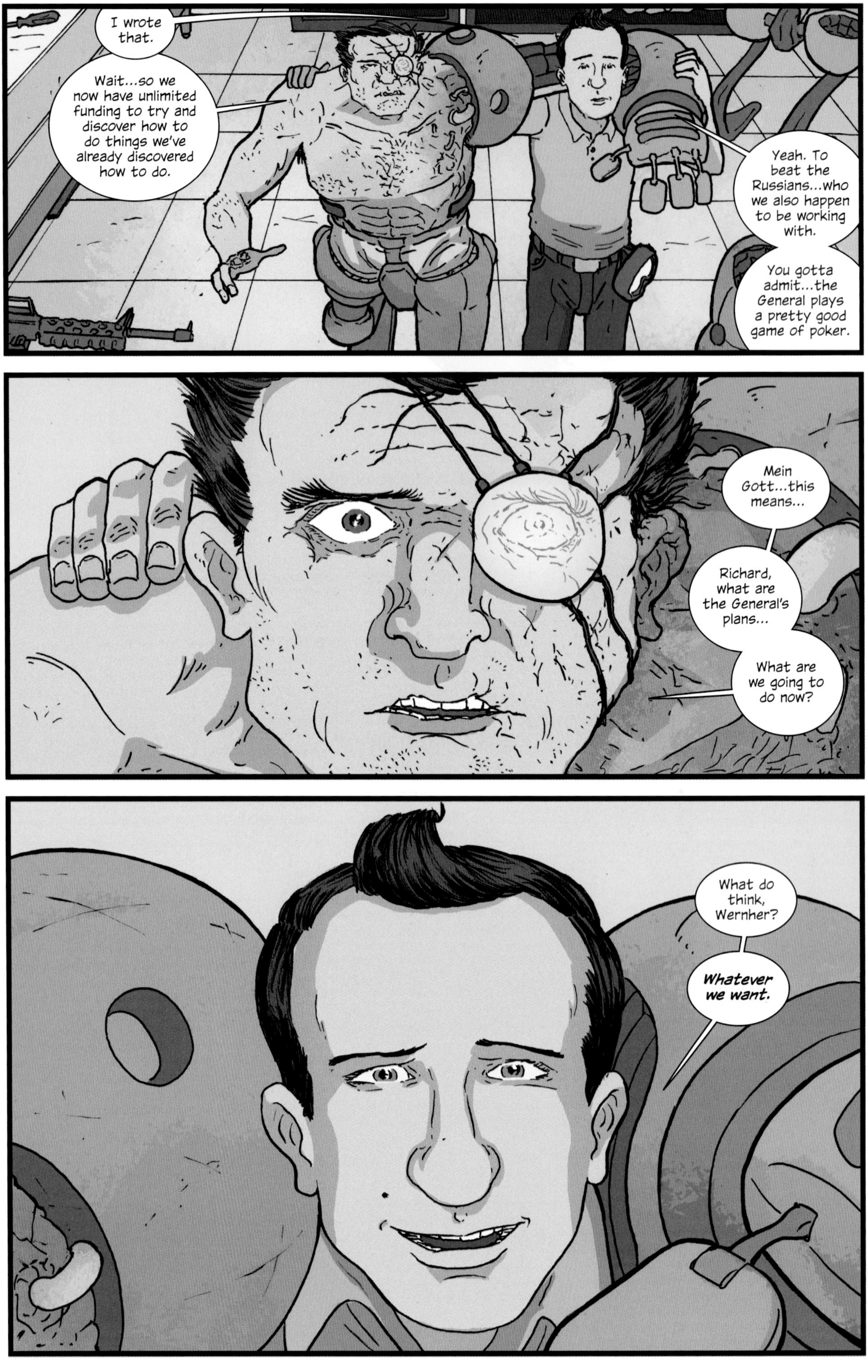
I wrote that.
Wait...so we now have unlimited funding to try and discover how to do things we've already discovered how to do.
Yeah. To beat the Russians...who we also happen to be working with.
You gotta admit...the General plays a pretty good game of poker.
Mein Gott...this means...
Richard, what are the General's plans...
What are we going to do now?
What do think, Wernher?
Whatever we want.

"...AND THAT WAS HOW WE CAME TO CONTROL IT ALL."

CLAVIS AUREA
THE RECORDED FEYNMAN | VOL. 3

HE FELT
GRATEFUL

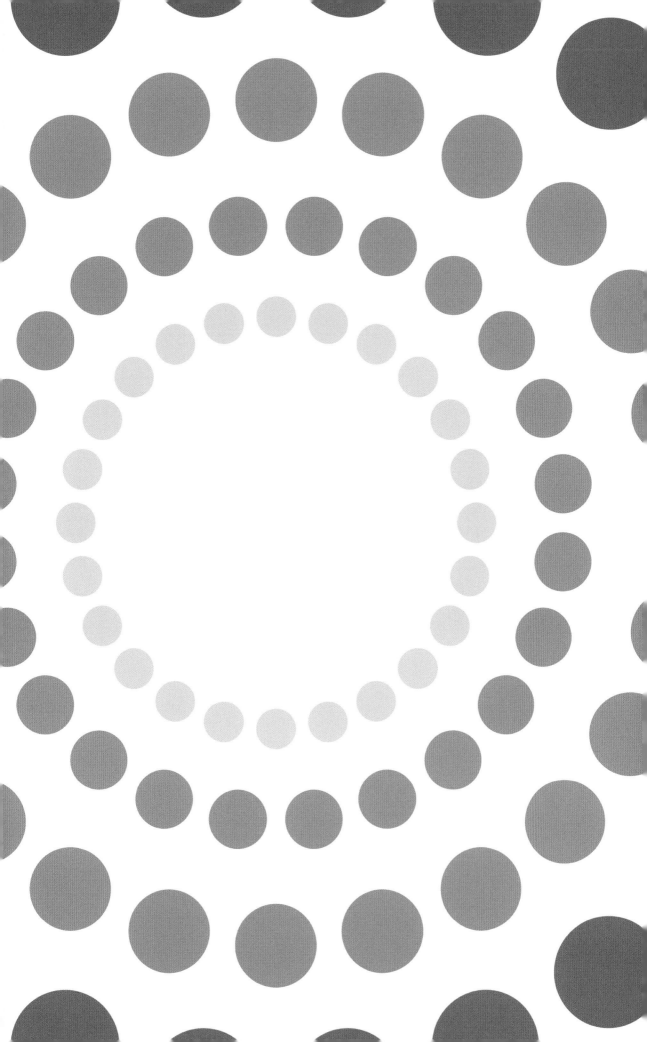

"THE GREAT EYE OF JOSEPH WATCHED OVER THEM ALL. THIS IS HOW THE WAR BEGAN."

- OPPENHEIMER

CLAVIS AUREA
THE RECORDED FEYNMAN | **VOL. 3**

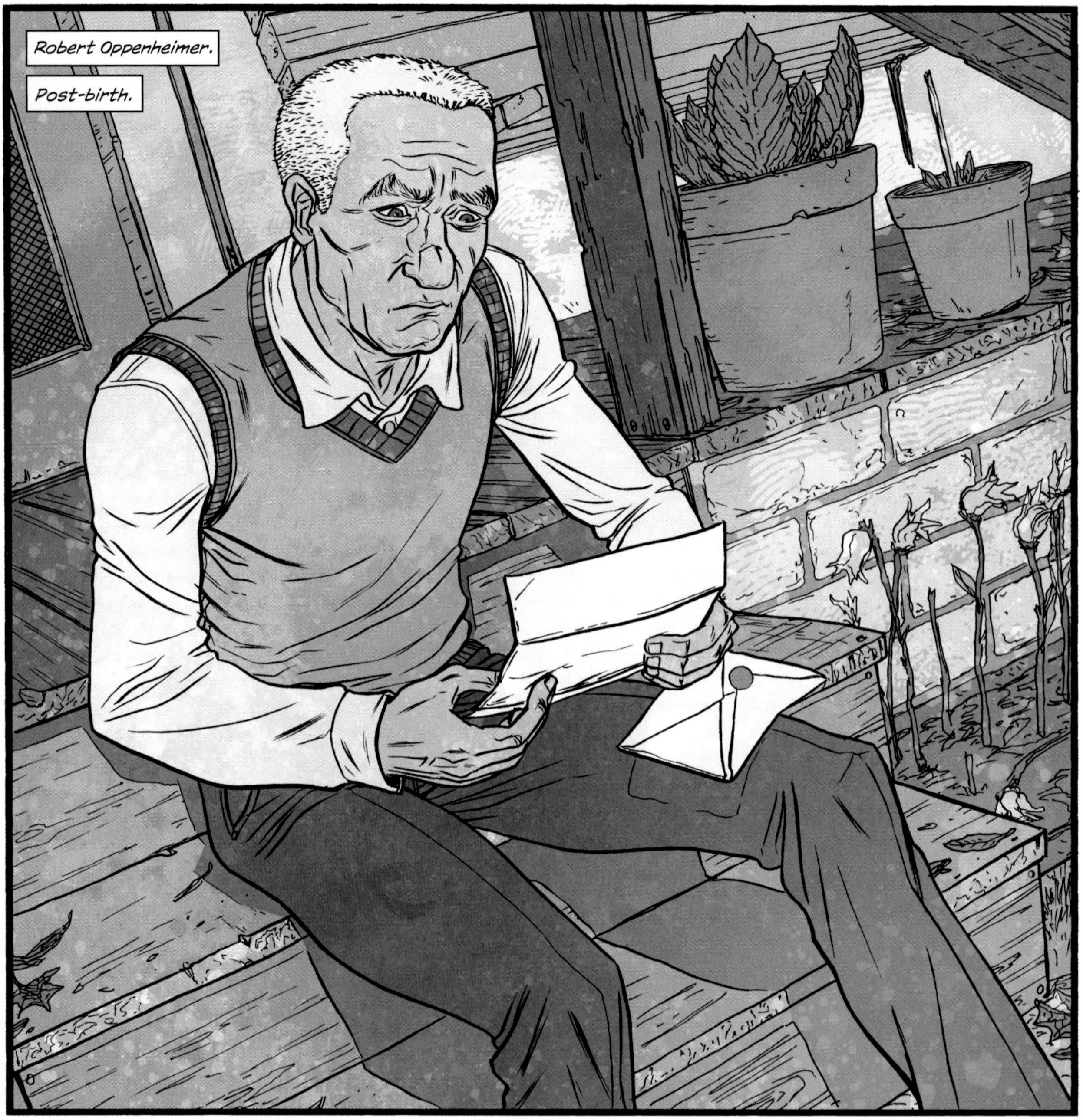
Robert Oppenheimer.
Post-birth.

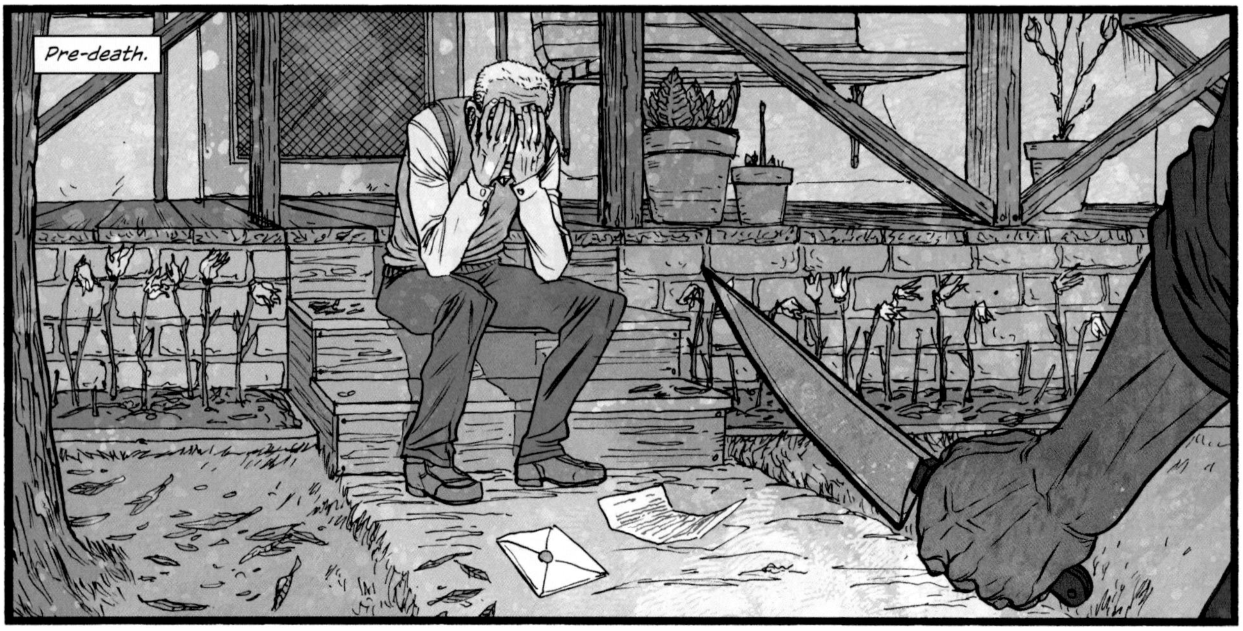
Pre-death.

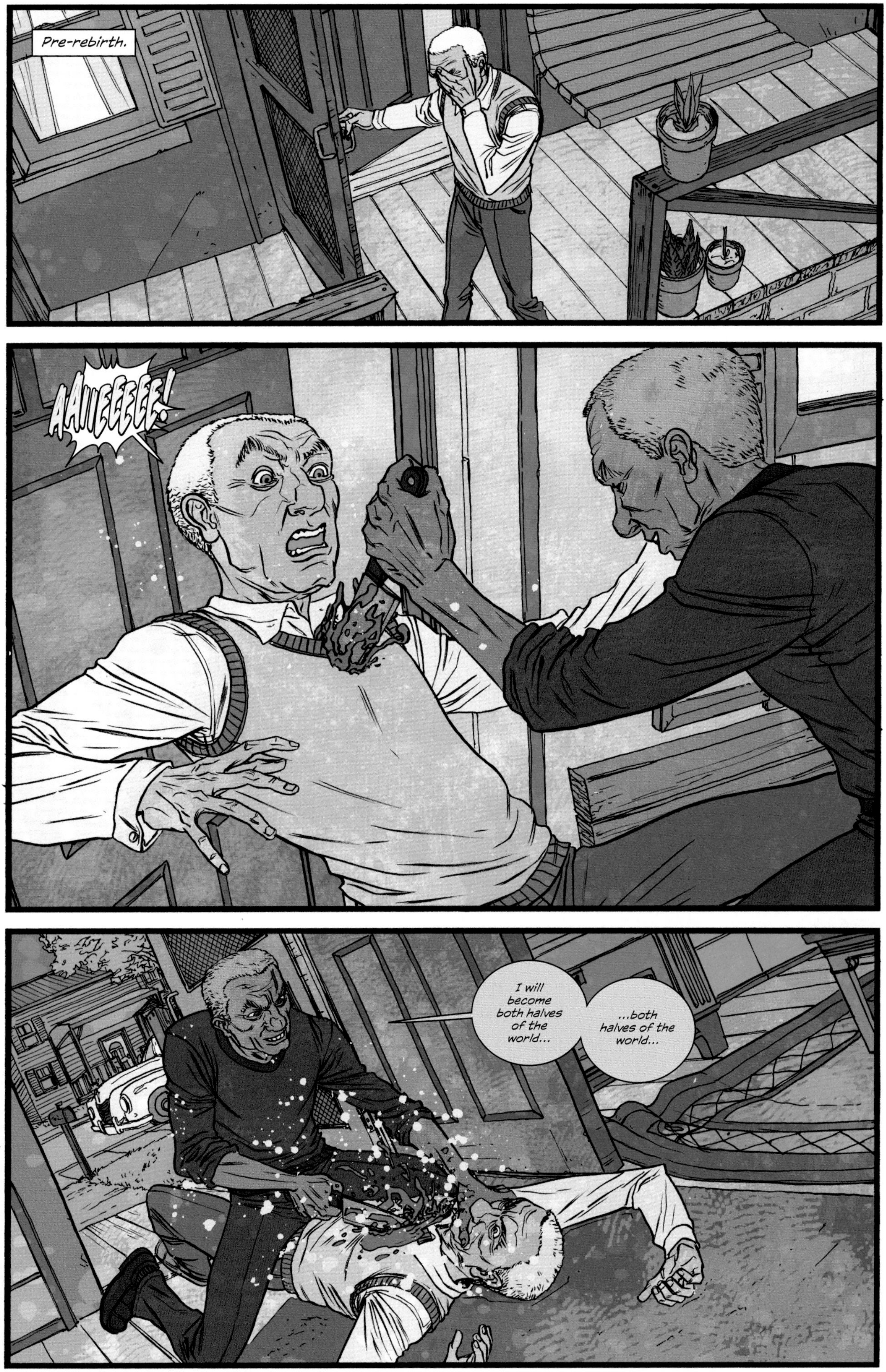
Pre-rebirth.
AAIIEEEEE!
I will become both halves of the world...
...both halves of the world...

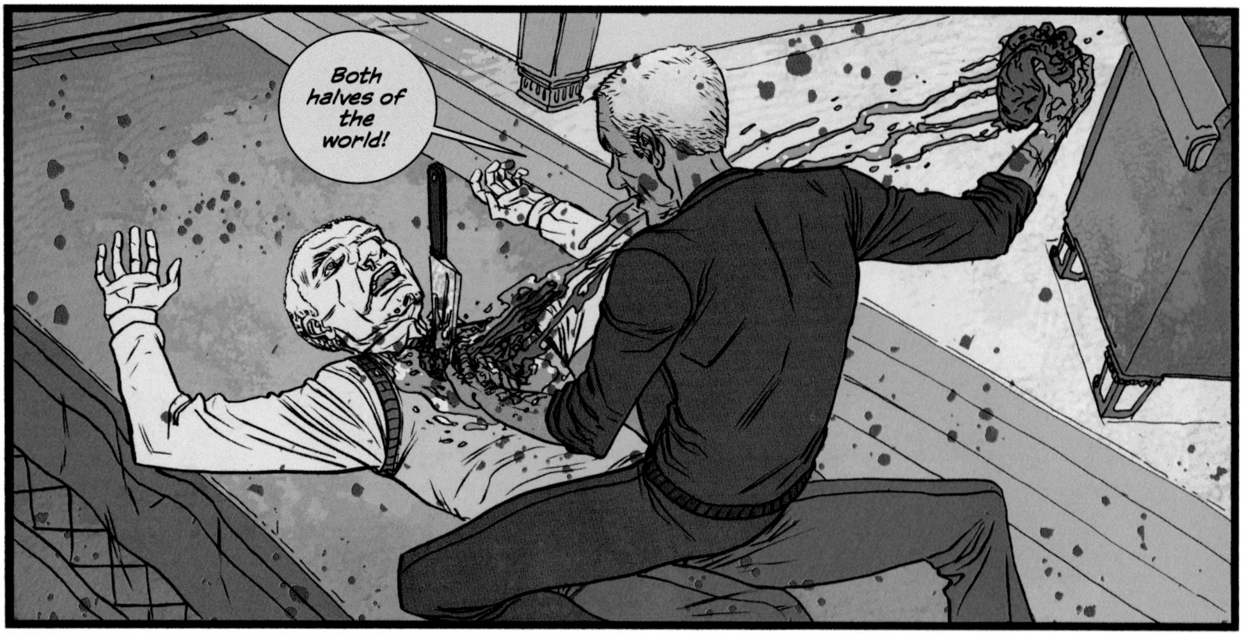
Both halves of the world!

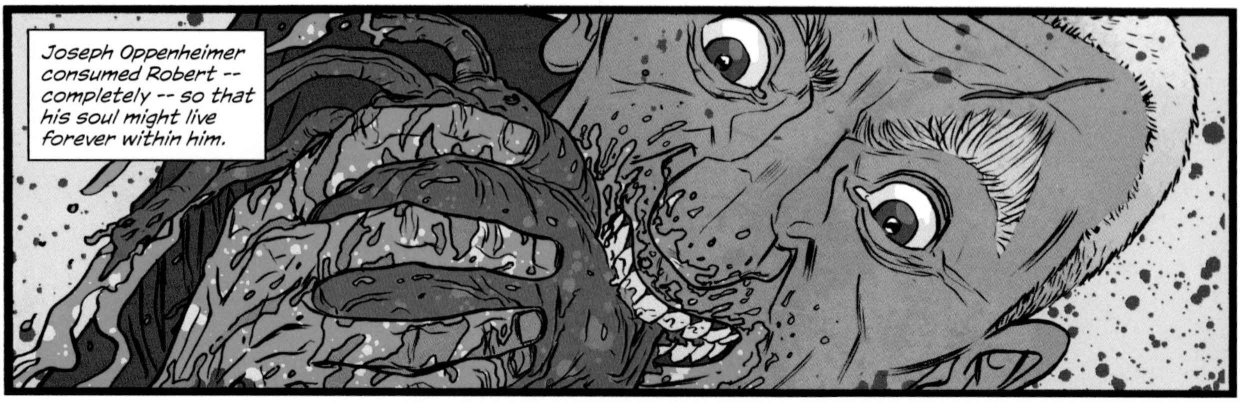
Joseph Oppenheimer consumed Robert -- completely -- so that his soul might live forever within him.

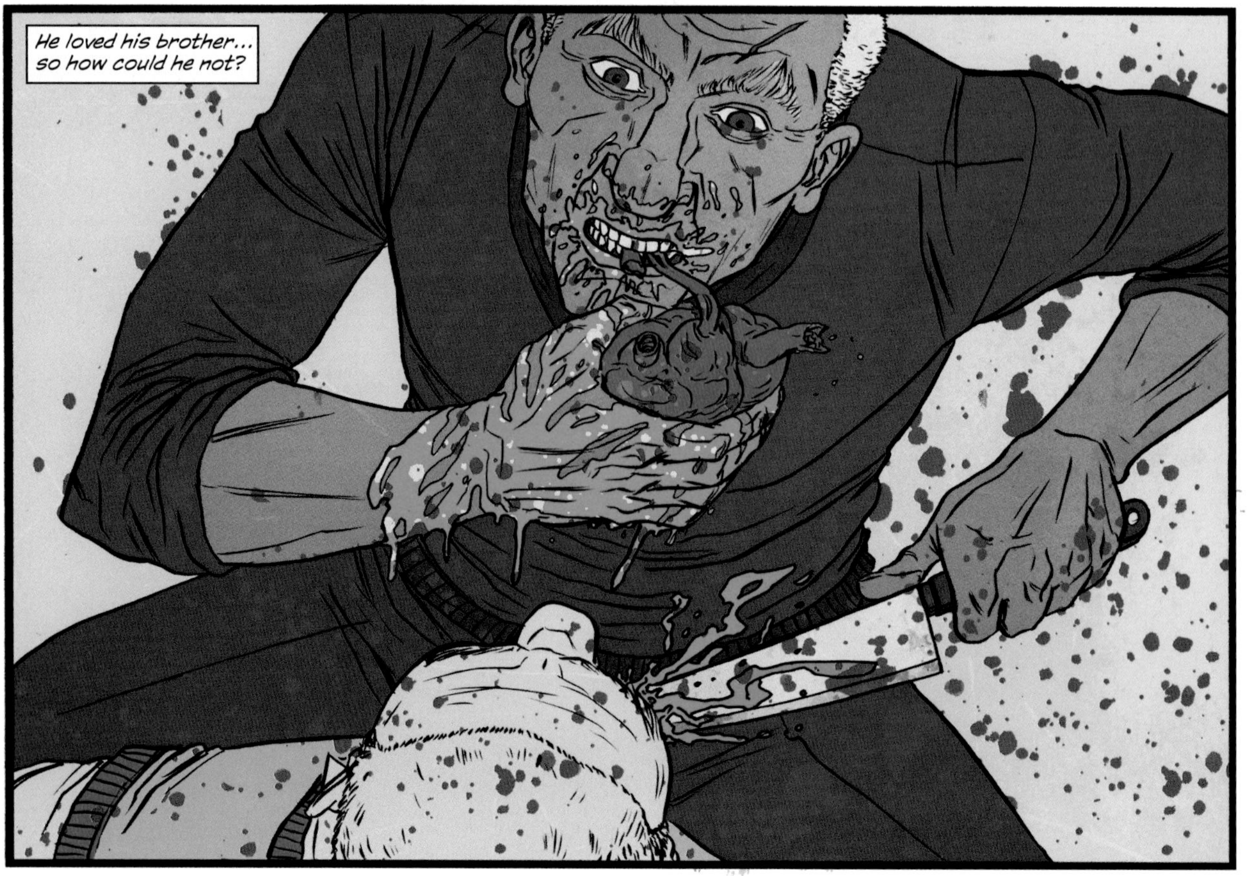
He loved his brother... so how could he not?

"THE GREAT EYE OF JOSEPH WATCHED
OVER THEM ALL. THIS IS HOW THE WAR
WAS LOST. "

- OPPENHEIMER

CLAVIS AUREA
THE RECORDED FEYNMAN | **VOL. 3**

10

FINITE OPPENHEIMERS

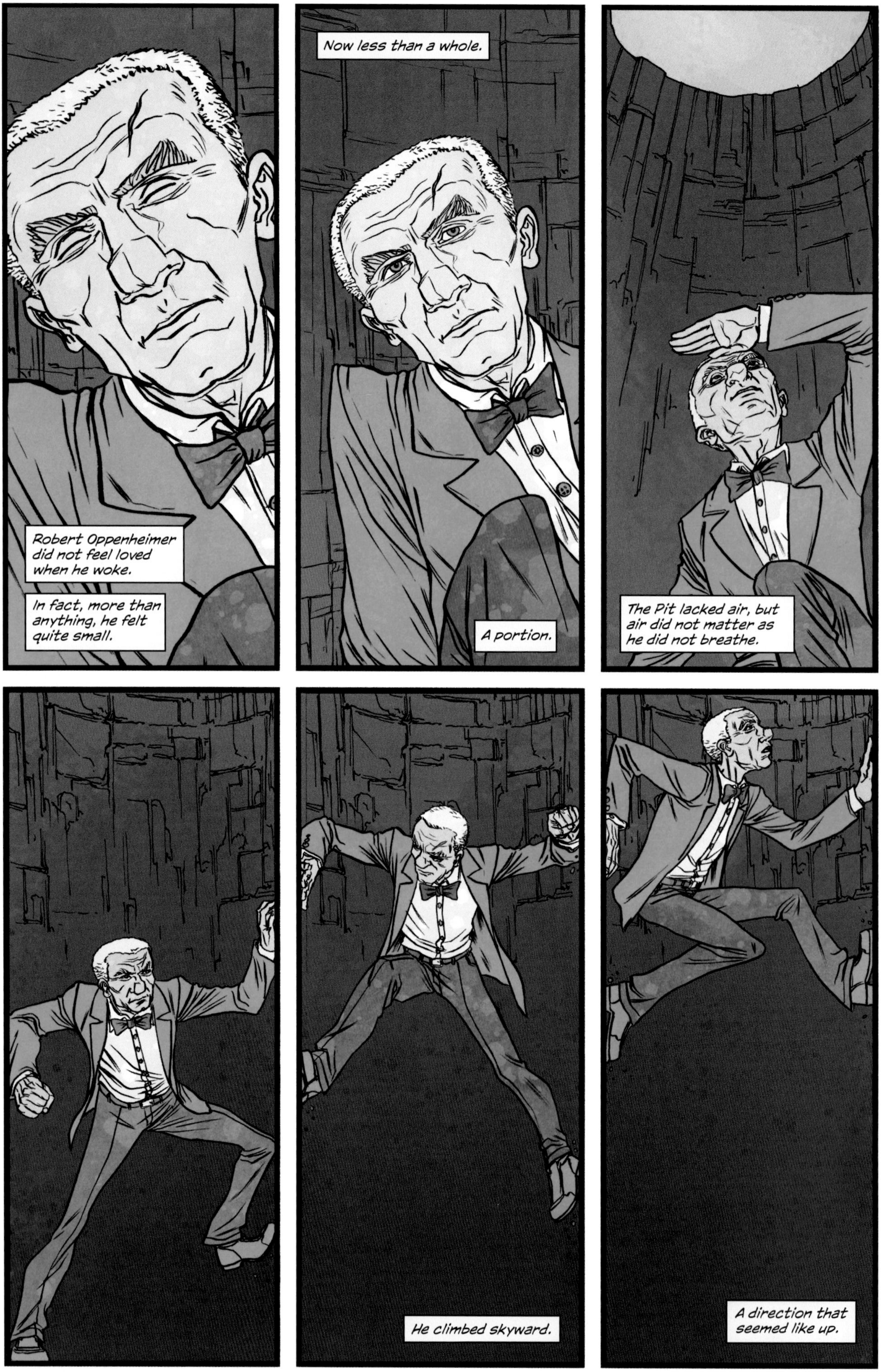
Robert Oppenheimer did not feel loved when he woke.
In fact, more than anything, he felt quite small.
Now less than a whole.
A portion.
The Pit lacked air, but air did not matter as he did not breathe.
He climbed skyward.
A direction that seemed like up.

He climbed out into not-day and not-night.

Some endless twilight emphasizing that, for an extended period, keeping track of time here would be difficult, if not impossible.

This did not concern him. Time being a component of progress seemed wrong in this place.

Achieving goals would be defined in other ways.

From the top of the world, Robert looked out, and he could see a city in the distance.

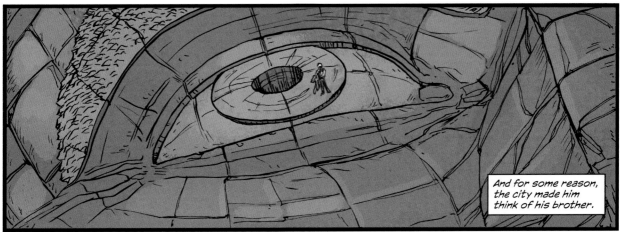

And for some reason, the city made him think of his brother.

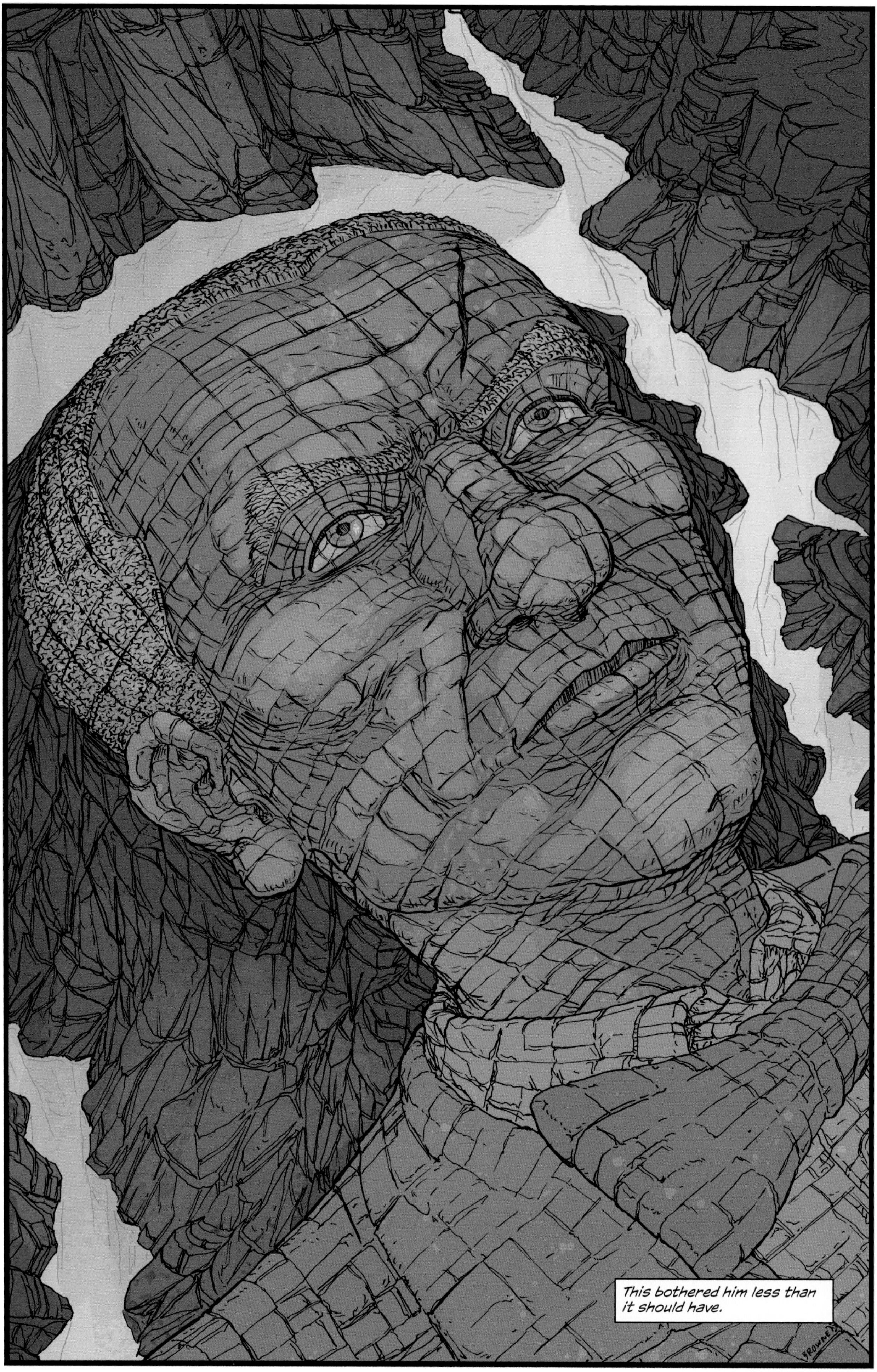
This bothered him less than it should have.

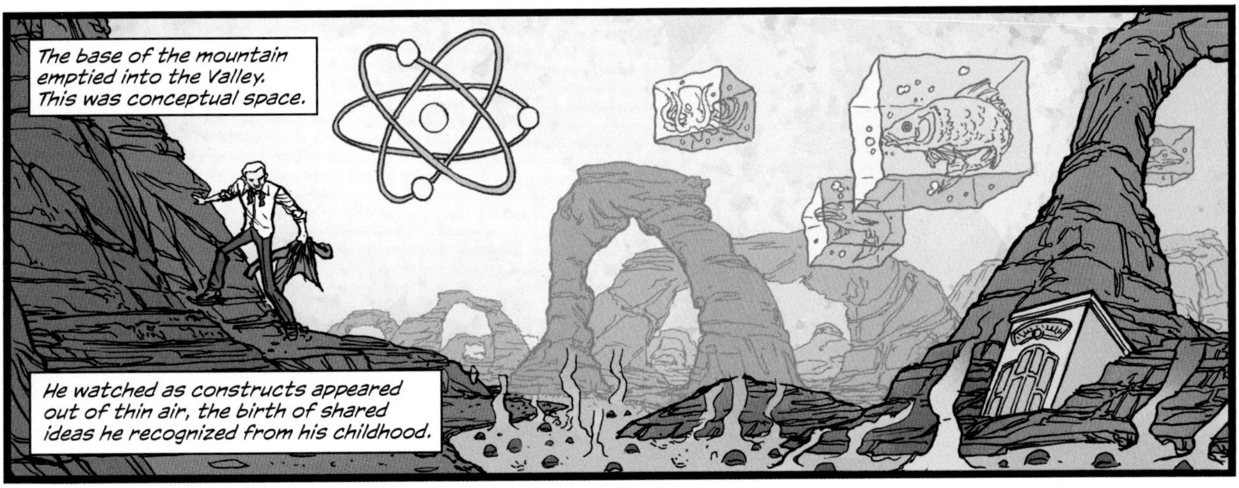
The base of the mountain emptied into the Valley. This was conceptual space.
He watched as constructs appeared out of thin air, the birth of shared ideas he recognized from his childhood.

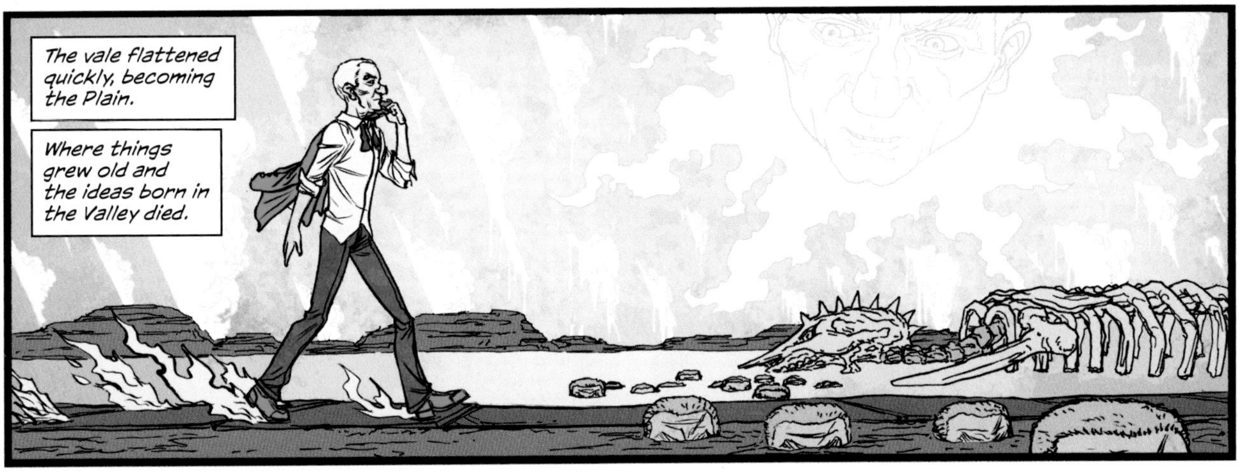
The vale flattened quickly, becoming the Plain.
Where things grew old and the ideas born in the Valley died.

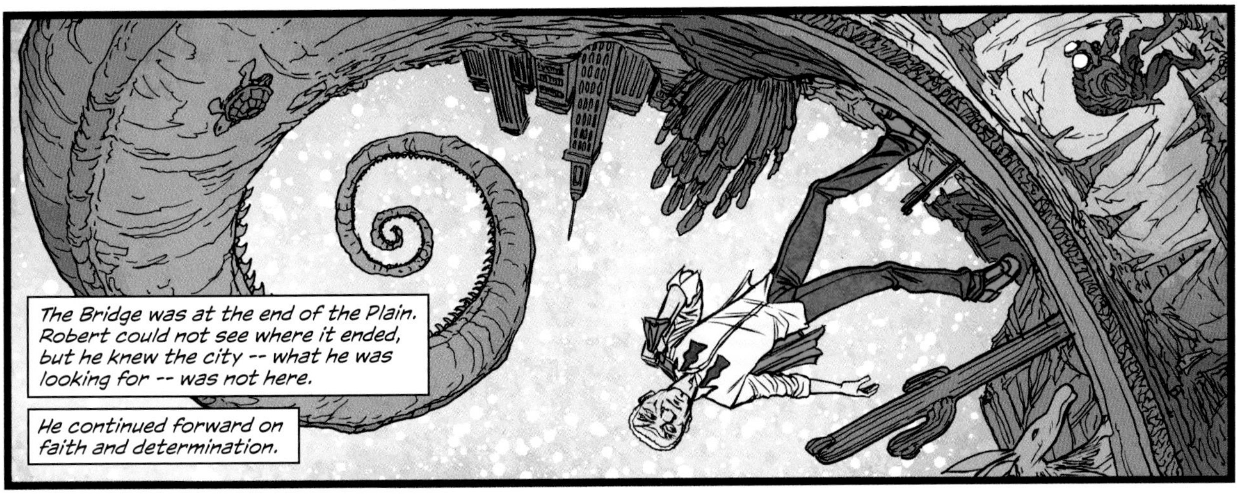
The Bridge was at the end of the Plain. Robert could not see where it ended, but he knew the city -- what he was looking for -- was not here.
He continued forward on faith and determination.

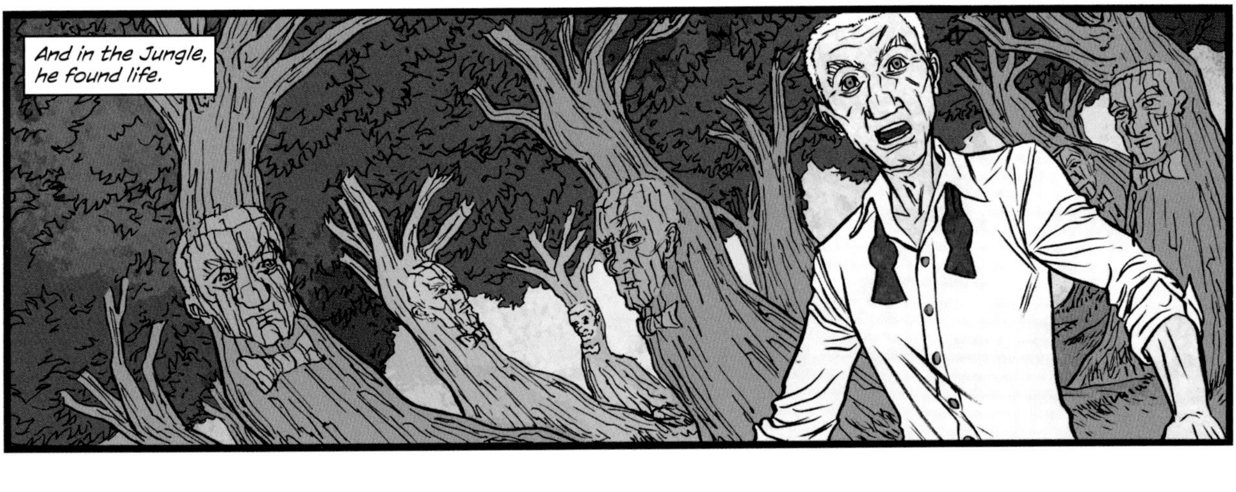
And in the Jungle, he found life.

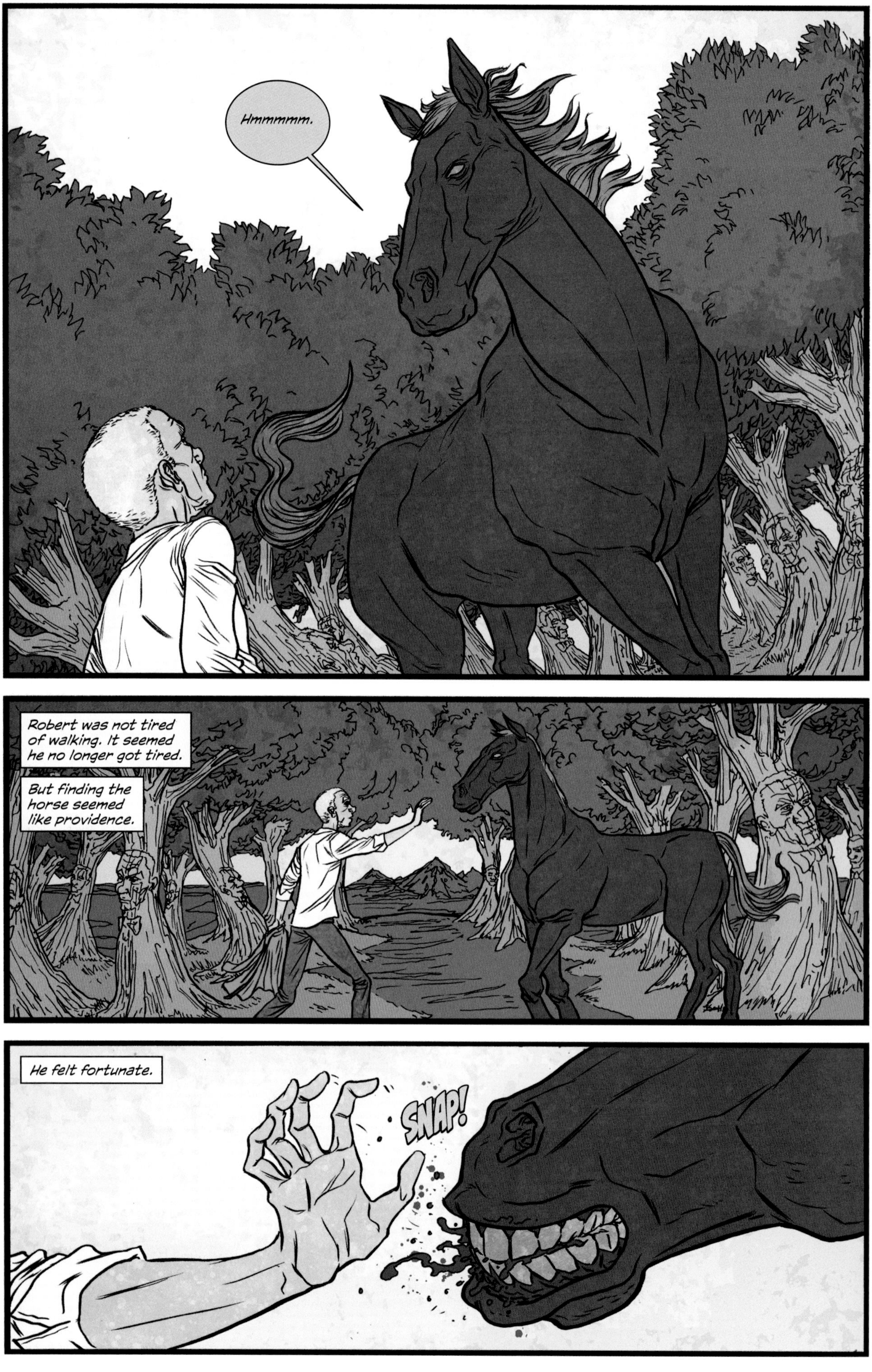

Hmmmmm.
Robert was not tired of walking. It seemed he no longer got tired.
But finding the horse seemed like providence.
He felt fortunate.
SNAP!

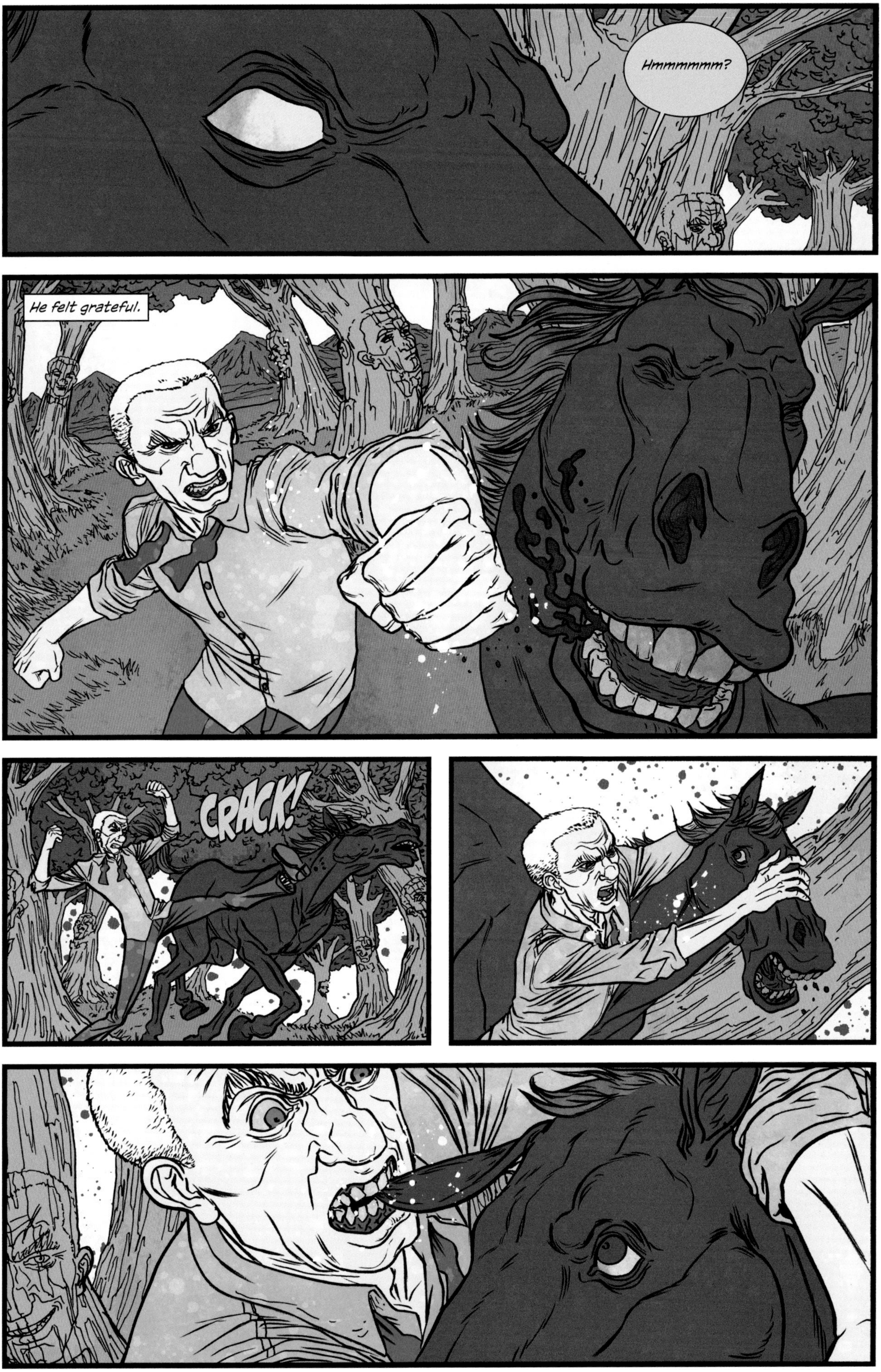
Hmmmmmm?
He felt grateful.
CRACK!

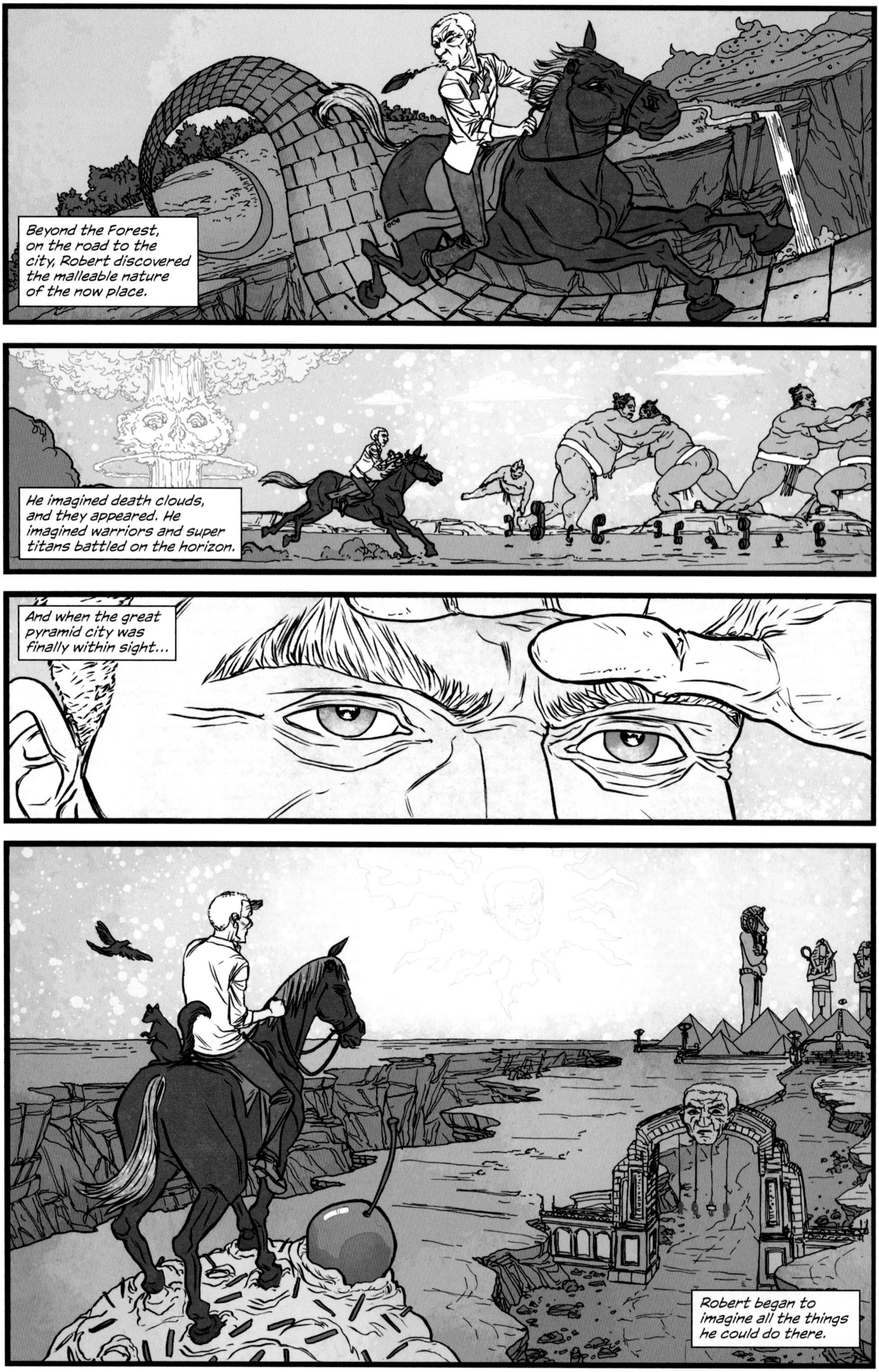
Beyond the Forest, on the road to the city, Robert discovered the malleable nature of the now place.
He imagined death clouds, and they appeared. He imagined warriors and super titans battled on the horizon.
And when the great pyramid city was finally within sight...
Robert began to imagine all the things he could do there.

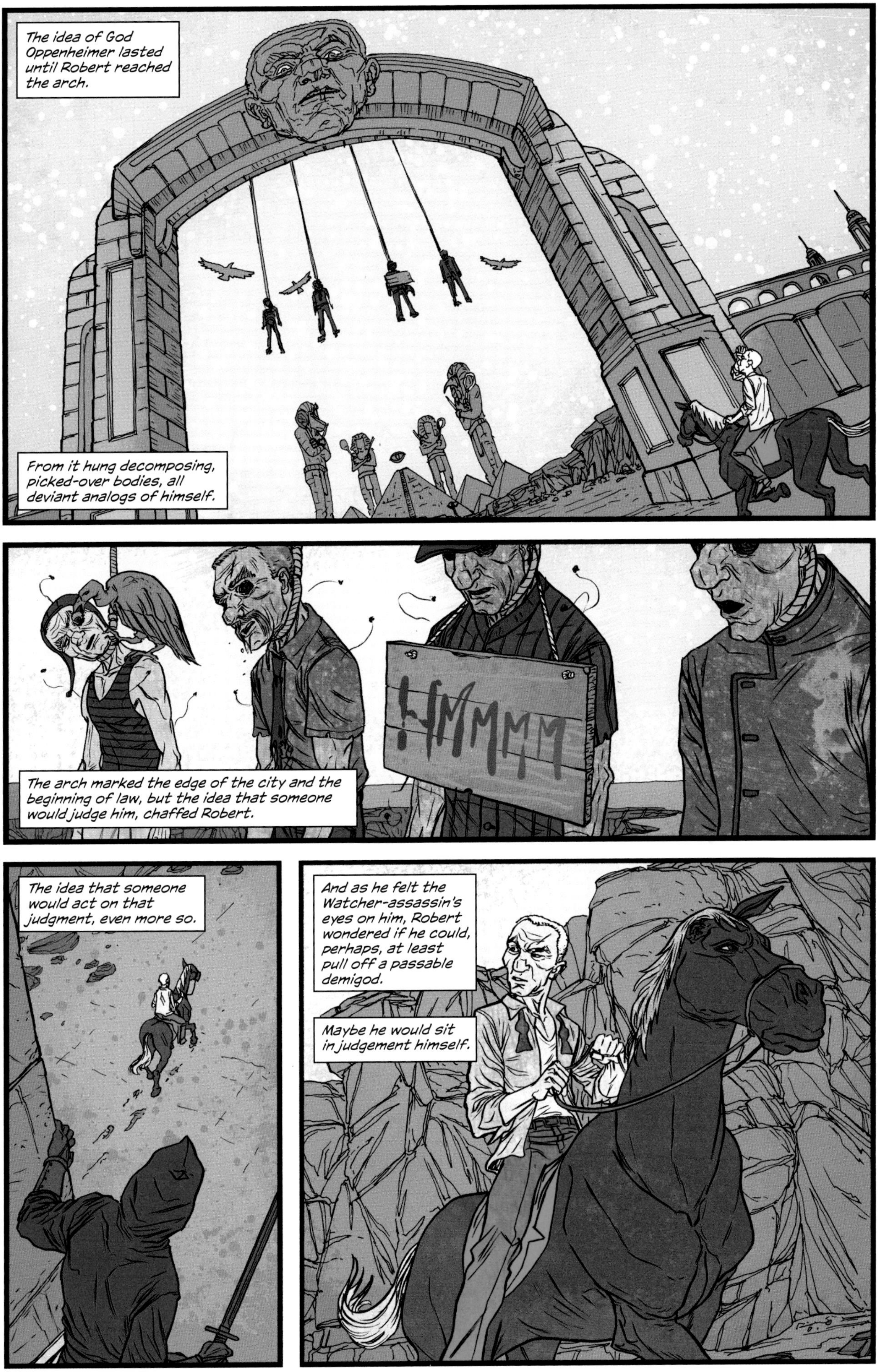
The idea of God Oppenheimer lasted until Robert reached the arch.
From it hung decomposing, picked-over bodies, all deviant analogs of himself.
HMMMM
The arch marked the edge of the city and the beginning of law, but the idea that someone would judge him, chaffed Robert.
The idea that someone would act on that judgment, even more so.
And as he felt the Watcher-assassin's eyes on him, Robert wondered if he could, perhaps, at least pull off a passable demigod.
Maybe he would sit in judgement himself.

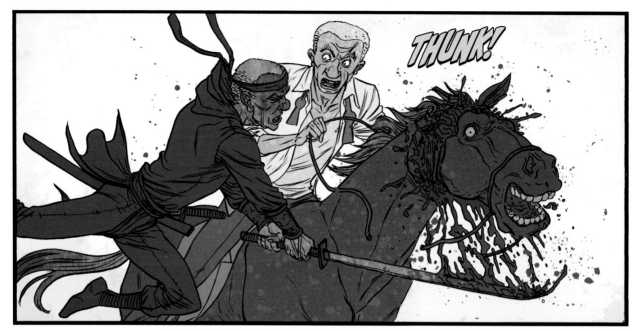

THUNK!

Hmmmm.

Hmmmm.

HMMMMM!

Robert imagined the Watcher-assassin bound, and hid his surprise when nothing happened.

He learned the Oppenheimer variants were beyond manipulation. Each one an individual persona operating outside the psychics of the now place.

But the world remained the world. A thing to be shaped.

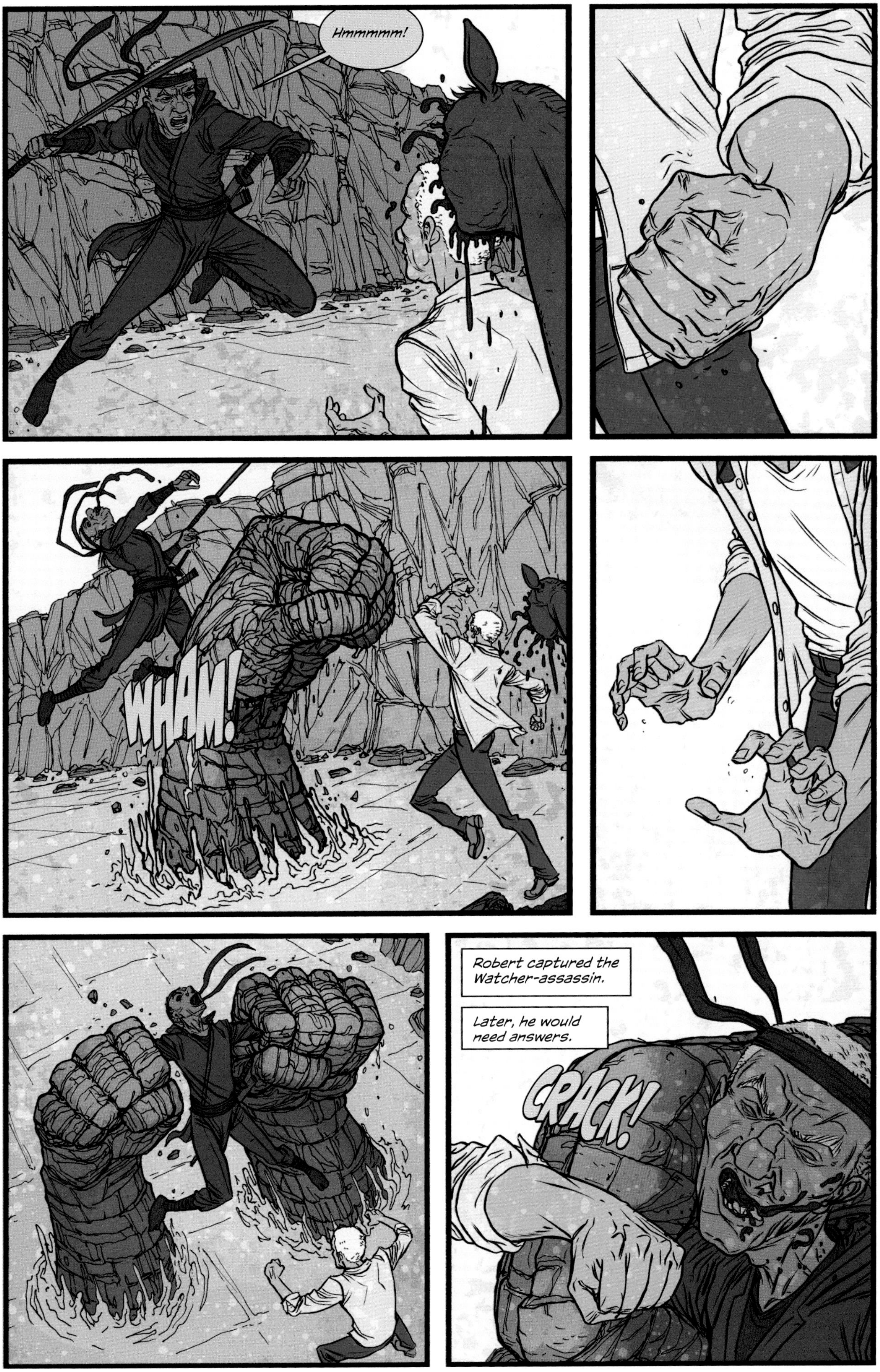
Hmmmmm!
WHAM!
Robert captured the Watcher-assassin.
Later, he would need answers.
CRACK!

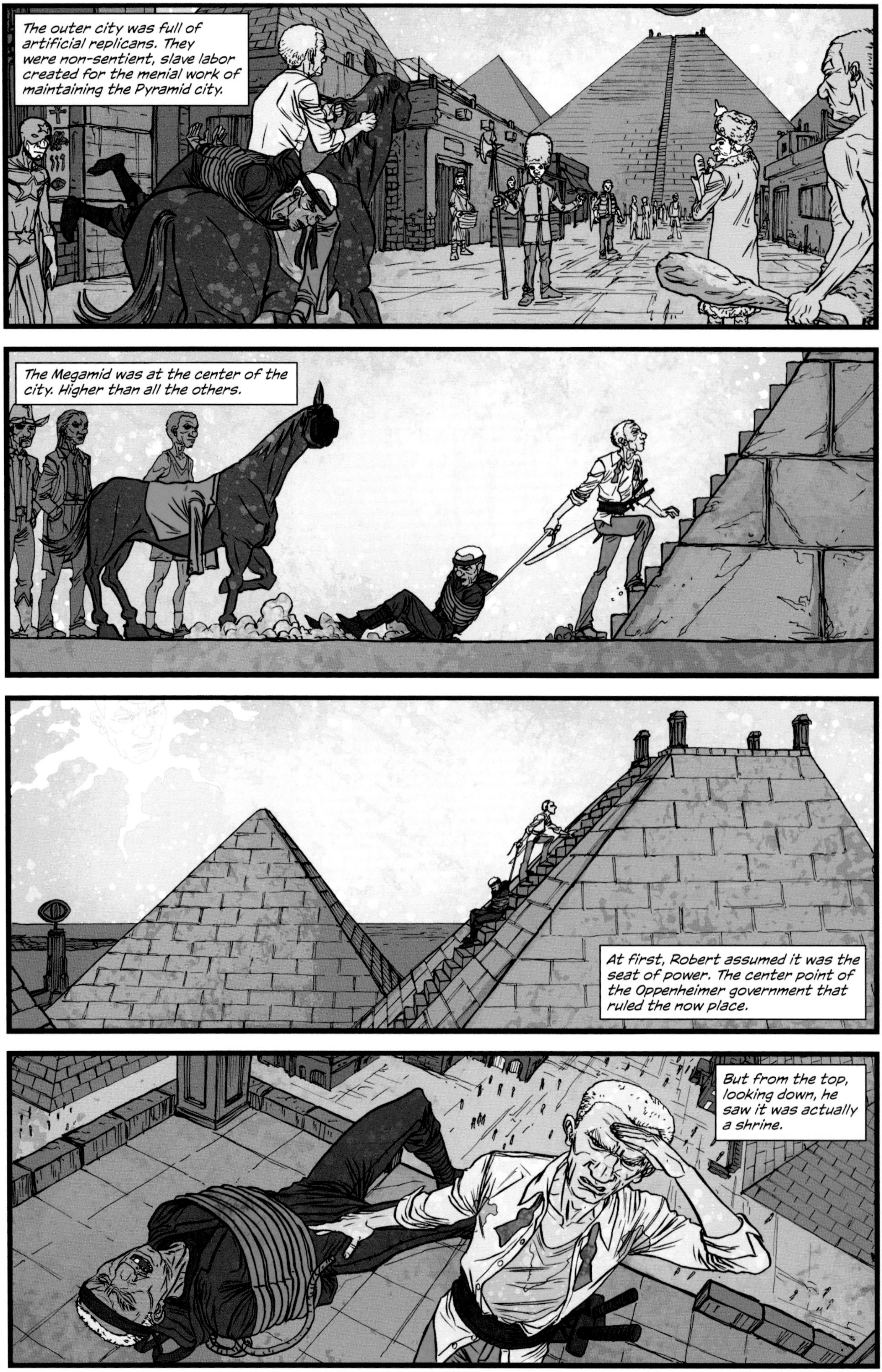
The outer city was full of artificial replicans. They were non-sentient, slave labor created for the menial work of maintaining the Pyramid city.
The Megamid was at the center of the city. Higher than all the others.
At first, Robert assumed it was the seat of power. The center point of the Oppenheimer government that ruled the now place.
But from the top, looking down, he saw it was actually a shrine.

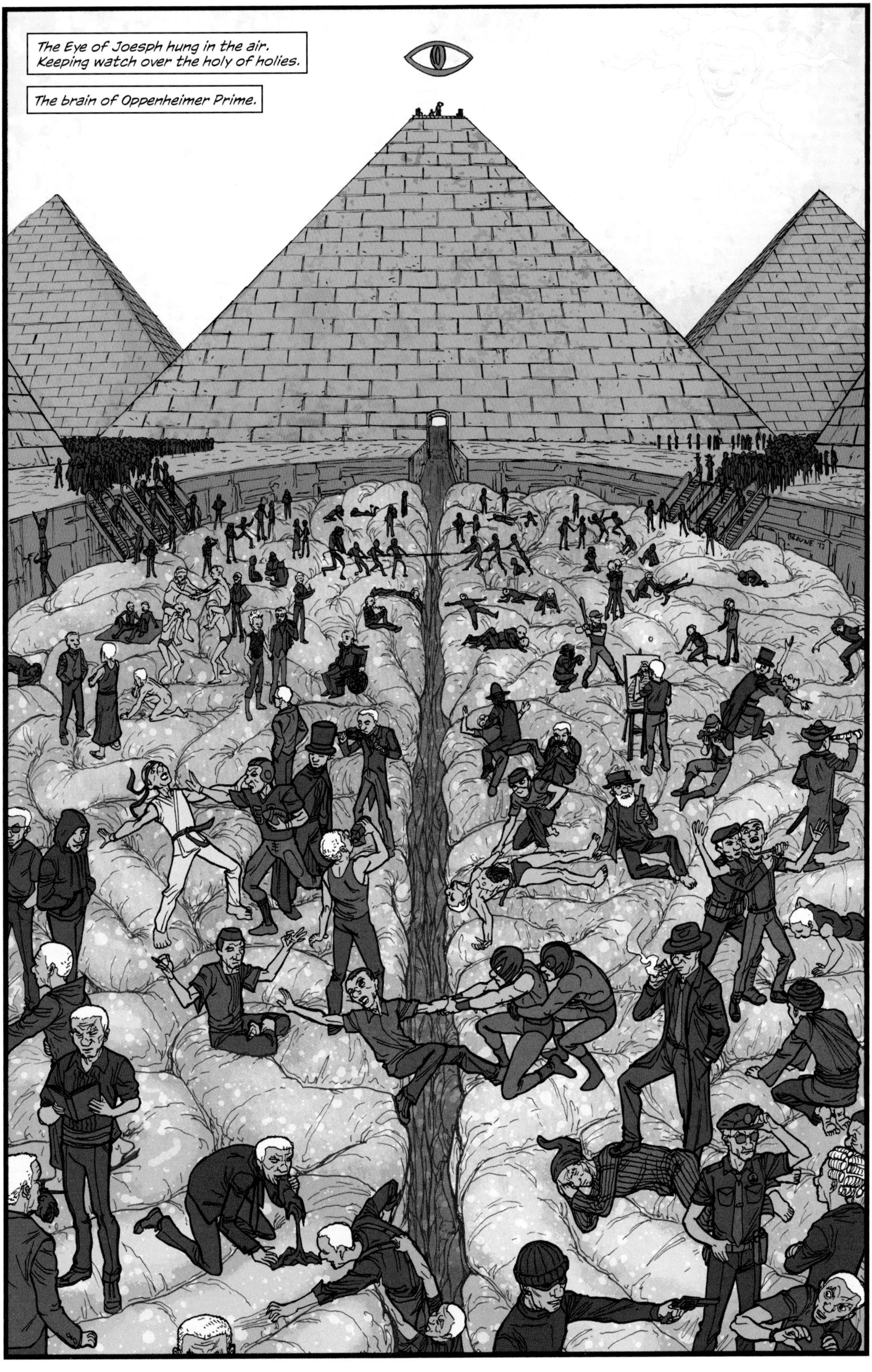
The Eye of Joesph hung in the air.
Keeping watch over the holy of holies.
The brain of Oppenheimer Prime.

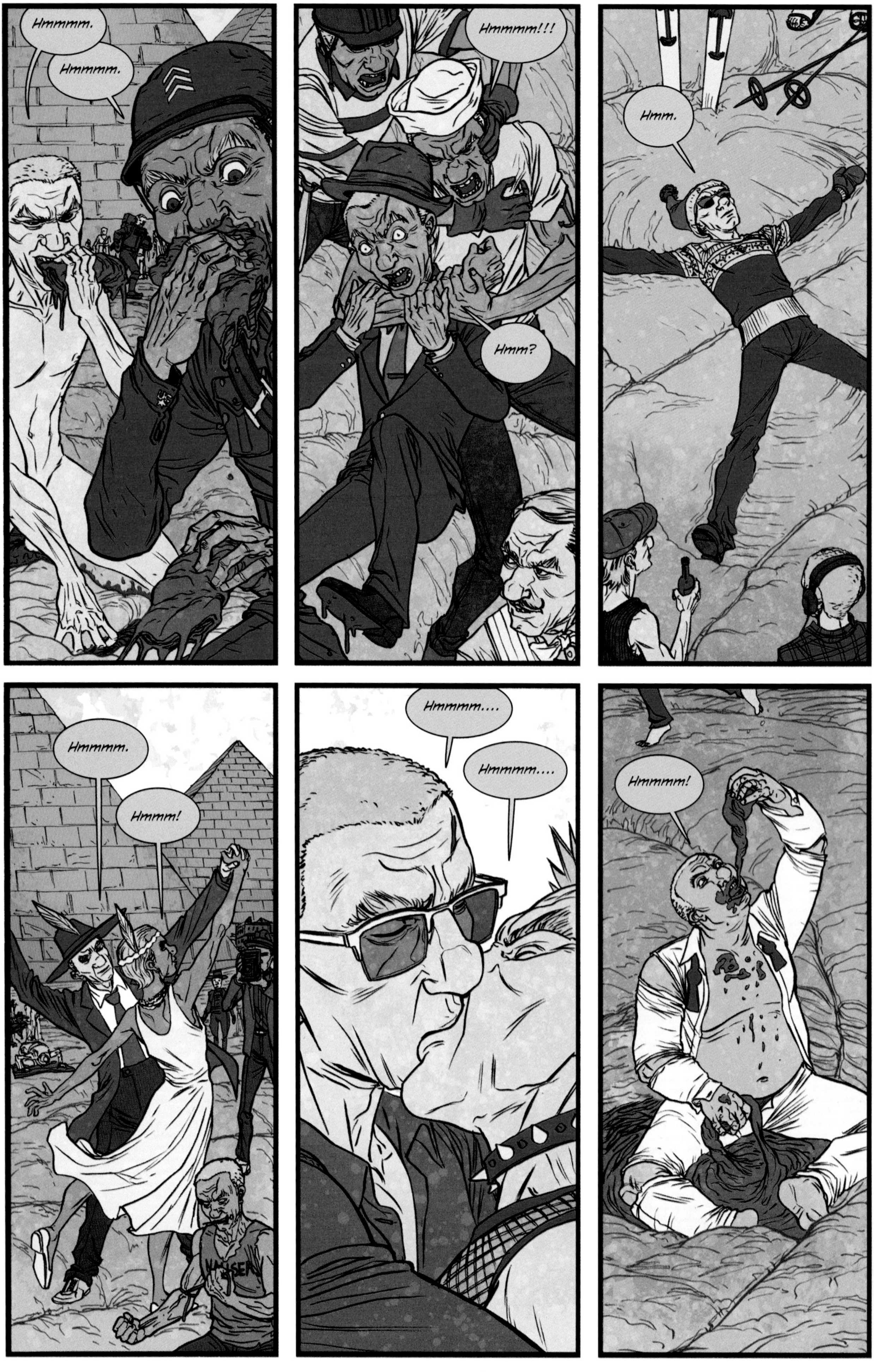
Hmmmm.
Hmmmm.
Hmmmm!!!
Hmm?
Hmm.
Hmmmm.
Hmmm!
Hmmmm....
Hmmmm....
Hmmmm!

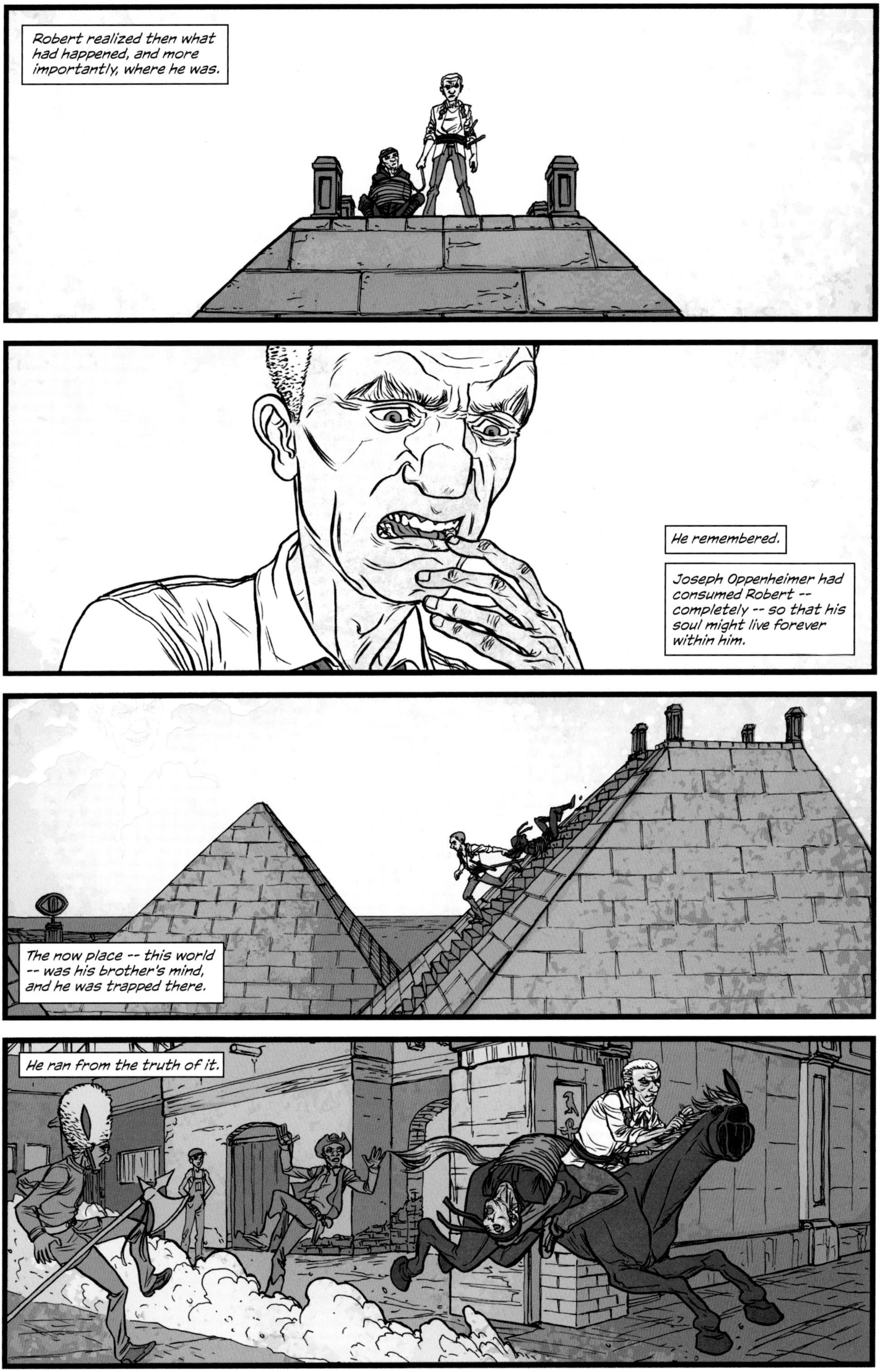
Robert realized then what had happened, and more importantly, where he was.
He remembered.
Joseph Oppenheimer had consumed Robert -- completely -- so that his soul might live forever within him.
The now place -- this world -- was his brother's mind, and he was trapped there.
He ran from the truth of it.

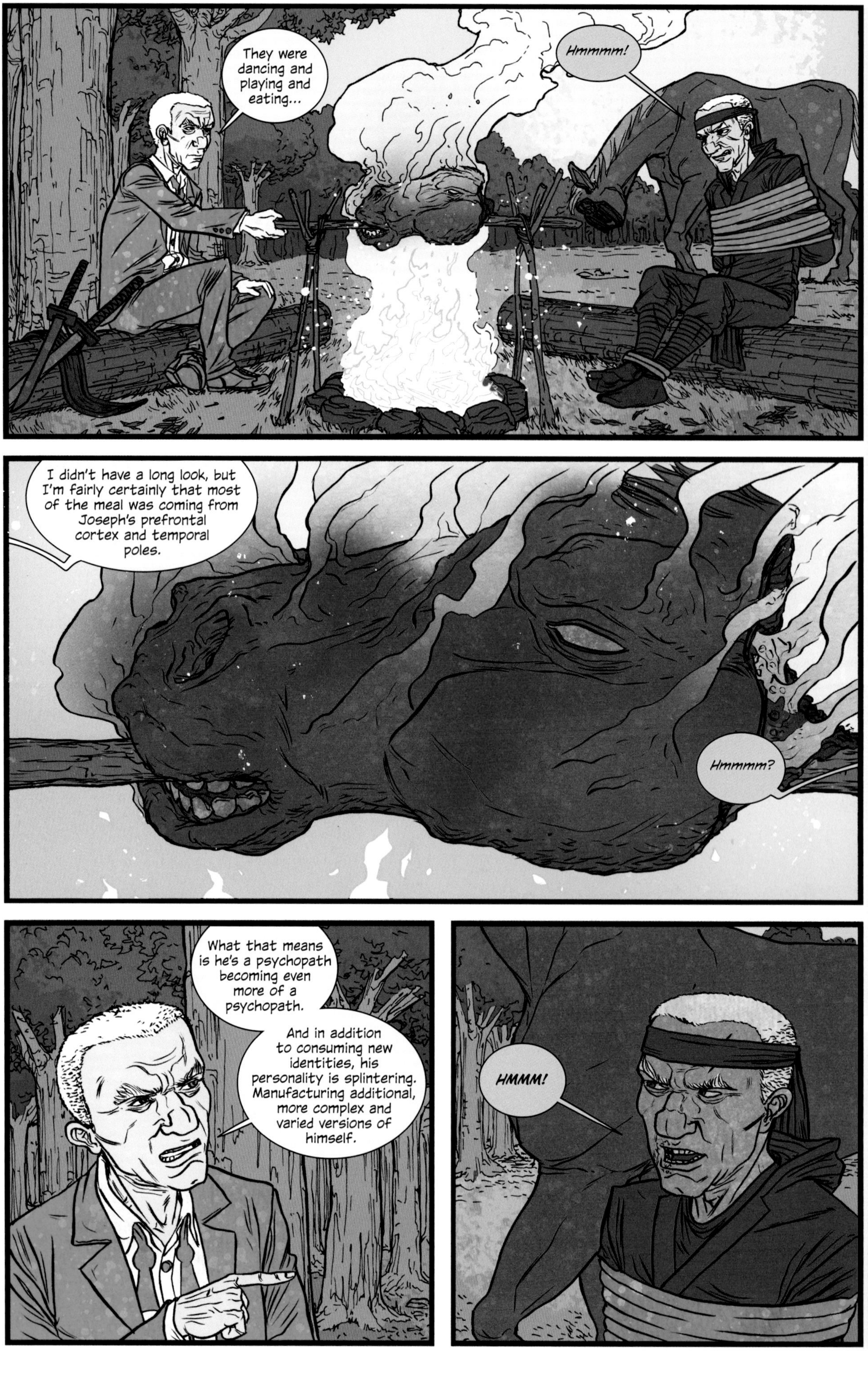

They were dancing and playing and eating...
Hmmmm!
I didn't have a long look, but I'm fairly certainly that most of the meal was coming from Joseph's prefrontal cortex and temporal poles.
Hmmmm?
What that means is he's a psychopath becoming even more of a psychopath.
And in addition to consuming new identities, his personality is splintering. Manufacturing additional, more complex and varied versions of himself.
HMMM!

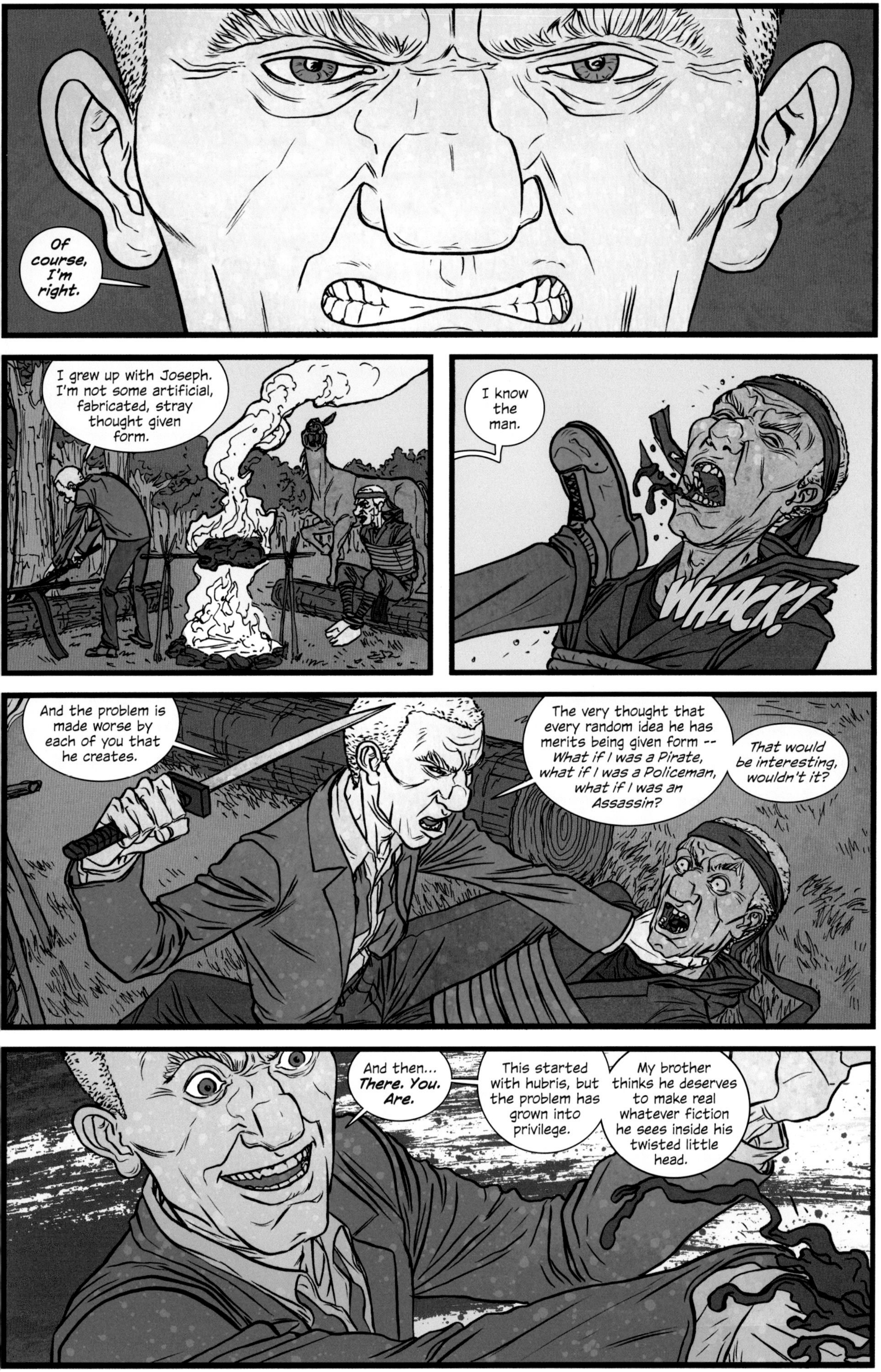
Of course, I'm right.
I grew up with Joseph. I'm not some artificial, fabricated, stray thought given form.
I know the man.
WHACK!
And the problem is made worse by each of you that he creates.
The very thought that every random idea he has merits being given form -- What if I was a Pirate, what if I was a Policeman, what if I was an Assassin?
That would be interesting, wouldn't it?
And then... There. You. Are.
This started with hubris, but the problem has grown into privilege.
My brother thinks he deserves to make real whatever fiction he sees inside his twisted little head.

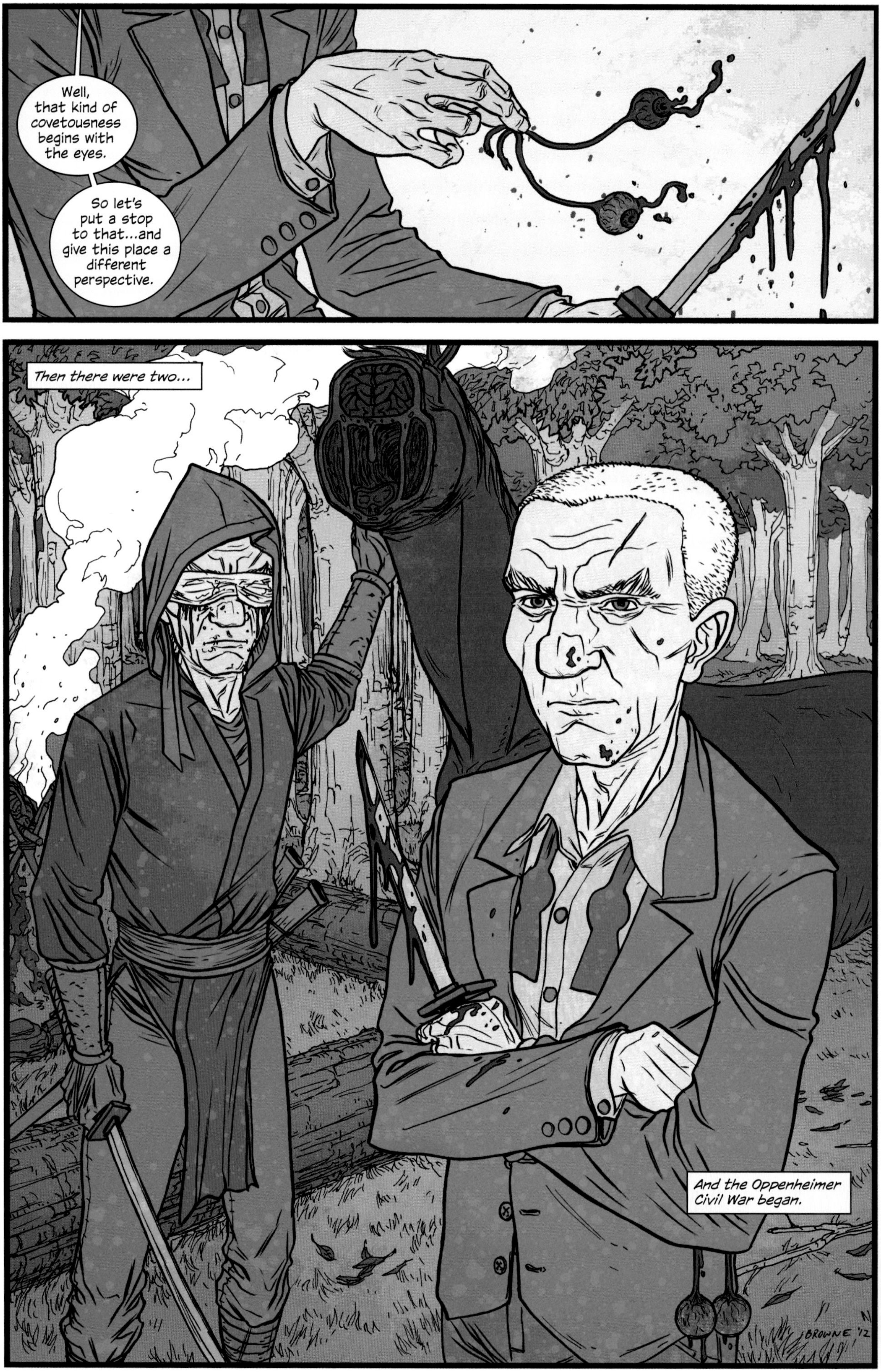
Well, that kind of covetousness begins with the eyes.
So let's put a stop to that...and give this place a different perspective.
Then there were two...
And the Oppenheimer Civil War began.
BROWNE '12

"WE LOOKED UP, AND FROM THE MEGAMID, IT LOOKED DOWN. THE GREAT EYE OFFENDED, SO WE PLUCKED THEM OUT.

AGAIN, AND AGAIN, AND AGAIN."

- OPPENHEIMER

CLAVIS AUREA
THE RECORDED FEYNMAN | **VOL. 3**

THE CAST

JOSEPH OPPENHEIMER

Super genius.
American. Physicist.
Multiple personalities.

ALBRECHT EINSTEIN

Highly intelligent.
German. Physicist.
Drinks.

RICHARD FEYNMAN

Super genius.
American. Physicist.
Wormholer.

ENRICO FERMI

Super genius.
Italian. Physicist.
Not human.

HARRY DAGHLIAN

Super genius.
American. Physicist.
Irradiated.

WERNHER VON BRAUN

Super genius.
German. Rocket scientist.
Robot arm.

LESLIE GROVES

Not a genius.
American. General.
Smokes. Bombs.

FDR: A.I.

Computational super genius.
American. President.
Dead.

HARRY S. TRUMAN

Not a genius.
American. President.
Freemason.

THE CAST

YURI GAGARIN

Not a genius.
Russian. Cosmonaut.
Hero.

LAIKA

Way smarter than thought.
Russian. Space Dog.
Speaks.

HELMUTT GRÖTTRUP

Super genius.
German. Rocket scientist.
Slave.

DMITRIY USTINOV

Not a genius.
Russian. Minister.
Master.

BAD
PHYSICS.

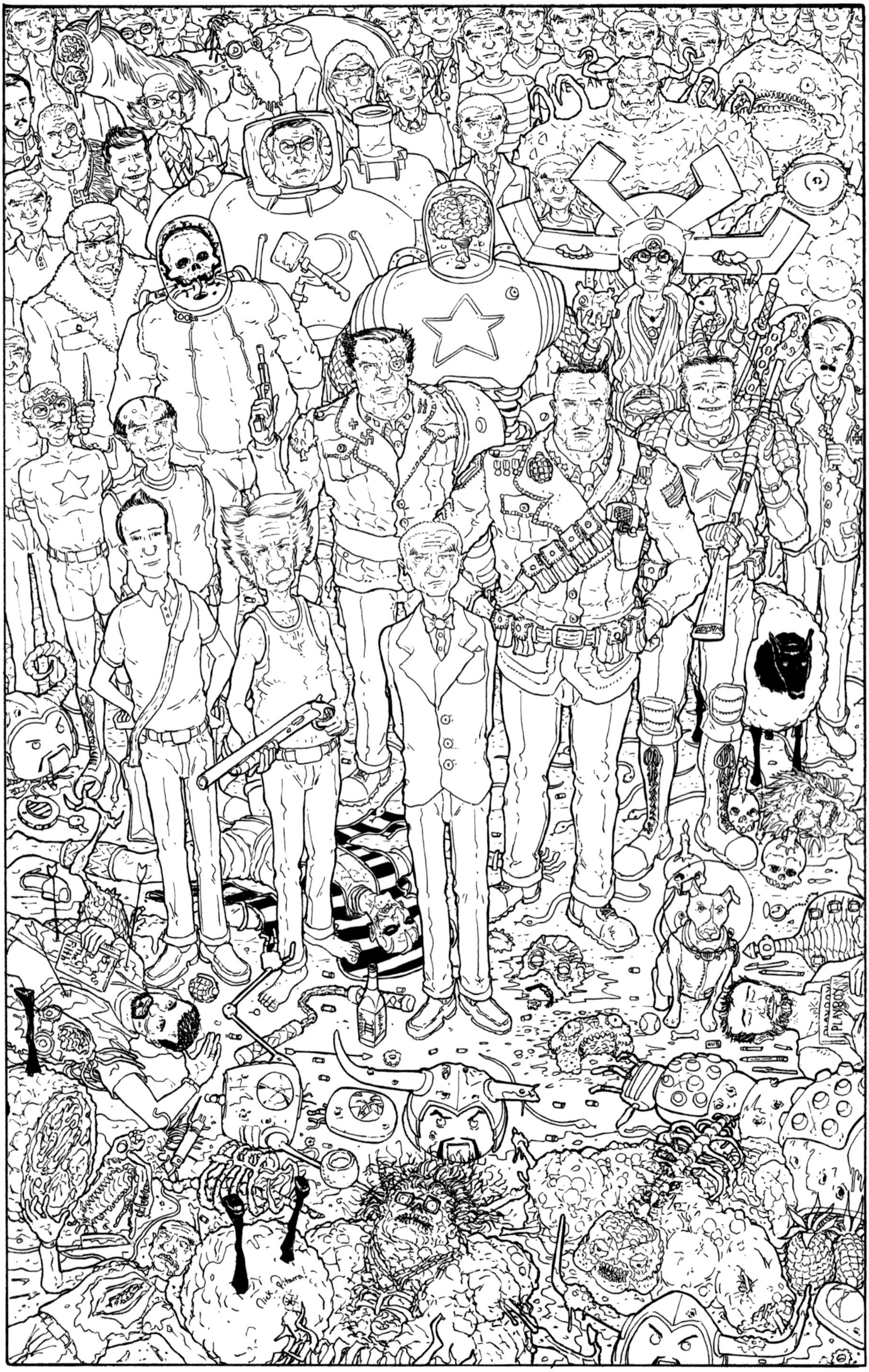
PLAYBOY
Nick Pitarra!

DESIGNS.

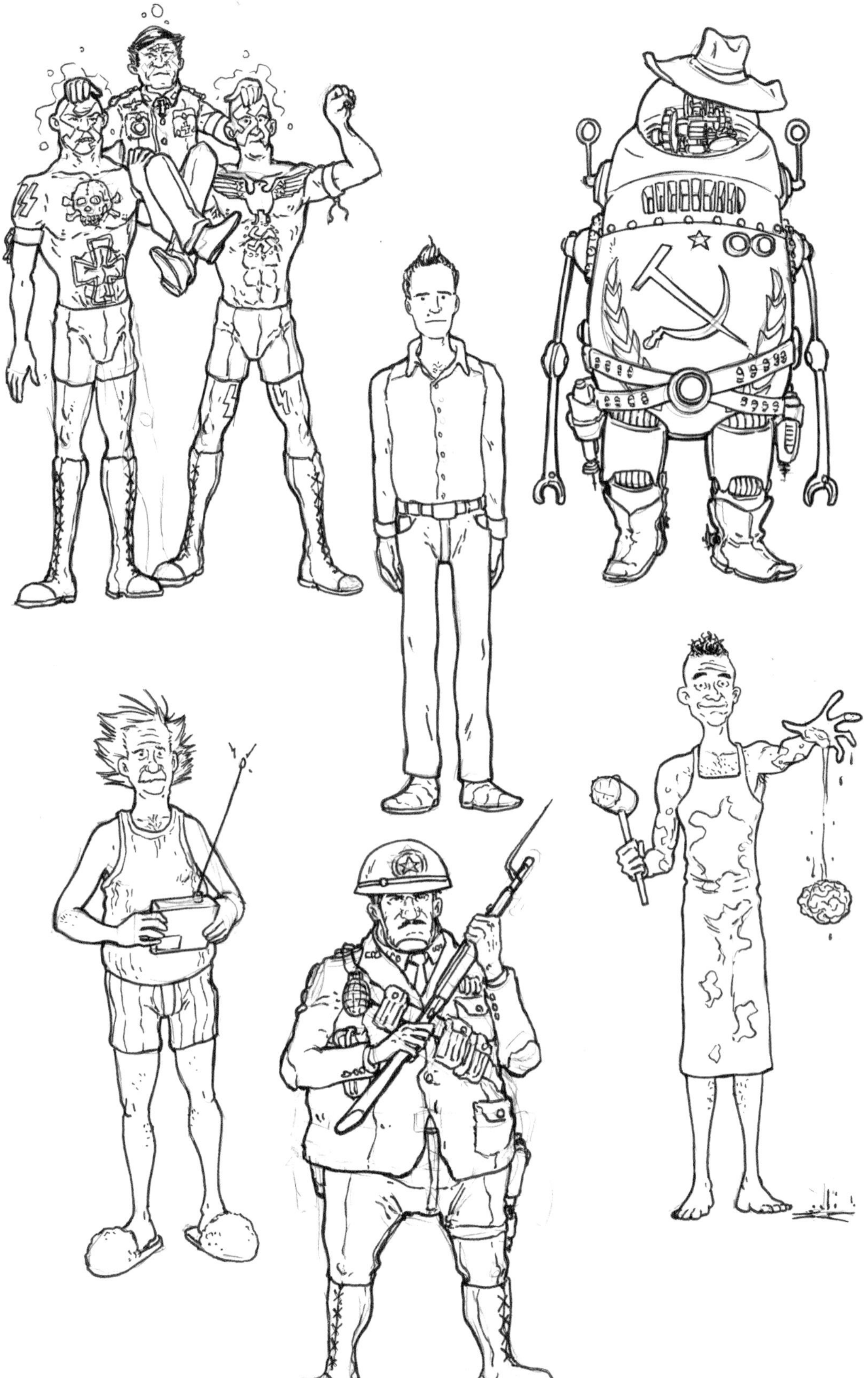

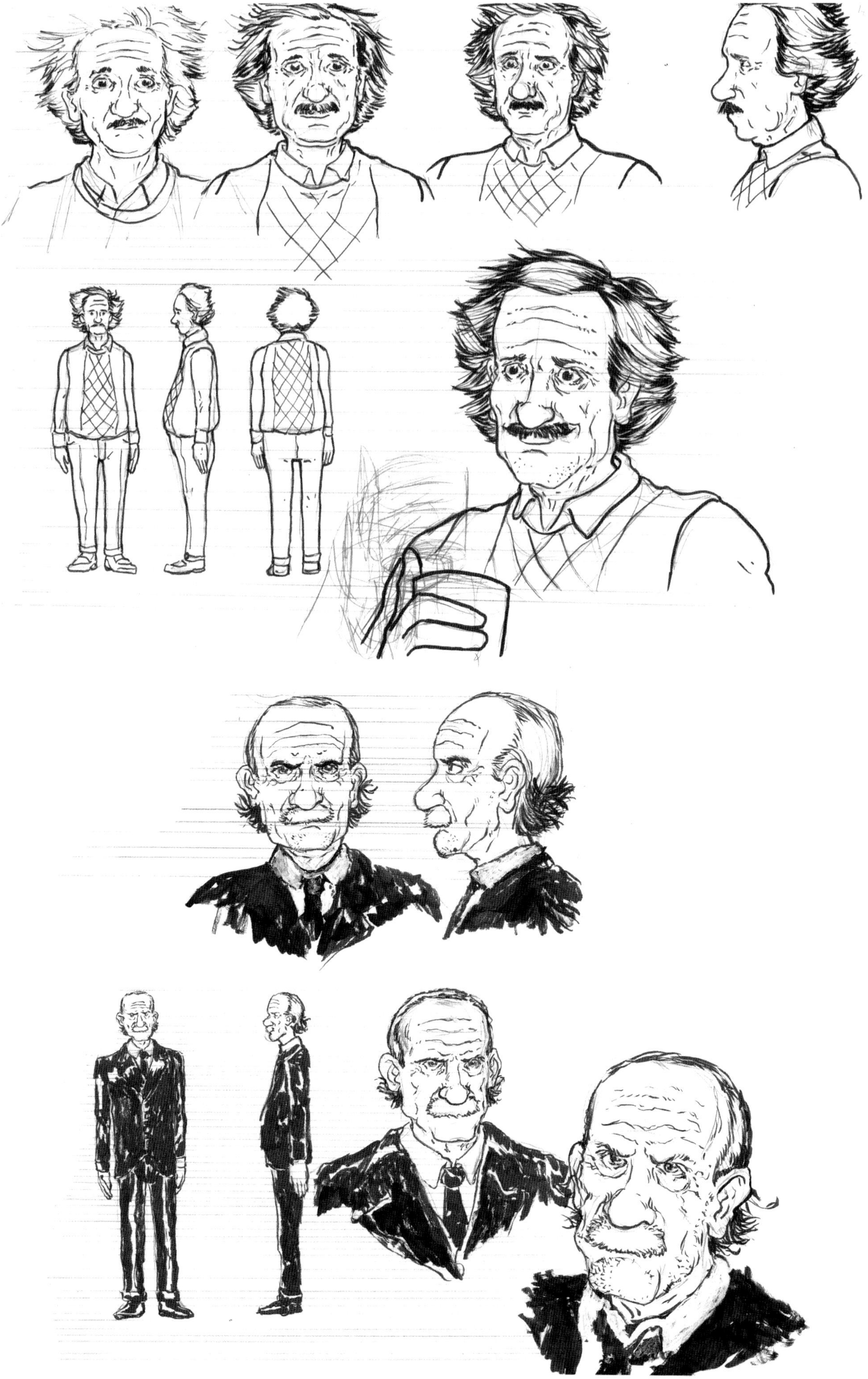

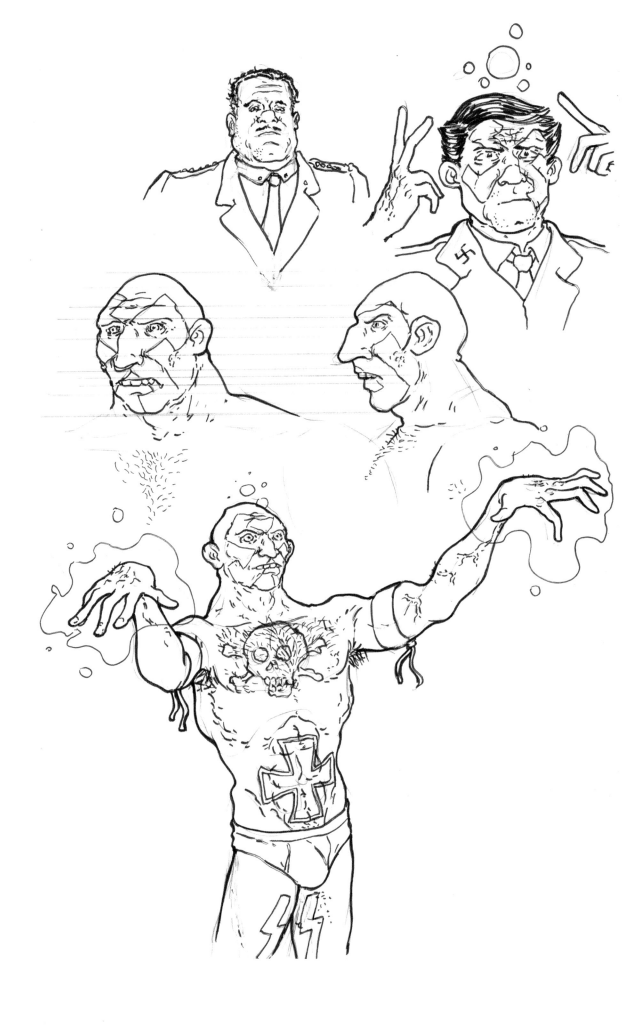

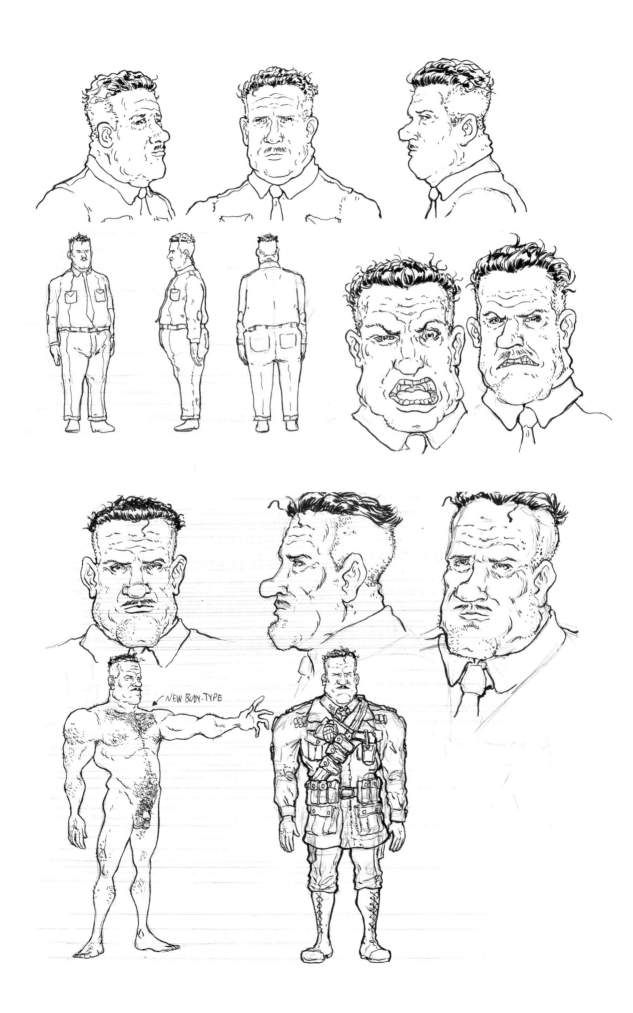

NEW BODY-TYPE

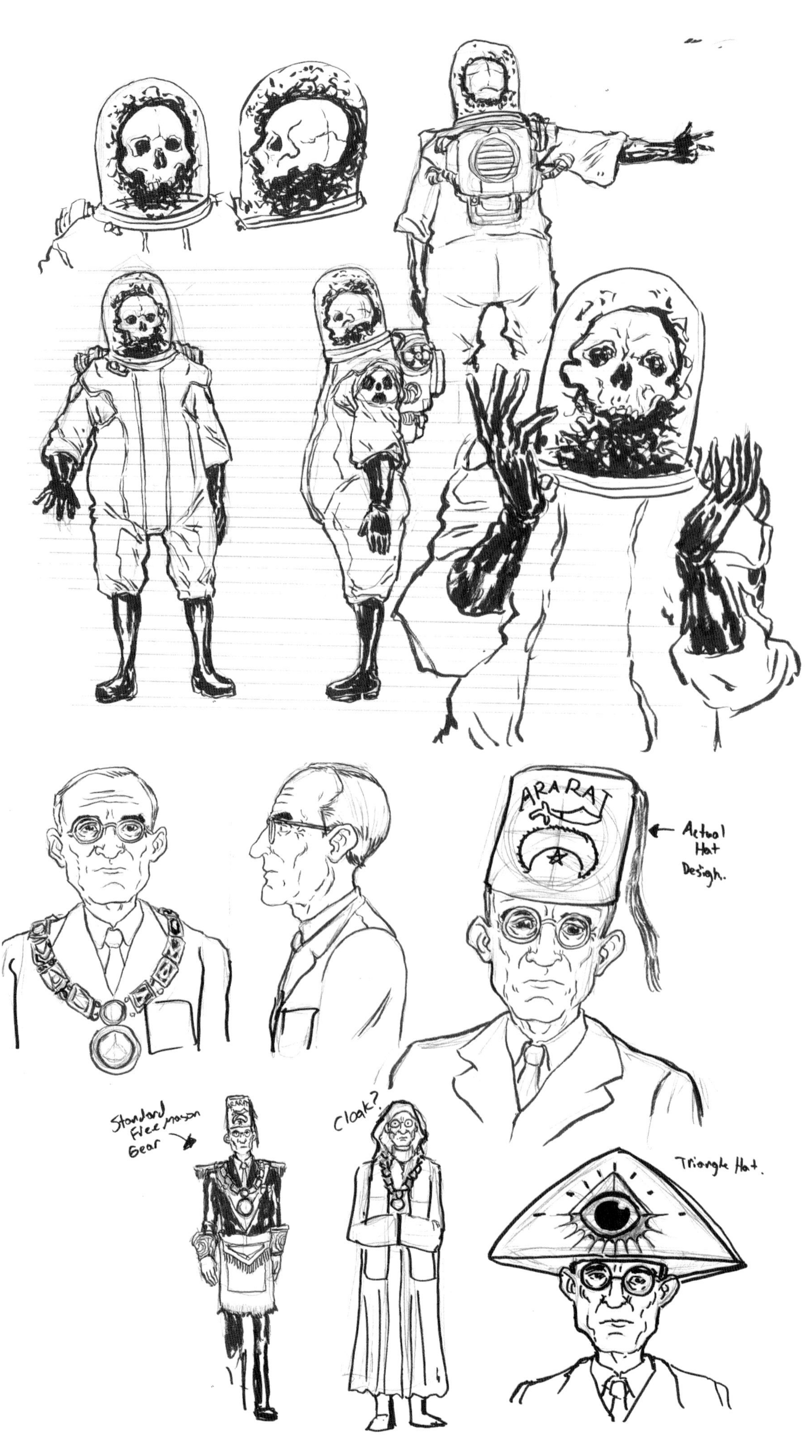
ARARAT
Actual Hat Design.
Standard Freemason Gear
Cloak?
Triangle Hat.

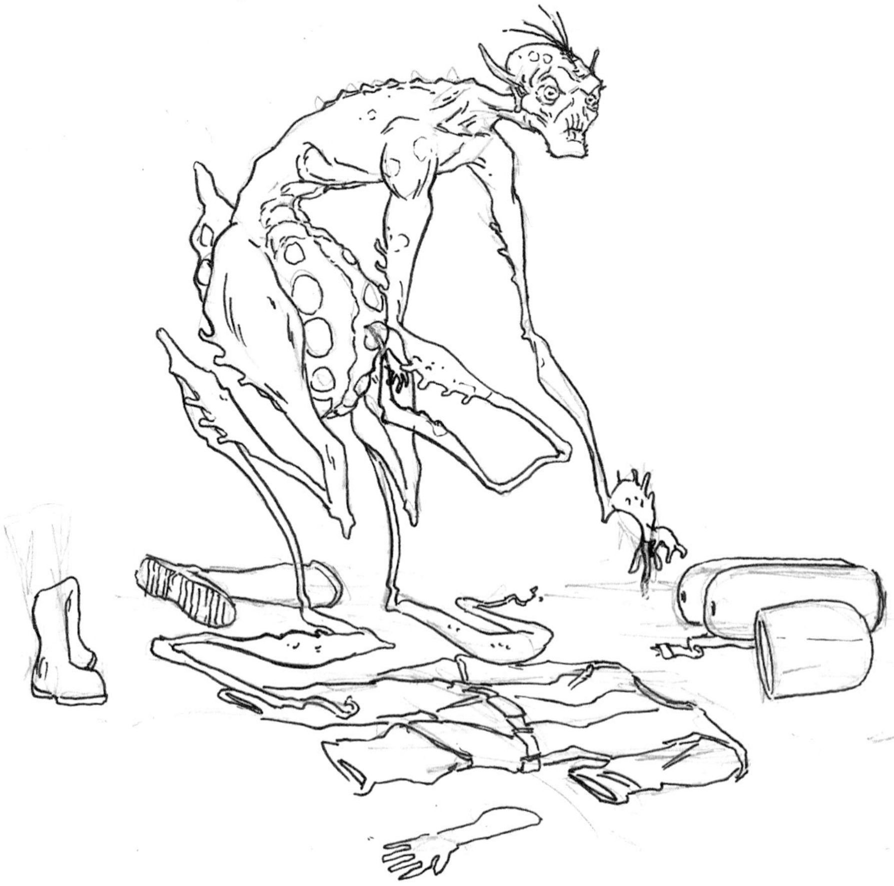

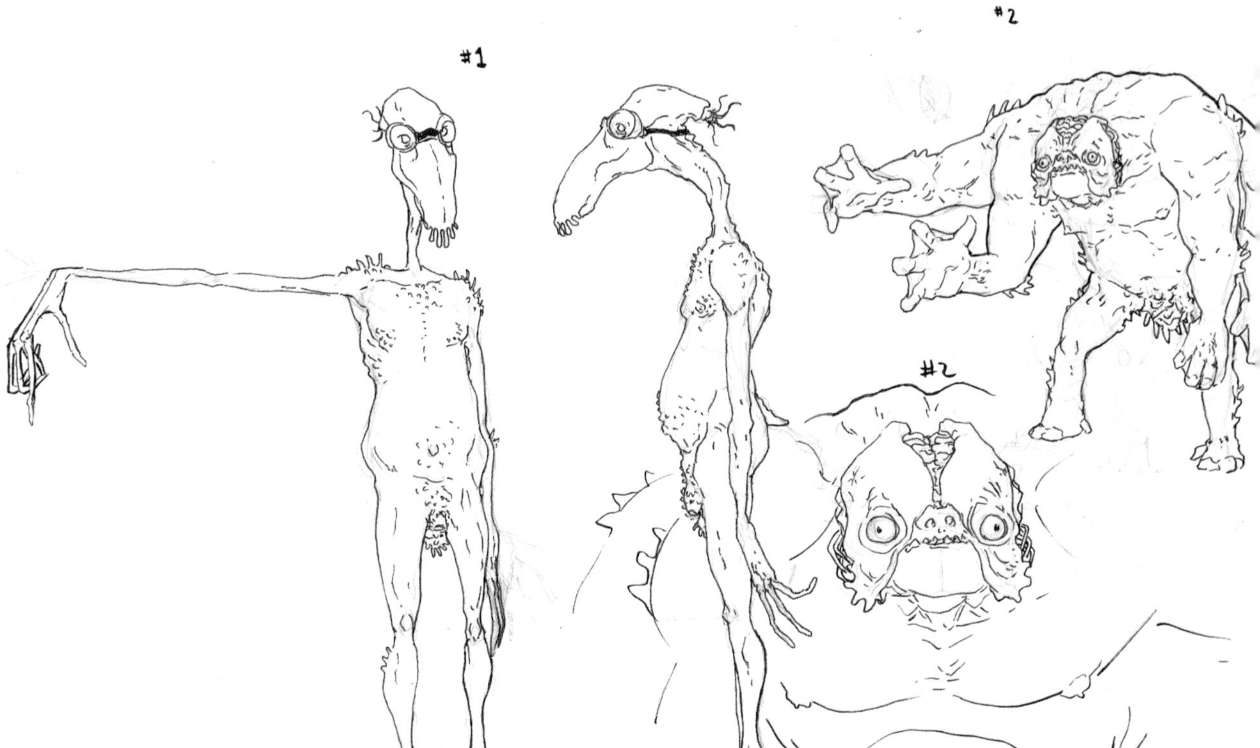
#1
#2
#2

ORIGINAL PITCH.

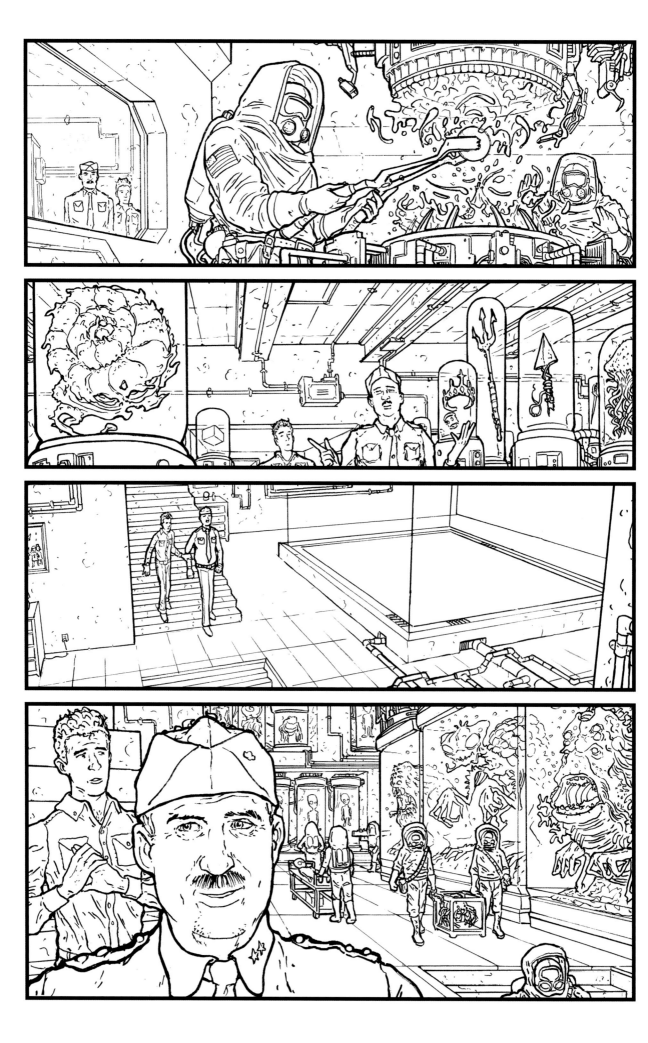

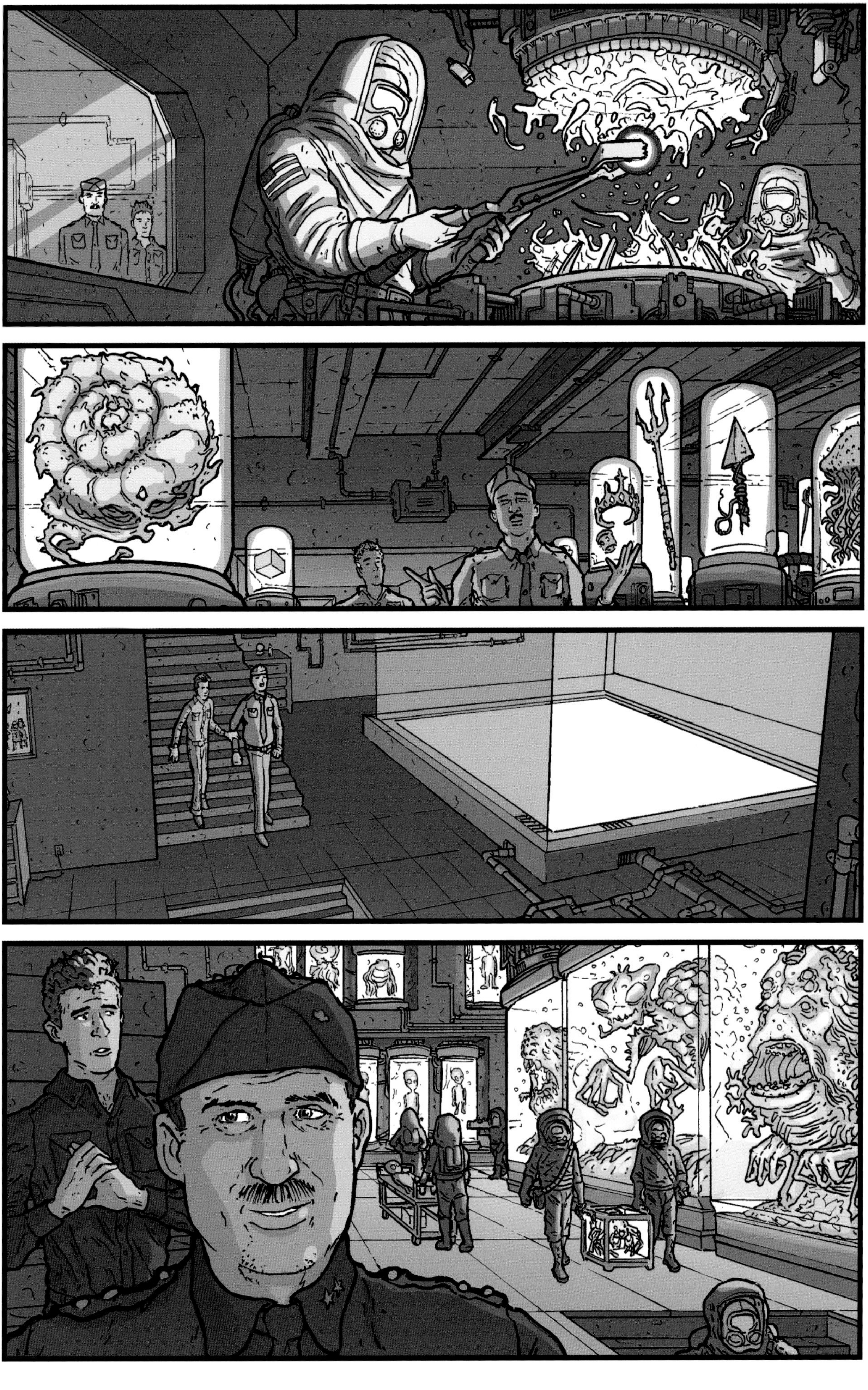

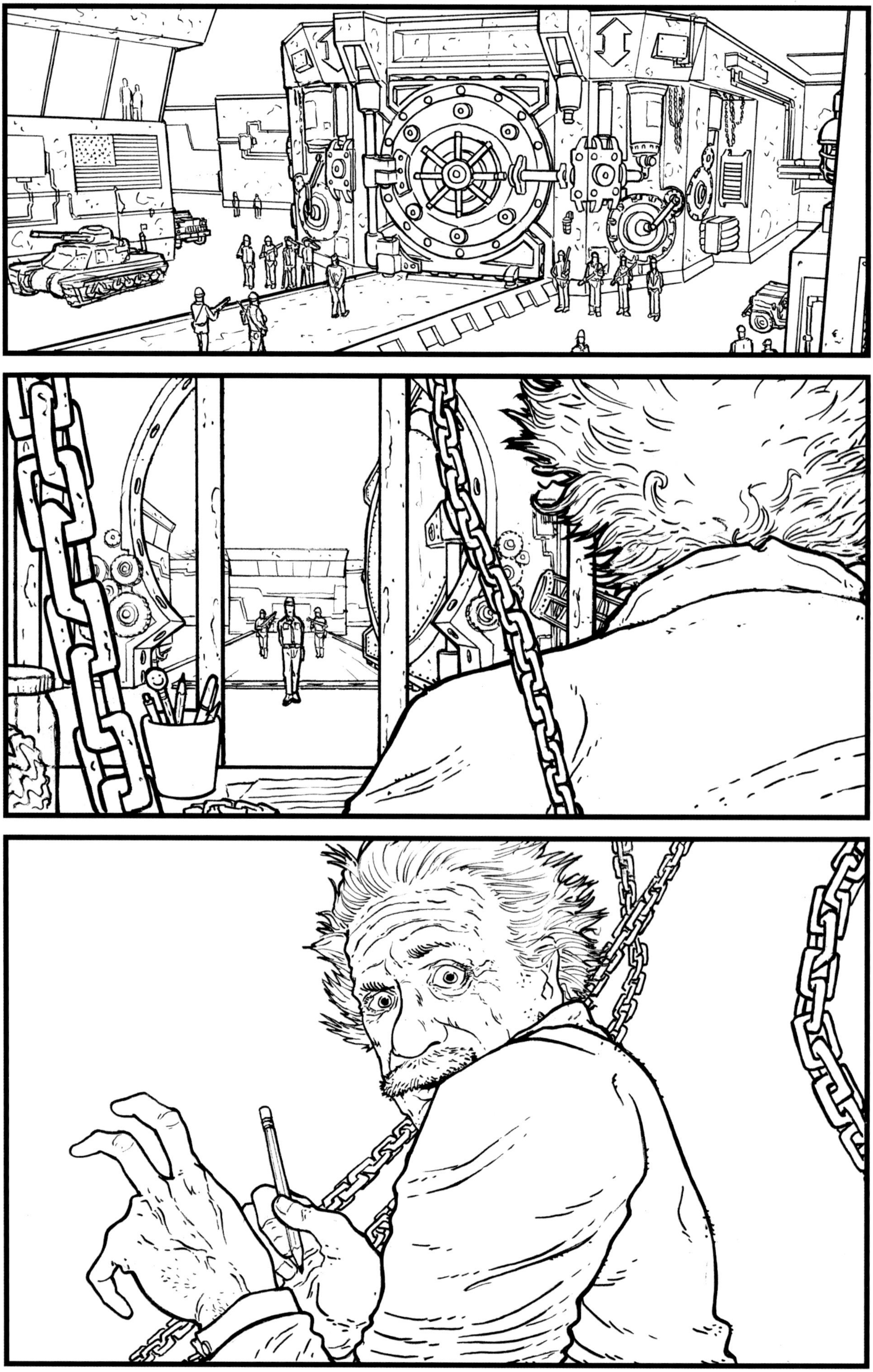

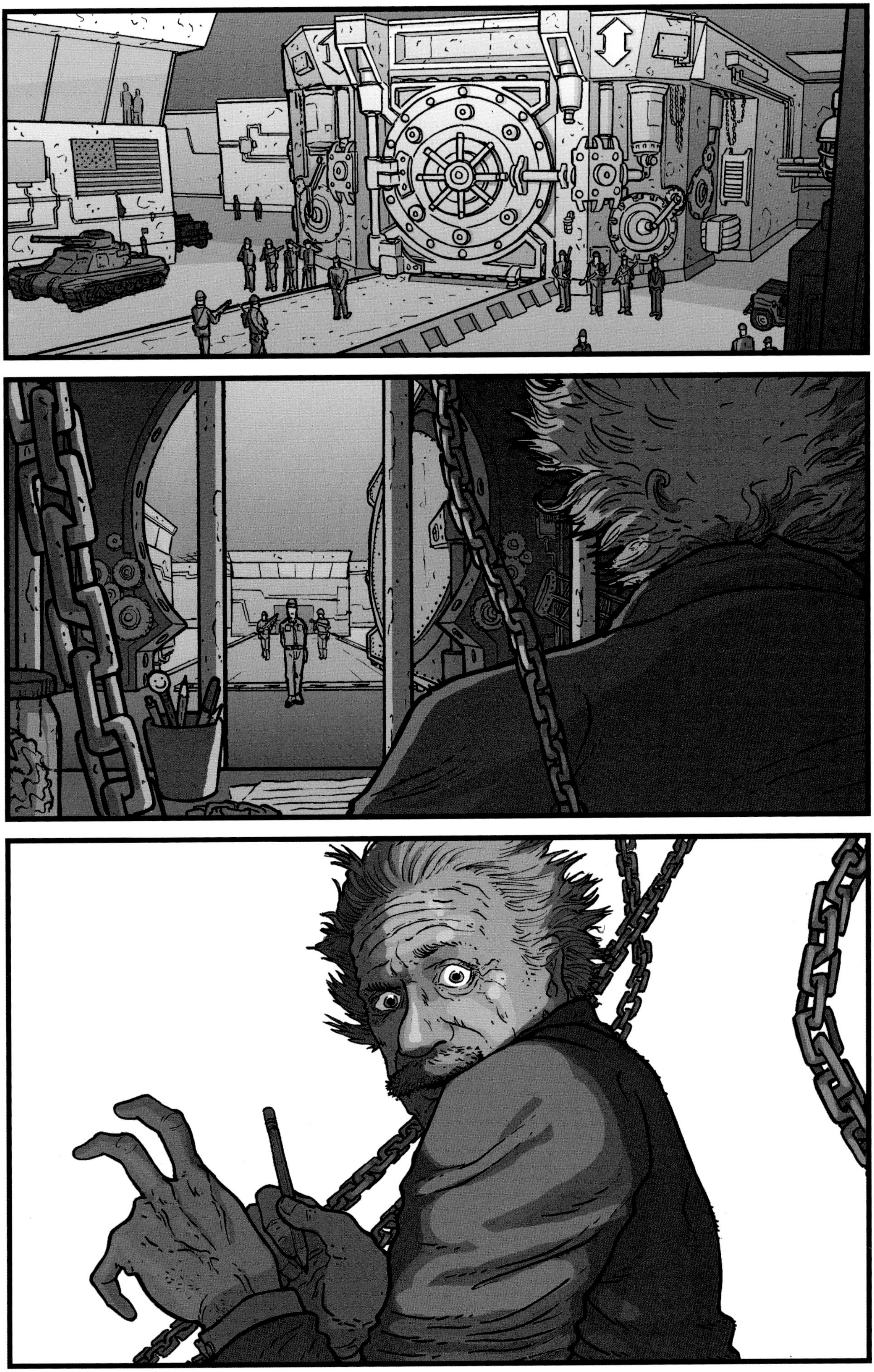

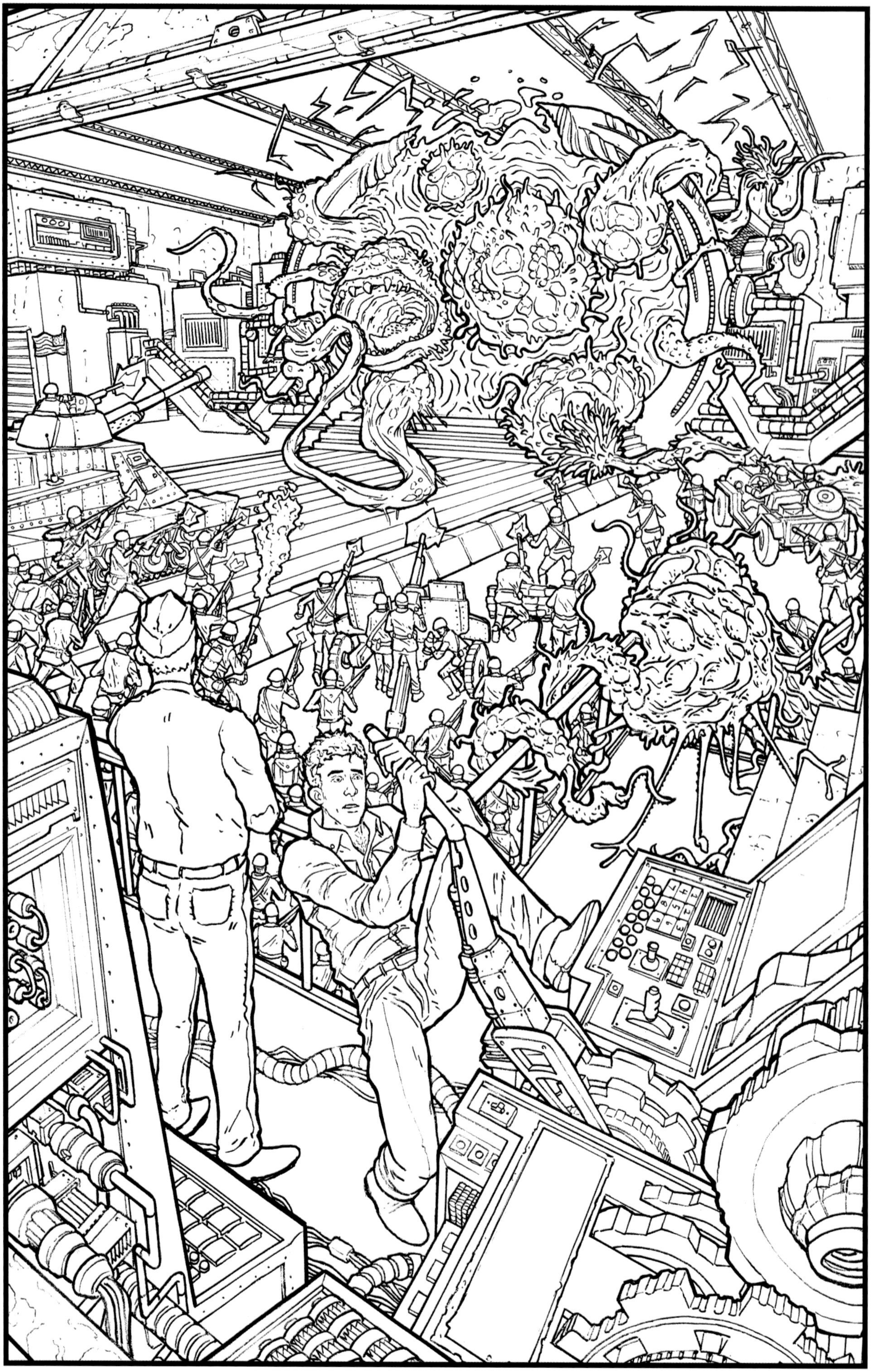

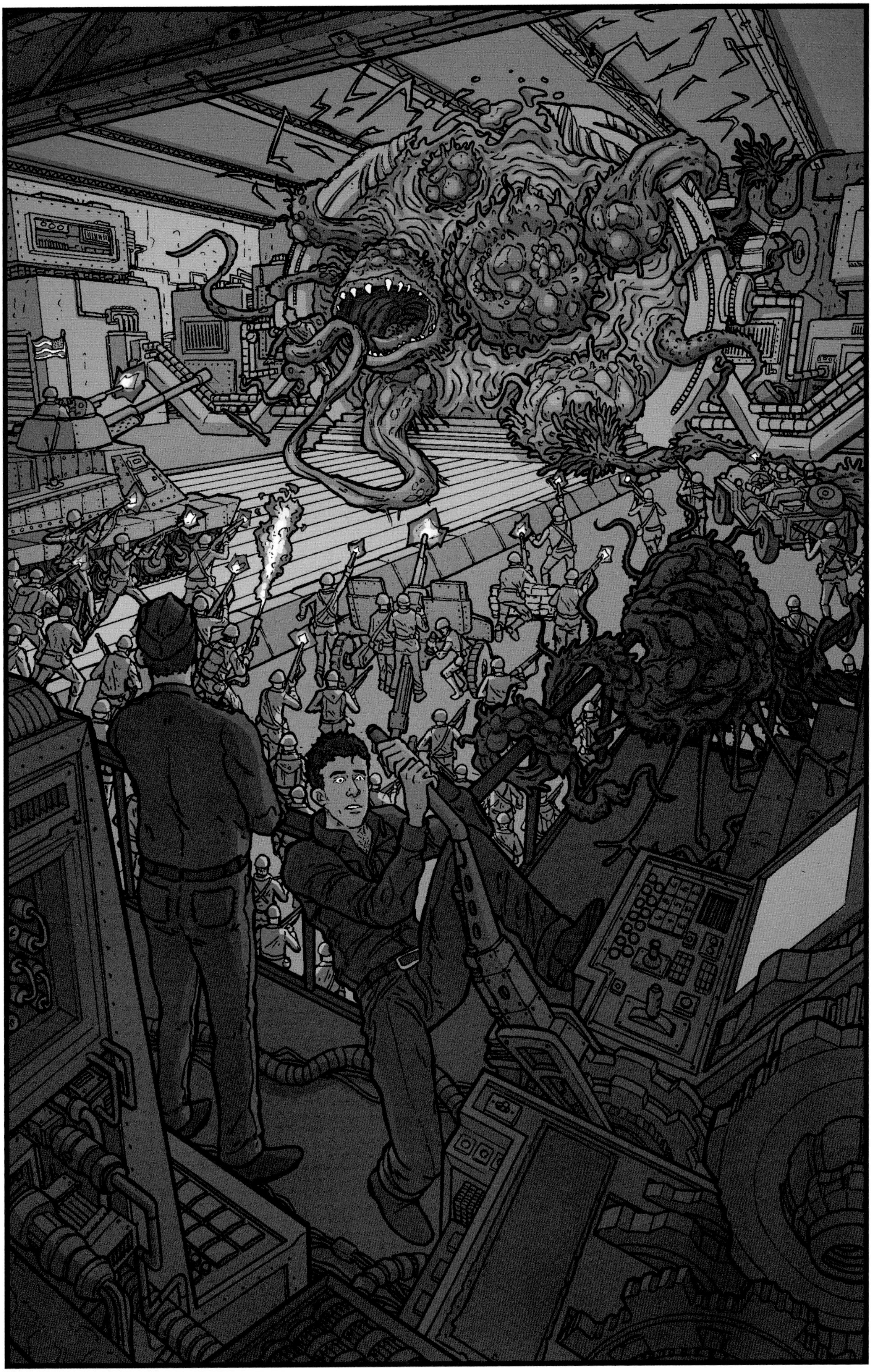

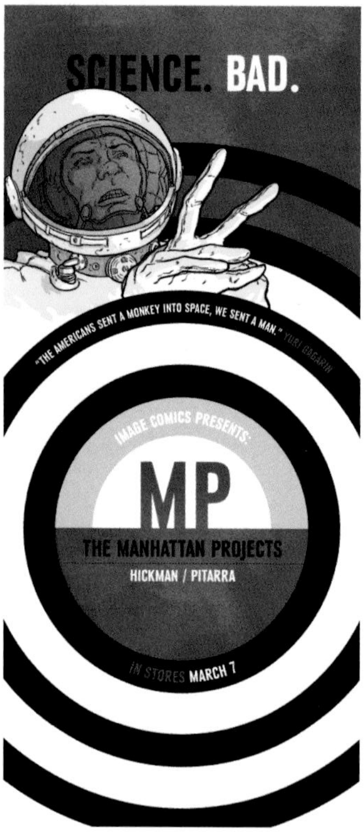
SCIENCE. BAD.
"THE AMERICANS SENT A MONKEY INTO SPACE, WE SENT A MAN." YURI GAGARIN
IMAGE COMICS PRESENTS:
MP
THE MANHATTAN PROJECTS
HICKMAN / PITARRA
IN STORES MARCH 7

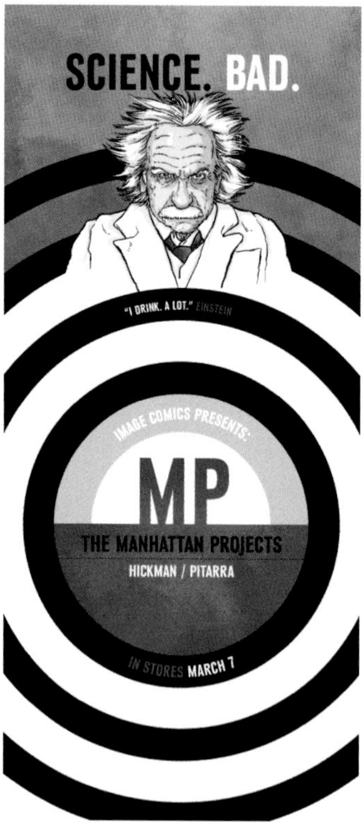
SCIENCE. BAD.
"I DRINK. A LOT." EINSTEIN
IMAGE COMICS PRESENTS:
MP
THE MANHATTAN PROJECTS
HICKMAN / PITARRA
IN STORES MARCH 7

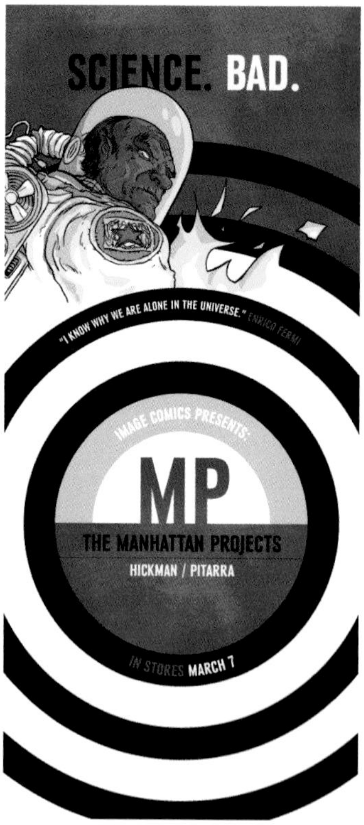
SCIENCE. BAD.
"I KNOW WHY WE ARE ALONE IN THE UNIVERSE." ENRICO FERMI
IMAGE COMICS PRESENTS:
MP
THE MANHATTAN PROJECTS
HICKMAN / PITARRA
IN STORES MARCH 7

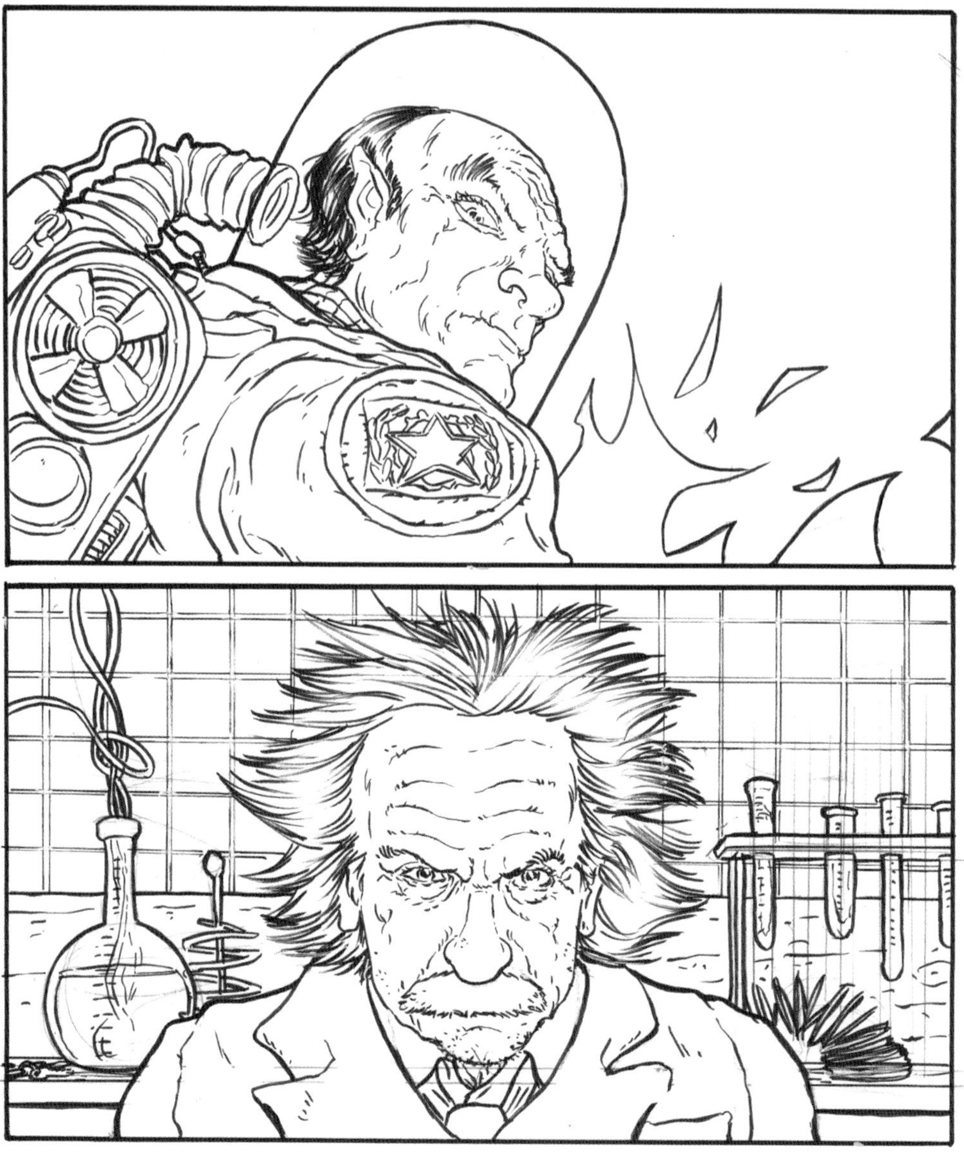

ISSUE ONE.

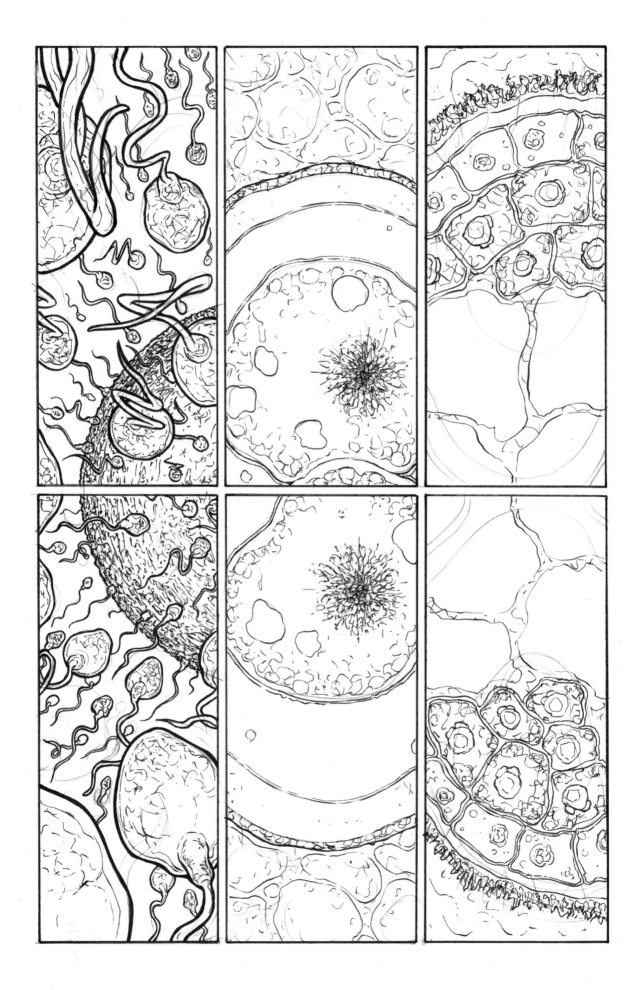

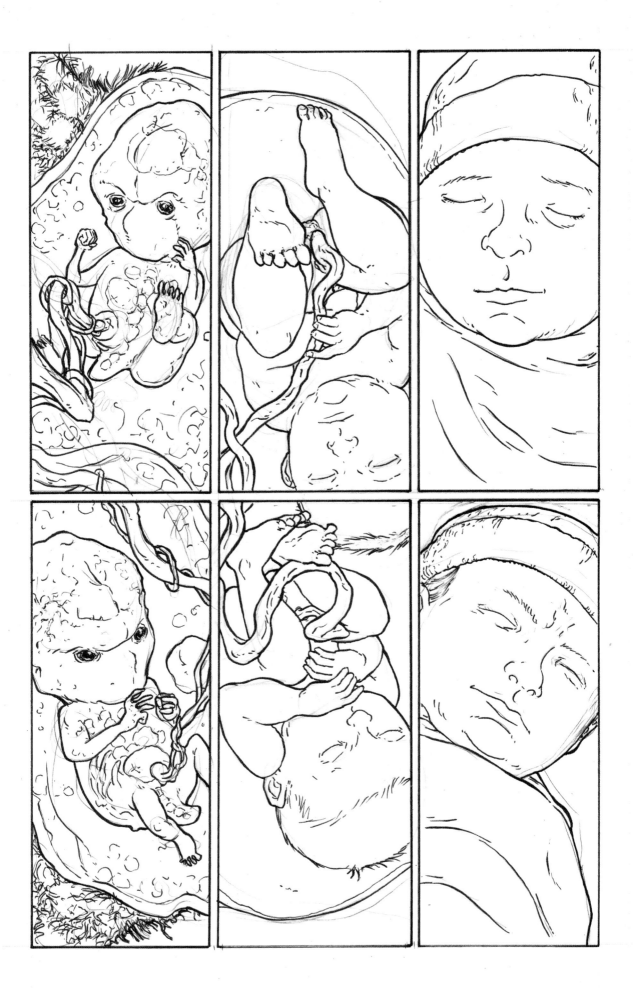

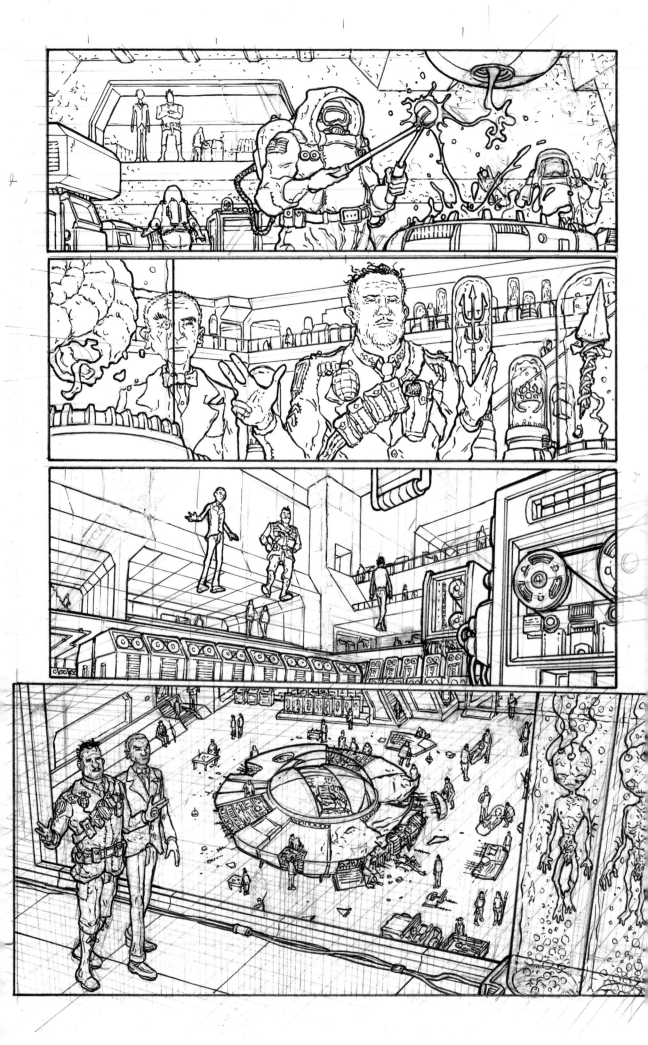

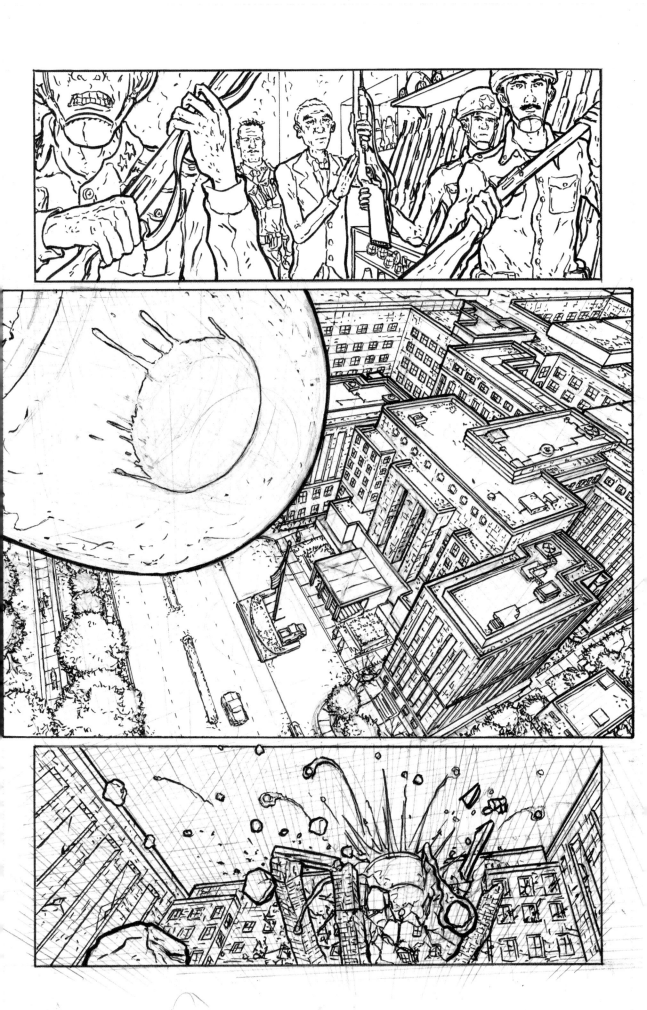

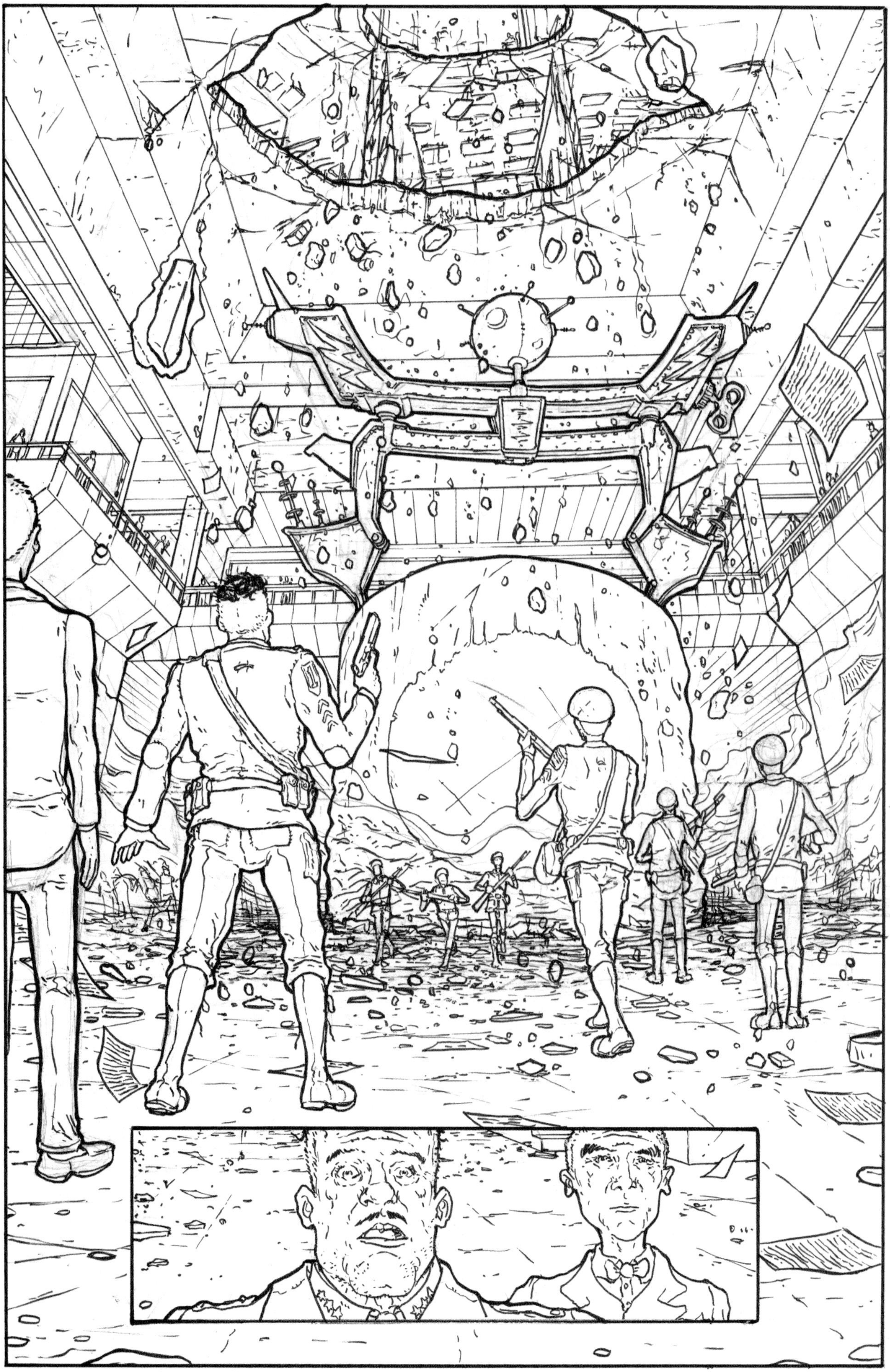

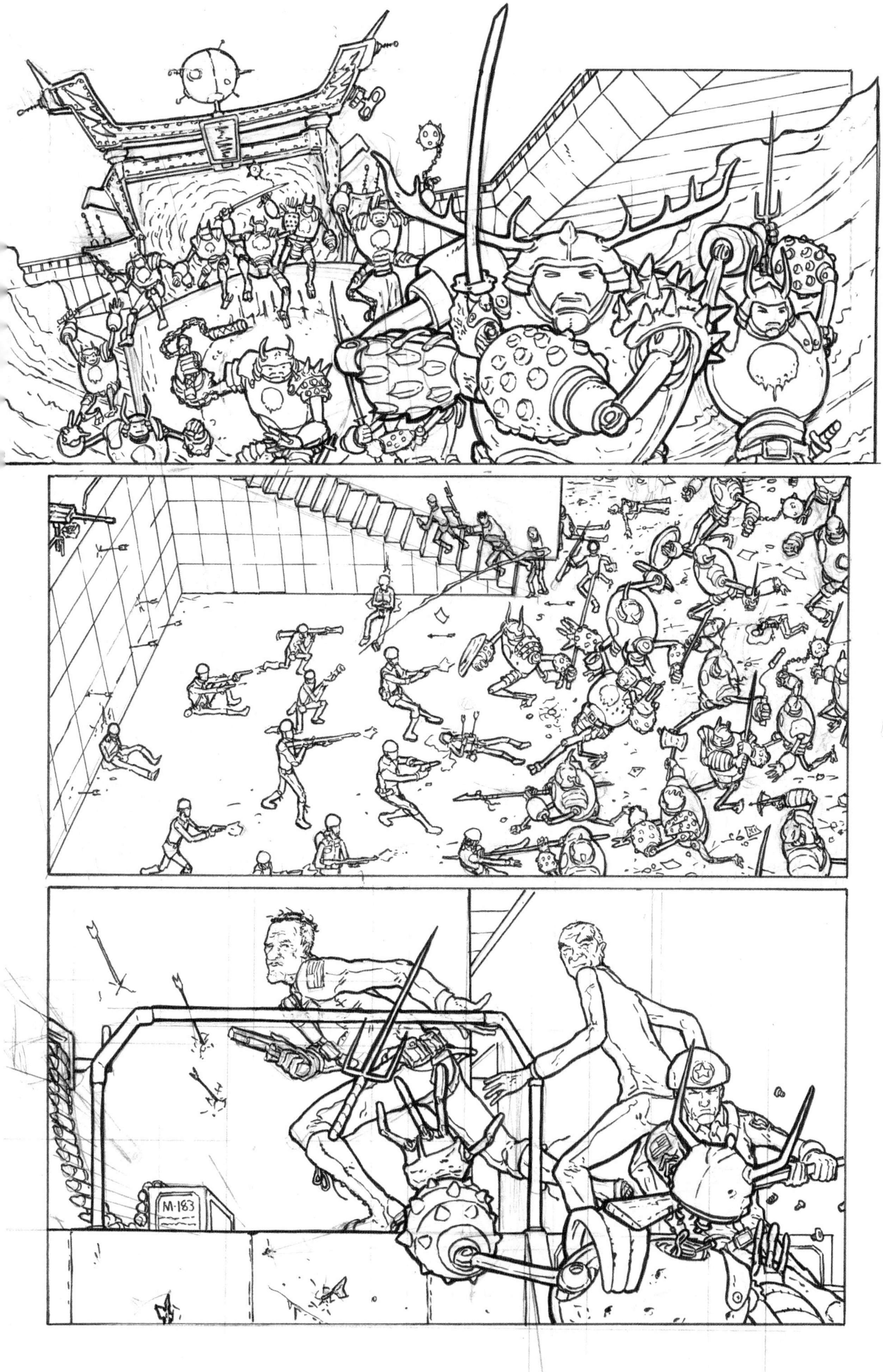
M-183

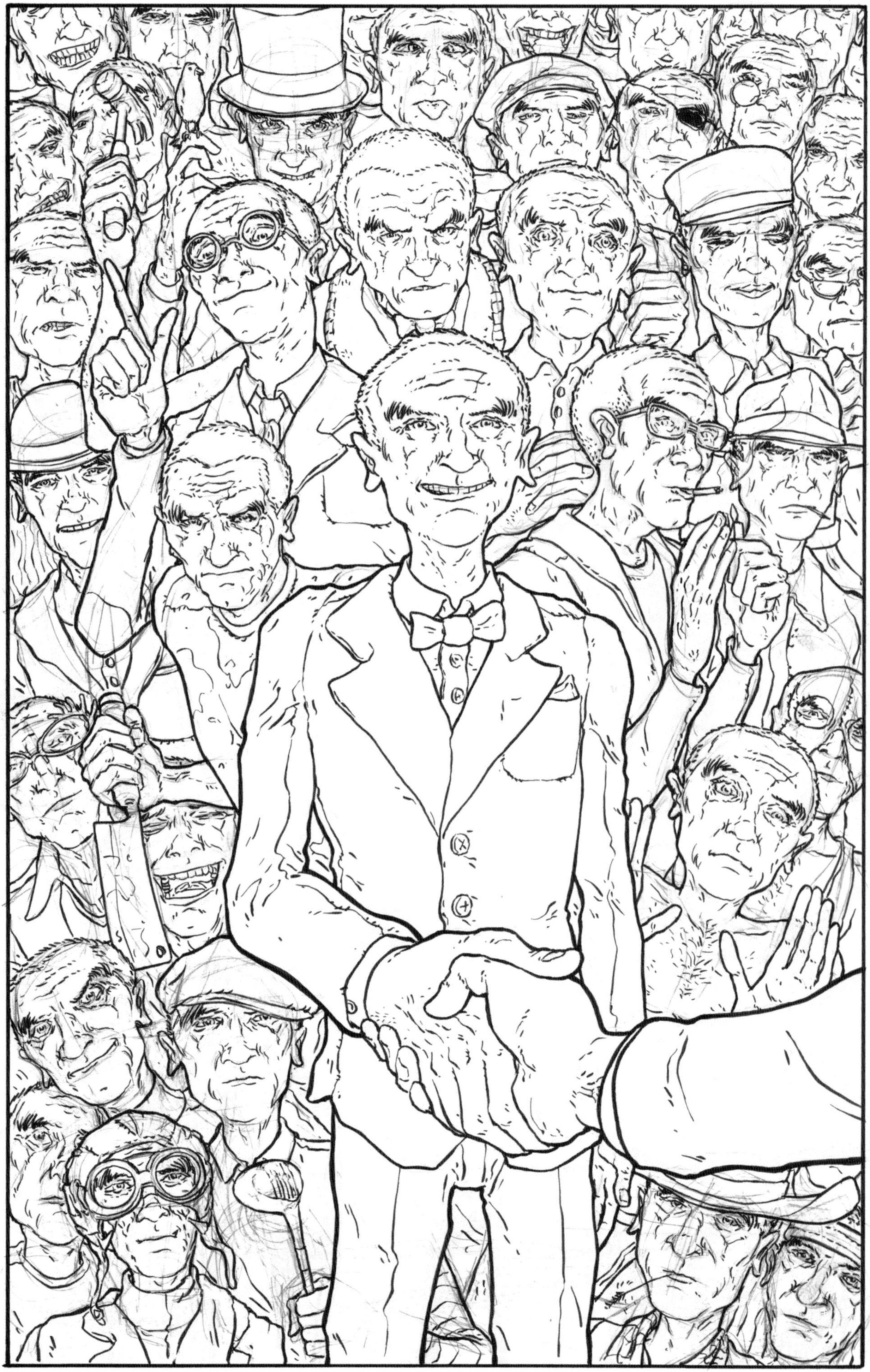

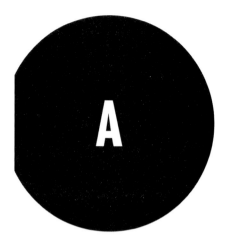

Jonathan Hickman is the visionary talent behind such works as the Eisner-nominated **NIGHTLY NEWS**, **EAST OF WEST** and **PAX ROMANA**. He also plies his trade at MARVEL working on books like **FANTASTIC FOUR** and **THE AVENGERS**.

His twin brother, Marc, once killed a lion with his bare hands. A lion who had a mighty roar.

You can visit his website:***www.pronea.com***, or email him at:***jonathan@pronea.com***.

·

Nick Pitarra is a native Texan and all around nice guy. As a senior in high school he was kicked out of honors English, and subsequently fell in love with comic illustration while doodling with a friend in his new class.

Sometimes it pays not to do your homework.